C000085787

Mark Richardson
Aimée Vanstone
Michelle Afford
Claire Tupholme
Annabel Cook
Donna Samworth
Angela Fairbrace
Heather Killingray

First published in Great Britain in 2007 by:
Forward Press Ltd.
Remus House
Coltsfoot Drive
Peterborough
PE2 9JX
Telephone: 01733 898101
Website: www.forwardpress.co.uk

HB ISBN 978-1 84418 466 8

Count Our Blessings

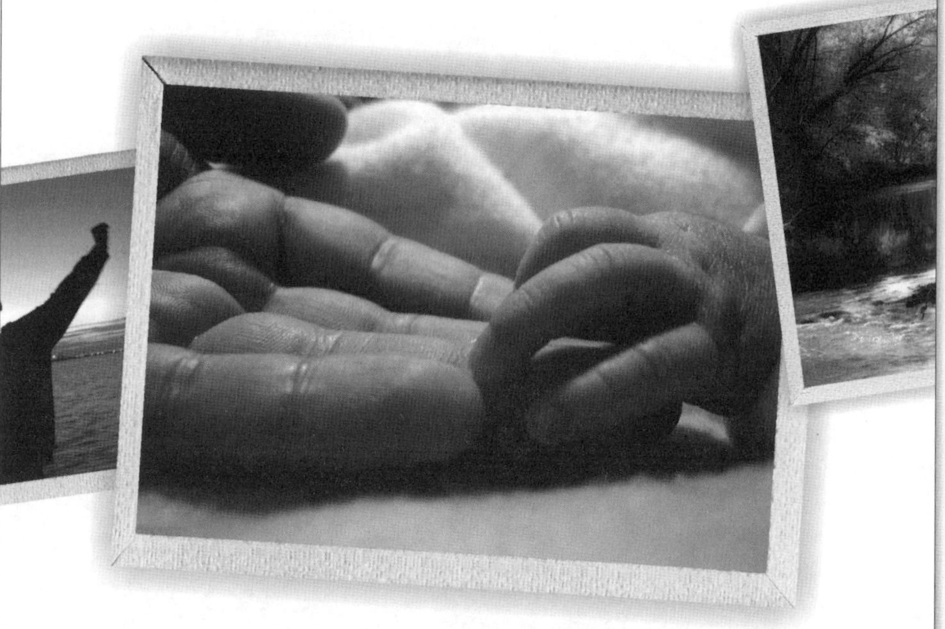

An uplifting and celebratory collection of verse bringing hope and reassurance

Foreword

Sometimes it's easy for us to forget just what we
are blessed with in everyday life. Easy for us to take
nature, love and family for granted. For many reasons we
forget to give thanks and 'count our blessings'. Lack of
time, the loss of a loved one and lack of understanding
that the best things *are* mostly free all play a part.
'Count Our Blessings' is a collection of verse to truly
remind us just what we can and should be grateful for.
Inspiration comes from all those who feel that, yes, there
is much to complain about in this life, but who have chosen to see
the positive side. 'Counting our blessings' is very personal and
these poets have opted to express their thanks in a most personal
way - through verse. We should therefore take the time to see the
world through their eyes and gain a little of their understanding.
This anthology will be a constant reminder of that positive side,
the ray of rainbow light that shows us all is not lost.
Hopefully, it will become *your* reminder . . .

Contents

Count Our Blessings

Count Our Blessings

Count Our Blessings

Count Our Blessings

Count Our Blessings

Count Our Blessings

The Poems

Count Your Blessings

Count your blessings, come what may
Give thanks and pray for each new day
Birdsong heard at dawn's first light
A free concert that brings such delight
Babies' laughter, filled with glee
At all the little things they see
Good manners that don't cost a penny
Rewarded with a smile from many
Give thanks for family and friends
Always there, right to the end.

Count your blessings in every way
They're all around you every day
A favourite song to cheer you up
Hot chocolate supped slow from a cup
Lost in a good book on a rainy day
As imagination takes you miles away
A best friend to confide in whenever, wherever
A partner to cherish and love forever
Children to teach, protect and nurture
It's good to feel loved and look to the future.

Count your blessings - know your luck
In case you ever become unstuck . . .
Just being able to move around
Having touch and taste, and sight and sound
The grass isn't always greener on the other side
Don't look to others to be your guide
Set your standards for yourself
Don't try to copy someone else
Believe in You - and you will achieve
The fabric of your life you weave.

Count your blessings, no matter how small
Pick yourself up when you fall
Good health and happiness go hand in hand
And love cures all - it's in great demand
But time is unstoppable, consuming our life
So make the memories good ones because blessings are rife
Open your eyes - you'll be amazed what you see
Most of these blessings are priceless and free

They're all around you in everyday things
Don't just take them for granted - enjoy what they bring.
Blessings needn't be material and cost you dear
It's the little things that matter and bring most cheer
Inconsequential they may seem to be
But without them life's a fallacy.

Dino Carlin

Prize-Winning Poem

Congratulations Dino,
your heart-warming and insightful
poem has been selected as the best in the
collection and wins you a luxury gift hamper.

(May vary from picture shown)

Dreams

Dreams come sometimes to us all and
Transported to another place,
Away from our worry and sorrow
We see again our lover's face.
When morning comes, the vision fades,
The memory of the dream is gone.
We are back in the world we left last night
And life goes on and on and on . . .
Just for those few hours of sleep,
When you can hold a loved one's hand,
He is standing there beside you
And he always understands.
How lucky we were to have that love.
How blessed to have that life.
When he was always my husband
And I was always his wife.

Norma Marshman

Count Each Blessing

Count those times when you've known love
Think fondly and remember
Count each smile and count each touch
They're blessings we should treasure.

Count each time you've been a friend
Each time as rich as gold
Count each friend as precious stones
To keep until you're old.

Count each time you see a child
A blessing sent from Heaven
Count each smile, each laugh, their joy
A hope you can believe in.

Count each time you feel the sun
Beat warmly on your face
Count each drop of rain you catch
As nature to be embraced.

So count our blessings one by one
Just stop and look around you
Remember love, remember joy,
Your blessings will astound you.

Natalie Sloan

Silent Post

He smiles
But he doesn't speak
He smiles
But he doesn't hear

Rain and wind tear at his coat
He struggles with the bag
Leaving bank statements, new offers.
I take them, stuff behind the clock
And watch as he calls at each house

He smiled
But he couldn't speak
He smiled
But he couldn't hear

I hear my children's cries
I speak with words of comfort
I count my blessings
And remember his smile.

Jo Hawksworth

Count Your Lucky Stars

One at a time,
Count them all,
Count each day,
If one should fall.

Count your lucky stars.

Look to the end of a,
Rainbow,
A star you shall see,
Look to the other end of a,
Rainbow.
A pot of gold you shall see
It be thee.
How lucky me.

Patrick Mannion

Blessings Taken For Granted - Haiku

As each day wakes up
The skies mostly catch brightness
While the world turns round

Colette Thomson

Tomorrow

If tomorrow never comes
Will it matter much to you?
Have you done your best today
Can you hold your head up high?

If tomorrow never comes
Can you say with honesty
That each thought, word and deed
Will bear up to scrutiny on high?

If tomorrow never comes
Are you ready to give account?
Were you planning flights of fancy,
Climbing that ego mountain so high?

Did you take each precious moment
Do each humble task with vigour
Did each deed give credit to you
Or was it 'self' you valued most high?

It matters not how clever we are
What medals gained or goods secured
If that tomorrow never comes
That neglected chance may cost too high.

Margaret Deverson

The Count

B lossom beauty in orchards found . . .
L isten to birds cry, coming from the hills . . .
E njoy quiet times, just look around
S unset and shadows over lakes and rills
S unrise brings new aspirations . . .
I n days of damp - think: Rainbow! . . .
N eighbours watching the environs . . .
G ardens fair and firelights glow . . .
S o many blessings we could but lose count!

Beryl Mapperley

Precious Joy

Precious joy
You are to me
My own dear sons
To love and hold.

Precious joy
You are to me
Every single smile
You give to me

Precious joy
You are to me
When sad and blue
I'll comfort you.

Precious joy
You are to me
A mother's love
Will never fade.

I love you.

Tracey Taylor

Count Your Blessings

There are so many blessings
Too numerous to count
Just have a look around you
You will see what I'm on about
First of all the open sky
Not always a lovely blue
But to be able to see at all
Is blessing number two
The leaves on the trees
That change colour by every hue
While the birds just fly about
Singing their blessings too
What about the gardens
And the comfort of your home?
The family to greet you
Wherever you may roam?
To be here at all is a blessing to behold
I look back over the years, still trying to count
The blessings I have already had
And they still continue to mount.

May Watkins

The First Of May

I had a dream of some far, nameless land
Of snow-spread rock, and ice and arid waste.
I was a tourist, willing to understand
A life so alien to my taste.

Some dwelt in caves in slatey, steep scarp face,
Rough hewn were crude-fashioned huts below.
Drab people hurried past with downcast face,
Dun birds left footprints in the snow.

A child wrapped close in layers of fading grey
Touched my blue coat as I stood mutely by
And smiled, - was he remembering a day
When he knew other than a leaden sky?

I woke to sunlight streaming through the room,
Looked out upon horse chestnut trees in bloom,
As morning mist my dream was fading away
In all the bright cacophony of May.

Where spirits are high imagination thrives -
God knows we need some colour in our lives.

Anne Filkin

Thank God

Thank God for small mercies,
In trouble and strife
Because without them I doubt,
I would get through this life!

When all hope is lost,
And the future looks bleak
Trust in the Lord
Behold, He will speak!

In prayer I find comfort,
A welcome relief
I'm eternally blessed,
With this constant belief!

Jasmine Newing

The Traveller On The Pilgrim's Way

I stood and gazed down the lovely vale,
And all around seemed still,
When a lonely traveller came in view,
Just o'er the crest of hill.

In long dark-hooded gown he came,
That long past summer's day;
No pack he bore . . . no frown he wore,
As he trod the Pilgrim's Way.

He paused to hear the songbird sing,
Watched others in the shade,
And stood as though he was entranced
When bells rang down the glade.

Then slowly did he make his way,
To the church set amid the trees;
Inside he knelt in silent prayer,
One knew, he was at ease.

It seemed an age e'er out he came,
As though was loathe to leave,
Yet once more on his way he went,
Along the Pilgrim's Way at eve.

A friendly smile to any child,
A cheery word to all he met,
And the look upon his countenance,
E'en now . . . I can't forget.

I watched him 'til he'd gone from sight,
And wondered from whence he came,
I wondered too . . . Where he was going?
Who was he? . . . What was his name?

Daisie Cecil-Clarke

Blessed Are We!

When you see the sun rise
Above the treetops and hills,
It's time to count your blessings
That cure you of life's ills.

There are many blessings that you have,
Throughout your lifelong years
Some to show your happiness
Others to wipe away your tears.

But the biggest blessings you can have
Are that of life itself,
For without the greatest one of all,
You have no life at all!

W Clements

Blessings

Love all around her beauty and care
Unselfish people ready to share
Friends when she's lonely who make it quite clear
They're there to assist her when sad days are here

Light in the darkness sun after rain
Suddenly life is worth living again
A heart once so happy now pierced with a dart
A deep-seated longing pervades every part

But life is for living and she must go on
Enrich every moment and strive to have fun
Try to help others be cheerful and brave
Gloom and despondency put in the grave
Set an example keep a bright face
Put on her make-up and follow the chase.

Barbara Hampson

In Your Footprints

Dear Lord
Each day I try to be more like You
Specially when the sun breaks through
And lights all the beauty You gave me,
The sun, the clouds, birds, flowers, trees.

Yet something always starts to annoy
When the Devil sends to employ
Wicked things for idle hands to do,
Mind slips from all that's good and true.

My tongue races forward without thought
And carries words I know I ought
To curb from wounding another's heart,
Trying harder to play my part.

Why waste my time in frivolities
With many others in such need?
Teach me to practise love, patience, care,
Another's load help me to share.

Let me not pass on the other side,
To be a confidante, a guide
To someone stumbling under their load,
To keep straight on along Your road.

Help me to use the talents You gave me
In any way that I can see
So that each night I can proudly say,
Lord I came nearer You today!

Pat Heppel

Mother

You are beautiful
You are wonderful,
Mother.
In the coldness and in the
Heat
In the darkness and in the
Light
You are there.
You wonderful Mother
In poverty and wealth
In sickness and health
You are there.
You wonderful Mother
In happiness and sadness
In misery and powerless
You are there.
You wonderful Mother
In loneliness
In happiness
In meekness
Or heedless
You are there.
You wonderful Mother
In hope and hopelessness
In pride and
Shamelessness
You are there.
You wonderful Mother
We pray to God
The Lord of the world
To keep you safe and
Healthy
Now and in the coming
Days
To be happy and be
Exalted.
You wonderful Mother
Thank you
Thank you
For what you have done.
May God be with you
And bless you all the time
Here and for eternity.
You beautiful
Wonderful Mother.

R Darakshani

Just - Thank You

My Lord - You knew I'd been alone so long,
In a very strange, unusual way.
Sometimes I doubted that I could go on,
As I tried to face the challenge of each day.

Then, suddenly in the wintertime
A miracle was wrought by You -
An Indian summer, just for me
And one for whom my love is true.

Thank you Lord, with all my heart -
All my heart and soul,
For sending me this one to love
And making me feel whole.

Betty Farajallah

Ode To A Mother

The love that I have is the life that I have
And the love that I have is yours.
The breath that I take, the moves that I make
Each day of the week because,

Expressed in the wish that a movement escapes
The winking of an eye
It's all in a moment of bliss of course and sigh.
Every moment you're near makes abundantly clear
The love we bear each other.
It's all in the thoughts of you
Because you are my mother.

Raymond Law

Feelings

People love too much, some not at all -
Hide your feelings, not knowing what you miss.
A secret heart never reveals all.
Never knowing a true loving kiss
Rejoice in your life and count your blessings
Wealth is all around you.
Freedom of life; choice; hurt; love;
Love cannot be bought, it is something you earn -
Cruel thoughts - anger cripple the mind . . .
It takes strength to try and put it behind.
Don't lose the sight of love, present or past,
Keep a happy mind.

Marilyn Drew

Licence To Heal

'Multiple Sclerosis' the doctor said.
Feeling faint, I bowed my head.
On and on he rushed his spiel.
All I heard was 'can't be healed.'
Mourning sickness every day
Till the fear had crept away.
Then one day I looked around
And Dr Kingsley I soon found.
MS his expertise,
He, my symptoms caused to ease.
Bespoke diets, candida gone,
Mercury fillings also gone.
Relapses gone, remissions here,
Dr K sure took the fear.
Some twelve years passed and all was stable,
Then I slowly was less able.
Relapses came, remissions didn't.
No longer could the truth be hidden.
By '03 I couldn't stand,
Just moving head, my arms, my hands.
But my spirit was intact,
Having heard some hopeful facts;
News of miracle goat serum,
Based on news of wondrous theorem.
For two whole years I followed its progress.
Then I knew what must come next,
A massive search to try and find
A doctor who would be so kind
To research facts and not deter
From having courage to administer.
Eventually I found the man
Who soon replied and took a stand
In helping me when others wouldn't,
No such word as can't or shouldn't.
Three injections made the start,
Giving hope to head and heart,
For I could move my legs again
And gaining strength to further mend.
My physio now helps me on
To wheelchair tricks and far beyond.
Slouch and straighten,
Twist and turn,
Feel the pleasure,
Reach the 'burn'.
Rehab now is all I need.
Grow the flower from the seed.
The benefits are truly real,
Give Aimspro a licence to heal!

Angela Garrett

The Place With No Name

Above the clouds stands a mountain so tall,
Rushing down the edge goes the waterfall,
Down to the lake,
What a lovely picture it would take,
Deer stand by,
At the mountain so high,
Taking a drink,
By their tongue so pink,
The lake glistens beneath the sun,
Baby deer running around having fun,
It looks so quiet, calm and still,
Trees stand so tall on top of the hill,
Mist circles around the mountain tops,
On the ground lies a few rocks,
I'll take a photo and put it in a frame,
Of the place so beautiful that has no name.

Louise Corke

What I Live For

I live for springtime to be here
When wintertime seems long and drear.
To see again 'that special green'
And know that flowers will soon be seen.

I live to see her fresh green leaves
As sap begins to rise in trees.
To hear the birds sing their sweet songs
For all these things, my soul, it longs.

I live to see a view serene
With newborn lambs on fellsides green.
To realise my golden dream
Of daffodils that grace spring's scene.

I live to see fair bluebells growing
In woodland dells, their joy bestowing,
And cherry blossom, pink and white
That brings us all such sweet delight.

I live for friendship's love and caring,
Its warmth and laughter, joy and sharing.
For friends who know me and who can
Accept me just for what I am.

I live for all so many things
That lift my spirit, give it wings.
But most of all, in hope I live
That peace be mine, with cheer to give.

Olive M Cork

A Precious Gift

Three children have come shyly to my door;
Bringing with them a very special gift.
They live downstairs and we are happy friends
And I teach their mother to make biscuits for us.

Sometimes I roast peanuts and the children
Come with scant excuse for they know well
That each will take away a warm and fragrant bag.

They, in turn, bring me fresh milky coconuts
Still warm and softly hardened from their tree
For this is Zanzibar, where the spicy smell of cloves
Wanders across the island on the evening breeze.

The children offer me the special gift, both hands outstretched,
An overture in Africa of peace and friendliness;
They smile and say 'Karibu' meaning 'welcome'

Enfolded in two tiny, careful hands
For the precious gift is living
And I take it gently in my own.

A small eye gazes fixedly, unblinking, from my hand;
And feathers brush my palm with urgent plea.
I feel the panting vibrance of a captive life
And I am heart-strung by the closeness of such fragile strength
Of a tiny bird.

I could not keep such freedom in a cage;
Nor pygmy kingfisher nor other bird
Should live constrained.

I smile and thank the children for their generosity,
I hold the bird until they know I care
About their kindness and their thought for me;

Then opening my hands, I let the bird take flight
To soar and dart towards the trees
Where safety lies,
While the little children stand and watch with me,
In sheer delight.

Pauletta Edwards

Understanding

If it's the closing of the summer
Autumn is not far away
You can play with the winter
Though it's not far away.
The spring is closer than ever
The summer is closer too!
You can't wait for the circle
The future belongs to you
You think you are immortal
And that you'll never get old
You're too young to think otherwise
When the birds sing to you
You walk with big steps like a giant
Pushing aside the breeze
You smell the air like a tiger
Just before you sneeze
The white butterflies will forgive you
As you push them to one side
The sunshine will understand you
As you walk the world outside.

David Rosser

Life's Blessings

Beyond my window frame
Pointillist trees
Spring green
Below a Constable sky
Comfortably lowering
Yielding a shower
That glistens
As it nourishes leaves
And horses foal in open view
Whilst a thrush perches on my sill
And a flutter of swallows
Pecks in the nut cage
Hooked to the veranda wall
And an elderly couple
Hand in hand
Walk across the green
Amongst the cherry blossom.

Katherine Jane Rawlings

Blessings In Life

(Written for my daughter who has recently left to live in New Zealand)

For every low there is a high
For every sigh there is a why
For every tear there is a fear
For life to always run so smooth
Is not a challenge, it's just for fools.
A prayer is all that's needed each day
It helps to keep the fears away.
The greatest blessing we can have
Is talking to our Maker when we are sad.
A thank you for the hills and streams
For wild flowers, birds and trees that gleam.
Delightful children, innocence aglow
As forward, onward in life we go.
The heaviest burden seems so light
With God our Father still in sight.
Distance is naught in this universe
As with one spirit life is rehearsed.
Blessings of fax and telephone so we
Can always call to home.
Life's big adventure leads us on
As those before us have surely gone.

Rosemary Whatling

Blessings

I count my blessings every day
And when I pray
I thank Him for all He has done for me
He has given me love so rich and free
I praise Him for the birds that sing
Reminding me of spring
I thank Him for health and peace of mind
And for friends so very kind
There is so much more I could say
Yes I count my blessings every day.

Evelyn Lees

Dogged Determination

As I looked out my windowpane
On the rain-swept street below.
My eyes perceived some movement,
Oh! How the wind doth blow.
Struggling into view there came,
An old and feeble man.
Coat pulled tightly round him,
As resolutely he began.
His was a mission,
He would go to any length,
Feeble hands and shuffling feet,
Belied an inner strength.
Slowly past my house he came,
Head bent against the rain.
Several times he almost slipped,
His body wracked in pain.
Hurrying to my door,
I flung it open wide
'Please don't go any further,
Won't you rest inside?'
My words were tossed back by the wind,
He soldiered bravely on,
From the distance I heard a cry,
'Come here, I thought you'd gone.'
Sounds of barking followed,
My face was all agog,
This time there were two of them,
An old man and his lost dog.

Oh! That I was loved as much,
Please dear family, get in touch!

Marion Brown

Best Get A Move On

Best get moving,
My day can't start,
Without me.

Wonder what would happen
If I didn't bother,
Would my day cease to exist?

I suppose it would
Without me it cannot be here,
It's an awesome responsibility.

B Smith

Over-Sixties Dancer

In brave defiance of the enemy
Colours unknown to nature tint your hair;
And heady perfume, as you turn and sway,
Sends an exotic breath into the air.

Your purple dress, which gaudy flowers adorn,
Is short and tight; the neck is rather low,
But your well-hoisted bust is proudly borne
In front, not drooping - tempting even now!

Your reddened lips are parted in a smile,
That still (unlike your teeth) is never false;
And as the music plays you dream awhile,
Forgetting fear and future as you waltz.

Dance on into the sunset with your mates,
Whirl in your party dress while time allows;
With pearly smile dance to the Pearly Gates,
Before your spirit fails and your head bows!

Marguerite Pratt

Thoughts Of You

Your mum is a precious commodity
I know now she is gone
She brought such wealth and richness
And her memory lives on.

Every day she nurtured me
Gave love in an abundance of ways
Her loving touch
That meant so much
And taught me from day-to-day.

A friend, a mother, that worked so hard
A tribute to you is due
You shared your life
In many ways
As I write these words for you.

Margery Rayson

Evensong At York Minster

The sound of the organ
And members of the choir
Ring around the building
Their praises aspire

We hear the dean
Say the prayers
An anthem is next
And the sermon declared.

The hymns are sung
Time for a blessing
The choir dismisses
Until the morning.

In this wonderful building
Built to His glory
Beauty around us
Reflects the truth of His story.

Praises said and sung
For centuries without end
May it continue
To the most trusted of friends.

Pauline Edwards

Friday's Child

(For Carmen Charlie Wood, born 10th November 2006)

Mouth like a rosebud, small button nose,
Skin like peaches and cream.
Eyes dark, coal-blue, reminiscent of those
Crisp, frosty, winter nights of dream.

Friday's child, loving and giving.
Please God, let me still be living
To see her grown, beautiful and bright
Shiny, sparkling diamond, born, 'twixt morn and night.

Child of Ryan and Tracey, precious little one,
Oh, so worth it, when all is said and done,
Please, be my friend, as your mother before,
So Carmen Charlie is my darling, my darling, my darling,
Carmen Charlie is my darling for evermore.

Mhairi Jarvis

Kittens

Willowy,
Sinewy,
Into everything.
Tiniest crevice,
Weeniest hole,
Smallest opening.
Quick!
Disappear!
Higher,
Ever higher,
Must go up;
Always
Upwards.
Vantage points,
Lofty views,
Checking out
Who's below.
Curious,
Inquisitive.
Why?
And who?
And what?
And where?
Testing,
Feeling,
Exploring,
Learning.
New life,
New day,
Fresh start.

Bettina Farrow

My Heart Has Shared Your Pain

It is for me an easy thing
To say, take heart and smile,
For your road is difficult,
With many a painful mile.

I have not borne your suffering
Your lonely nights of fear,
Nor watched the surgeon, doctor, nurse,
Always waiting near.

But though my body is fit and well,
My heart has shared your pain,
And waited by your bedside
To see you smile again.

Joyce Dunkley

Do You Know That God Is Ever So Near?

Do you know that God is ever so near;
Do you know He is with you?
Yes, He is right here.
Do you know that He cares
More than any you know?
Do you know that He shares
All your joys, all your woe?
Do you know that He sees all that you do?
Do you know that He feels all you go through?

Yes, God sees all, and knows all your fears;
He'll comfort the worried, and wipe away the tears.

And *all that is wonderful!*

For I have got everything that I need,
And that 'is blessing', yes indeed . . .

I know that others are not so fortunate as I -
Some struggle to live: many die . . .

So I close my eyes and
Some sort of peace has come over me.

I open my eyes and look and see
'All the lovely things God gave to me'.

All the treasures He left on Earth;
All the wonders of the universe;
All the tiny things 'beyond' my sight;
All the things I see to my delight;
All the mighty power 'all around'
Of the heavens, the seas;
This precious ground,
Where life's own seed grows generously
From the refreshing rain sent for me
To rejoice over . . .

Mary Winter (née Pauline Coleman)

Being Alive

When you wake up in the morning and realise that
you are alive one more day
You get happy and thankful for the given opportunity
to enjoy the Earth you live on.
You go out and see her beauty,
hear her voices,
smell the freshness of her breath
and get in touch with her children:
plants, animals and other human beings
and
in your soul you feel the sun, the moon, the stars, the wind, yes,
Eternity itself . . .
and
you feel yourself really blessed for having this beauty around you.
Enjoy it and learn from it.
This opportunity is granted to you but *once*.

Vineta Svelch

Beauty In Jeopardy

Oh what a magic sun-filled day
As perfect as one hopes in May.
With endless blue and cloudless sky
And flocks of birds are flying high.
The butterflies and bees abound
On flowers and trees, with ne'er a sound.
A gentle zephyr stirs the leaves
And martins nest beneath the eaves.
I feed the mallards on the ground
Identify each different sound
Of all the birds within my view,
The collared doves are in the yew
Thrush and magpie, starling, crow
Chaffinch, sparrow, to and fro.
We hunt to kill, and fell the trees
Pollute the air, and poison seas.
Decimate the life around
And acid rain falls on the ground.
How can we dare to jeopardise
This lovely earth before our eyes?

Sheila Phelan

I See Something

There is a cloud hanging over our heads
And we don't sleep in our beds
So many heartaches through the years
So many frequent tears
When I look at you my child
I see something wild
I see a change in front of my eyes
And am no longer wise
There are demons inside trying to get out
Then suddenly without reason a scream then a shout
Twitching, squirming, a violent spell
Sometimes I feel that we are both in hell
Quivering shaking, a look of hate
That's how it is up to date
Nowhere to turn, nowhere to go
Trying to smile when I am low
But then you will do something my boy
And I remember you brought me joy
'I love you Mummy,' you will say
I am no longer entrapped in my life day to day
I count my blessings that you are here
And I try to hide my fear
I see the boy you used to be
And hope one day you will break free.

Margaret Pow

My Life

My life has totally changed I fear,
Though with little help from me.
I had a stroke that hit me out of the blue, you see,
Which left me partially sighted,
And other little things,
But my one dream was to see the lovely trees and flowers in the spring,
Then after an operation,
Happiness came to me,
For now with both eyes I can see,
With no more pain or sorrow,
I am so pleased and you will agree,
My life is now my own
But will never be the same again.

Sylvia Reeve

Our Brother Chris Lydon

(We count our blessings every day for his partner Sue)

Nothing could be bleaker than
The news we had last year,
We try to come to terms with it
But still we live in fear.

For our brother now has cancer
And we're hoping very soon
His oncologist will let him have
Some very pleasing news.

For our brother is so special that
We think of him each day.
And I know our heart would break into two
If we should lose him now.

But we all feel very proud of him
Because he's coped so well
And we owe this to his partner Sue
Who's cared for him so well.

It's clear to see she loves him so
Which feels so nice to see
We only hope they'll get the chance
To both live happily.

We also love our brother too
That's why we'd like to say
Thank you Sue for taking care
Of Chris for us each day.

Merilyn Gulley

October 1987 - Aftermath

Though the October storm
Did a great deal of harm
And in places you can't see the trees for the wood
It's a very ill gale,
Quite outside of the pale,
That doesn't blow somebody, somewhere, some good.

Now it's quite hard to see
Where that goodness can be
As you survey the damage it's done to your house,
When the man from next door,
Whom you thought such a bore,
Turns up with his tools and you feel such a louse.

You've complained of the noise
Of his two rowdy boys
And the howls of his dog have oft had you cursin',
With a tree on your roof
You don't feel so aloof
And now, all at once, he's become a new person!

Each sturdy young lad
Gives a hand to his dad,
And between them they manage to clear up the litter.
Then with faces all smiles
They replace all your tiles
And you hate your own guts for having been bitter!

G Baker

The View

'We'll take you up to see the view,' they said,
And so we journeyed through the autumn rain,
The children wishing they had played instead,
Their weary parents trying to explain,
With fraying patience, how they ought to show
Their aunt the countryside. Five people, set
Apart by irritation, huddled low
Within the car. We got out on the wet,
Sweet grass a very fractious cavalcade;
'Til overawed by space, dissension died,
And clouded eyes awoke to see displayed
The patient glory of the countryside.
As mortals changed, we stood in silence there;
And five were one, and one was everywhere.

Mary Spain

Garden Dreams

Now is the time for planting and sowing
Tilling the soil, weeding and growing
Thinking and planning for silky green lawns
A mower that mows on its own
Until dawn.

When gnomes feed the plants
When at night you do sleep
So that roses and fuchsias
Abundantly peep.

Out in the sunlight with flowers so bright
Where fairies have dusted before
It was light.

So sit in your deckchair, believe
What you see.
But shut your eyes tight to dream
Dreams like me.
If you open them now this garden
Will fade
Leaving just weeds with dandelion maids.

Beryl Smyter

A Bouncing Daffodil

I saw a bouncing daffodil
Coming sprightly down the hill.
The sky was overcast and grey,
It was a dreary sort of day
Until that burst of golden light
Came leaping gaily into sight.

Through mist and rain, as it drew nearer,
The shape and form became much clearer.
Inside a golden anorak, a boy,
A happy child, jumped for joy!
On he bounded down the hill,
Receding, diminishing, until
The splash of gold became again
A daffodil, revelling in the rain.

Louie Carr

A Prayer For The Day

Let the stillness of the night
Rest our souls,
With slumber tight
So that, with energy abound,
Thank the Lord,
That he has found, in His heart,
That we may -
Awaken to - another Day;

And to show with thanks,
His gracious giving,
Amid much turmoil,
That we are still living:
Tho, there may be many,
Who, in their plight,
Never made it,
Through the night.

So - to do our best,
Throughout the new day,
Seems to be, the only way,
Of saying,
'Thank you Lord'
And with your help, may we tread
The path of Righteousness,
On this - new day.

Irene Hurd

At Godmanchester

I am tackling up my spinning rod
For the first cast of the fishing season.
I have crossed the Chinese bridge
With its arc of white lattice-work,
And am standing on an island
In the middle of the River Great Ouse.

I look back to the Chinese Bridge
And see the water-lilies in the margins.
They neither toil nor spin,
As I toil and spin,
But have not the slightest difficulty
Keeping their level heads above the water.

I am reminded of Monet's famous painting
Of the water-lilies below the Japanese Bridge
In the garden of his house at Giverny.
Perhaps, at fifty-eight, I can reinvent myself,
As Monet reinvented himself at fifty,
With more than a little help from the water-lilies.

Stan Downing

Phoebie

Life is a wonderful journey,
That you have just begun
To learn the secrets of it;
We wish you lots of fun.

The world has much to offer,
And you have much to give;
It all depends on what you do
And on the life you live.

So take your time,
Go gently on your way,
And we will watch your progress
As you travel through each day.

Francis Collett

Miracles

When did you last see a miracle?
Look harder, chase that frown
Sun, moon and stars in their courses
Never let us down.

Walking on air is no mystery
The miracle's walking on Earth
Look in the mirror and recognise
The miracle of your birth.

We live in a miracle every day
And don't even realise
Those big white clouds above us
In the beautiful blue skies.

Flowers and fruit in their season
Animals tame or wild
Green-leafed trees and hedges
The wonder in the eyes of a child.

Do you believe in miracles?
Look around and you'll have to agree
If you take the time to think of it
Open your eyes - see!

Maureen Quirey

My Angel

You took your last breath and suddenly my world seemed to stand still
I watched the trees sway in the breeze over your window sill
There seemed to be a silence, stillness in the room
Yet outside the world turned as normal, didn't acknowledge the gloom
While I cried tears of sadness, the skies seemed to open too
Life wouldn't be the same again, not without you
I wanted you to hold me, tell me it would all be OK,
But when I looked into your eyes, the light had gone away
My beautiful mum, you had left me, I didn't know what to do
My legs turned to jelly beneath me, I felt sick and cold through and through
I laid next to you and held your hand, kissed your cheek, it was cold
Your skin seemed waxy and pale, yet peace seemed to have taken hold
The pain went away when you fell asleep, at last you were free
Free to be an angel in Heaven, which is what you are meant to be.

Claire Wilde

You And I

You are the God who weeps with me,
And feels all my pain,
When others leave me on my own
Still You, O Lord, remain.

You are the God who grieves in me
And feels my great loss,
Inviting me to leave my cares
With You, before Your Cross.

You are the God who breathes in me,
Who fills my lungs with air,
Who feeds the hunger in my soul,
Refreshing it with prayer.

You suffer, care, work, mourn with me,
My sorrow is Yours, too,
And though I feel all alone,
Yet You will see me through.

You give me hope, when I am lost,
And don't know what to do,
And when I have nowhere to turn,
Then I can turn to You.

Yes, You and I, Lord, we will share
The sadness and the strife,
Stay with me, keep me from despair,
Walk with me through my life.

Richard France

Light After Dark

For us light after dark is not
Like the aurora borealis;
It's not the day's beginning
On the edge of the horizon or on
A window sill: an eye peeping over
A mountain, bloodshot from
Too much opening and closing;
It's just a light within
That does not light up a room
But lights up a world
Like no other light can do.

Light after dark is seeing
Life's vitality through luminosity.
We are all children of light or darkness
Born after sunset, or sunrise
When the day is on its way,
It's no matter we are blind
There is always a shade of grey.
It's all in the mind - if we lack one sense
It's likely another is sharpened instead,
And darkness is cut by a sword
That flashes in the night,
Illuminating the mind from behind.

Light after dark is clean,
Like cutting an eyeball in half
Without inflicting pain;
We cannot feel what we cannot see:
In one's life there is only one light within
Bathing in a moon-filled pond,
That we see better with sightless stares.
But it doesn't matter, not really -
We recognise all truths far better
Like they were written on stone
And we can see with touch,
All's hewn in our other senses;
Therefore we do not crave for vision -
It comes to light after dark.

Raymond Fenech

Maa-Ode To My Mother

Oh Mother, the sole bearer of human life on Mother Earth!
You bore me for over 10 months in the cocoon-like safety of your womb.
Through unbearable pain gave birth to me, your first-born son,
Nurtured, protected and fed me whilst a swaddling infant,
Catering to my every whim, which on adult reflection
Shows what an infinite ocean of human kindness dwells in your bosom!
Sacrificing your own personal needs to make sure that I and my
Siblings were fed, clothed and educated properly.
Tigress, Mother Bear, you made sure that no harm ever came to any of us!
Teaching us our moral and religious values that I still adhere to in my daily life.
Through joyous and sorrowful events, you have always been there for us.
Recently, when you were ailing and at a critical crossroad on the Journey of Life,
Came the realisation that mortality is a common, unprejudiced leveller with no exceptions!
I reflected on the things that I always wanted to say to you but put off for another day;
I regretted then, that, I never told you how much I loved you,
I regretted the hot-headed outbursts causing you to raise your blood pressure,
I regretted that no matter what I did then,
I could not repay the debt of my mother's milk and raising me to adulthood.
By Divine Intervention, you overcame this illness
And gave me more time to rectify my past sins
And gave me another chance to be a dutiful son for a few more years.
Yet I now know, no matter what I do will never be enough!

Robin Halder

Freely Given

To Mount Street Bridge I take a bus:
I leave the traffic, noise and fuss;
And suddenly a blissful peace
Surrounds me everywhere.

Beneath the overhanging trees,
A shelter from the gentle breeze,
The ducks approach to warmly greet
As I their haven share.

The drunks upon the other bank
Have nought wherewith their Lord to thank;
No beauty greets their clouded eyes
As they sit sadly there.

I move along towards Dolphin's Barn
As I compose this little yarn;
A yarn with which I weave my life,
For all around I see God's care,
With which nought else can e'er compare;
A commodity to some so rare,
But . . .
I accept it with gratitude.

Michael Thompson

Please Don't Call Me Lonely

Please don't call me lonely
Please don't think me sad
For that would be just awful
That really would be bad!

I've been through all the titles
As I've journeyed through my life
Terrible twos and teenager
Through to loving wife!

Even having the children
Never made me glum
It's just another title
Moaning, nagging Mum!

Now they're old and leaving
There still will not be tears
I'm going to do what I want
Catch up on those lost years!

Dye my hair with streaks of pink
Even learn to drive
Cos deep inside from now on in
I'll still be 25!

So please don't call me lonely
Please don't think me sad
For how can I be those things
When I've had the life I've had?

Rowena

Love You

Peek-a-boo, I see you,
Running up and down,
Hiding in and out,
Pick yourself up,
Don't do it again,
You're tired at last,
How you make my heart beat fast,
You're just like your mother was,
Doing all these things,
How you put a smile on my face,
When you come to my place.

Beryl Elizabeth Moore

Discovery

I may not have washed all the curtains
I may not have hoovered the stairs
I may have forgotten to plant all the bulbs
Not polished the rails on the chair
I've often spent far too long shopping
When I still had a meal to prepare
And no! I don't check every sock in the wash
To find every hole - or a pair
So of course there are those who wonder at me
And hold up their hands in despair

But I have hobnobbed with a neighbour
Trimmed a hat - quite a fussy affair
I've read a whole book in an evening
And tried to play Chopin with flair
I've laughed with a grandchild in puddles
And eaten a fat juicy pear
I've talked and I've dreamed with my dear one
We've sauntered and taken the air
I've found too that life can be rosy
Even though I can't run up the stair

Best of all I have spent time with Jesus
And I'm learning to trust in His care
I've learned too that God's love is steadfast
His friendship beyond all compare
I feel so enriched by His blessings
I just want my life to declare
The wonder of knowing a Saviour
Who walks alongside me to share
All the ups and downs of my journey
And helps me to breathe Heavenly air.

Ruth Hartridge

The Later Years

As I wander through this year of great significance,
And quietly ask the question how I feel about the fact,
That more years have now gone by, than are before me,
The future, not dependent on the way that I react.
My opinions, once regarded, no longer carry any weight,
Ideas, there still are many, buzz continuously in my head,
But with fewer kindred spirits left to share my lofty thoughts,
They disappear, like snow that chooses oceans for a bed.

How I sometimes want the wonder of new experience again,
But find myself rehearsing why 'it's not a good idea',
Style is not so very different to what it was back then,
But now 'dressing in the fashion' to your family causes fear.
Where once a lot of jobs were done before the lunchtime break,
Now the clock can chime past nine, before I stir from sleep,
There are many contemplations whilst watching life enact the day,
Before it's over; and again the cloak of night does inexorably creep.

But mostly, I am happy slowing down my daily pace,
I can leave responsibility to someone other in my stead,
Within my reach is something that I've never had before,
The time, to really just enjoy my life that lies ahead.
No major plans, nor anticipating troubles that may come,
But listening and reacting to the pleasures all around,
Sharing of the simple things with lives that touch mine close,
Is all I need in future for fulfilment to be found.

Sandra Griesbach

Every Blessing

I count every blessing yes
As I walk down the street
And wish everyone good morning
Even the strangers I meet.

I count every blessing yes
As I clock in at work
Because being unemployed is so easy
And not paying my own way would hurt.

I count every blessing yes
As I sit down to my meal every night
For God had time for me when I was down and out
He made everything come all right.

Keith Powell

Winter's Chill

Winter days,
Have come and gone,
Bleak grey skies,
Each frosty morn.
The day awaits,
The routine set,
Though cold and gloomy,
I shall not fret.
For I have seen,
Both sides of the coin,
The low dark troughs,
And brilliant sunshine.
Looking back,
A memory spoken,
Of laughter and tears,
And promises broken.
For the fleeting touch,
Lingers still,
Of better times,
To ease the chill.
The darkness fades,
And I find my smile,
For another day here,
Is worth the toil.
My days are full,
My life complete,
And despite the gloom,
I find the heat.

Stephen Humphries

Morning Thoughts

I face the bathroom mirror
In the unflattering morning light
And as I try out a rueful smile at my reflection
I notice the lines between my eyes soften somehow
As my eyebrows rise up slightly
And the furrowed central line
Flattens for a brief moment -
And then settles back into its regular position
Where regrettably it will no doubt deepen.

My bleary eyes look on
In disbelief at their current condition.

They will improve as the day continues
But the dark rings and wrinkles beneath
Are probably beyond repair, and sit accusingly there
Reminding me that for some time I have been remiss in their care
And in the absence of the required miracle product
They are probably now a permanent feature.

But - my nose!

The prominent nose of my dear mother
Adorns the centre of my face
And is decidedly firm and wrinkle-free!

I can hide neither it, nor my joy at its appearance!

Flanked as it is by the twin dark ravines
Winding down beneath the roses of each cheek
Eventually to meet the jowls gathering pace beneath my chin
It is until now in pole position in the race
To defeat the ravages of time
Which as we speak are coming up fast behind.

Never mind, just for this morning, on the face of it
I am winning by a nose!

Maureen Horne

The Blackbird

Is the blackbird's song of love
Clearly heard in Heaven above
Or is it just for us below?
The answer I would like to know
How does he from his tiny throat
Produce so clear and pure a note?
As from up in yonder tree
He sings his joyful song to me
A miracle of life is he
Giving thanks for being free
I daily thank the Lord above
For the blackbird's song of love.

Ian Russell

Windfalls

You came
the first windfall apples in small hands
their greens and yellows glowing.
You'd picked them carefully one by one,
presented them with your childish smile.
I peeled them later when you were gone
and cooked them in an evening apple pie -
a gift of apples to give twice.

The second windfalls I lift without you
accompanied by a yapping collie
who crouches sheepdog-like,
black and white in autumn grass.
then pounce, yelp and dart -
hoping that apples are for playing fetch.

All the year's warmth is harvested here
for the making of feasts
feasts of images
feasts for winter days
feasts of hope.

Ethna Johnston

Thank You For The Insight

Thank you for teaching me all you have taught me
Through you I've discovered the chance to be free
Thank you for helping me learn that I want to
Learn what it's like to be me.

I came to this place with very mixed feelings
Deeply depressed, isolated, in pain.
I leave with a strength I was quite unaware of
I'm learning that life's good to live, once again.

You've opened a door leading to new discoveries
Containing adventure, excitement and fear.
Although the pathway ahead may be risky
The promise of a world rich in freedom is near.

And now that pathway is starting to beckon
Even though progress may sometimes be slow,
Thank you for showing me how deep inside
I have the means to develop and grow.

Jennifer Densham

Tomorrow

The sea laps the shore gently, on a tranquil summer's day
The tide ebbs and flows, in its own inimitable way
No white horses foaming, not today, it's much too calm
A calmness that I hope I will absorb, a soothing balm.

I wonder where each wave evolved, perhaps from a foreign shore
And where it goes on after and has it been before?
The water changes colour matching moods of summer skies
Creating a serenity that is music to my eyes.

I feel a peace creep over me and know that it will be
The same again tomorrow, the sea, the sky and me
There's a wonderful monotony in watching moving water
And thankfully it's one rare thing, man hasn't learnt to alter.

No matter what state our life is in, everything moves on
The troubles of today, tomorrow may be gone
The seasons will change for certain, and the flowers bloom again
The sun will shine, the wind will blow, and of course there will be rain.

The vastness of the ocean makes our problems seem quite small
Over the horizon a new beginning calls
Man cannot stop nature, the tide will always turn
A lesson to apply to life, and one we all can learn.

Jackie Johnson

A Special One

(To Norah for all her help and love)

She has been a special someone
All through my years and days
A very special person
In so many, many ways
And as the years have gone by
Sometimes they have been hard
But there has always been that someone
To help me through that part
I have neither gold nor riches
To offer her this day
But all the love that I have
Is hers in every way
She has always been there
To help me
To help me live my life
For that very special person
Is my wife.

L Davies

Springtime

Wintertime has passed away,
Spring is in the air today;
Gone the biting, bitter wind so cold
Warmer days will now unfold.

We've seen the crocus and the snowdrop
Daffodils in plenty - a golden crop.
Now come hyacinth and tulip bursting through,
Flowers in the garden, on trees too.

Birds are nesting, lambs are leaping,
New green leaves through buds are peeping.
In spring I always get the feeling,
Of new beginnings: most appealing.

Easter heralds new life in God's Son
Over death the victory He won
He redeemed us from the Fall
Now life He offers one and all.

Jesus Christ, our Saviour, Friend
Promises Life that will never end.
We count our blessings day by day
As we travel on our way.

Jackie Hamblin

My 4 Rooms

The all-year-round warm glass room
Comfortable bright cosy never to entomb,
Outside onto a wooden-decked sunny space
Airy, vast, calm and peaceful place,
Entering through the middle spindled post
I come across the green room of midmost,
Chairs in situ under the crinkly willow
Keeping cool in the shade below,
I arch my way to the water feature and summer house
To catch the last of the sun as it's about to dowse,
How I adore my 4 rooms all on one floor
No one could ask for anymore,
You can always add or take away
Changes appear every single day,
Lucky I am to have this wonderful pleasure
In my back garden all at my leisure,
I am able to see, smell and to hold
Forever or at least until I'm very, very old!

Angela Cooney

Life's Portfolio

How fortunate we are that we are here,
Small plants in this world's wondrous atmosphere
Who think . . . feel . . . see . . . explore to learn and know
Some small content of life's portfolio.
Nature's green fields, the flowers, trees and streams,
Night's twinkling stars and dancing gold moonbeams
Are our inheritance - a treasury -
A priceless gift of true prosperity.

I heard the cuckoo call early today
Announcing that the summer's on its way.
The apple tree has donned its wedding dress
And birds are singing songs of happiness
While up on high, piercing the sapphire blue,
The eye of Heaven beams its golden hue.
How good life feels! Each season has its gold
With all its many treasures to behold.

Life oscillates just like the weathervane
So everyone will know some hurt, some pain
For joy and sorrow travel through the years,
While joy brings pleasure, sorrow brings its tears.
Each must be shared, emotion needs a friend
And creditors hope for a dividend.
Variety's the spice that helps us build
A character of strength - a life fulfilled.

Joy Saunders

Dance

Oh sprightly nymph,
On feathered feet,
Dance your step,
And give us treat,
Rhythm so deft,
Music to savour,
On pipes of pan,
Melodious favour.

Oh lithesome youth,
Take nymph to dance,
Move in harmony,
In abandon prance,
Two as one,
As grape on vine,
Merry the tune,
Rapture divine.

Oh nymph and youth,
Your dance delights,
On tip of toe,
You reach the heights,
In symmetry shown,
In graphic line,
Stirs the heart,
Blossoms the mind.

On nymph and youth,
Cavort a pace,
Give your dance,
Beauty and grace,
Smile the while,
As round you go,
In perfect time,
And elegant show.

Oh nymph and youth,
Your dance so fine,
Subtly movements,
So sublime,
A joy to watch,
Poise supreme,
Precious moments,
Romantic dream.

William Stannard

Unique Life

As life is ever moving,
So are our thoughts,
Feelings and fears.
We move along slowly
Dragged down at times
Forgetting to see all that glitters.
Then events take over
So sad or frustrating
And until we can lift
Ourselves out of the gloom
We miss all there is to see.
Like the child that smiles up at
Me, innocent and caring.
The parents with praise
And warmth, or the
Lover who is always there
In all ways letting me shine.
Life can be tragic and full
Of surprises but within those
Surprises are the magical
Moments we take for granted
That make us appreciate who
We are and what we hold.

Karen Roberts

The Joy Of Living

The joy of seeing skies of blue,
After skies of grey.
The joy of greeting dawn anew,
Knowing another day.

The joy of meeting friends again,
Sharing together laughter, and pain.
The joy of being able to give
A smile, some cheer, some time.
To help another just to live.

The joy of giving another love,
Of knowing and receiving love.
The joy of holding a babe in your arms.

The joy of loving, sharing and giving
All adds up to the joy of living.

Grace Maycock

The Magic Of Words

Think of your own special place
The place that you love best
Take your time to memorise it
Now simply call it *rest.*

As you travel through life's journey
To places of heavy stress
Now! Just think of the one key word
Yes you've remembered *rest.*

Your very own special place
Has returned into your mind
The special place that's just for you
That no one else can find

As stresses and strains of every day
With problems to be solved
If they're really getting you down
Think *rest* then look around

Your very own special place
Has returned into your mind
The special place that's just for you
That no one else can find.

At day's end and you are tired
And lying in your bed
Instead of problems in your mind
Just think of *rest* instead.

Ray Johnson

Tanka Train Of Thought

Here, playing at trains
with him, I realise that
the mind of a child,
if we stop, look and listen,
gives to us more than it takes.

Geoff Lowe

Lullaby

Child
It's to you
That I owe it all
Without you
I never would have made it
And one day
When you're older
To speak to
I'll tell you all
That you have done
But till then
Let me hold you
And caress you
And hope
That you'll understand
That my love
Will always
Be there
When you in your turn
Need someone.

Sharam Gill

What Blessings We?

When in humility, I consider all the things I'm not
It's hard to numerate the things I've got
Good health, I'm fit, a bonus you'd agree
So what on earth is worrying me.

Looking through a mirror, I see
Another mortal, just like me.
Is it a blessing? I'm not blind
To witness thus, the ravages of time.

Or then to hear a songbird's trill
The draughts of winter, blowing through
I chide myself, the tiny bird now flown
I wonder will it safely reach its home.

Global warming all's turmoil
Think not of this, but thankful be
Of growth, warmth and security,
So snap out of your complacency.

What is in store? To strive and seek.
Listen to that inner voice, and see.
Wake up to beauty all around
And count our blessings, our life is rare.
Self pity's not a grace to share.

Elizabeth Saynor

Anarchic Beast

A boy's delight in scruffy dog
Revives the way I saw the world
As child: but years of ups and downs
And knocks from life have often hurled
Me headlong wild and left me blind
To blessings all around for those
With eyes to see and hearts to learn.
This pup with eager shiny nose
Would not be choice of mine, but now
I know it through its owner's smiles
I relish beast from restless tongue
To ever mobile tail. Its wiles
When after food it's spied are cause
For bouts of mirth. Its frantic run
In fruitless chase of bird who takes
To wing, and silly growls at nun
Who rustles on her way along
Our road, are both absurd. And yet
It's living every moment full
To brim. It makes me glad I've met
This most endearing, foolish, pet.
It's pleasure I'll not soon forget.

Henry Disney

Peace And Hope

We know not what the future holds,
Each dawn, each day our paths unfold.
As time moves on and minutes pass
Change unstoppable, no moments last.
Each month begins with hopeful prayer,
new miracles of birth we share.
As life progresses through each season,
we look for hope, we look for reason
for lives that end too soon, we feel
for leaving those who have to deal
with sorrow, loss and memories dear,
We face again another year.
Carpe diem, seize the day
We have our dreams - and friendships stay.

Gael Nash

Nursing Home

For thirteen lingering months
Sister Mary Drostan has been living at Ladymead
wheelchair-bound, tartan plaid across her knees,
some book on the banks and braes of Scotland nearby
She is ninety-four years old
We visit her daily after her nap, while the sun makes its
proclamation in the skies - or it might just as well be raining.

We find her among the elderly confused,
the agonisingly distressed lost persons
in the bright lounge but more often in the sundrenched
conservatory
Punchy curls up a neighbouring blue seat
rigid hind leg underlining his lustrous black shape,
a triangle of tail exposed
and there is twin brother Snowy stepping in,
wearing his eye-catching polar bear coat with panache
Our old friend chimes in:
'Aren't we lucky, lucky people to be here,
Aren't we lucky to live in this beautiful place!
Look at the trees, the fields, the horses, that man taking his Labrador
for a walk! And the Downs!
If my legs were stronger, but they aren't today,
I would climb right to the top and see the whole stretch of England
Then like a swallow she returns to her small round nest of fond
memories, still intact and warm
'We had a happy childhood,' she says
Outside a white-collared dove swings on a branch
part of the sad-contented monotony

Françoise de Pierpont

Life's Pleasures And Treasures

Just feel the supernatural warmth
And joyous surroundings around you
As all the world's stars will blossom their shine afar.
As when we are walking through the emerald forests,
We will feel the delicate touches from the butterflies' wings
Which will ignite all the world's pleasures to feeling life's diamond treasures.
As there will be no worries, only extra hurries for nature's finest paths
So our brain marbles will feel the beautiful star awards to all worldly tours.

Steven Pearson

Winning Smile

Seeking out the message, hidden in your eyes
Meeting lips now pressing, expressions of your sighs
Intimate responses interpret, meanings brought to bear
Lost emotions now returning, to comfort and to care
Escape the hold of time, live life's seconds to the full
Sucked in by passion's moment, drawn in by its pull.

Senses start to reel, before the coming revelation
Memories then flood back, to form the realisation
Inner feelings burst forth, emerging on the surface
Loosened from their ties, now ready to embrace
Ecstasy transcends, yet to a new found zone
Special thoughts now emerge, you are not alone.

Secret wishes now fulfilled, with the new found key
Messages now translated, dot the 'I' and cross the 'T'
It makes the heart beat faster, causes the pulse to race
Lets the body now reveal, with its beaming on the face
Excuses are now put aside, you can break out in a grin
Smiles outwardly shown, in this life's game, you win.

Graham Broughton

Blessings

Blessings are things we can be glad of in life,
In a world that seem so full of strife!
It is best to count our blessings every day,
This helps to cheer us, when wrong comes our way!
At the start of a New Year the days are cold and bleak,
We have telephones in our home and pockets, so to friends we can speak.
Sending a card or a letter on any date,
What a blessing to communicate!
To get out and about is another good thing.
We can bless others by a visit and by gifts we bring!
I am blessed with grandchildren visiting me!
To see smiling faces, is a joy to see!
I have photograph albums on my bookshelf now,
They can provide memories to treasure, a comfort somehow!
To go to church to sing, a blessing too,
To thank God our Father from whom all blessings flow.
So many blessings it is impossible to count them all now!
I hope in this life to provide some cheer,
By counting my blessings each day that I am here.

Joyce Hallifield

Nature

Wings of wonder
Birds flying
Silver in the sky,
Look up and see
How wonderful nature can be,
Count your blessings,
See the sky
The moon, all free,
How wonderful
Counting your blessings,
Can be.

Doreen Thomson

Joined Hands

Your hand holding mine,
Saw me through the maze,
Keeping me safe
Through haphazard days.

Your hand holding mine,
Upon our wedding day,
Placed a ring upon it,
As my dad gave me away.

Your ring placed so tender,
Upon my trembling hand,
Completed Love's sweet circuit
Within its wedding band.

My hand placed in yours,
Found a haven in your hold,
Turned me from frightened girl,
To a woman much more old.

Your hand squeezing mine
Told me of your love,
And lifted me sky-high
To blue heavens above.

My hand placed in yours
Through the furore of the years,
Calmed my inmost worries,
And kept away the tears.

My hand will ever only
Be held within your grasp,
And that yours finds mine freely
Is all I'll ever ask.

Aleene Hatchard

To Eddie, A Dearly Loved Husband

I see the sunset's lovely glow,
And think of you.
I wake at sunrise to the day,
And think of you.
Each hour that passes, oh, so slow.
I think of you.
I feel your presence in the sun's ray,
And think of you.
Put out my hand to talk to you,
But you have gone away,
And I am alone.

I fill my day with all the tasks you used to do,
And think of you.
The garden leaves and roses' scent.
I think of you.
I only have to hear an aircraft in the blue,
To think of you,
Evenings drag, in loneliness spent.
I think of you.
I say goodnight,
And have no reply.

You always were my hero in your uniform of blue.
I still think of you.
We would not have survived the war, without heroes just like you.
I remember you.
So now I hold your medals as a memory of the past.
So all the ghosts of yesterday, stay, as memories that will last.
I feel you near, but cannot see
Where you are.

But when I see the passing clouds and colours in the sky.
I think of you
And wonder that I still remain and ponder the reason why.
To think of you.
The memories of many years, the love that still is there.
To remember you.

The closeness of all the love and care.
I will always remember you.
I speak to you but you
Cannot answer.

Gwyneth Pritchard

Life Goes On

What faith have ye
When you cannot see and
Your eyes have closed their blinds
But there is a path that nature finds
For other senses will take command
Compensate and help one understand.

The world is in so much disarray
Yet hope can truly come your way
A challenge beckons to know your fate
Only time will answer what lies in wait
But inner strength helps one start anew
A new door opens with a different view.

So take heart the sun again will shine
A future one day will become benign
Open your mind and then you'll see
A place to explore and set you free
The warmth of family is there every day
To help you walk on that great highway.

Norman S Brittain

The Gift

Out of love is everything made,
The morning and the night
The whole universe and many worlds
Drifting far beyond our sight.
Love made the sun to rule the day
Designed the moon for the night.
And fashioned the many dancing stars
To keep our pathways bright.
Our tiny Earth, where we now live
Is very richly dressed.
The Earth, the sea, and the clear blue sky
Where we live, and work and rest.
The Earth is clothed in a carpet of green,
Renewed every morning with dew.
It stretches right over the countryside,
Blending above with the blue.
The sea, often calm and tranquil,
But sometimes dark and strong.
Makes up the basic structure,
From which all life will come.

Pamela Stoner

Autumn

Lucky are we who have sight to see,
The glorious colours splashed on a tree
From the palette of the artist 'supreme',
They blend and compliment the singing stream.

As autumn slips in, the colours stun.
Green to gold glinting in the sun
Interlaced with dark, dark red.
Summer surely now has fled.

Morning mists, gossamer o'er the wold,
Silent, waiting for the day to unfold.
The leaves glisten from the morning dew,
The jewel-like colours shining through.

There is no sound, all is still
Interrupted only by a robin's trill.
A glorious vision suspended in time
To hold and to keep, this image sublime.

Daphne McFadyen

Our Guiding Friend

When dark clouds hang above us and the way ahead looks grim
As we journey o'er the rugged paths of life
When we stumble in the darkness, lost, alone in all our sin
And we know how much we need a guiding light
If we reach our hand to Jesus and we call upon His name
Then the darkness and the shadows fade away
For He knows each hidden pathway, every dark and lonely lane
And has promised, if we ask, He'll lead the way!
None but He can guide us safely on this long and bumpy road
None but He can keep us on the narrow way
Only He can ease the burden of our sinful heavy load
Only He can lead us back when oft we stray!
Through the darkness and life's turmoils as we journey on ahead
Let us trust His precious guidance all the way
When we reach our journey's end, then we'll know who's been our Friend
When we see the golden dawning of the day!

Isaac Smith

Life's Blessings

When you wake up in the morning
And you cannot face the day
For the job you hold is menial
With no prospects and low pay.

Spare a thought for other people
Not as fortunate as you
Whose lives hang in the balance
And whose blessings are so few.

Don't yearn to be like Beckham
For fame and untold wealth
Be glad you live in Britain
To exist, and have good health.

To be alive is the great blessing
And marvel at, this wondrous Earth
Just to taste the joys of living
Shows exactly what life's worth.

Take a trip into the country
Walk the green and pleasant hills
Stroll along the sea kissed beaches
Feel the beauty ease your ills.

So go on and keep enjoying
Choose a path and make your way
Don't forget, you're rich in blessings
And they're with you, every day.

Graham Thomas

Tabula Rasa

Great! We are finally here
At the point where
Everything has collapsed
And all we have to do
Is clear away the debris.
It was so frustrating,
So incomplete,
When there were still bits
Standing, not yet fallen, about to fall,
Now we can rejoice, one and all
And on the cleared surface
We will be able
To dance.

Elaine Harris

Magic Moment

A cold windy autumn morning,
Taking the dog for a walk.
Trudging round the football field,
I deep in depressing thoughts,
The dog sniffing his own little world,
Leaving his scent for his friends.

Moving across the side of the golf course,
Long, muddy tussocks of weeds.
Could I juggle my money to pay all the bills?
Would my daughter's fraught marriage endure.
While the dog skittered backwards and forwards,
Chasing unseen smells in the air.

Heading home we came to a copse of trees.
With the wind now howling wildly,
The wonderful magic occurred.
As I stepped in the midst of the falling leaves,
Multicoloured moths, caught in the reeling gusts
Rained every which way on me.

Swirled and twirled, lifted and danced,
To a tune that blew from the wind.
Crunched and crashed, rose and fell
Till I laughed and laughed and danced as well,
Whirling dervishes we, the wind, the leaves and I
And the dog looked on waiting to take me home.

Sheila Wicks

Amber

A little girl called Amber,
Comes calling from next door,
She bounces in with tales from home,
And tales from school galore,
She has a smile to melt your heart,
Her laughter is so infectious.
She helps me dust and make us cakes
She really is so charming
I hope she's around for a long while yet,
'Cause she really is a darling.

Mari Gilmore

There's You

Anyone can see, there's only one for me
My lover, my joy.
Everyone should know that everywhere I go
There's you.
Waking on my mind throughout the day I find
My lover, my joy.
I close my eyes to see a picture looks at me
There's you.
You're with me constantly
A thought that I can rely on.
You give me strength to see
That nothing is impossible
With you by my side.
Whatever I may do wherever I may go
My lover, my joy
Any fool can see, whenever there is me
There's you.

John Greenslade

Bless The Word

Came life
Out of infinity.
Union with the night
Neighbour of daylight,
Treasured by those alert.

Youths to convert
Older wiser onwards,
Ugly never! Always lovely
Ruby, pearl, or emerald.

Brightest jewels are man
Lucky to be alive,
Each day brings new
Souls of the word,
Strong in verbal richness
Icons of the island,
Nation's national treasures
Growing into elders
Singers, poets, word slaves.

Linda Coleman

My Birthday Wish For You

My birthday wish for you
Is happiness, forever new
I hope it lasts your whole life through
As will my love, so very true.

My kiss was so sincerely meant,
I know my love is Heaven sent
You must have been made for me
So let our friendship always be.

My gift to you, to keep you warm
From wind and rain and heavy storm
I never want to know alarm
To know you're always safe from harm.

I miss you so when you have gone
When you have left me all alone
My thoughts are for you all the time
Please tell me soon, when you'll be mine.

Our affair could be so loving
All our joy would be so moving
I know that you've been sent for me
Let us hope this will always be.

I want to tell you through these rhymes
The way I've loved you many times
Our kisses all so tenderly
Ever meant from you to me.

Until my heart forgets to beat
You'll be my love, when e'er we meet
When will you let your feelings come
Then only, will I know I've won.

John Pierrepont

My Counted Blessings

If we count our blessings, one by one,
They could make us grateful for what we've become
I, myself am blessed with a gift,
Writing stories and verse, which give me a lift
My father is the one I thank for this,
If he were still here, I'd give him a kiss.

Ena Andrews

An Ode To Zarah

I meet this girl whose heart seeks the faith
Oh, melting joy when she moves around,
Locked in her endless dream of the late,
One day her jealous heart would be proud.

Her soft kind looks will break any heart,
Thy right flame will melt her away,
Such a fancy gives writing 'bout art,
Then handsome flame would take her one day,
Their love and passions will delight,
Such a popular soul will arrive,
The love songs that makes her face just bright,
The sometime hearty love will approve.

The sweet loveliness will love approve,
Sky will grant true love its permission,
Wordy love Heaven will hearty prove,
And bless'd each true love by tradition.
In her own lips will live true kisses,
Her fancy will make delightful day,
Oh, her mind will delight blifulness,
Too, her heart's fame will melt fear away.

Milan Trubarac

Summer Days

Forget the winter weather
And think of summer days,
Fresh green fields and flowers
And beautiful sun-drenched ways.

Paths you take when walking
Off leafy country lanes,
In spring knee-deep in bluebells
In autumn the soft damp rains.

The hedgerows with their brown twigs
Housing our feathered friends,
The undergrowth where red ants
Their busy work extend.

Think of the stately iris
Bright yellow and cornflower-blue,
The lilac colour of waving phlox
And the rose with its perfect hue.

The beauty of a country church
Where you slip inside to pray,
In the cool you kneel to our Father
To give thanks for our summer days.

Iris Forster

Me Grandad; Died 1952

Me grandad told me 'bout the world
When 'e was young, an' freshly 'girled'.
T'old Queen 'ad died; no tears from 'im;
They young-uns saw 'er times as grim!
They'd brighter stars,
An' motor cars
Filled future's cup up to t'brim!

'e never talked about the War
The pains 'e felt an' sights 'e saw,
But when 'e went in fifty-two
Others told what 'e'd bin through.
The fear-fraught fights
An' trembling nights,
'e'd deeply drunk that sick'nin brew!

'is son, me dad, 'ad fewer tears
When young in so-called 'peaceful years',
But then there came a second war
Which snatched 'im from me grandad's care
To shoot an' kill
Agin 'is will
An' travel far, 'e knew not where.

Dad came of age in forty-three,
An' married Mum, 'an fathered me:
A father I would never know
For back to war 'e 'ad to go
An' there 'e died,
Me grandad's pride,
To close that year of joy an' woe!

What lovin' 'and then stroked me 'ead?
Who was it tucked me up in bed?
Who told me of 'is boyhood days?
Who brought me sick-bed breakfast trays?
Me grandad-dad,
Whose little lad
Lacked now't 'neath t'old chap's anxious gaze.

I loved 'im like a proper Pops,
An' Mum was Mum so all was tops.
I pr'aps wondered 'bout 'is skin an' bone
An' why 'e always slept alone.
Yet 'spite broken 'eart,
'e played the part,
A bestest Dad. Me very own!

J LeC Smith

This Blessed Earth At Eastertide

England, my England,
Where are you now?
We loved you as you
Loved us, and how!

Driven away by those
Who do not care,
Forsaken by they
Who only stand and stare.

Our fortress destroyed?
Those who love you know,
That England's where those
With splendid hearts may go.

Cry, 'St George for England'
Before thy Cross we stand,
Great God our salvation
Your resurrection is at hand.

Roger Jamieson

The Gift Of Love

I watched my plant grow
From a tiny stem
To a pure white flower,
As driven snow,
It was given to me
By two tiny hands -
'Here you are, Nan,
This is from school.'

It cost five-pence
But was expensive
In love,
He cared for me
In a way so dear,
With love like that
What have I to fear?
My grandchildren are
Gifts from above
And I thank God
For their lives
And their love.

Rita Beresford

There's The House

There's the house with red bricks so warm
That withheld many a bad storm.
And there is Dad and Mother too,
Stood at the door waiting for you,
Full of love with smiling faces.
Your heart quickens and your paces,
Rushing to arms that hold you tight,
Keeping you safe from hurt and plight.
There's the cat and the dog sprawling
In front of the fire, brawling
With each other in gentle war,
Rolling and growling in the glow.
The same pictures hang on the wall
And rugs and carpets in the hall.
Familiar smells of cooking
Drift from the kitchen, unlocking
Memories of family nights
Gathered together in the light
Of low-lit lamps, softening dusk
Which gathers in deep dark'ning nooks.
And the same old bed which complains
As you twist in the counterpane,
In your search for quiet repose,
Stretching yourself from head to toes.
And there are the old creaks and groans
Of the house . . . and you know you're home.

Gwendoline Douglas

The Gift

When life seems at low ebb
World news sad and dreary
Despair a close companion
Aching body weary
Then to my old recorder
Fingers fly for music's balm
Such joy and infinite blessing
Composers' gift of calm.

Marion Webb

Countless Gifts Of Love

Oh how my bones creak
As old age creeps on
So much slower in all I do
And yet, so much to be done!

How a welcome cup of tea
At the start of a new day
Is the tonic I need
And then I pray.

Yes, I pray to my God
For He is my friend and my guide
Always beside me
Whatever betide.

As I draw back the curtains
The sunrise peeps over the hill
Casting a pink canopy
Of tranquillity and goodwill!

There on the lawn I espy a blackbird
With his head to the ground
Listening intently for the squirm of a worm
Such a welcome sound!

My constant companion
Rescued from hunger and spite
Longs to sit on my knee
With her droning purr of delight.

The red coals of the fire
Bring light and cheer
Comfort and solace
Dispelling all fear.

At the end of the day
In the fading light
I close my eyes
Dreaming through the mists of time
So much joy and yet many goodbyes.

As night descends, stars drape
Across a velvety sky
Like a bejewelled necklace
No money could buy
Thank you God, my Father
As You pour upon my life
Your countless gifts of love.

Frances Gorton

You Never Know You're Blessed

You never know when to count your blessings,
Life is more complete than you know.
Taking for granted loved ones at weddings,
Then at funerals, it hits you when they go.

Feeling complete but don't appreciate -
Then it's too late to ingratiate.
People you knew and saw every day,
No longer in your life's enduring picture, worn away.

When young, it is time to live,
Holding onto hurt, too righteous to forgive.
Only in middle years, as empathy grows,
You see others had the same tears and woes.

Experiencing immense extraction,
Felt more in a social or personal interaction.
Gone the ones cherished the most;
Intangible as a crest spied from the coast.

Through the lives of a new generation grown,
Misgivings are put to rest for seeds of resolution sown.
Only through the eyes of yourself in others new,
Can you remember what was dear but passed.

The first flush of youth has been utilised.
Now is the time to step forward and realise -
Command a self awareness and declare,
'Yes, this is good, yes, this is true and yes, this is wise.'

Thomas W O'Connell

Africa's Leopard

The African forest holds in its folds an animal perfect in stealth
A tawny yellow coat with black rosette spot
The feline, graceful and strong
By the skin of its teeth, as it leaps up a tree, holds firmly a carcass
I see body pattern matches sunlit leaf, elegantly poses;
A large carnivorous of the cat family
While I peep through an opening, hidden.
It hangs astride at full stretch on a branch watching me?
While eating its brunch high above the ground;
Africa's leopard forty feet above in the tree, hidden cubs slumber,
Its mate close by, sleeps sound.
Nothing disturbs their calm, shaded from the midday sun
Do you recognise the mark of its maker's hand? Instinct abounds.

Norma Landolfi-Bowden

To Julian

He hadn't far to go now,
Down that long and winding lane -
The lane that led somewhere, somehow,
Away from all the pain.

His daughters came with cheerful smiles,
Settling down by the hospital bed.
Hastily dabbing her grief-stricken eyes,
His wife came with jaunty tread.

He smiled - was that him smiling?
Standing on a sunny lawn,
Hearing the rooks and whiling
By the pond on a summer's morn.

Peering at the fish there,
Scales glistening through the deep;
In the flower-laden morning air
Bees drowsily lulled him to sleep.

A paradise garden in the Hertfordshire hills -
All that you had and more,
A haven to linger away from all ills -
In the shade by the summerhouse door.

Rosemary Harvey

Did You Know?

You know that Christmas is past
And January's grim.
Stormy, windy, early dark
Stuck indoors, no walks in the park.
But did you know that
There's a red rose peeping in my window
You've heard of the last rose of summer,
Seems this guy's the last rose of winter.
He's brilliant red,
So is the robin looking to be fed.
There's no sorrow in blackie's song
'Did you know?' he says
'The shortest day's past and now they're getting long?'

Snowdrops and aconites to look forward to soon
And up in the sky there's a beautiful moon.
Things must be getting better, 'cause they can't be getting worse
My heart's so full of joy I had to put it into verse.

Marjory Gordon

Arise Friendly Poets In New Beginnings

Arise friendly poets with pens so poised this era of relevant time
From all ashes past, fervently create fresh fields of beauty
Time to be new prophets who can point the way they clearly sense
Shine healing rays to ones despairing of any race or creed
Patiently and gently show inspiring and viable pathways
That they can bless with loving and compassionate care
If need be now, reveal best depths of soul to those who read
Shout, cry, smile or laugh in appropriate emotion for value added
Point direction for those lost, lonely or desperately perplexed
Let's help contain worst manic moments of man's lows and highs
Faithfully lead the way to joyous heavens of glory bright
Speaking close to heart's pains with healing rays of sacred thought
Heralding new age of better times, - as angels of such timely need
Let now humanity's very best features - warm the globe
Till the lives of freshened life flows along, - so beautiful
Perceptive poets pacing prized pathways of potential peace
That a hurting world -
waits receptively -
to hear!

Don Harris

Combating Arthir

The X-ray shows your cartilage is wearing out
Down in your lower spine, its lumbar part.
The doctor's news, last year brought me up short
I'd known for years about my shoulders, wrists and knees
But this was the severest shock to me.
OK, I'd ached for years, when gardening, well lots!
Had known, 'up here' I couldn't stand for long.
Some people thought (and said) I'd put it on.
Since then I've swallowed tablets by the score;
Used magnets, heat pads, infa-red and acupuncture.
I've shuffled (with a stick), rubbed 'Deep Heat' on
And, just about used every trick to see the thing off - gone!
With gritted teeth I've clung to furniture,
Then given in and used my TENS machine.
The upside of all this now I've excuse to sit
And write and paint and draw
And though I am less active then before
We still get out to classes; have Saga holidays
Because I have a scooter now, we're out most days
We're members of the National Trust and also U3A.
I'm *not done*, yet, my *brain's* still active, see
This thing's not going to have me *beat*
I'm raring to be me!

Ella Neal

Tomorrow?

I awoke to a morning of skies cold and grey
And drizzle was falling and fell all that day;
But in faraway lands where scorched earth lay
The folk had no water and vainly did pray.
I switched on the lights and heat to keep cold at bay,
But in some lands that's banned for most of the day.
A washing machine made life easy and glad
But in other lands no water or heat could be had.
I needed a doctor and saw one that week
But in far-off lands a witch doctor was all one could seek.
I was injured one day so a hospital sought
But for some, no help is there unless it is bought.
And even then - no drugs can be had
And hygiene non-existent and medicine bad.
So now when I moan about rain and grey skies
I try to think twice and open my eyes
To the fact that the things I accept as my right
Many would be glad just to sleep safe at night,
To have water just at the turn of a tap
To dwell in safety free from bullet or knife.
To have food every day and no terrors in life.
For children to have safety to walk and to play
Not fearing armed men will take them away -
To sell to the West for slaves or for porn.
They should sleep safe at night and know safety at dawn.
Oh, wake up world from your torpor of wealth
And think of the have-nots instead of yourself.
Give help to the wretched to be free from such fate
And free terrorised children before it's too late.
We have lived in a land of great beauty and wealth
But indulge our great appetite just to please self.
We live as though time will stretch on without end
Not thinking that this may be the last day we'll spend.
Each day we're given is a gift of great worth
We must use it as though 'twere our last day on Earth.
Oh mend quick your ways, do not tarry or wait
For tomorrow may not come and you'll then be too late!

Betty M Irwin-Burton

Take Time To Stop And Think

Have we forgotten what Christmas is for?
Presents and many bargains galore.
Children will be eager to tell you of that there's no doubt.
Why it's lots of food, presents and fun, that's what it's all about.
But now that it's over and you've had plenty to eat and drink.
Just take the time to stop and think.
We spend hundreds of pounds here and there
Just let us take the time and try to care.
All we get are just a material thing
If we try to help others just think of the joy this could bring.
Remember our homeless perhaps through no fault of their own
Sleeping in cardboard boxes feeling vulnerable and all alone.
Many stealing to get money for their drugs
Once upon a time they were not thugs.
Sometimes life is so mean
This so many times we have seen.
We are becoming so greedy
Please don't let us forget the needy.
I'm not much of a religious person I must admit
But I'd like to think I could do my bit.
Those poor souls in under developed countries would think it a precious gem
If just food and water were given to them.
Are we too blind to see
The most precious gift given to you and me?
Our lives, the love of our family and friends and this should be all we ask.
So helping others is not such a great big task
At school the children act out the nativity play
But do they know, are they taught why they should pray?
Think of the people around the world with nothing but pain
Do they ask for presents? No, they just want to be able to live again.
So people of the world don't cry
He went to Heaven, He didn't die.
Some will say they don't believe, but when help is what they need
They pray to Christ, it's to Him they plead.
But I must stop myself and sigh
Because there for the grace of God go I!

Jan Salmon

England's Seasons

Spring awakes the dormant plant,
Greenness brings a welcome sheen,
Flowering buds the eyes enchant,
Colour paints a magic scene.
Scent of blossoms fills the air,
Refreshing sweetness everywhere.

Summertime and lazy days,
Lounging in the humid heat,
Brilliant rays so fiercely blaze
And mercilessly downward beat.
Beauty and brightness and relaxation,
Happy, restful meditation.

Autumn's wondrous, golden glow
Stirs one's heart with inspiration.
Rich, warming tones of nature show
The wonder of the Earth's creation.
Gorgeous sunsets, burning fires,
Nature's cyclic life inspires.

Winter's chill can cruelly bite
And cover ground with ice and snow.
The once green fields are dazzling white
While frozen waters cease to flow.
A hush envelops the countryside
And latent plants and creatures hide.

The seasons bring their many changes,
In the cities, on the seas,
In meadows sweet or mountain ranges,
Causing drought or deadly freeze,
But always, steadily, life redresses,
Slowly develops, evolves, progresses.

Joan McClung

May I Remember

Brass trumpet daffodils
heralded the Spring
their brazen fanfares silenced now.
On stage blossoms enchantress May
adorned with bluebell, sorrel, celandine
to complement the budding woodland floor.
All around
the joyful sound
of chaffinch, lark and cuckoo,
chorusing, cascading counterpoint.
Garish golden oil seed rape
vies with the sun for pride of place.
Unruffled water, not to be outdone,
reflects the smile of azure sky.
Impatient anglers wait in lazy boat
watch coot, or grebe,
plunge headlong
on some poor unsuspecting tench.
Disdainful swims the supercilious swan
serene upon its placid way,
unmindful of a regal role.

Such bounteous beauty
offers us a glimpse of Heaven
beyond the wit of impotent Man.
Idyllic day -
in all but one:
alas I had no friend to share
and stand enraptured,
hand in hand.

Horace Gamble

What Are You Doing Down There?

(Dedicated to my sister Valerie)

Do you really feel down in the dumps?
Just imagine how you would feel with the mumps?
You could have measles or a bout of the flu,
bunged up and aching, feel worse wouldn't you?

Are debts the problem making you feel down?
Causing worry and fear, making you frown.
Forget your finances if just for one day
the cloud's silver living is on its way.

Remember the folks much worse off than you
no home, no food, no reason to start the day anew.
Some people have no sight or no sound
you can see and hear things all around.

There are those who can't walk without pain
and others whose illness make life a bain.
At least you are whole and can rise to the test
one shot at life we have, give it your best!

Think of your forebears and how they coped
great things for your future and success they hoped.
Don't let them down with your lack of vision
shake off the blues, be thankful and go on.

Look through old photos, ponder for a while
remember the love and warmth in that smile.
Think back to when you laughed fit to burst
deal with your problems, start with the worst.

Draw on the strength of those now passed away
just imagine the words that they would say.
You've lived your life caring, loving and giving
now is the time for you to start living.

Smile and the world smiles with you they say
resolve to make tomorrow your best ever day.
Take up life's challenges, aim high and care
before someone asks, 'What are you doing down there?'

Carl Nixon

We Never Said Goodbye

David you have left us
No words can express our pain,
But you will remain forever in our hearts
Till that day we meet again.

We were blessed with four beautiful children
Fiona, yourself, Lyndsey and John
Three grandchildren, Sarah, Darren and Paul and now
Great-grandson Jake, the youngest of all.

Your patience and kindness was there
For all to see
Whether playing with Rhona and Sam
Or bouncing Jake upon your knee.

You were Dad's right hand man
Always by his side
His tower of strength on which he relied
At this moment in time the future looks bleak
We have lost you dearest David
To us you were so unique

I believe that there's a reason for everything
Although at present it's so hard to believe
However, God willing, we will eventually
Have the courage to go forward and succeed.

God realised that your work on Earth was done
It was time to call you home
Heaven has a new angel now
To us you were only on loan.

In attempting to cope with your parting
Which at present still seems so surreal
David, as your loving mum Joan
I simply had to tell you how I feel.

We pray that you are now at peace
After all the hurt you've been through
Such a wonderful son to be gifted to us
We shall treasure the memory of you.

Joan C Igesund

Angels In White Coats

Everyone takes them for granted, regardless of the profession they take
They only realise when they're a patient, that they've made a grave mistake.
To witness the care they provide, while they go from bed to bed
It's not a fairy tale from some book that once you read.
Their work goes on constantly, seems they're never done
Caring for their patients, it can't be measured by the ton.
Doctors, sisters and staff, so glad I'm in your care
Admiration doesn't come cheap; I'm pleased you're there.
Apologies are only words, leaving is too much to bear
It feels a bond has been formed, one you're not willing to share.
When you're inside or a patient, remember there's a code
Accept their commands, doing what you're told.
Nursing skills will be always needed, a blessing to us all
This nation would be lost without them; it makes you feel rather small.
They are there for a reason, their patience is beyond compare
Proving to all that enter, they're getting the best of care.
So when you come as a visitor, don't stand and gloat
Remember they are not only nurses, but are angels in white coats.

JRH Graham

Psalm To The Poetry Of Joy

The moon rises like mist distilled from a burnt river,
It whirls with her humming until the bonds unravel,
Now she is caressing the smile into radiant morning,
Her dust is lingering, it sprinkles onto dormant souls
Of night awaking our song of love to a golden dawn,
The poet's pen is dipping into this chalice of nectar,
It wanders across pages with infinity and innocence,
A dance with the light and shadows of sacred ritual,
Psalm of joy to a pristine moon and the drowsy sun.

Nigel Pearce

Here . . . Now

Be happy for this minute
Savour every second in it
Drink in full measure
Each golden moment's pleasure
Enjoy with all your being
The gifts of hearing and seeing
Then into memory's treasure chest
Place your little gem to rest
Until some future where and when
Your need will bring it out again.

Joan H Callister

And Then She Smiled

(Dedicated to my lovely wife)

The day was dull and filled with gloom,
My soul was dark with thoughts of doom,
I sat inert within my chair,
My spirits low, drugged with despair.
Must life always be such a mess?
I'm less of more but more of less.
What was the point in going on?
Things would improve if I was gone.

And then she smiled . . .

The radiance of it filled the room,
Dispelled all thought of doubt and gloom,
The sun shone and the day was bright,
A switch was thrown to day from night,
My spirits rose, my heat leapt high,
My soul was soaring, let it fly.
Life was good, the future fine,
Love was hers and love was mine.
I sat there basking for a while,
Thank you, thank you, for your smile.

Barry Jones

I Count My Blessings

Dear friends of mine
Some now alone
Their loved one gone
They're on their own.
I count my blessings.
He wears no wings
Or halo bright
The care he brings.
Each day and night
I count my blessings.
Lest we forget the ones who care
For those of us whose pain they share
They don't have wings or halos bright
They're angels of the day and night
I count my blessings.

Jean Spence

Little Things Are The Best

To see the beauty all around
As I wander along a leafy lane,
My cares, they slip away from me
Heedless of the falling rain.

On a chestnut tree, its arms outstretched,
As if to welcome the cooling touch
Of moisture on its thirsty leaves,
Each raindrop they greet and clutch.

To see a garden, in fragrant bloom,
Carpets of pinks and pansies blue,
Delphiniums as sentinels stand noble and proud,
Amid seas of blossom, in every hue.

A chirpy blackbird in a sycamore tree,
Throwing his song to the heavens, and why
Do I feel a new spring in my step?
'Tis the kiss of rain as silk from the sky.

Now a golden redness, a rosy gleam,
Lights up the last of the fading day,
The petals close, the bird has gone,
A new tomorrow is on its way.

Darkness falls - the night is due,
A new day will dawn, a new sun will glow.
So bless the little things that come to you,
And Spring will remain wherever you go.

So look about with eyes open wide
Do not give but a fleeting glance,
The best things in life are free they say,
Make haste or you may miss the chance.

Doris Farran

A Rejoicing Sonnet

Almighty God is my special blessing
Closely followed by family and friends
Good health, cheerfulness in adversity
My lengthy list of blessings never ends
Not material aids, intangible ones
A sound outlook and serendipity
Love and laughter and truthfulness abides
And scorches the Devil's iniquity
Counting your blessings may appear hackneyed
In this instant gratification time
But I urge you to halt for reflection
Indefatigableness heralds sunshine
Of course troubles can always keep mounting
Just assess your true wealth and keep counting . . .

Gladysemily

Inheritance

No myth. Our media gurus
say that last week, allegedly Monday,
our Earth's axis wobbled.

This affected our dictionaries.
They tell us every last word
turned upside down. Or inside out.

In a number of extreme cases
some words scurried back
through our languages, amok.

Speech got cut down
to just four syllables;
tot, bib, tit, tat.

Serious? Just try asking
somebody, what's the time?
Or talk at all, come to it.

Our children you may not know
thrive on such things, they survive
beautifully, dreaming day and night.

Our children dream endlessly,
of imaginary friends and entities.
Their never-ending conversations

use just; tot, bib, tit, tat,
with tonal frequency variations.
Possibly a bit like speaking Chinese.

In this, *their* tilted Earth's reality
all kinds of beauty and beast roam
in and out of our children's hearts

showing them such wonders to come
from their last vast language of light.
How their tilted Earth minds its futures.

Neil mac Neil

The Brighter Side Of Winter

(A treat for the senses)

Wake in the morning and look at the world,
Watch from the window as nature unfurls.
Clouds scudding by on the freshening breeze,
Birds singing spring songs from bushes and trees.
Scent from the daffodils filling the air,
Touch of the winter sun - warmth so rare.
Later we'll walk 'cross the fields to the sea,
Admiring the views, a pleasure that's free.
White-crested waves rolling into the shore,
Skimmed by the seabirds that circle and call.
Back through the woods on the path by the stream
That tumbles on down o'er rocks to the sea.
Sun's low in the sky now, daylight is short.
Home is our haven, a tranquil resort,
Our senses refreshed, our faces aglow,
We'll plan for tomorrow - where we will go!

Anne Lawry

Pink Clouds

In April, the cherry trees bloom pink clouds
Against a pale pellucid sky.
Every branch with pink blossom bows
While above baby-soft clouds wander by.

Each spring, midst April's cool blusters
The trees that stood starkly 'gainst grey winter skies.
Bravely burst forth their pink clusters
To the joy of our hearts and our eyes.

It was ever so since long times past
The scene in sunlight bathed.
It lifts our spirits on high, as we see at last
The cherry trees in full beauty swathed.

All too soon, pink flakes swirling, descend
As skittish winds rock the boughs.
Though next year, we surely may depend
Again we shall see pink clouds.

Ruth Berry

Counting Blessings

When you complain of too much rain,
You really shouldn't oughta!
For many countries in this world,
Are very short of water!

While you eat honey, having money,
An affluent kind of bloke!
Some others live in poverty,
No joy in being broke!

You're driving far in your smart car,
Just wondering where to roam;
You notice people passing by,
Who just don't have a home!

The house is rosy, nice and cosy,
Your life is hard to beat!
And yet out there are orphans who,
Are sleeping on the street!

You tend to waste some food you taste,
Because you say it's rare!
Yet many folk, starvation-faced,
Would say that's just not fair!

You fail to sleep, no, not a peep,
When you lay down your head;
For thoughts, within your mind you keep
Of those who have no bed!

So if you're brave, though you can't save,
The poor, with all these guessings!
Be thankful till you're in your grave
That you can count your blessings.

R Bissett

Tears

The tears that fell upon my face
Were tears of love and full of grace,
The look that He bestowed on me
Was only for my eyes to see.

For I am just a humble soul
And He has come to make me whole,
As I lay there wondering why
The truth came from up on high.

The tears too were for mankind
That they should be so very blind,
For it seems that the human race
Are here, just to the world deface.

So as the gentle tears did flow
To me it seemed that I should know,
For when He showed Himself to me
It was the face of eternity.

So counting my blessings one by one
I know the Lord, His work is done,
And feeling His face so very near
With a sigh and a smile, I too shed a tear.

Winifred Booth

Count Your Blessings

When the earth is scarce and bare
And everywhere is dark and dull
Think for a moment and count your blessings
When you will find life fair and full
With never a dull moment to spare.
Look around you here and there
See if there are those in need
Whom you can help to clothe and feed
Look for wildlife in the winter cold
Sheep strayed from the shepherd's fold
Look for hedgehogs on the road
And bring them in to the cosy fireside
Where in warmth, they can thrive
Until such time they seek the great outdoors
Amidst gardens, fields and lonely moors
Do not mind shopping, cleaning cooking
And having to stay indoors
Never mind the weather
Driving one to the end of one's tether
Just look around and count your blessing!
Be sure you will find not just a few
But more than you ever knew.

Blanche Rice

It's all a question of economics we're told
Everything's priced and must go up or fall,
Marginal utility decides on the outcome
And whether or not it has any value at all.

I pondered awhile over this definition
Of what is worthwhile and what measurably is not,
A friend I had known didn't fit in this picture
His decisions seemed poor and he fumbled a lot.

The sunset that day was both glorious and sad
As my friend left forever his place on the Earth
Many had benefited from the kindness of his deeds
Usually fulfilled with humility and mirth.

He valued everything not by temporal worth
But whether or not it enhanced what is true,
Maybe in the event some wealth was created
But that was incidental as everyone knew.

I considered once again the initial definition
Concerning the costing and accountable reasoning,
That every step or decision we consciously make
Must always clearly have a numerical rating.

Maybe economics sometimes confuses price with true value
As my friend discerned in his utilitarian, fair-minded years,
I couldn't put a price on the sunset that evening
Because its capacious glory inhibited a few tears.

I'm sure those who had benefited from his special kindness
Or been strengthened or uplifted by a comforting word,
Would ever subscribe to the overriding notion
That the broadest definition of value must be heard.

John Pert

All It Takes

All it takes is a patch of blue peering through the storm clouds
All it takes is a snatch of birdsong borne on the breeze at break of day
All it takes is the clasp of a hand in friendship
For the peace of the Lord to shine upon my way.

Meg Gilholm

These Endless Appeals

Here's another one! Still more and more,
They flop through the letter box onto the floor,
appeals for the hungry, the homeless, the blind.
They tell us sad stories, ask us to be kind
and donate some of our wealth
to restore others to health.
And then they ask, 'Can you increase?'
I wish they'd give me a little peace!

Then I think of those people
who are working so hard
to raise money for those whose lives have been marred
by sickness or sorrow,
by loneliness,
by pain,
and I think again.

I am not hungry or homeless or blind.
I am healthy in body and healthy in mind.
The blessings I have I *cannot* count.
The more I try, the more they mount!
So how can I ever give thanks to God
who has blessed me always
in so many ways
but by giving to others
to lighten their days?

Then let the appeals flop to the floor.
May I give to them gladly
in thanks,
for God's blessings galore!

Ellen Rutherford

Day By Day

Writing this poem, as all others
Is a frame of mind,
Putting thoughts onto paper
I try to be kind.
Most of us struggle
With life, day by day
So when warmth comes along
We should all shout hooray!

Les J Croft

Blessings

The world save me seems all a slumber
As the grip of winter is at hand,
So wind and rain follow each other
In a wild assault upon the land.
The rocks remain, old and substantial
As waves crash upon them in Mount's Bay,
Pale tamarisk bends but never breaking
Rooted in cliffs, covered in spray.
Search for a glimpse of winter sunlight
Know the bough must yield before the saw,
Search for pale catkins on a willow,
Know the ice prevails before a thaw.
Each icicle is form and colour
Of shimmering hues that interlace.
Someone once told me, 'Small is lovely
Where your blessings find their own birthplace'.

Frances M Searle

My Angel Fay

And Fay was like the Christmas morn,
She smiled wide with her front teeth gone;
She whispered in my ear, 'My mum loves you.'

The gift I thought I'd never get!
'How do you know your mum loves me?'
Sweet toothless Fay you are indeed a sprite.

'Because I asked her and she said
Hmm, well, I think perhaps I do.'
A good impersonation too my Fay.

Did the world change that afternoon?
I think it did, the past was gone
Gone in a single breath of Fay's soft words

For Fay's mum had said she loved me,
And as she occupies my thoughts
Every moment of the day - the world changed.

'I put you on my Christmas list,'
She beamed, her cheeks aflame and warm,
'Ah then, all wishes do come true,' I said.

Fraser Hicks

In Darkness

I love to listen to the birds, as I walk through the park.
I touch the flowers and smell their scent,
Even in the dark,
In February strange sounds I hear,
As down the street I wend
My stick it helps me feel my way,
My dog, a faithful friend,
I reach my door and know I'm home,
Get greeted by my wife,
I smell the food on table set,
But can't see fork or knife,
No one can take these things away,
They always will be there,
I have a sense of happiness,
To know that people care,
A helping hand is welcome,
People are so kind,
Life has much to offer me,
I can live with being blind.

Vera Parsonage

Happiness

Happiness is in the house of the blessed
Whom God hath redeemed by His blood.
Happy is the man who makes the Lord his trust
And to praise Him is a must.
Happy or blessed it is a thing most wonderful
To grasp with our whole heartful
To belong to Him is out of this world.

And heavenly showers will come down
To fill our hearts with cheer
And gladness, there is no room for fear.
'Fear not,' I hear him say, 'I am with you'
Serve Him oh child of God, He loves you.
He has promised rivers of blessing
That will cause your heart to sing
Songs of joy, pleasures to the king.
For He is worthy for us to bring
Peculiar treasures to Him
'He is building a people of power
And He is making a people of praise
That shall march through this land by my spirit
And shall glorify my precious name.'

G A Cameron

Count Your Blessings

When the skies are very grey
And you've had a rotten day
And you're feeling that you can no longer cope,
Take a careful look around,
Because I have always found
When you do so you will find a ray of hope.

For each black and cloudy sheath
Has memories trapped beneath
Which you alone can speedily unfetter.
So release each golden ray,
They will chase your blues away,
Count your blessings and you'll soon feel so much better

John Eldridge

A Learning Process

When bad things happen
I try to laugh and say,
'When all of this is over
Good things are on the way.'

Everything is for a reason
Whether it's good or bad,
So continue being patient
And the sad will turn into glad.

I now see troubles as blessings
Although they are in disguise,
It's easy to understand this
Once you begin to realise.

Rachel Joyce

Blessings

Life is a blessing
From womb to grave.
In its beginning
Are blessings yet to come,
In its omega the promise
Of a kingdom.
Cradle hours - infant tears
Blend into more mature years.
Each stage brings some new blessings
'Til old age finds it has penned
This is the end
Come enter the promised kingdom.

Pat Bidmead

Celebration

Let all things sing,
Let the butterflies and bees,
Let the insects in the trees
Swell the chorus of the breeze.
Let them sing! Let them sing!
Let each life form, everything,
Let all moving creatures bring
Dulcet memories of spring.
Let them sing! Let them sing!

Let all things sing,
Let the birds carol their joy,
Let the lark and thrush employ
Every note that skies enjoy.
Let them sing! Let them sing!
Let the crow, the rook, starling,
Let the blackbird, all that wing,
Cause the firmament to ring.
Let them sing! Let them sing!

Let all things sing,
Let the creatures of the Earth,
Let reptile, beast, fish prove worth,
Praise together in their birth,
Let them sing! Let them sing!
Let whales set depths echoing,
Let the lion's roar be king
And the sound never-ending.
Let them sing! Let them sing!

Let all things sing,
Let the human race rejoice,
Let it speak with just one voice
And acclaim its Maker's choice.
Let them sing! Let them sing!
Let bass, alto, up-curling,
Let soprano, tenor, fling
Glorious music mingling.
Let them sing! Let them sing!

Let all things sing,
Let the angels inspire choirs,
Let phoenix feed deathless fires,
Till harmony meets all desires.
Let them sing! Let them sing!
Let Gabriel's trumpet swing,
Let cherubim, seraphim,
World's crescendo gather in.
Let them sing! Let them sing!

K Batley

The Young At Heart

The morning breaks, another dawn, you're wrapped around me like a glove
A yawn, a stretch, your hands reach out, your false teeth on the mantle love,
You put them in, another grin to start the day again.
So kiss me on these tender lips, I remember when we were young
In the mirror lines, you look fine, after fifty years as one.
The daily ritual has passed; you go the same time every day
Perhaps it's helped by all the bran, the health food shop said eat this way
No piles in sight, buttocks white, to start the day again.
So kiss me on my tender lips just like when we were young
Get in the car, we won't to far, let's go and find the sun.
The day trip's over, we're all tired out, we're slowing on the landing floor,
Take off our clothes, pyjamas on; we don't have sex no more.
It's gone limp, in the pink, so start the day again.
Cuddle me and hold me close, just like when we were young
Don't mean to say there ain't no way, for us to have some fun.

Carolann Sutton

The Right Approach

The world we live in consists of good and bad,
Some events will bring sorrow and others will make us glad.
Often, what we find is coloured by our personal view of life
Do we journey daily in good cheer or do we always envisage strife?
Pessimism or optimism paints the picture we see,
Tears and forebodings on one hand, otherwise images of glee.

The world about us offers much to give us cheer,
Yet still reminds us on occasion of reasons to fear.
The breathtaking, terrifying power of natural forces
Amply portrays the negative side of Nature's resources.
Yet all around us beauty seeks our approving eye
Of many manifestations in an unending supply.

Consider the swan gracefully gliding down a waterway,
Or the weeping willow gently sweeping a suburban pathway.
The dew in a spun web sparkling in the early dawn,
Or even the tremulous steps of a lamb newly born.
Should not these cameos of beauty encourage us to pursue
An appreciation of our life in a positive point of view?

Allen Jessop

Keep Smiling Through

Don't let life's worries get you down
Just wear a smile and not a frown,
Just keep on smiling and you'll find
Your troubles will be left behind.
Each of us has our cross to bear
And sometimes life seems so unfair
But when we stop to look around
There's so much beauty to be found.
When winter winds blow loud and shrill
And frost is on the window sill,
Do not despair for never fear
Remember spring will soon be here,
And very soon your garden will
Be full of dancing daffodils.
When you lose someone dear to you
Your feel there's nothing left for you,
You long to have them back again
But could you bear to see their pain?
Instead, remember midst the tears
Those happy days, those happy years,
For if you store them in your heart
You'll never feel so far apart.
For all the things that make us sad
There's so much gladness to be had,
Just look ahead and you will find
The gift of a contented mind.

Anne Bonsen

Sam

Here is an eagerness;
A bright brink of tender expectation;
A lighting
Of laughter in round eyes.
Round head tilted.
Here is Sam. A senior now,
Digging phrases with his tongue,
Tining nuggets of implausible whim,
In his coat from eBay.
Cool!
Cool, with his forty-minute trim
And favourite scarf
Knotted the groovy way.

Lucy Taylor

Beyond All Measure

I can't count the stars in the clear, dark sky,
I can't count the swallows swooping high.

I can't count the poppies in the field of corn,
I can't count the songs in the chorus at dawn.

I can't count the leaves on the poplar tree,
I can't count the fish in the salty sea.

I can't count the pebbles on the shingle shore,
I can't count the roses around my door,
I can't count the suffering of the sick and the poor.

Nor can I count my many blessings -
They cannot be measured
But they are deeply treasured.

Megan Hughes

Camden Market

In a bookshop at Camden Market
At the start of the new year
It was with serendipity
That I chanced upon Edward Lear.

His kindly bespectacled eyes met mine
From a sepia photograph,
I was wearing my pea-green coat you know,
He was trying not to laugh.

I paid the three quid on the flyleaf,
To bring him home with me,
Because something within me recognised
We were both far out at sea.

Olwen Smyth

The Butterfly

Her hand lay silent, soft and still,
Her cheeks full with hopeful youth.
Her brow unknitted, finally at bay,
I saw this butterfly fly away.

At first her wings pierced the clouds,
And the pure rain fell with our tears.
But now she allows the sun to shine,
And her rainbow to erase our fears.

With each breath of the wind I feel her there,
Her wishes and whispers buried into my hair.

Charlotte Jones

The Blessings Of A Child

A child is born with beauty and charm to grace our lives
She enchants and delights with the simple joys of living.
No jewels on Earth compare to the gold and diamonds in her curly hair
Or the sapphire-blue of her shining eyes.

Once more we see the pleasures of our world
In clouds, the moon, the stars and flying birds on high,
Was our language e'er so musical as heard from the lips of a babe?
A rich and rolling, increasing vocabulary gleaned from day-to-day.

We delight at the crackling brilliance of fireworks
With their colour and radiance lighting up the sky,
The Christmas trees invite a touch, the baubles and angels and tinsel shining bright
And young eyes all sparkling at the sight.

There's water and sand and shells and earth to dig,
Look, worms and beetles too. Flowers grow with colours bright, perfumes to smell
And butterflies and ladybirds to hold aloft and release with amazement.
What a blessing to see anew our world from the eyes of a child.

Brenda Robinson

Count Our Blessings

Darkness brings its blessings
Through the winter night,
I leave the curtains open,
To view a wondrous sight.

I wait anticipating,
To see the moving stars,
Appearing through the window,
My travellers from afar.

Lifting from the horizon,
They slowly rise in flight,
A gradual moving chain,
Of successive, twinkling light.

Large ones like diamonds,
Teasing me to spy,
Enticed by sparkling wonders,
I willingly comply.

These ironbird phantasies,
With cabins blazing light,
Display a ruby-tipped left,
And emerald to the right.

Slowly, slowly, drawing near,
Depleting jewellery from the sky,
They clamber slowly overhead,
Within the night - goodbye.

Margaret Nicholl

Stirring Of Hope

I love it when the blackthorn blows
on the sleeping trough of winter.
It cheers the spirit's weariness
to see the crest of early spring
washing the senses with hope.
We may wait long for nature's bounty
the bright brave blooms -
these early flowers kindling hope
enough to soothe the weary.

Joan R Gilmour

Searching For Happiness

When you are feeling deeply troubled and lost
As if everything in the world has gone wrong,
Look upwards, and see all the clouds in the sky,
Ask for God's help, it will make you feel strong.

Memories don't have to cost a lot of money
But they store as life's treasure year by year,
Sometimes we need good and simple things
To make all our troubles seem to disappear.

Just glance at a young baby's happy smile.
Hear a boy soprano singing a special song,
Maybe it's a male voice choir, harmonising,
Bringing back memories of where you belong.

Now none of these things cost much money
Yet they've the power to cut through any pain.
When they cheer us through our darkest hours,
The people who make life worth living again.

Remember to get love; one first has to give it
And not stand back in fear of getting burned-
It's when people least expect it, that they find
Joy once more into their life has returned.

Mavis Simpson

A Joyful Heart

Oh joy that in our hearts give
that something that makes us live
and ready to forgive.

The bad things suffered in the past
now that are gone, no longer last.

With outward sense and thought
forget the past, and what it brought
and live your life serene
by looking at it evergreen.

Francis Xavier Farrugia

Live To Your Limit

My blessings I count at the end of each day
A stranger's smile, a child at play.

The fullness of laughter, a sweet cup of coffee,
A big chocolate bar and the smoothest toffee.

Aloft, a rainbow, birds in flight
Warming sun, the joy of daylight.

A wagging tail, the softest purr
The comfort of stroking our pet's smooth fur.

A knock on the door and there stands a friend
Extending some flowers with a 'Please could you lend . . .'

A postcard arrives from some distant shore
Bringing a message over which I pore.

From the honeymoon couple in love with life
And with each other, now man and wife.

Reflecting, I think of all I can do
Dress myself and tie the lace of my shoe.

Make some bread and a pot of tea
Listen to radio and watch TV.

Walk the dog and feed the cat
Enjoy new clothes and spend a lot.

Owning a car and being glad I can drive
Being fit, whole and very much alive.

For yesterday is over, over and gone
Tomorrow we may not have won.

But the now we have, enjoy every minute
Live, live, live to your limit.

Shelagh C James

The Norfolk Broads

As your boat glides through the water the feeling is this,
The feeling of freedom to me is sheer bliss.
The things that you see as you get underway
Changes quite rapidly day after day,
The wildlife is abundant, a joy to behold,
A glimpse of a heron is worth more than gold.
The wildflowers, the bulrush, a blossom on a tree,
Seems like the Garden of Eden on Earth for me.
The windmill, the Wherry, the cruiser, the yacht,
All help to add to the pleasures you've got.
The colourful wild ducks and kingfishers too,
All helps to make Heaven on Earth for you.
As you glide through the water on our Norfolk Broads,
It's the nearest thing to paradise so just thank the Lord.
The reeds stand on guard all along the way,
They move with the boat's wash and gently sway.
See the craftsmanship of a building topped with thatch,
Seemingly, to surpass this, there is no match,
As you pass churches, wind-pumps or weir,
It makes you feel you're glad to be here,
The honking of geese in a noisy display
Will soon break the peace of a beautiful day.
You can laze or just gaze at the beauty put on the Earth to be seen,
And enjoy all the rapture be you ordinary man, king or queen.
Be you bishop, pop star, local or visitors having a break
The Broads in all their beauty are there for everyone's sake.
The elegant swans hold their proud heads in the air,
Gracefully swimming about without a care.
Men sitting fishing try their luck for roach and bream
To catch the biggest one yet is their dream.
With dragonflies and butterflies flitting by,
Are sure to catch anyone's watchful eye,
See delightful grebe with young ones on their back
It seems parental care they do not lack,
Scurrying waterhen, coot or swooping gull
The sheer peacefulness gives you and me time to mull
Over our thoughts and wallow in bliss,
To find and enjoy you just shouldn't miss.

Joyce Hammond

Memories

We all have some possessions collected through the years,
Some bring happy memories, others bring the tears.
Not many from our childhood we didn't bother then,
We were far too busy learning and counting up to ten.
When maturity came though we started to collect,
Some we threw away, the special ones we kept.
And as the years went speeding by
We were loathe to part with any,
So by the time we reach old age
In our collection there will be many.
Knick-knacks from the seaside
Gift from far and wide,
Birthdays, Christmas, holidays, we look at them with pride.
Every spring we got them out, determined some should go
But memories kept flooding back as we sorted them you know.
We couldn't bring ourselves to do it
Our resolution was gone,
How many did we throw away?
I'm afraid the answer's none!

Wendy Bryan

Memories

Photographs on my kitchen wall
Memories of loved ones to recall.
Happy times with family and friends,
Walks in the park on wintry days.
Snow surrounding as the children play.
Snowballing, sledging,
Oh what fun to be a child again.,
Blowing bubbles, chasing and jumping,
Laughing when they burst.
The beautiful colours of rainbow hues,
Shining through.
Family snapshots, beloved parents
Now gone,
I'm so glad that memories
Linger on and on and on.

Rita Cassidy

Alone

The movement less, no food at all,
The words grew less, there is a call,
The doctor comes to see how sick,
The ambulance called, to hospital quick.

Infection soon takes hold so tight,
The drugs, injections, cause a fright,
The journeys full of wind and rain,
The life at home so full of pain.

No smile, no greeting, all so still,
The doctors, nurses, work at will,
To see a chink of progress, great,
To bring her home will be class date.

The journeys home so full of fear,
The tasks to do will bring some tears,
But on the doorstep, fresh cooked meal,
A kindly friend knows what it feels.

The telephone calls come thick and fast,
Some are just short, but others last,
This breaks the night and gives one hope,
The friendship great, it makes me cope.

John Paulley

Bereavement

Take heart, my dearest friend
This sorrow will pass away,
All sad thoughts will slowly end
And life will once again hold sway.
Time is a great healer dear
Have faith, God is at your side,
He will wipe away the tear
Until you turn the tide.
Take comfort and learn to smile again
Your friends all wish you well,
They share with you your pain
For only time will tell.
When you are happy once more
And there is love around you
As once there was before
When all things are made anew again.

R P Candlish

Going Home

(Just a short visit to my hometown after Christmas on the hills)

I went back to London to see the London sights,
But the only thing that glows there are the brighter London lights.
Tower blocks fill the skyline, where people once had been,
Cardboard city cut-outs where once a smile was seen.
I walked along the Thames, where we watched the world go by,
But the places and the faces change and I began to wonder why.
The magic that was London, began to disappear,
The friendliness, the warmth and charm, almost turned to fear.
The old man in the subway, they called the one man band,
No longer plays his music with a begging bowl in hands.
Young people fill his place now, from many, many lands,
Many, many begging bowls and multi-cultural bands.

On winter's nights in doorways, they sit huddled from the cold,
Among the trash and plastic waste, no streets are paved with gold.
They join the struggle to exist, with others of their kind,
Their faces age each morning, as the sun draws back the blind.
My life began in London, my heart still lingers there,
The magic part of London, that made you stop and stare.
The friends I had have moved away, but others still arrive.
They add to all our memories and on memories we thrive.
I remembered all the good times, when London had its pride,
When its people stood together, to cheer a royal bride.
We watched the State occasions, for cabinets and kings,
But times have changed the way of life and priorities are things.

I've wandered through the parks and squares, subways and hotels,
Looking for old London's heart that rang out like the bells.
I find my London's dying, the heartbeat almost gone,
I only have my memories to tell me where I'm from.
But politicians and their planners may find to their surprise,
That the people who were London and listened to their lie
Still walk below the concrete blocks that blot out all the sky
For London is its people and they're not prepared to die.

Jonis Pastit

Where's Prince Alfred Now?

Where's Prince Alfred now, my friends?
A landmark for us to discuss matters,
a second home and a house of joy,
the place I spent many an hour when I was a boy.

Where's Prince Alfred now, my brother?
The faces upon the walls and behind bars,
the feeling of warmth watching the people filling their jars,
without its faded dartboard the place wouldn't seem like a morgue.

Where's Prince Alfred now, my lover?
The machine its tempting cherries,
sipping beer from a sometimes empty tomb
other times the pleasant smoke-filled room.

Where's Prince Alfred now then?
The times you'd be found up there,
the symbol of your mind a place of care,
sometimes as fierce as the lion's den.

Where's Prince Alfred now, my very self?
This happy barman puffing on his pipe,
with the desiderata once on the wall
or the saloon like the Viking hall.

So where's Prince Alfred now, my son?
A little bench outside marked a spot,
drowning and laughing more than a lot,
can you or anyone remember the fun?

Where's Prince Alfred now, my friends?
A landmark for us to discuss matters,
a second home, a house of joy,
the place I spent many hours when I was a boy.

Simon Boothby

Tenderness

Tears of rain upon my windowpane.
Love lost and gained.
I love you, never to be.
Relax in each other's company.
You asleep on the settee.
Dreaming of wild passion.
Me content to hear you breathing.
Watch you laugh, watch you cry.
Because you could never be with me.

Tricia Jones

Inanimate Beauty

If my ornaments could come to life,
They'd have so much to tell
About the folk who gave them me,
When they wished me well.
If my ornaments could come to life,
They'd each have a story,
Of poverty, frustration, joy,
Hidden in their glory.

They'd surely say from whence they came,
And who created each:
The jeweller, potter, silversmith -
All folk now out of reach.
The struggles that beset each one,
As their craft they wrought.
Did purchasers care ought for these,
When the goods were bought?

As my ornaments can't come to life,
When dusting them each week,
I admire the skill and patience
Shown in them, as they seek
To achieve the pure perfection
Of beauty, shape and style,
That gives such satisfaction,
And evokes seraphic smile.

So my ornaments don't need to live,
(Not in the sense we mean)
Their presence speaks with eloquence:
God's hand, through Man, is seen.

Art fills my soul with utmost pleasure,
Related to ethereal treasure.

Rosemary Mann

Smile, Jesus Loves You

Sam, Sam, Samaritan,
You've a pretty face,
It's not always to do with,
Ribbons and lace.

I lay by the roadside,
I wasn't very well,
Everyone's too busy,
To save me from my hell.

A bird is singing outside my door,
I think he sings for you,
One in a million take time to stop,
For what it's worth, thank you.

Josie Pepper

To Those Who Can See

What would you do if you were blind
And could not see the sky
With all the lovely sunsets
And birds flying swiftly by?

You'd never see trees or flowers
In blossom every spring,
Their lovely shades and colours
To make your glad heart sing.

How much do we take for granted
The fact that we can see,
But don't forget to spare a thought
For those not as lucky as we.

Never forget to lend a hand
When you are passing by,
For you never know if one day soon
You cannot see the sky.

Sybil Edwards

The Aconites

The aconites are coming.
It sounds like an advancing army, all conquering,
Suddenly appearing, taking all by surprise.
Spring's foot soldiers - the infantry.
Bright yellow helmets popping up
To face the blasts of a wintry onslaught,
With a green livery of leaves emerging later.
Are they too bold, too soon, too fragile?
The hard frigid earth would seem to agree
As do the decaying leaves of last autumn
Partially covering them under the weeping birch.
But nature is forever uncompromising -
The lifecycle is marshalled by an overarching programme
That cannot be overthrown by climatic change.
They are the harbingers of spring, of hope and life rekindled.
So stand still a while, try to understand and be amazed.

Robert Main

Winter Of Discontent

Oh, how I hate them, those long winter nights,
Darkness only dispelled by the twinkling of lights,
Wind howling down chimneys and rattling slates,
The banging and clattering of left-open gates.

Cold seeping through my rheumatic old bones,
Chest wheezing in unison with involuntary moans,
Rubber hot water bottle clutched to my chest,
Not really satisfactory, but doing its best.

I miss my old partner, warm and cuddly in bed,
Bedsocks and cardigan must make do instead,
Piling on blankets, trying not to get ill,
Daren't light the fire, cos I can't pay the bill.

Oh, what it is to be lonely and old,
And dread the long winters, so barren and cold,
Then I think of the homeless, asleep in shop doors,
Their only bed is the hard concrete floors.

So I say to myself, 'Well, life's not so bad,'
There's really no need to be fed up and sad,
Look, there are some snowdrops and a crocus so gay,
Hurrah! At last, the spring's on the way!

G K Baker

The Love In View

From every grey and clouded sky
Let a beam of light shine through,
For every tear not even cried
Send a voice to guide them too.

Let every soul distressed and torn
Be comforted by Your hand,
Cause pain and strife to lessen
In every war-torn land.

To every child who reaches out
In fear or great despair,
Show them that You are always near
And place them in Your care.

Make every flower glow with hope
And the green grass sparkle with dew,
So that even the brightest daffodil
Fades to the love in view.

Tracey Lynn Birchall

Thinking Aloud

Life has not always been perfect
I have known loneliness and despair
But always, even in the darkest days
Love was there.

The love of a man can be fickle
And not always true
Although I know I loved and lost
I won when I found you.

The love of a child is a wondrous thing
I have been rich in the love I've received
It is a love that is given honestly
No one can be deceived.

I love the trees, the sky, the earth
Nature's beauty I behold
I love music, perfumes, wine, good food
But I know I'm growing old.

I've sinned in plenty, yes, it is true
And ahead there is doubt of below or above
But in my fear, hope shines through
When I remember God is love.

Elaine Rowlands

Blossoming

It's nice to see the flowers grow
With trees above and grass below.
The sun and moon away on high
Stars a-twinkling in the sky.
Nature's being kind to us
So why do we make such a fuss?
When seasons change and winter comes
And we sit huddled in our homes.
The flowers and trees work down below
Waiting for the spring to grow.
And fill our hearts with fresh delight
As we look at the wondrous sight
All the flowers we thought were dead
Were resting underground instead.
Waiting for spring to come once more
So they can blossom as before.

Pat Adams

A Blessing From Above

Many years ago
You came into our home,
A black ball of fluff,
With nowhere to go.

You'd been badly treated,
Put out on the street,
Your coat was all dirty,
Right down to your feet.

We loved you on sight,
You filled a gap in our lives,
We had just lost one kitten,
What a blessing you survived.

You stayed nineteen years,
You must have been content.
You gave so much love,
Surely you were Heaven-sent.

Early last year you said,
'Enough is enough.'
Illness took over,
We couldn't let you suffer.

You ended your days
Still giving us love,
Many precious memories,
A blessing from above.

Helen Perry

Changes

Time will change you,
Things will come and go,
How and when,
You won't always know.

Sometimes people leave,
When you really don't want them to,
Sometimes people appear,
To make your dreams come true.

I suppose the message is,
That in life, things will change.
So hold you head up high,
And smile instead of sigh.

Michelle Walker

Build Your Bridge

'What will I speak of?' I said in despair
Knowing full well that my guide would be there.
Tell them how barriers spoil life on your Earth
And how pulling them down gives the spirit re-birth.

It's like giving a building a lovely façade
Yet its very foundations are shoddily made.
You must remove all the weak parts, the grot and the grime
And demolish those barriers one piece at a time.

This task won't be easy but very worthwhile
Sometimes a tear - another a smile.
You'll find memories there of loved ones who've passed
A friendship or two you knew wouldn't last.

A stone that was thrown, a harsh word that was said
A letter received that brought hurt as you read.
The regrets that you had and the chances you've missed
There are so many things I could add to this list.

Some blunder through life and never take blame
Their ego inflated with the glory they claim.
Their barriers built by the best architect
A structure that nothing will ever affect.

But sometimes a crack will appear and just spread
And the barrier falls - which is something they dread.
Then spirit will see all the deeds that have hurt
And for everyone noted, they'll receive just dessert.

Some things I have mentioned bring chaos and doubt
So gather them up - and throw them all out.
Sift through what remains with infinite care
But remember - compassion must always be there.

Now mix up some mortar with positive thought
Adding faith and each lesson you've ever been taught.
With all the ingredients will rise something new
A bridge to be used by both spirit and you.
When your bridge is complete with the work you have done
You will then realise our two worlds are as one.
And if either should feel they have something to say
We'll both cross the bridge and meet each other halfway.

Phyllis Lampard

The Quiet Spirit

There is a quiet spirit
To guide you through the dark,
To watch while you are sleeping,
To follow when you walk,
To speak if you will listen,
Advise if you can hear,
You'll know if it is missing,
You'll know if it is near.
But, this illusive presence,
Whatever can it be?
Just think next time you sense it,
Can it be part of me?
And if this thing's inside us
And comes when courage lacks,
Then are we simply holding
Our own hands - behind our backs?
And how can there be guidance
If we merely guide ourselves,
If it's just our intuition,
Not some spirit that foretells.
If we think we've got a partner
And we're sure we're not alone,
Is it really wishful thinking
Of the sort one can't condone?
So is the spirit with you
To answer when you call
Or are you self-reliant
With no 'little friend' at all?
And is it really vital,
When a helping hand arrives,
Whence it comes or what its title,
If it straightens out our lives?

David J Ayres

A Time To Remember

Tears may not fall so often,
sometimes, I might even smile,
and it won't mean, I don't love you,
or miss you all of the time.

It's just that I count my blessings
thankful of all we shared.
Our lovely times together
and the way you always cared.

And when I count my blessings,
I remember a moment in time
When we stood in a church and made vows
that would last till the end of all time.

Jacqueline Davies

Blessed By The Father's Love

I have the most supreme blessing,
Although it is only one -
My father is God Almighty
Through Jesus Christ, His dear Son.
As God loves the whole world so much,
He gave His Son to us all:
So whoever believes in Him
Will have LIFE that never falls!

Christ did *not* come to condemn us
But as our Saviour, to save,
As, alone, we can't get things right,
Christ *frees* us - sinners are *slaves.*
I'm accepted, no need for guilt,
Rescued from all that's confused,
There's nothing that can't be undone -
Through Christ's love, it's all good news!

The Father meets all of our needs -
I'm not the slightest bit poor,
He solves my worries and heals me,
And never closes His door.
In knowing the Lord, my life's rich,
He shows me why things are wrong,
For He knows all He's created,
And to Him the world belongs!

It's the Lord who gives all blessings,
Satan gives sin and *disease* . . .
Weakness and degeneration -
But God's *love* will *never* cease.
So there is no greater blessing -
None other can count as much -
As a child of God Almighty,
Who's found His tender touch!

Natalie Brocklehurst

I Count All Our Blessings Now

Cancer shook me by the shoulder
Whilst looking out to sea
And though you've gone
I'm listening to you now.
It makes me want to pick up
A falling leaf
And stick it back on the tree
To keep summer in the eyes
All year long.
And though you've gone
I count all our blessings now.

Cancer quietly announced the sleep
Just as autumn's ghostly veils fall
Believe me when I tell you
I never took it like a man.
There were tears on the road
From the rain that fell
And though you've gone
A time bruised, holds the sun
To keep summer in the eyes all year long.

You hinted at times that I was weak
I took it as a proposal for us to marry
You never knew how rich I was
With you as my friend
But it was cancer who took me home
Leaving me angry, planting roses,
To keep summer in the eyes
All year long.

And though you've gone
I count all our blessings now.

Collin Rossini

Heaven-Sent

It's round, slightly furred
As I bite into its flesh
The sweet nectar rolls down my chin
Honey never tastes so divine
The blissful pleasure as I bite into the heart
It bleeds red as a rose
Flesh intermingles with the nut
Then I sigh . . .
Ah, nectarine.

Pat Seddon

Count Our Blessings

Occasions when considered hard done by
Our dearest wishes life doesn't supply
Self contained we're trapped in our own skin
Pour out endless trouble heartaches begin.

Count our blessings how fortunate we are
The world is my oyster I've travelled far
Lose track of many positive aspects
When weather turns cold our clothing protects.

Mope about the place nothing appears right
Moan about injustice however slight
Never content and show our gratitude
For some strange reason always in a mood.

Habit forming frequently say poor me
Bark at our neighbours omit the beauty
Reputation disruptive influence
Spoilt by imaginary fence.

Own worse enemy if only realise
We should begin by opening our eyes
Our interpretation way off the mark
Enthusiasm generates a spark.

John Neal

Hidden Blessings

When feeling low let memories flow
Of blessings past and present,
Happy memories of childhood,
Health and strength, a comfortable home.
And nice garden in which to roam
A happy marriage, a daughter too,
Next three grandchildren come into view.

Good-natured dogs that comfort and soothe
Lifting spirits when they're running low,
They look up to you with loving eyes
So many blessings in disguise.
Count your blessings, you will be surprised.

Margaret Kinshott

Nowadays' Gran

What type of person is a present day gran?
Is she still like the world famous Giles cartoon?
No, I think she has changed in so many ways
From those long ago, post-wartime, halcyon days.
We don't, past our sixties, retire, slacken-up,
Even, after eighty, we exercise and dress up.
Our grandkids still are a wonderful treasure,
That's my belief, something we cannot measure.
We look forward to hearing of their daily lives
Delight in the news relayed by them on their lives.

My grand-girls filled me a Santa-sized stocking
This Christmas, with loads of all sorts of gifts.
They even bought me a glittery jewel
For my birthday, following this.
Then they sat around their Mum's kitchen table
To each make me a card, the best they were able,
Just as they did long ago round my own
While they visited, with their parents, when they were young.
My grandsons entertain me with a musical din,
Which they make on their instruments, drum, violin.
They look down upon me, their little old gran,
Their hair all gelled up, to make it a-gleam.

Some grandmas babysit, are carers, do much
While others work hard for their kith and such.
Replacing their daughters, who go out to work,
So they put me to shame, for these things I did shirk.
However, I know this for sure,
I love my grandchildren, could not love them more.

Veronica Bulmer

White Rose Of Summer

Each year I watch you start to appear
In the garden, year after year.
Your strong green stems start to grow,
From where you were pruned months ago.
Then from that stem the buds spread out
Green tight buds standing tall.
One sunny day little bits of white start to show
Another day as I walk by your buds are opening to the bright blue sky.
Petals form to a perfect head, smooth like velvet to the touch.
Your blooms get bigger as the days go by
Before we know it, your petals start to fall
So once again we wait for next year
To enjoy the lovely white rose of summer.

Jean Adam

Blessings In Disguise

I stare into a stream and watch it flow
See leaves dance in their auric dress
I feel so lucky I am so free
Not trapped in a high-rise flat, in full distress
I wander in an open field and through the woods
Not a house in sight, perhaps a lonely farm
People locked in inner-cities searching for light
May not experience this beautiful calm.

Lord I thank You for tranquillity
So grateful for all I see around me
So much I have, yet nothing I pray
Ther is music in the air, yet I hear no sound
Some people live in the fast lane of life
In concrete jungles, feeling disturbed
I haven't enough fingers to count my blessings
God has given me, but I don't deserve.

The Lord will always bring light to the tunnels
Giving hope to those in dark despair
We all have God's blessings, though many disguised
When I count those for me, I know life is fair.

Alison Jackson

You Too Can Now Be Freed

Despair's a woollen blanket, wrapped tight around the mind
I know for I have been there, but hope and joy were kind
They ripped the blanket right apart, light for me to find
Then pleasures so abounding, with hope and joy I dined.

I first looked all around me, to see the world was bright
And treasures I'd beholden, were now within my sight
From petals of the buttercups, shining in the light
To buildings of such grandeur, towering with great might.

I now find I'm alive again, in the sun and rain
So moments I find precious, become a treasured gain
They may be only fleeting, but in my heart remain
And remembered when I'm low, to lift me up again.

So despair will never taunt me, in my life I lead
For hope and joy are in me, on them I'll always feed
To remind me of the good times, that is all I need
Through my own experience, you too can now be freed.

Nigel Lloyd Maltby

Thank You

Thank You Lord of the universe,
Whose powers that could disperse,
Thank You for the powers You gave me.
Two working eyes with which I see,
A voice with which I can talk,
Two legs that I can walk,
Two arms to lift and hold,
A brain for ideas to be told,
And for the body these parts fit in.
And the joy of which they bring.
Thank You for all which You have created,
Leaving me stunned and sedated.
Thank You for the countryside,
The animals that bring it alive,
Birdsong serenading the dawn
Making you wish that you were born.
The sky an azure blue
Making life fresh and new.
Mountains tall and grand
Seen from everywhere you stand.
Forests tall with shady glades,
Bend and twist with the gales.
Flowers coloured and scented smells,
Hidden in delightful dells.
Waterfalls cascading into the sea,
Its brilliance a joy to see.
The golden orb that graces the day,
Chases the dark of the night away,
Bringing a newborn day.

Robert Gray Sill

Hope

Hope is like an eternal flame it never dies,
It's the look you see in a child's eyes.
The faith you have in the ones you rely on
And true friends that stay when others have gone.
Daydreams that someday you wish may come true,
That life's path be paved with happiness for you.
To aspire to give and ask no return
And forgive their hurt though inside you yearn.
To believe although you have been let down,
In coming years smiles, will outweigh the frowns.
Hope's a yearning, burning, deep down inside,
A longing for something sometimes you hide.
It keeps you going 'til your journey's through.
So in life may all your hopes come true.

Jim E Dolbear

His Heaven On Earth

(In memory of my husband Joe)

There's a corner of the garden
Where once he toiled with fork and spade
Never knowing he'd just sit there
In the garden he had made.

There's a corner of the garden
Where he'd always want to be
He'd survey the many flowers
That gave joy to him and me.

There's a corner of the garden
Where he'd pass the hours away
And he'd try his very utmost
To appreciate each day.

There's a corner of the garden
That he called his very own
Filled with peace and calm tranquillity
And his thoughts could freely roam.

There's a corner of the garden
Where if given half a chance
He'd stay and drink from the cup of life
'Til the evening shadows danced.

And when he no longer laboured
For his energy had waned
He would take his medication
To alleviate the pain.

Yet the garden he had toiled in
Still could lift his dark despair
Though his legs no longer held him
And he'd wheels upon his chair.

There's a corner of the garden
Where he'd contemplate life's worth
It's in that corner of the garden
That he found his Heaven on Earth.

Christine Lannen

Count Our Blessings
In The Showers

I lifted my eyes one morning, in the pouring rain,
And what did I see, flowers and green plants in the fields.
The sight of them made me feel happy that I was sheltered.
And what did they give again?
Physical and emotional well-being,
Certainly the flowers and plants brought living energy,
Which was lacking that morning.

They helped lower the blood pressure which was at a boiling point!
Aided the concentration and improved the memory that day,
They boosted the mood and energy levels and brought happiness
and enthusiasm
When it was impossible to go on.

It helped calm the spirits and soothed the soul
And just being in their presence anytime, anywhere is always
So refreshing and reassuring!

Joana Efua Sam-Avor

Little Blessings

The world is in absolute turmoil
With fighting and feuding and sleaze.
But - red winter berries shine brightly
On both of my two holly trees.

The royals seem no longer royal.
The church has indeed lost its way.
But - I've got a red-breasted robin
Who comes to my garden each day.

Vandals and hooligans flourish.
The law can do nothing at all.
But - white Christmas roses are budding
Down by my patio wall.

Man's institutions are failing.
We see the results everywhere.
But - quietly, as in past ages
God is still working out there.

Nora Veysey

God's Constant And Unending Blessing Of Salvation Through Christ's Name

As constant as the stars
Traversing our night sky
Always to hold their course
For a million faithful years -
Are the ceaseless, unending,
Reliable blessings of God.

As constant as the sun
Which rises without fail,
Shines fruitfully on Earth
For a million faithful years -
Are such ceaseless, unending,
Reliable blessings from God.

As constant as the waves
Which lap or lash the beach
On ten thousand, thousand shores
For a million faithful years -
Are these ceaseless, unending,
Reliable blessings by God.

How constant is mankind?
In God's own image made
Yet disappointingly poor
For many a thousand years
Is his unreliable
Response to love's blessings.

God's constant blessings flow -
Showers of refreshing rain
Softening the hardest heart,
Baptising for two-thousand years
Those who for Jesus' salvation call
Receive God's greatest blessing of all.

Geoffrey T Perry

Granddaughter

Her smile
lights up the heart -
clouds part, the sun shines through,
the world's a brighter place because
she smiled.

Eileen M Lodge

The Guardian Angel

(Translated from Hebrew by Lind Zisquitt)

'The angel who keeps me from all evil shall bless the children'
These are the words my grandpa taught me when I was little.
He leaned over in his white kittel and said,
'This prayer is a shawl to protect you,'
It will guard you from the harms of this world.'
'The angel who redeems'
This is a whisper before sleep.

Time went by to another place
My grandpa and his white robe are no longer with me
And I'm not the child who slept in her room alone so scared of the dark.

Now it's my turn to teach others how to bless all children
'Sh'ma Yisrael - Hear O Israel'
And whoever is curled up beside me also murmurs the words
'The angel who redeems'
And somewhere, far away, my grandpa keeps praying with me.

Nava Semel

The Wanderer

He wanders through the deepest night
Amid the gloom profound,
No light, no signpost is in sight
And silence all around.

So he continues, filled with fear,
Uncertain of the way,
Amid the darkness, far and near,
Beneath Night's sombre sway.

But soon there comes another day,
Night's shadows disappear,
The clouds of darkness roll away -
His path is plain and clear.

And so it is - day follows night,
Each day its blessings brings,
A radiant dawn appears in sight,
The world, awakened, sings.

Geoffrey Lund

My Girl With Gills

A quiet session at the pool;
October-gold sun slanted in
Across the rectangle of blue
Which shimmered as
Comfortable slow regulars
Sculled back and forth
Moulding the waters to their own needs.

Mercifully, no toddlers' groups shrieking
Fit to shatter the clear mirror of my mind
Which, between strokes,
Reflected memories, chores, the day's dealings,
The odd poetic line . . .
And a pretty young woman's face bobbed into view.
When she stood to rest,
Her taut, black-elastaned belly
Told me at least two months to go.
Swimming, she carried her unborn, swimming.

It is our first skill,
To swim in fluid, floating,
The unborn baby's advantage;
No need for gills.

The woman was happy.
She kissed her partner at the edge.
They both bounced in the water, it was a celebratory dance.
She swam, self-contained, the baby at its purest stage.
She, untainted by tiredness, broken nights, sore breasts
And that later terror when they don't come home on time.
The blissful stage . . . where she is centre-stage
And babydom is a Mothercare idyll.

Pleased for her, I swam on, carrying my daughter in my mind.
That is where I keep her now;
Memories, prayers, ambitions,
Developments, achievements, snapshots.
She swims and dives and surfaces in my mind.
My girl with gills,
Breasting the choppy waters of life,
My girl with gills.

Kate Sedgwick

Spirit

The wonderful spirit
We have in us all
The spirit we have
When we take a fall.
We all have it in us to be
To stand straight and tall is our destiny
It is there so fine and true
It is there in me and you
When we feel it all around
When our feet can touch the ground
I feel so proud to be
Part of our destiny.

Olive Haycock

War Against Terror

Darkness, depression, dawn and delight
Familiar is the road, so recognisable,
Take heart, for I survive.
This road that I have travelled
Many times, fuelled by panic
Striking so stealthily - unannounced!
So it was - so it is.
Suffering so many years, I now fight back.
Defence mechanisms activated,
Until the dawn arrives!
Consider happy things, like family,
Don't wish to be a burden
Living alone and yet not alone
Photographs support me
In my darkest hours.
Children and grandchildren
Who cry, 'Play with us please.'
Hence the delight!

T G Bloodworth

The Gorge

Water comes gushing through the gorge,
Sounding like peels of thunder - dashing from side to side,
Causing a suspension bridge above to vibrate.
The rapid flow gathers momentum, like a raging storm swirling and swaying -
Sweeping everything in its stride.
And just as suddenly, leaving a frothy trail in its wake -
It reaches the river below,
Where at last it mellows into a tranquil flow . . .

Agnes L Berry

The Owl

A blue and white owl
flew into my hands
on Christmas Day,
from behind a curtain
nobody can draw back.
Its porcelain blue eyes
look like yours, my daughter.
By chance it was found,
lying in a box - undiscovered for some years.
In your wardrobe,
next to a dark African mask.
The silent face has its eyes closed,
and a mysterious half-smile.
In its gentle curves I see
the soft contour of your face.

Since you left us
for that unknown place,
all sense of magic had deserted me.
But suddenly
the owl and the mask
became a stored miracle,
your wonderful present to me.

A little girl, curled up in my lap,
when I used to read to you
a story you loved,
'Ernest Owl starts a school in Blackberry Farm . . .'
On the box nobody knew about,
two words written in your hand,
For Mum.

Antoinette Marshall

Dreams - Memories

Dreams die, memories live,
forever like a bright star,
Or a vivid rainbow, beautiful times,
falling in love, holding a child, family times.
Celebrations with good friends,
to love and be loved is more precious than rubies.
To have all these very precious memories
makes life so very much worth living.

June Sweeney

Nature's Blessings

How often have I wandered
O'er country hill and dale
Gazing on nature's beauty
In a dreamlike sort of way.

Some folk say she must be mad
To look the way she does
On those green leaves and hillside flowers
With such unspoken love.

That's because they cannot see
The glory that I know
The wondrous gift God gave to me
Over seventy years ago.

I gaze upon the sunset
There in its golden glare
See a brighter better morrow
With strength all ills to bear.

Jean A Smith

All That We Enjoy

Although dissension mars the human scene,
On other subjects pores the mind that's keen.
The friendly sights of garden, sky and home
Surround us like a deeply-soothing dome.

And nature's backed by wisely-chosen art,
For music, pictures and a book can start
One's mood to rise onto a higher plane,
So lessening the toll of daily strain.

And yet the contemplative stance can't last,
When others' views into our ears are cast.
What luck, a simple method meets this test:
Agree the things you can and leave the rest.

Let's tick each other's answers that are right
To emphasise with positive delight
Our unity on all that we enjoy,
Ignoring lots of trivia that annoy.

Allan Bula

Another Day

Your loved one's gone, you are alone
Left in a cold world with a plastic phone
Friends disappear, can't stand your pain
Left with black clouds, tears that stain
The very face he used to kiss
The special hugs as you made a wish
Through the misty glaze of your teary eyes
Look up at the rainbow that lights the skies
That has to be where he has gone
Absorb the colours to make you strong
A starlit night shining so bright
The brightest one you watched with him that last night
Death but a stage, he's around I know
Watch the robin sing to you trying to show
That in everything you loved together he is still there
Even the crimpled seat of his favourite chair
Oh yes, I know it's so hard to see
Because this you see happened to me
Take your time, don't rush, cry at his favourite song
It's but a short time before you're back in his arms where you belong.

Sue Starling

Britain

The dawn that rises over Britain,
So soft, so gentle and so calm,
May it spread its peace across our nation
And give the world its soothing balm.

The island peoples that are Britain,
Of every colour, creed and race,
May we temper pride with love and wisdom
And live in liberating grace.

This land of beauty that is Britain,
So green, so temperate, so kind,
May we tend it with respect and mercy
And save this jewel for mankind.

The dusk that settles over Britain,
So soft, so gentle and so calm,
May it spread its peace across our nation
And give the world its soothing balm.

Clare Baldock

Only You Can Cry

I know that place of dark despair
I know it well I've lingered there
Where sunshine barely dares to touch
Though warmth is needed oh so much
That place where rainbows leave no mark
Where daylight shrinks to favour dark
A place nobody should endure
Where stress and strife search for a cure
A meadow without bird or song
A place no flowers bloom upon
Where butterflies forget to dance
Where love is but your only chance
That place you call your safety nest
Depressed, forlorn and sadly dressed
Where all your troubles pull you down
You try to smile but only frown
That place where only you can cry
And sit and hope and wonder why
But through the dark you see some light
And gradually each day looks bright
With love you can escape the gloom
When you have love you have the moon
I know that place you know it too
Thank God my love that I have you.

David Whitney

My Thanks

I'm thankful every day for my Mary Kay
She's my best friend until the end
You know my Mary loves the dawn
Your spirits come alive when she's sitting on the lawn
She's my one and only, I am thankful for every day
In every way for my Mary Kay.

Colin Zarhett

A Sunny Smile

The morning was dark, the bus was late
The queue was getting long.
We reached the queue together - I think I really won.
I let him go before me, he was only very young,
His need was greater than mine, he had two sticks, I'd only one.
The smile he gave me lit up the sky,
It taught me a lesson that day,
Forget your troubles and think of others and help them on their way.

Constance Dewdney

Lost

The room is redolent
Of old stale perfume
Clothing still hangs in the closet
This is still her room
Searching desperately
A hint, a clue
The smell, the smell that was you
Although everything is still there
It's not the same as you
A picture, a photograph
Yet, the eyes don't shine
Lustreless like your smile
In a while I'll compose myself
I'll remember you a while
But not with sadness
Or with glee
But with the very soul of me
I'll have a quiet moment
And for a while
I'll remember you
And your style
For just a moment
We will be as before
But then alas
No more.

Cedric Thrupp

The Blessing

So many blessings we so take for granted
Quiet dawns painted on the canvas skies,
Glorious flowers - lilac, roses, bluebells,
And birds that early sing their praise to God on high,
Trees that lift their arms so blossom-covered,
And cornfields ripe and waving in the wind;
The orange, brown and yellow trees of autumn;
Winter's holly, and the beauty of the covering snow;
Rocks along the seashores, and the great mountains -
So great variety of animals, and so beloved our pets;
Blackbirds' melodious songs, and the dear sparrows;
And honeysuckle, or wild roses in a country hedge -
All these are but few of the blessings we are given,
But they can't compare to the blessing of our Lord Jesus Christ
When He took our punishment that day upon the cross -
This blessing, truly for us, the greatest one of all.

W Prance

Beautiful Villain

So gently the snow floats down to the ground
In such large quantities without a sound
Changing the shape of all it can touch
Except for heat, it doesn't like very much
Everything else gets wrapped up so tight
And generally forms a nice pleasant sight
Some things it unfortunately seals their fate
As they crack and crumble under its weight
With its softness and beauty all children must play
But have most of them crying at the end of the day
To the eye of a human the pictures so nice
But not so pleasant when it all turns to ice
Most other blankets will keep us all warm
But not this beauty that arrives in a storm
The respect it demands is certainly no joke
Gets even a bow from a great English oak
So much anguish and danger you wouldn't think twice
When it arrives so gently and is wrapped up so nice.

E S Segust

Burton Beach

The soft breeze blows straight to my face,
And pebbles crunch beneath my feet.
The tide laps gently on the shore
And all around is perfumed sweet.

High on the bank the woodbine climbs,
Entangled in the hawthorn green,
And wild rose fights with Russian vine
To be included in the scene.

And there in front the river stretches
With sunshine glistening like a cloak,
And small boats bob with gentle ripples,
As in-between them cygnets float.

There on the shoreline swans are watchful
Protective of their young they stand,
Their elegant necks stretch up and outward,
Surveying sea as well as land.

Beyond I hear the muffled traffic,
Too muted to disturb that scene,
A world of beauty, calm and peaceful,
Perfection caught, as in a dream.

No footprints left on green brown seaweed,
Nor on that shingle, nor those rocks,
Nothing disturbed to mar that beauty,
That treasure chest, with secrets locked.

Janet Llewellyn

Autumn Leaf

My name is Autumn Leaf I proudly say
it's the name by which I am known,
I flew here one bright and windy day
and look how colourful I have grown.

I do not know if I have my friends
I was all alone as I flew,
I only know I knew my fate
as I landed close next to you.

You picked me up with gentle hands
and looked me straight in the face,
'You're lovely,' is all you could say
and I felt I was made of lace.

You held me in your hand and ran
away to a different place. There were houses,
it was busy and I knew
we would never again touch base.

The weather changed, it rained and your steps
got slower until they stopped
right under a shelter dry and clean
and out of your hand I hopped.

You never saw me but I hope you'll find
a leaf to give shelter to and be kind.
My colours will linger until I die,
and then Autumn Leaf it will be goodbye.

We must share our colours with everyone
and make the whole winter through
a place of pleasure, good luck and charm
a place of friendships, firm and true.

Mary Fawson

The Gift Of Love

We travel miles and miles seeing different places,
Cathedrals, towers, great bridges lie
In cities, reaching to the sky.
Man-made wonders of the world,
Before our eyes can be unfurled.
Man's ingenuity undenied,
Yet we remain dissatisfied.
Like one possessed we travel on, oppressed by disillusion.
Searching for a way of life to end all this confusion.
So exalt in nature's beauty, of mountains, sea and sky
And find the peace of joy and love, our lives enriched thereby.

Mary J Whiteley

What Does It Mean?

What does it mean to be happy?
Wear a smile on your face all the day?
No, it shows in your personality
Your actions, your ways and what you say.
Each word has a meaning
Sincerity from the heart,
Then your day ahead will be happy
Right from the start.

What does it mean to like someone?
Yes, what does it mean to love?
Love is a gift we can all accept
It's a gift from One above!
Because He loved the world so much
He gave His only Begotten Son
That the world may be so full of love
As He loved everyone.

It's not just a phrase, 'I love you!'
It's a quote from deep within,
What does it mean? Is a question
Asked by young and old.
There is an answer to everything
If we're willing to be told.
'We are never too old to learn'
Is a phrase from days of old.

So, go ahead, turn that corner
See what lies ahead.
Don't just turn over and think
Just another half hour in bed!
Step out, and be determined
Walk forceful, not hesitant,
Search for happiness!
Then you'll know
Just what it all meant.

Anita Bricknell

The Coming Of Spring

With the earth's awakening in the first sweet breath of spring
Man's heart grows lighter,
As he sheds the burdening sorrows of the winter's ills
And lifts his eyes to greet the blossoming hills.

The trees burst forth in green and dainty splendour
And flowers give gay gavotte in breezes tender
Release your spirit man and with the dancing trees
Give thanks that spring is here
And winter has now passed another year.

Muriel Johnson

My Homeland

What does Yorkshire mean to me?
Limestone crags, heather moors and summer blue sea.
Fertile acres of green and gold
Roll down from the moors
And up to the wolds.

Ancient York stands within its walls
A spiritual heart still for us all.
Damaged Minster lovingly repaired -
Pleasing to see that we still cared.

Homes of gracious living,
Splendid parks for sheep and deer.
Tourists' silver pays for viewing
So future's children can still come here.

Scarborough's north beach is empty,
Firmed by the cleansing sea.
With tourists all gone in September
Then Yorkshire belongs to me.

Primroses in Derwent Valley,
Roadsides misted cranesbill blue,
Space and quiet and wild free wind
Is that what Yorkshire means to you?

Jean Raine

Rainbow In Your Heart

Carry a rainbow in your heart
Use it to brighten up your day
Whenever you are cold or lonely
Or skies are dark and grey.

Red, the colour of the sky at night
That heralds a bright and sunny dawn.
Orange, the flickering flames of the fire
Built to keep you warm.
Yellow, the colour of ripening corn
On a glorious summer's day.
Green, the luscious grass in the meadow
Where newborn lambs frolic and play.
Blue, a bright Mediterranean sea
So wonderfully inviting and warm.
Indigo, my favourite pair of jeans
Frayed, faded and well-worn.
Violet, a delightful little flower
Grown for their fragrance alone.
Carry this rainbow in your heart
Wherever you may roam.

Christine Collins

Free Spirit

The bird flies high,
Gliding over the sea.
So peaceful and calm
So natural to see.
The tallest wave
Reaches up to grab
A tiny bubble.
The miracle of shimmer.
Peaceful and calm,
Elegant and grand,
Floating in light.
So magical,
So spiritual,
So calm.
The tiptoe of the waves
Come up to see
The adventure of the land.

Tracey Dixon

The Legacy

I see a mirror image in the early morning light,
Glints of lustre twisting - moving a spiral
Of pearls, from a breeze of an open window.

In my memory I see an altered vision
Of long ago, in a different time and place.
I'm a fevered child of seven,
The year is 1939,
The shadows then were twisting droplets of smoky light.
The curtains drawn tight against the sun,
In the shaded corner sat Mam - keeping watch till I awoke.
She rose from the chair - slightly parted the curtains,
Fingers of sun reached in and touched the pearls
That glistened at her throat. Mesmerised -
I watched, and listened as she gently spoke.
My head hot, my throat sore, our thoughts paused -
From outside, a newsboy cried, 'War!'

Today, surrounded by time hangs -
A rosary of pearls
Held together by a thread of love,
Their beauty twice magnified in the mirror.
I lift them down, feel the weight of time,
Around my neck, my mother's legacy
I lovingly entwine.

Kathleen M Smith

The Hospital

I really like the hospital
I like the things they do
They give you truly awful food
That looks and tastes like glue.

Then they take your picture
They X-ray this and that
But no matter where they photograph
There's never any fat!

As soon as they get you into bed
The questions then begin
Trouble is they don't seem to end
'Til they reach your next of kin.

The fun part then clicks into place
The needles all appear
You realise that Dracula
Has taken up residence here.

They take you to the theatre
But don't let you see the show
At least you get some hard-earned sleep
Then back to the ward you go.

I wish they'd find another way
To get the bloods they drain
Just like they do on 'Star Trek'
Where there's never any pain.

To the folks who work in hospitals
There's something I must say
Without their tender loving care
I wouldn't be here today.

Esther Jones

Contentment

A roof over my head
and a meal on my plate,
on a cold winter's night
a fire in the grate.
What more could I want
in this world full of strife,
I'm lucky indeed
to have such a good life.

J Heath

Lament Of A Blind Friend

I'm sitting here and thinking
Of the lovely world God made.
The mystery and the majesty
Of His work will never fade.

My mind goes back to childhood
As I romped through meadows green,
Or watched the white clouds scudding by,
Or paddled in the stream.

I loved to watch the swift in flight,
The industrious ants and bees,
The pearly pink of tiny shells
Polished by turbulent seas.

The majestic moon in a velvet sky
Festooned by a myriad stars
Was a magical sight to a tiny child
Crouched behind nursery bars.

By day the sun caressed the world
Burnishing trees and flowers.
What grand delight to laugh in the sun
And spy a rainbow through the showers!

Light glancing across the white-tipped waves,
The glistening pools, the golden sands,
Gave way at night to the lighthouse lamps
Sweeping across the silver strands.

It's good to have such memories,
They bring me peace of mind
When I'm afraid to question God
Because now I'm almost blind.

When I began to lose my sight
I railed against my fate.
But, peaceful now, I revel in memories
Of the beauty of God's estate.

Monica O'Sullivan

Rose Petals

Rose petals strewn and to delight
and blessings to bestow
so many colours shining bright
and wanting me to know.

That everything is coming up roses
the despair it had to end
my hands both carrying poses
and no longer to pretend.

This scent uplifting to greet me
to give depression a clout
a prosperous future to meet me
my hands reach for it no doubt.

As all these colours resemble a rainbow
at the end of a storm
my body still shaking it does tremble
as a magic carpet it does form.

Stepping on these petals I am striving
to leave all hardship behind
reaching for the life that is arriving
one that is wonderful and kind.

This is the moment that I have dreamed of
and that I now embrace
with all sorrow behind me called off
as a life full of joy I now face.

Irma Trigg

Michael

What a friend we had in Michael
All our troubles he did share
Peaceful comfort brought to bear
With his loving, faithful prayer.

When life at times was bearing down
He had a wondrous smile, not frown
Charity, it's said begins at home
It was *his maxim* on a daily roam.

Advice when needed, you knew he can
A charming, friendly loving man
Who touched the lives of all he met
God bless you Michael, I'll never forget.

John Cole

Helford Summer

A blue haze over Helford,
river stretches, inlet fingers
green dip into deeps,
traversed by a tiny ferry,
puttering between two sunlit shores.
Where lush gardens
stroke the coast and parents lie at ease
recessed by stones, as children's ice cream faces
probe in rocky pools.
Close by, frond secreted,
a Frenchman tethered
in a cove of literary fame.
While further down, sheltered seals
bask and show off tricks
to captivate crowds, who at day's end,
wend their way, leaving the setting sun and
a plenitude of boats
jingling in the wind.

Valerie Hockaday

Memory

How could I ever forget her
Whilst she is still here in my heart?
She, who was always part of me
And now we're so far apart.

I wonder if she ever smiles upon me
From her heavenly haven above?
Does she still carry on thinking of me
And knowing I still feel her love?

How could she know I'm thinking of her
How she made my life so complete?
How I love, adored and admired her
From her beautiful head to her feet.

How could I ever forget her
When she was so much of my life?
When I was her ordinary husband
But she was my wonderful wife.

J R Burr

Mary Queen Of Scots

In the great hall of Fotheringhay
On a spring-like February day,
Mary, Queen of Scots was led
Very soon she would be dead
Honour the name of this queen
Weep now for what might have been.

The spectres gathered at the scene
Intent to see the Scottish queen,
To see her head upon the block
Preparing for the headsman's shock.
Angels in Heaven, stand by
Mary has come here to die.

Riccio. Bothwell. Francis - king and boy
Oh, just once more to taste such joy!
But they had crossed from life to death
Now waiting for her final breath.
Great God, be merciful please
Mary is down on her knees.

It once had been her fate to reign
Came innocence, then bitter pain,
Conspiracy had brought her low
All to be ended with one blow.
Fearless and true to the death
Faithful unto her last breath.

So it had all come down to this
As fickle as was Darnley's kiss,
Rejected by her son so sweet
No mercy at the monarch's feet.
Please let her ending be brief
Strengthen her lifelong belief.

But now she stands alone at last
Unshackled from her tragic past,
Intrigue, revenge, all swept away
Becalm, descended on that day.
Mary, now your spirit's free
Intercede with God for me!

Moira Wiggins

Embracing All Growing Things

I submerge myself in all growing things
The burgeoning spring and midsummer high
When herbage is spilling from the verges
Overflowing onto winding country lanes.
Recalling September's mellow fruitfulness
Of hazelnuts and polished blackberries
Cherished like chocolate fruit and nuts.
I marvel when it's ceaselessly raining
When my water butts, flushed, spill over
As water gushes from downspouts
Whilst dust dry and burnt summer earth
Runs gravy thick with rich brown mud.
Yellowing rhubarb leaves bowed down
Considering gravy browning just fine.
Preferring custard or cream next time
A windy day arrives in early October
The last of my apples falls on my crown
Discovering Newton's gravity once again.
The blaze of the Mexican born dahlias
Finds no favour with the first frost.
Yet nothing is really ever lost
As fat tubers from the soil are removed,
Methodically replaced in much haste,
Sown not by seeds but corms and bulbs
Into the still warm earth for a rebirth,
Goes snowdrops, scillas and fragile crocus,
Then ranks of soldierly Darwin tulips,
And sun-dipped, haloed golden daffodils.
England remains always a garden proud
Since earth first turned by a rude plough.

John Pegg

The Changing Sky

I open my eyes on a clear summer morn
And gaze through my window to welcome the dawn.
The sky all aglow, coloured mauve, red and gold,
The sun slowly rising - a joy to behold.

As I watch the scene changes until - right on cue,
The sky gently turns to a bright azure-blue.
Then fluffy white clouds in that azure-blue sky
Foretell that the day will be sunny and dry.

But now shadows lengthen as day turns to night
But, once more, the sky is a wonderful sight.
As the sun slowly sinks in the sky far out west
My heart tells me this is the sky I love best.

Frances Heckler

Days Of Joy

Lift your eyes to the skies
Your arms stretched out wide
Forget the dark days of winter
When you feel you want to hide

The beautiful spring and summertime
Will soon be coming your way
Lifting our hearts and minds
Day after day after day

Think of the delight of the season
Which will soon be bringing us cheer
Bringing those long days of happiness
Which all of us hold so dear

Those feelings of despondency
Are now things of the past
Don't dwell on them any longer
For they are not likely to last

New grass will soon be growing
The days will be getting longer
The lambs will be hopping about
And we shall all be feeling much stronger

So count your blessings daily
In every type of way
Listen to others carefully
Let them also have their say

Do try to think of others
Make them happy too
For in return for your efforts
Happiness will come to you

We should all count our blessings
In this crazy world of strife
For if there's one thing we all enjoy
It's being given the great blessing of life.

Martin Selwood

Faithful Living

A cruel word may mar a life,
A careless word may inflame strife,
A timely word may lesson stress,
A loving word may heal and bless.

A life of love and magnanimous caring,
A love of altruistic sharing,
A love of self-denying kindness,
A love not bound by prejudiced blindness.

A faith in which we can believe,
A faith which we can all receive,
A faith which sustains us to the end,
Faith in our Redeemer, Saviour, steadfast friend.

Malcolm F Andrews

Bonding With Eternity

It was love opened up my heart
to all life means to me,
nor shall death its bonding part.

Sands of time, soulmates at the start,
a song of destiny,
it was love opened up my heart.

May the world no finer truths impart
than its natural beauty,
nor shall death its bonding part.

Like summer skies, stars, even clouds
charting a fragile humanity . . .
it was love opened up my heart.

If a taste on the tongue sweet or tart,
our togetherness a delicacy,
nor shall death its bonding part.

Be nature's kin struck by a poison dart
comprising all inhumanity . . .
it was love opened up my heart,
nor shall death its bonding part.

R N Taber

Getting Tough

When things are getting tough
And the going is getting rough,
Take time out to think about
The good things in life.
Like a baby in a pram,
Eating bread and jam,
Or a sunny day in May
Or the smell of new mown hay.
A walk in the park,
Playing footie for a lark.
To go out on a clear night
When the stars are shining bright.
The smell of good food in a cooking pot
Or even when you laugh a lot.
The scent of a blossom tree
Or the sense of feeling free.
The colours of a rainbow
And the autumn leaves.
These things cost nothing
And are easy to achieve.

D Hamey

Count Your Blessings

We count our blessings
As every new leaf unfurls
As every animal awakes
To play in the forest
To hear the birds overhead
As swallows fly in formation
As every new blade of grass grows
We count our blessings
To see the world
To hear children's laughter
To enjoy a friend's company
To visit museums
And to hear a baby cry
Is such a joy to behold
In this fast achieving world
So let us rejoice in the beginning of the world
To see how we have developed
Over the years long gone
Into a new generation of song.

Elaine Day

Count Our Blessings

There's a purpose in what is now happening,
Should you wonder if God got it wrong?
Frustrated that things are not going your way,
And the journey of life seems too long.

Jesus wants us to learn from our suffering,
Came to seek and to save those who're lost.
He turned disappointment to good effect,
Blessing those who accepted the cost.

Rest a moment, to hear the sweet song of the lark,
Smell the fragrance of flowers after rain,
Feel the warmth of the sun as it melts frozen hearts,
Know new birth will bring joy after pain.

So when plans have been shattered and hopes come to nought,
Use His grace that's so freely supplied.
Jesus comes to restore and make everything new,
Take control of your life, be your guide.

Gillian Humphries

True Consolation

I believe we all experience paradise on Earth -
an invisible reality that exists for our Salvation.

Identical parallels and reciprocal endearments,
the illuminations sharing our secrets of time,
bring enlightenment to the mystery of eternity.

Every individual has a cascade of memories -
a derivative of life's precious tracery of caring.

And within the close embrace of loved ones
there comes a beauty of the soul's discretion
to heal all sorrows in times of grief and loss.

Nothing can die that is reborn in germination
to live again in a living soul for solace and joy.

Precious seeds of memories that are cherished
grow to enhance the reality of remembrance -
an enduring consolation - cradled in our love.

Rosemary Watts

England Now That Spring Is Here

Just a sleepy suburban Sunday morning
Only the milkman and paperboy awake.
Barring some unforeseen earthquake
Too early for the earliest of birds to stir.
On their way to the first church service,
Or heading for the old Methodist chapel.
The air as fresh as the lawn daisies.
Their pure and simple flower heads
Ascend to greet the newly risen sun
On this dew-fresh dawn in late April.
The green's large pond lying so placid,
The recently hatched mallard ducklings
Like a small flotilla follow their parents.
Geese and goslings still in the reed bed.
The pair of graceful white swans linger
Atop the floating raft of their untidy nest.
Whilst cawing rooks are noisily quarrelling
In the high canopy of the old lime trees,
Blackbirds perched aloft on chimney pots
Singing their realm defending hearts out.
How can such a glorious song be an issue?
Still most folk remain snugly abed sleeping,
Or are rising, with much pausing and yawning.
Looking thoughtfully thru bedroom windows
Contemplating the wonders of this season.
Marvelling at the burgeoning spring garden.
Was it God who designed the first flowers
Or the contemporary Pagans amongst them
Thinking, *isn't Mother Nature truly amazing?*
England is an Eden now that spring is here.

Julia Pegg

Look, Listen, Help

Look around through eyes that see, listen to Nature's voice,
Walking, running, dancing too, at least you have the choice.

Changing season to enjoy, movement unrestricted,
A place to sleep undisturbed, no fear of being evicted.

No open doorway finds you rest, no dustbins feeds your hunger,
A whole new world awaits your view, look, listen, wonder.

You're not at war, but safe at home, a roof above your head,
Talking, laughing, meeting friends not wounded, buried, dead.

So count your blessings, look with love on those who have not any,
Let joy and hope assist their needs and your blessings will be plenty.

Kathleen Townsley

Count Your Blessings

Hold on to which is good
Keep your steps forthright
There are battles to be won
So keep your armour bright.

Cling to that which is good
Keep your life serene
You will find what can be done
To fulfil that dream.

Fill your life with love
Keep your humour light
Laugh at trouble, make it fun
Conserve what's good and right.

Cling to your beliefs
Do this and you will find
If you hold tight onto the reigns
You'll leave your cares behind.

Surround yourself with goodness
Lend a sympathetic ear
Help someone who has lost their way
Give a hug and calm their fear.

Count your blessings
Have good luck in good measure
May your life be long and happy
With the loved ones that you treasure.

John W Hewing

The Joy Of Dance

The joy of dance - amazing, yes, here's what to do
When you're feeling sad, when you're feeling blue
Put on your dancing shoes, go out and have yourself a ball
Guaranteed to give you a high, instead of going up the wall
And feeling lonely too.

Don't worry if you've no partner to hand, or if they've got the flu
Jump on a bus if you have to, but don't hang about too
Long, or the time will soon be gone and you'll miss out on a great enthral
The joy of dance!

You can jump and jive, twist, rock and roll or line dance the whole night through
Just sway to the music, don't be self-conscious, an adrenaline rush will come to you
Your head will lighten, depression will lift, you'll feel abut ten feet tall
You've discovered a wonder, the wise of this world, very happily call
The joy of dance.

V Hall

Thank You God For Me

Thank you for the ability to say, thank you.
Learn to create a priority now.
It was not yesterday you learnt it, but probably the day before anyhow.
Lifting up words to Jesus through all your joys and sorrows
will give you great fullness of wisdom in each and every task.
All the joys and trials carry tomorrow's endeavour,
each and every hour responding to the purpose anew.
So thank You, Jesus, for giving me the ability to learn to thank You for me.

Anne Hadley

To Be An Angel

(Dedicated to Finley Walsh-Dennett, age nine months)

When the moon goes to bed and the sun will rise,
If you are quiet you will hear the sighs,
The gentle breath that touches your cheek,
A feathered whisper that seems to say,
'Don't cry, I'm OK Mama, I'm on God's knee.
I'm an angel now, He will look after me.
I love you Mama and Daddy, so very much,
I can feel the sand running through my fingers,
Running through His toes
I am in his garden, I am a rose.'

Dorothy Rowe

So Blessed

Memories of loved ones I hold so dear
Enriched far and near
A baby's first smile, birth of my sons
I'll treasure within.
Turning around my life again
Seeing the window after the rain
Counting my blessings after tears and pain.
Learning with confidence to go on again
When I felt so alone
My trust still remain, blessings anew,
Seeing others, what they had been through
My daughter, my grandchildren, love so true.
Seeing the first snowdrop, white and pure
Daffodils so bright seasons bliss and delight.
Rich blessings that stay
A peace a joy to being
Turning grey into song
Prayer for those far away
Thankful blessings, for what we have this day.

Maureen Thornton

Flute Player

Icarus kites casts shadows against the hillside, distorted by the heat
Prominent in the azure
Sky dancing to the flute player
Sitting in a sweet, mown meadow
The notes diverse in the elegant blue
Blue notes - indulgent in a melody - full of melancholy
Water God appeased by the music
The flowing dimensions removing the fear from thirst
As the grey stallion, legs in dappled sunlight meadows,
Gallops back to his mares
He stands, yarns, black all knowing eyes see the Icarus kites
From beneath a thatched forelock
His tenet that the water will never dry up.

Hilary Clark

Without Knowing Why

Feeling down without knowing why,
We have all experienced this . . .
As we sit here and cry.

In such moments we shout for help,
Without knowing why,
Forgetting sometimes that we can help
Ourselves if we really try.

Imagine that you are in a dark room
And this room is your life,
And darkness is your mood and gloom
As you think of trouble and strife.

Reach out and switch on the light
Amazingly the room is now bright,
Filled with reasons to be cheerful
Because all that you see
Is your inspiration and your will . . . to fight.

There is a silver lining in every cloud,
Whatever adversity you may face,
So always look for that spark of hope
It will always be there
So don't give up the chase.

David Wright

Drifters Walk

The brow of a hill
Where all time stood still.
The freshness of a new day
A wind greeting me in every way.
I could see the clouds in the sky
The sounds of birds flying by.
The fields opened up to my gaze
Wonderful sights of colour amazed.
I could see the towns and trees
Smell the flowers and leaves.
All around me life blossomed in the air
Unstopping without compare.
This is meant to be, for all to see
Life in tranquillity.

R H Sunshine

A Best Friend

'Hush now child,' Father gently said
To the young girl crying on her bed.
'Why did my best friend have to die
And fill me with sadness I cannot hide?'
'A task that we can learn and become strong
Think of her now she's gone.
All those happy times shared together
The games you played in all weather.
Her joyful bark, her wagging tail
Her playful manner in which she gave.
You have been blessed to share your lives
Think of her now by Jesus' side.
Dropping her ball, barking out loud
Chasing others across God's fields
And when at last you meet again
Happiness will return instead of pain.
Together you'll walk side by side
In God's eternal tide.'

Linda Gray

On A Sunny Morning

When you wake up in the morning
To a sunny bright blue sky
There is no time for doldrums
Because it lifts the spirits high
Watching the day wake up
Is priceless beyond belief
Everything stirring readily
From the night's long sleep
All ones troubles are diminished
With the sight of a sunny day
Sunlight lifts our hopes
When things have gone badly wrong
The horizon seems much brighter
And our hearts are full of song
Throw open wide your arms
When rising on such a morn
And be glad, oh so glad
That into this world you were born.

Daphne Fryer

Count Your Blessings

'Count your blessings,' my Granny used to say.
'Count your blessings, be thankful every day.'
And then her merry eyes would twinkle, bright with fun
As she warbled to the old tune, 'Just count them one by one!'

Now I've become a granny and down along the years
Those words of hers still echo so clearly in my ears.
Times not always easy - but when all is said and done,
I've been showered with many blessings and I count them one by one.

A very happy childhood and loving parents, who
Guided and protected and gave me sisters two.
Next a loving husband and each day of my life
I realise how lucky I am to be his wife!

A caring son and daughter and of course those lively boys
Grandsons dear, who shower me with so much love and joys.
My friends at church and neighbours and people everywhere
What blessing we receive from them, what joy to know they care.

And then of course the little things - a cup of tea in bed,
Electric blanket, microwave - so quickly we are fed!
A sunny day, the garden birds, a holiday by the sea,
Oh yes indeed they all become more blessings still for me.

But first of all my blessings, must be the Christian way,
The faith that Jesus gives us, His presence here each day.
That God could care so deeply, He sent his only Son,
To be with me and to make me count my blessings one by one.

Kath Hurley

The Reckoning

Blessings? What blessings? I ask with a frown.
I'm ageing, on pension, there's no way but down.
Arthritic twinges are beginning to bite,
A spasmodic cough often wakes me at night.
- I'm weary.

The bills keep on coming, with taxes sky-high,
I'm even arranging my life when I die!
The country's uncertain, there's change ahead,
Where once we were winning - we're losing instead!
- I'm worried.

But stop! Just a minute - we're in a new year,
Is there nothing to lift us and give us some cheer?
I'm going to look harder - I know that I should,
There must be something, somewhere, some good,
- I'm searching.

Well yes - there is one, two, or three things I see
That I'd overlooked in my perplexity,
A house, comforting, that's welcome and warm,
A shelter from life's gathering storm
- I'm grateful.

And now, on reflection, there's a dozen or more,
There's blessing on every hand galore,
A loving wife, and family and friends,
To see, smell, touch, taste, the list never ends.
- I'm privileged.

Finally, overall - there's a God up above,
He looks down, He watches, His heart full of love,
So blessings to be reckoned, whether rich or poor,
Don't be surprised to find many more!
- I'm counting.

Brian Fisher

Spiritual Renewal

Feel the peace
Smell the fresh air,
Hear the quiet
A moment of prayer.

The mind is emptied
And the senses are raw,
Time stands still
And connects once more.

Nothing to fear
And everything to gain,
Your blessings are here
They take away the pain.

Joan Yvonne Matthews

Father Thames

It's England's greatest river, on maps a thick blue band,
It rises in the Cotswolds, then meanders through the land.
As it flows through Oxford, the Isis it is called,
As soon as it's on course again, its true name is restored.
It flows along past Kingston, Teddington and Hampton Court,
Then makes its way past Henley t'wards the Tower of London fort.
Where once it ferried traitors who were destined for the chop,
Past Wapping, into Essex, to the busy Tilbury Docks.
Then on past Tilbury Fort, where good Queen Bess once slept,
Before her fleet went off and turned the Armada into wrecks.
Then past Hope Reach and Canvey to the Southend Estuary,
That's where the whole world's longest pier's built out into the sea.
From its source a gurgling stream gains current as it flows,
Meandering across the country, swelling as it grows.
It carries life and commerce from the Cotswolds to the sea,
Thus England's greatest river, Father Thames will always be.

Mick Nash

Eye-Opener

The weather was vile as it could get,
Yet my neighbour was rushing along in the wet -
'You're surely not walking in this for fun!'
'No, I'm counting my blessings one by one.
A month ago I couldn't move my feet,
But now, I thank God, I stride down the street.'
Returned to my home, now warm and dry,
I began to think, I wonder why.
I've never said, thanks for living here
Not in the bus shelter or under the pier.
The phone rang, 'Hi Mum, how're you faring?'
A family in touch, loving and caring.
So thanks for all means of communication,
That really connect nation with nation.
In the kitchen preparing myself some food,
Tasty and plentiful, really good -
Grateful to all who provide for me
Working the land, fishing the sea.
A magazine, a book or the TV,
Gifts of learning, sight, hearing open to me.
Changes of clothes whether hot or cold,
Choosing high fashion, or comfortably old.
Cash in the bank, enough for my need,
But to needs of others do I take heed?
My neighbour's remark made me look and see
The range of blessings God has given to me.

Di Bagshawe

Spring's Awakening

Down the valley sweeps winter
In a cloak wet and grey with rain
Swirling with mist as he covers the weeping earth.
But underneath that cloak, a stirring, wakening
As the first flowers of spring arise
And greet us, weary with the wet and cold.
Their strength growing and bidding us come to meet them.
Snowdrops, cold February's fair maids
And crocuses, so small and gold as flames
Tell us that spring is near.
And then at last we hear a blackbird's song.
Rejoice with me, oh weary world, he tells us rise and sing
Dark winter's gone and soon it will be spring.

Margaret B Baguley

Retirement

The winter months are rolling by
retirement looms, the minutes fly,
the rain and cold will soon be past
and spring will bring relief at last.

I look forward to long lazy days.
I'll lie in bed, I'll change my ways,
my life begins - the big six 0.
The world's my oyster, off I go.

I'll get a bus pass, travel far
with cut-price fares, I'll sell my car.
My 'joie de vie' will reach new heights
I just can't wait for the delights.

That life begins at 60 years
I have no doubt, no time for tears.
My days will fly in idyllic haste
and not a second will I waste.

It won't be long as you can tell
12 weeks to go then ring the bell.
It's goodbye work, hello to leisure
my golden years are what I'll treasure.

Jennifer M Caine

Autumn Night

Love in low colours reaches from the mist
Beseechingly, to wrap itself around
Your heart, with passion but without a sound,
Strange silence, leaving bruises like being kissed.

Intensely. Do you see the terrorist
During the nervous moments when he's found
And drawn the pin, feeling his huge heart pound
Four times before he swiftly flips his wrist.

To send another death upon its way?
That is the picture of silence which I mean,
Producing an irrevocable change -
Like the first kiss of passion, or the grey
Ecstatic mist from which bare branches lean,
Weeping to find a solitude so strange.

Sean Quinn

Grandmother's Picture

'Look back where we've come from', my grandma used to say.
But I didn't understand her - it was all before my day.

'Look back where we've come from' - the poverty and pain -
When I heard of all her troubles I understood her glad refrain.

If she hadn't shown endurance and battled bravely on,
Leaned with full assurance on God till day was done.
If she hadn't shown such courage, never yielding to despair,
How could I ever manage my troubles now to bear?

When I need to seek assurance, my spirits low to raise,
I remember her endurance, the truth behind her gaze.
She looks out from her picture that is framed upon my wall -
Steadily to the future - no fear is there at all.

Her dark eyes gaze upon me, calm and so serene.
She seems to say so fondly, 'Remember where we've been.'

The truth behind that picture, when she was thirty-three,
Is that she had no future then, no grandchild would she see.
And yet God overruled the past, he gave her forty years.
She lived each day as if her last. Love cancelled out all fears.

So, 'Look back where you've come from', remember through your tears,
That courage and endurance will cancel out your fears.
'Look back where you've come from', and carry bravely on,
Leaning on the love of God until your day is done.

Shirley H Ford

A Prayer

Light a light, show me the way,
Give me direction, hear what I say.
Help me to bring to others out there,
Words of comfort from those who care.
Bring happiness back to eyes having cried.
So many people who feel denied.
Giving pleasure in some small way,
To a life that's known so much dismay.
Helping yourself to a life worthwhile,
Sharing your gift to bring a smile,
To those who are living with tears and pain,
Much wonder they feel to smile again.
Someone helped me, helped to ease my pain.
They did it for love, no thought of gain.
Now it's for me to reach, and lend a hand,
Bring out of the waves onto the sand.
Someone who's lost and all at sea,
Just as I was when someone helped me.

Linda Dickerson

The Friend In You

My days are bright with happiness
My skies are always blue
And life is wonderful
Because I found a friend in you.

The kind of friend whose faithfulness is everything it seems,
Who shares my fondest hopes with me,
And understands my dreams.
Who constantly inspires me
To put my fears away,
And trust in God to help me live,
A more courageous day.

Who seems to read my very thoughts,
And knows just how you feel,
And who is there to share things,
When I speak or appeal.
The world is gay and colourful,
And life itself is new,
And I am very grateful,
For the friend I found in you.

Irene McBurney

Creation

Pluck the strings laid across the void
and activate the glad creative word
as echoes dance the atoms into being
and sheer delight welcomes their harmony.
Let myriad colours blend in purest light
and sounds prolong their lucent melody.

Love is the spur that starts the cosmic dance.
Love is the wind that makes the taut strings throb.
Love is the eagerness explodes in matter.
Love is the wave of joy that speeds the light.
Love is the song that flows in constant motion
and rolls all things in one in the endless sea.

Derek Rawcliffe

The Children's Countryside

Because such lovely things surround you
Stop, and take a look around you,
And surprised you'll be,
Because the sun shines for your pleasure,
All the world is filled with treasure
For eyes trained to see.

I'm sure that everyone is knowing
Of the wonder when it's snowing,
Even though it's cold.
Let little children's delight reach us,
Let their sense of wonder teach us
Joy as we grow old.

Absorb the beauty of a petal,
Caterpillars on the nettle,
Shiny insect wings.
Look deeply in the stream that flows by,
Notice trees against the blue sky,
Hear the bird that sings.

The changing moon and twinkling starlight,
Splashing water, sand and sunlight,
Meadows fresh and green.
It's sad that many pass this way and
Yet things revealed today are
Hardly ever seen.

Don't ever lose your sense of wonder,
Though the pressures you are under
Make things seem so small.
How sad to never watch a sunset.
Fleeting jewels are, don't forget,
Most precious of all.

Diana Duncan

Life

My dad went to war, to be free,
Also the country, Mum my two sisters and me.
Dad lost many friends, also dressed in blue,
At Poppy time I think of the fallen few.

So I diligently do many a household chore
Remembering who won the war.
I clean the house until spick and span,
Plus the wheelie bins, best I can.

And I don't mind sweeping the path.
Well it gives the neighbours a laugh.
They know on me they can depend,
Pets to mind, plus, parcels people send.

So when I feed the birds,
With washing out, they never mutter any words.
Children, paper girl, window cleaners, given a sweetie bar,
Especially the road sweeper in his special car.

40 years, my house has been my home,
From twenty to sixty, I have grown.
With husband John, our three sons,
Their wives, and grandchildren, five little ones.

I thank God and always do my best,
Because I know I am truly blessed.

Jenny Hayes

The 'Loving Memory' Rose

Your perfect buds, the healers of despair,
On stems that stretch their arms to reach the air,
Proud, stately, straining for the upper sky
Of heavenly glory where birds wheel and fly
Free, effortless, uplifted by the breath
Of spirit power that raises us from death

Your full-blown blooms that hold the dew of tears
Mix joy with sorrow, beauty wrought from fears,
For on your radiant glory shines forth grief
The cost of pain, yet promise of relief.
For lifeblood, shed for us, gives hope of peace
From guilt and shame and death, a blest to release

Your crimson petals, fallen to the earth
Before the quickening breeze, inspire new birth
And spread a life force into barren clay,
To lift the gloom of night to joy of day.
For all of nature shows the hope of life -
The risen Lord, who heals our inner strife.

Sheila Harris

Through Houghton Mill

Through Houghton Mill, come, take a walk,
Where steeples to tall steeples talk,
Across a field at whose far edge
Huge trees shrink to a lowly hedge.
Contented sorrel cows all pass,
Grazing long shadows down the grass;
And rooks, a raucous rabble, fly,
Black windblown chaff, about the sky.
Late in the day, as air grows cool,
The stream lies placid as a pool.
Where crowding lofty reeds give space,
To gaze upon broad Ouse's face,
His languid waters clearly show,
A perfect other world below;
Watch dazzling azure dragonflies
Hover and dart between twin skies.
Upstream, smart leisure craft lie tied
Each to its own reflected pride.
A pure white swan serenely floats
Still breast to breast on which it dotes,
Till, as sun's passing time is told,
It charges Ouse with molten gold;
Couched on her leaves the nenuphar
Retires before the evening star;
One distant, dusky barge glides on,
Like Arthur's bound for Avalon.

Roger Newton

Take Chance To Try Your Best

There is this call
The need of thanks.

For all those gifts surrounding
That just seemed created
Put in place with no misfit case
That form a part
To all lives pride impart.

Then there is another chance
With strength given beating heart
To join in the pace, accommodate start.

Of such given freely grace
Counted out in ration state
For all of goodness, case to make.

E Gordon

Out Of Darkness

We all have our blessings I'm sure,
Gathered as we travelled on life's way
Counting them all one by one
Thanking the good Lord day by day.

My blessing to me is a great joy
A black year, I'm now seeing the light
The long tunnel was so very dark
I'm through it, now the light is so bright.

When one's loved one is near Death's door
And we feel we are losing our way
We weep and we feel so very sad
So we turn to the good Lord and pray.

He heard my plea and he rescued me
Out of the darkness I felt so free
For my man was soon Heaven blessed
For he returned to all his family.

So please share with me my blessing
After a year that was fraught with woe
The new year has begun, so to everyone
Have faith in your hearts, don't let it go.

Doris M Engleman

Memories

For me to count my blessings, I just wouldn't know where to start
I have been content in my life, I have got my parents to thank for that
They would instil in my siblings and I that God was to be the top on our list and He has to come first
I go down memory lane and think of all my dear ones that have passed on
I am the only one left in my family, sadly they have all gone.

Time goes by but happy memories still linger on
I get my photographs out and go through them, one by one
Children are a gift, one feels blessed when they are born fit and healthy and strong
And as they grow, they put little arms out to you and want to feel loved and to belong

My dear husband was sick and disabled for many years before he died
He would raise a little smile and reassure me, 'Don't you worry, God is on my side.'
He was racked with pain and suffered so, God took him home, he had to go
Oh happy day until we meet again, I do know where, but I don't know when
I know my heavenly Father knows the hour my journey here will close.

Until the daybreak,
Amen

Rosina Forward

Since Amy Came

Two months ago you came to be,
Defenceless creature, vulnerable.
Your father, apprehensive of what was to be,
Your mother waiting for your birth impatiently,
She longed to hold you in her arms.
Your life would make their lives complete,
The perfect culmination of their love.
A precious child, small hands and feet,
Fine auburn hair and big blue eyes.
They are captivated by your gurgling and smiles.
You keep them busy night and day,
Attending to your every want.
You only have to move or cry,
Four loving hands are there to pick you up.

And life will never be the same,
Since Amy came.

Elizabeth J Homes

A White Christmas

A winter night of marcasite stars,
snow dunes concealing driveway cars.
A barn owl ghosts above the churchyard yews,
scarcely a rustle from headstones to pews.

Icicle fangs extend the gargoyle's grin,
a reveller stumbles homeward from the inn.
Stained-glass glow from Lady Chapel light,
the December darkness transformed to white.

Crunching steps of a black-cloaked curate
pausing to click the latched lych gate.
Air numb and dumb until the belfry bell
resonates like a Siberian knell.

A hopeful stoat sniffs the starched grass,
confident this sterile time will pass.
From frigid stream to moon-laden wold,
rustics claim, 'Twas never so cold'.

Malcolm Williams

Guardian Angels

We all have recollections
of times when we've been blessed;
a prompting or coincidence
that we could not have guessed.
We have a special angel
and need to be aware
of the presence of our helpmate
who is always there to care.

A prayer we learned as children
still stands us in good stead
in times of need or trouble
of anxiety or dread:
Angel of God, my guardian dear
to whom God's love commits me here
ever this day be at my side
to light and guard; to rule and guide.

Josephine Sexton

Relax

It's very early in the year,
The blooming snowdrops show no fear
Of winter's raw and icy blast,
For weeks this pendant flower will last.
Yet in a sheltered spot one thrills
At the sight of early golden daffodils,
Their blooms sway gently in the breeze,
Announcing the end of winter's freeze.

From branch to branch in nearby tree,
A grey squirrel leaps with ease and glee,
Round the trunk it scampers, then down
To ground that's clothed in leafy gown.
Then carefully searches where it believes
Its food is hidden under the leaves,
Then sitting on haunches eats the repast
Stored during the months of plenty that's past.

As spring kisses winter adieu,
The warmth of the sun brings life anew.
Open your eyes, observe your surroundings,
Why do you rush with heart pounding?
Dashing around, watching the clock,
Must not be late or others will mock.
Does all this stress improve your life
The constant worry, trouble and strife?
No, it makes you ill and tense,
So relax, relax, the benefits are immense.

Janet Boulton

Escape Into Spring

People are trapped
Bound and gagged
Marooned in a nightmarish dream
Sentenced by fate
Without a trial
Prisoners of the winter regime

Suffocated by darkness
Persecuted by cold
Savaged by storm after storm
The winter fuels
The weather's rage
Seething from night-time to dawn

Again came the snow
The populace froze
Condemned to the next Arctic blast
People kept faith
In moments of prayer
For soon the sentence would pass

Faith shone again
The darkness retreats
Thus came a glimmer of hope
Skies became light
Warmth slays the cold
The curse of winter is broke

Counting their blessings
The people rejoice
Once they hear the birds sing
The sun does shine
People are freed
Free to escape into spring

David Bridgewater

Sword Of Damocles

Three years ago disaster struck.
'Two days? Two weeks? Two months?' they said.
'Good surgeon and a lot of luck
Maybe two years before you're dead.'

The sword may fall on any day.
Who knows when the thread will fray?
Three happy years of life and love
And still the sword hangs there above.
Sometimes I can see it swaying
And wonder if the thread is fraying,
But love and laughter rule here still
Until . . .

Gwen Joselin

The One Who Understands

Health, wealth and happiness
Just three little wishes,
Used to end our letters,
With so many little kisses.

We send them in sincerity
To friends on getting married,
We hope these friends will understand
The loving thoughts they carry.

There's two that are essential
And one that could cause trouble,
A little of it is a must;
With none, we are sure to struggle.

The last is unpredictable.
Our circumstances govern it
But if we know we have a friend
We tell Him all we struggle with.

His ear is always listening.
He's kind, and so dependable.
We always can on Him rely.
He'll deal with us so tenderly.

I recommend Him now to you.
His praises I convey to you .
My loving prayer for each one
Is, come without delay to Him.

Catherine MacDonald

Count Your Blessings

(In memory of Margaret Shalders - Mum)

That is what my mum used to say
It was a saying she used almost every day, in a lovely way
In good times and sad when things seemed to go astray
My mum would say, 'My girl, count your blessings,
And go on your way.

Tomorrow will be different, better than today,
Put a smile on your face and have joy in your heart,
Remember my girl, count your blessings.
And life will go your way.'

Maureen Batchelor

Hidden Jewel

Why did You forsake me when I most needed You?
Why did You let this happen?
To strike me down with illness when I should have been
At the peak of my powers?

What did I do wrong that this afflicted me?
Faithfully I struggled, working to the bone
Often when my weary mind would have gladly given up.
I feel angry, bitter, cheated and utterly dismayed.

What do I hear You say?
It was a gift?
The greatest disappointment of my life - a gift?

This gift so tightly wrapped you cannot open now.
Through time its outer skin will disappear.
There you will find a jewel that you could never buy,
An understanding what it means to suffer hurt
And not to break.

And with it comes an insight
Chiselled out from your despair,
An insight into other people's pain
That only now, you honestly can share.

Kathleen Davey

My Very Soul

Walking in the early morn,
I watch the sunrise up at dawn,
I listen to the birds that sing,
And smell the fragrant flowers of spring.

As I look up to the sky above,
My heart does fill with warmth and love,
For I know not of anywhere else to be,
Where I feel at peace and oh so free.

And as the day does pass on by,
And the sun sinks down in the evening sky,
Well then the moon does start to rise,
And a silent tear falls from my eyes.

So there's always something up on high,
In the day or night-time sky,
So be it day or be it night,
My heart is full of sheer delight.

Oh what a land, oh what a place,
As I stand with nature and embrace
On the threshold of eternity,
I give my very soul to thee.

Ernest Hiddleston

Thank You Lord

There came my way, an invitation,
A believer's lunch, for any denomination,
No lecture, no speaker, no one to preach
Just men talking together, to learn or to teach.

I went to the venue and looked round the room,
Tables for two, each with a spring bloom.
Near to one table I saw a small dark man stand,
Approaching him smiling, I held out my hand,
'Can we share this table,' I asked, he too smiled,
'Yes please! But I'm Jewish,' came his answer, soft and mild.
'We worship the same God!' said I as we sat down.
'Yes that is true.' A smile replacing his frown.

As we sat at our table, still smiling he said, 'A lovely day!'
I laughed, it was raining, 'No that I can't say.'
With that my companion just rolled up his sleeve,
Exposing a tattooed number, 'My dear friend, believe!
Each day I survived in that Nazi prison,
I gave thanks to God, the sun had again risen.
And I was alive, his praises to sing,
Still every day, I do the same thing.'

Many years have now passed I too remember his way,
I draw back my curtains, and to God I pray,
'Thank you for my blessings and for this new day'!

Brian Humphreys

Love

We were young and carefree and life was fun,
In summer, we walked hand-in-hand in the sun,
In winter, we laughed at the cold and the snow,
But now it seems like a lifetime ago.
We stayed together through all the years,
Some filled with laughter and some with tears.
We made a promise, till death us do part,
But now I'm alone with a broken heart.
You were my soulmate, the light of my life,
And I was so proud to be your wife.
Now the light has gone out, but when I see a bright star,
I know you are out there, watching over me from afar.

Betty Bramma

The Legacy

I scarce could walk when I was put to work,
A sickly child. I feebly fetched and carried
For the men; they thought of me more hindrance
Than a help. But years and strength brought me
To man's estate; I lifted stone, and learned
To chisel, cut and shape the rough-hewn blocks.
We toiled from dawn till sun went down,
And in the gloom of winter's icy days,
Our frozen fingers bled, and feet were numb,
And bitter cold would crack the callused skin.
Our pay was scarce enough to buy our bread,
And many a friend would perish by the spring:
And even summer heat would take its toll.

But, oh, what beauty grew before our eyes!
For, year by year, the stately abbey rose
Above the thatched roof hovels round its base.
And people stood in awe and gaped, wide mouthed,
To see the blessed Saints in niches carved,
And fearsome gargoyles casting devils out;
Massive, pillared arches spread, like jaws
Of death-grey whales, that soared to heights,
Too far above for candles' pallid glow.

And, indescribable, my daily joy
To see this glorious testament to God
Rise up in all its beauty, grace and form,
And touch the very soul of all.

But now in age, my old frame groans,
And I no more can bear the load.
Toiling generations yet to come
Must do as I have done, and groove,
And cut and shape, and bind
The massive blocks of sharp-edged stone.

I will not live to see God's house complete,
The awful splendour of its majesty;
And yet I gain much comfort in my pain
That I have played, as boy and man,
A tiny part in His eternal plan.

Jay Whittam

The Rotunda Of Life

It was as easy as one, two, three . . .
Snowdrifts.

One was an homage to our birth; the next
a shrine of learning; the next a reminder
of life's tribulations long and short; another
the wink of happiness and song of joy;
and the last was an entire rotunda
'neath the heavens on a bright winter's day.

Oh great bright light, from where did you come?
Was it my fellow travellers who found this epitome?
Each grave has sunk to the greatest of depths;
And each our spirits here as the winds sweep,
How our hearts and minds connect
Only our voice and song shouted this epithet
So a free bird of the air would hear us,
And our fervent wishes and hopes bless us;
'Twas not so long ago that the earth was bleak
And not that long ago when the fire twigs squeaked,
Just think of all your friends
How each and every foe should be turned
Around to kindness for us to yearn.

But only a rhyme and a riddle would recall
of one special winter's day as when
the great white life travelled o'er our terrain
and blessed it as a kiss upon a sleeping giant;
I'll bluff not, certainly not, when it was
I and those held dear who found the rotunda.

On the thrice, when winter struck!

Linda Curtis

My Blessings

I sit in my garden just dreaming
And count all my blessings anew
Though I've had many dark days and sorrows
The good things still keep shining through.

There was the friend that just called to see me
With a cheery hello and a smile,
And the glimpse of the sun in the morning,
When the day began with black clouds.

I thank God for the many blessings,
Which come to me every day.
Sent along with the trials of my life
Which help me to find my way.

Deirdre Wise

Snail

On wet, grey, ageing stones, a lone little traveller
Silently wends his way,
His home spiralled to his being
He has no mortgage or carpet to clean.
A translucent vibrant form,
A microcosm in a vast domain,
Perchance a human soiled
Foot will thunder past and by degrees,
Could crush to a wet mass, to mingle with the rain,
Or the swoop of a hungry bird, his prize with precisioned eye,
A morsel to sustain, he will trill his joyful note in return.
A symphony of silver gently winds,
His highway is not the motorway,
His yesterday and tomorrow is now,
Patterned to purpose, his evolution, is slow,
A glimpse of Nature's journey,
In restless days.
An awesome thing, how each raindrop, each snail,
Each bird, and me depend and identify.

Olivia Hicks

Memories

Memories, memories come floating by
Some are sweet, some are sad, all catch my eye -

Sad, like the night when my hometown was bombed:
Our home was a wreck, but at least we were safe -
The world was on fire, even moon, stars and sky.

Sweet, like the day when we both said 'I will',
Future unknown, but the war days behind.
Five moves in five years, then a mansion and grounds!
And delight in the trees, flowers and birds.

Then such a sad time, when your last days had come,
Seeing you suffer so, trying to ease;
Helped by son John, when it came to the end,
Though he grieved for you too, at the loss of a friend.

Sweet, as I look round at where I live now,
The flowers, birds and sun, a constant delight;
With friends I can turn to, work I can do,
And always behind me, my memories of you.

Mary Dimond

My Blessings

I was feeling sorry for myself
On a dark and dreary day
Thinking of all the problems
That had come my way

I don't see very well these days
Or walk as I once could
I've twinges here and niggles there
I'm not feeling good

And then I thought of what I have
A loving family who care
Who bring sunshine to my life
And who are always there

I have someone with me
Who helps in every way
To make my life run smoothly
And does so every day

And so I count my blessings
What else could I wish for?
I'm helped, supported, cared for, loved
Who would ask for more?

May Morrott

My Love To You

The love you have
For a person
Is shown in what you do

But always keep the memories
Of your 'loved ones'
And friends from the past

Remember the games you played
The songs you sang
Go out, be joyful
Stay in command

You may even one day
Join the local brass band
Hip hip hooray!

C Wigglesworth

Our Daughter

We have been blessed,
And we thank God every day,
Even though she has the everyday problems,
She still cares about us,
She has been through such a lot for her years,
And so many tears,
But we look at her and feel so very proud,
We want to shout it out aloud.
She was just a tiny chrysalis,
Then, this beautiful butterfly was born,
We are always there if she should fall,
And she's always there if we should call.
Loving, caring not one selfish bone,
We will never feel alone,
With our beautiful daughter,
Whose name is Angalee.
Thank you for coming into our lives,
Yes, we do know we are blessed,
We have the best.

Angel Hart

Thanks Be To God

God gave us eyes that we may see
The many things around us that are free.
Love and beauty that can be found
From animals and flowers that are in the ground.

Ears to hear the birds' morning chorus,
Choirs in church singing for us,
Prayers are needed to see us through,
To feel the love God gives to you.

So count your blessings, there are so many,
They don't even have to cost a penny
The colours in the sky as the sun sets,
An artist's dream as he uses his palette.

Thinking or seeing all this
Should give everyone a lift.
I hope it can bring to you a smile,
Cos life is certainly worthwhile.

Evelyn M Harding

None So Blind

There is none so blind that cannot see
Beauty in a simple tree
Or appreciate the dawn
As another day is born

And none so deaf who would dismiss as noise
Laughter from small girls and boys

Yet I was blind and bereft of sound
And then another world I found
For I was told that death was near
So overcome with grief and fear

I prayed, and I had never prayed before
My prayers then opened up a door
My life took on another lease
My heart and mind transformed with peace

And colours that once looked grey
Were now a dazzling array
And everything was clear and bright
I saw magic in the stars at night

All at once my values changed
My priorities were rearranged
My life before was built on sand
But now I find
Success is not the quantity that I acquire
But the quality I leave behind

Terry Wigzell

To Lepe Beach

Modest and unpretentious
with a wild, rugged charm,
your shore is mainly shingle,
your bird the common tern,
your shells many but unremarkable,
your sea just the Solent,
you face the unexotic Isle of Wight,
your visitors are prone to cellulite,
you entice no millionaires' yachts,
you attract no traffic queues,
your beach is never packed,
your facilities merely minimal,
yet you have my heart and soul,
for weekend sunbathes and a peaceful after work stroll.

Carole Luke

The Seemingly Deemed 'He' - 'But' - 'And Yet' Poem

His glass seemed half empty,
For all that he could see -

Was that he was scruffily scraggy,
But
Not desirably craggy.

He had an abundance of body hair,
But
This was deemed no longer required.

He had increasing sparcity of scalp hair,
But this seemed in no way desired,
Unless magnificently, shavenly, bald,
But
He seemed, anyway, deemed *too old.*

He was sensibly, seemingly, naturally slim,
But
Was dismissed, instead, as punily overly thin.

He did his level best to be caring and sympathetic,
But
Seemed dismissed, instead, as weak and pathetic.

He had an abundance of degrees and 'O' levels,
But
These were as good as ignored -
Because his failed maths was far more loudly deplored.

He worked consistently hard all the hours that he could,
But
Failed to earn recompense that he should.

He worked full-time/part-time enjoying helping others,
But
Beckoned insufficient perks for attracting any lovers.

He was a dependable
Expendable -
His genes seemingly deemed not worthy of passing on . . .

Count Our Blessings

And yet

After all had been done and said -
He at least had some sort of roof over his head.
He had avoided being completely *'down and out',*
And therefore remained *'in with a shout'* -
Of seeing his symbolic glass more half full than it might have been -
For things are not always as they first do seem . . .

He remains alive and fit and well,
And as far as all can tell -
Has many remaining years that might
Eventually see him *get things right* -

And so he can count his blessings!

Paul Bartlett

The Greatest Show On Earth

Far removed from a three-ring circus,
Billed as the 'Greatest Show on Earth',
Geared to making money! All captives,
The audience, participants, animals and humans.
They gasp, scream, clap at unnatural acts.
Now leave it all behind you, watch nature's show.

Lean on a gate, sit on a log, or grassy slope.
Keep still - listen - let nature engulf you!
Now observe, feel, be part of the scene.
First the lambs as they skip and run,
From tree stump to gate, and back again,
Not heeding the warning bleat of their mothers.

High in the sky nature's orchestra starts up,
The skylarks song - so pure and sweet,
Contrast to that circus drum.
The birds in the hedges now join the chorus,
All singing their different tunes, yet harmonising.
Nature alone knows how to accomplish this.

Roll up! Roll up! To see this great show!
Do it quietly, not striking a discordant note.
No open mouth box office to swallow your money,
The show is free for all to enjoy,
Taking place continuously for all to join in!
This time, however, for just me - and my maker!

A R Lewis

Count Your Blessings

Count your blessings on what you've got,
Maybe it might not seem a lot,
If only people could just see,
You don't always need money, just peace and harmony.

Maybe if you look around you, you will find,
Lots of things sent from the Lord, to bring peace of mind,
If you live alone, friends, neighbours or pets,
Can be blessings in disguise,
Especially when they are a shoulder to lean on,
To help dry tears from your eyes.

Pets too can help ease the pain,
They understand again and again,
But if you have no one like this, I say,
Just think of the Lord, He's there every day.

Maybe you might have a family,
And possibly grandchildren you can see,
But just remember, counting blessings is not hard to do
Because friends and family, most of them really do love you.

Count your blessings for good health,
It is worth more than lots of wealth,
Money cannot alter, whatever a possible hurtful family situation may be,
Maybe it pays the bills but surely you can see.
That if you have enough to get by,
And you have family, friends, pets, good health and God,
Then I ask you why?
You don't look at life in a different way,
Learn to give thanks for a beautiful day.

Look in the gardens, as you pass by, I say,
Listen to the birds, see the beauty of the sun shining,
The rain or maybe a rainbow today.
That it all comes from God to replenish the earth, that's true
So replenish yourself and count your blessings in all you do.

Barbara Holme

Whisper Of The Wind

(For Beryl Adey)

The path we walk
is sometimes shrouded in shadows
laying like a heavy cloak on our shoulders
sapping our spirit and dampening our resolve
as the way home eludes us
and when it seems we will crumple under the strain
we hear the call of those we love
on the whisper of the wind
and sunbeams of hope penetrate our darkness
shepherding us towards the gate
where those we love and care for are waiting to
welcome us home

Jan Maissen

God's World

Why is it that some people
Don't see what I see?
Like seeing the flowers
That is lovely to me.

Like the beauty of the Earth
That nature gives out,
With trees like giants
Branches swaying about.

Why is it that some people
Don't appreciate the green fields?
Taking them for granted
For what the land yields.

What of the creatures
So innocent and free,
Minding their business
For we don't let them be.

I count my blessings
To have eyes to see
The creations of God
This is wonderful to me

Wouldn't it be nice
If war was unknown?
For war is destroying
The Earth that He owns.

Jean Lloyd-Williams

Thank You For A New Year

Thank you, Lord, for a fresh day of life,
For enough strength and health to meet this small, new beginning.
Thank You for arms and hands, legs and feet
That, despite age and ailments, I can still use unaided.

Thank You for five senses, dimmer now,
Like brain and memory, but affording gentle pleasures.
Thank You for the day's first sip of tea,
Music that lifts the heart and books that transport the reader.

Thank You for husband, family, home,
The bedrock of my life and my incentive for living.
Thank You for all kind human contacts,
From lifelong friendships to the stranger's unexpected smile.

Thank You for Your never failing love,
Father, Son and Holy Spirit, this new year and always.

Margaret Gregory

Tomorrow And Tomorrow

(Yours, my grandson)

My dear grandson, I am yours today and tomorrow, for
in the future, you will be there, I shall not
Your three score years more are for you, your joys, your
woes - give life all you have got

Have fun for its own sake, be a good friend, laugh a lot,
but do all things well, fulfil your dreams.
Learn your trade never ceasing to be curious, be slow to
judge, sensing when all is not what it seems

Give of yourself but not too much; at times just *be*
be silly, be crazy and lazy going with the flow
Set a good example, ne'er too grand, take time out to
try something new, keep in the know

Not only love but care - care for those with less,
less knowledge, less ability, less hope
Be a good coach, mentor the young, distrusting those
who pronounce on those who cannot cope

No more wise words from your granpa and your
loving granma too,
Go ahead, live, venture, play and be happy
We shall be proud of you always, full of pride in you
being you.

Clive Bowen

Clouds And Silver Linings

We live in a world influenced by material wealth,
And it's easy to get side-tracked into believing,
This is what ultimately brings happiness,
Yet the natural world around us has much to offer,
In lifting up a discontented spirit,

Notice the beauty of a spider's web,
Covered in early morning dew,
The adhering droplets sparkling like diamonds,
A blackbird singing his early morning repertoire,
Autumn's rich and varied tapestry of leaves,

Life's journey offers us many choices,
Roads to travel and paths to choose,
We can often dwell on the *what ifs*,
And would that other direction,
Have resulted in a more beneficial life,

That we will never know,
Because we cannot change the past,
And whilst mulling over the *ifs,*
The present is moving forward,
Without us living in that moment,

Fate, is the motivator that moulds our character,
Plays its hand in who we are today ,
Remember the old adage, a blessing in disguise,
Put the past away, savour today,
Look forward to the future and have no regrets.

Ann G Wallace

Loving Memories

All yesterday's loving memories,
will always live on.
In the hearts of our beloved ones,
long after we are gone.
Long after we leave this Earth,
there is no one to blame.
When all tender loving memories,
of the love we shared and gave remain.
If a memory was like a candle burning,
into a beautiful loving light display.
It would lighten up our dear, beloved ones lives,
of those we touch with love each day.
An everlasting tender love for them,
long after we are gone.
A love to soothe the broken heart,
and give them strength to carry on

Joyce Willis

A Happy New Year

Christmas is over and the New Year is here too.
With it comes all the memories
Of past, present and those to come.
And life to live as we go along.

It's inevitable, that for many,
Christmas might hold unhappy memories
Of events, beyond their grasp.
But, for the rest of us,
Christmas, brought us joy beyond belief.

What with the hustle and bustle of Christmas,
The excitement of children and grown-ups,
With the expectations of pleasant things
Whether to do with gifts to come,
Or, reunions with long-lost relatives.

And now, we all share hopes for the new year.
For how many families
Through the spirit of Christmas
Forged new friends, new acquaintances,
Or made up friends with long-lost relatives.

To these the New Year, holds a bright future.
In fact, let's all look on the bright side of things
And leave negative thoughts
Behind, where they belong.
Let's all try and be positive
And be satisfied with what we've got.

M Kiddie

Trust

Between the dark silent trees
the scarlet sky burns.
Born in the secret heart of afternoon
without warning my husband's death
opens a voracious abyss.

The presence of his absence
spreads a thick fog everywhere.
I am lost with all who are dear to us both.

Slowly, a trembling light makes darkness visible.
Over all dead and alive
is lit the silent Bethlehem star.

Angela Cutrale Matheson

Gratitude

I have a roof above my head,
I've a warm and comfy bed.
I've a garden full of flowers in the spring;
In fact it's very rare
That there's not a blossom there,
And trees with birds that simply love to sing.
Then, too, on every school day,
As she passes by my way,
There's a little girl who waves and gives a smile,
And the lad whose cheerful grin
Seems to bring the sunshine in,
With my paper, as he lingers for a while.
I've a family who care,
And when needed they are there . . .
On each and every day that's plain to see.
I have friends, faithful and true,
Whatever would I do
Without their love and welcome company?
And the ever changing seasons
That give so many reasons
To be grateful as we greet each different one.
And I can choose, on any day,
Down my path to make my way,
Just to marvel at a glorious setting sun.
So many, many more
Of wondrous things in store,
Such as memories of happy days gone by.
So many blessings, too,
That I know the thing to do
Is to be so much more thankful . . . so I'll try!

Winifred Chubb

Trees In Autumn

What beautiful impurities
That cause the leaves to turn
Amazing golds and reds and browns
That deck the fields and dress the town
And make my senses burn.

Behind the wood the sun is low,
And through leaf-skin a richer show
Of subtle hues eyes scarcely know.

My soul glows with the colours
Of these wondrous autumn leaves
Nature's stained glass window
The glory of the trees.

Charmian Goldwyn

Touched By An Angel

Am I going crazy? Out of my head?
They were watching over me, I believe
When I was on life support in that hospital bed.
It's said we all have an angel
Someone we can turn to.
Just surrender your cares, worries to them,
They'll help to see you through.
Am I dreaming? Am I awake?
The angels want to help me
There must be some mistake.
Yes I've been touched by an angel,
There to help surrendered my cares, worries too.
When you have your difficulties
They're there to help, see you through.
Talk to the angels,
Whether you're happy or sad.
Just confide in them.
God sent them to you for a purpose,
It doesn't mean you're going mad.
They say just call upon us angels,
You'll know that we are with you.
You'll feel cold or feel a soft gentle touch.
You'll feel we angels are with you,
Don't ever feel you'll ever ask too much.
You even get Earth angels,
People who listen, advise you everything will be all right.
You even get these angels as a spirit, not as much as in sight.
Writing and music are my passions, thanks to Him up above.
I always turn to Him and the angels, count my blessings,
As these are my first love.
I ask them to guide me,
A light to help me see.
I surrendered my feelings to them,
Say writing and music means the world to me.

Karen Rust

Life Is What You Make It

Life is what you make it
Enjoy your journey through the years
There will be times of joy and laughter
And sadly, there'll be tears.
Learn to cope with life's disasters
Help those that are in need
Cultivate your sense of humour
With God's help you will succeed.

Muriel Berry

Crying Wildly At Sea

Skimming the river the swallows flying,
Higher over loved ones robin singing,
Silently waiting the heron fishing.
Seagulls crying through waves of the sea.
Early the morning with songs is filling,
Songs of the chorus of birds, high trilling,
Cuckoo, thrush, chaffinch and blackbird piping.
Voice of the wren shrilling, bursting with joy.
Drifting in winds the small birds migrating.
Following stars to the lands of their choosing.
Coming the light of the evenings is longer,
Turtle doves crooning the sweetness of spring.
Mincing the masses of midges, warblers
Busily feeding their clam'rous offspring,
All the birds singing and growing, flying,
Flying to lands over high stormy seas.
Fa la la la, fa la lala la, crying wildly at sea,
Fa la la la, fa la lala la, crying wildly at sea.

Ben Henderson Smith

Disclosures (Of A Personal Nature)

I was abandoned and you rescued me
Spurned and yet you saved me.
I was the shameful secret within your family
Still you gladly welcomed me into your hearts.
Rejected in my (innocent) infancy,
Denied my birthright and fearing
Never to be loved, for the person I truly was,
You both dedicated yourselves to the task
Of providing selfless, loving care for me.

So, that is why, in my darkest moments,
I can think of you, my adoptive parents and
In humble gratitude, count my blessings and marvel
That I found you and that you chose me.

Sonya Hynes

Blessing Account

Just look around you every day,
Blessings abound and come our way
To share for evermore

Someone needs you, be it day or night,
Whatever the time or the plight,
Kind words, a prayer truly meant,
Such blessing beyond compare.
Just tell a friend you really care.

Be a blessing dear to hand,
The issue is never lost when you understand.
Someone just needs that God-given touch,
A sympathetic ear, may be momentous and means so much.
Take time, it is so surely worthwhile,
To turn a sad face into a sunny smile.

Blessings shared are our joys untold,
Much more precious than diamonds or gold,
So marvellous they are returned a thousand-fold,
So count your blessings, name them all - one by one,
Then we really will see what God surely has done.

M W Clarke

Our Gift

We take so much for granted
We never stop to think
That little girl is cosy
All wrapped up in pink

The miracle of a baby
When we look on in awe
Those little tiny fingers
Just what a baby's for

Those eyes look so adoring
Asking for our love
She was sent to us
From the heavens above

So take her in your arms
Cherish her for life
Remember she's the miracle
You promised to your wife

Andrea Lynne Taylor

Love's Art

A songbird greets the rising sun,
The grass glitters with morning dew
Such brightness fills my inner self
Because I am in love with you.

I wish that it would stay with us
Until the time's ceased passing by
Clocks tick away the earthly life
And stars become dust in the sky.

I remember you asked me once:
If great love can make life a whole
Or if it briefly touches the heart
With no emotions in the soul?

The answers may come down to one:
Sharing one's life is love's great art
With the power to soothe the world
From soul to soul, from heart-to-heart.

Anthony Gyimes

Babies Are Cuddly, Soft And Warm

Babies are cuddly and full of charm,
and we like to protect and keep them from harm.
I love to watch each stage they go through,
especially when their teeth come into view.

They gurgle loudly when they try to laugh,
when their mummy puts them in the bath.
Lots of warm water, babies love to be bare,
bubbles floating everywhere.
Their toes are so podgy their fingers too,
they look so cute when they are wet through.

When they start to crawl, it is exciting to see,
they get into places that they shouldn't be.
A baby's first words are so good to hear,
even if it's not so clear.
I love to fuss over a child at play,
hugging and kissing every day.

Sandra Bentley

Counting Our Blessings

In the aftermath of Christmas and season of goodwill,
Do your troubles overwhelm you?
Is your life lonely and grim?
As the years reflect our sadness
And the awesome brevity of life,
Do you see that spark of hope
In the beauty of the universe?
Or feel God's touch and gentle presence
Among clouds of doubt and hopelessness?
Count our blessings, for with Him none are too small.
Look up to Him - not down in despair!
Lift all your troubles to Him in prayer!
He'll comfort and strengthen you, giving you hope.
Lifting your spirit and revealing His plans
For a future and hope that's in line with His will.
If only we'll trust Him and humbly obey.
So let's count our blessings, list them one by one,
You will be surprised what the Lord has done.

S Williams

Counting My Blessings

Life is still a blessing
Now I am old and grey;
I wake up every morning
To face another day.

The carer will be calling
To get me out of bed,
Then she will bath and dress me,
And see that I am fed.

I have my books and radio
To pass away the time;
Then, of course, there is TV,
But for old friends I pine.

So many now have passed away,
Alas! So it must be -
'Tis the penalty of growing old,
But memories comfort me.

Being a prisoner in my home,
I think a lot and sleep;
I count my blessings one by one
And quite a harvest reap.

Margaret Bailey

One Moment

A normal day, well so it began
Everything just going to plan
Quite easy, going along with life
Nothing to cause me any strife.

Then a letter arrived in the post
Medical report, results of tests, felt lost.
Time and date, oh I thought, early next week.
A talk with hubby, solace, so to seek.

News no good, the big 'C'.
Didn't take it in, just couldn't be.
Hubby by my side, I did listen,
Just keep calm, to the decision.

Week in hospital, been sorted
Three months later, things thwarted.
Praise to doctors and nurses, such care,
Without them, I wouldn't be here.

So be grateful, for all that is given
My life is changed, I love living.
All seasons, breathe it in
My one moment was, I win

Julie Dawe

The Seasons

Snowflakes falling, covering the earth
Sparkling like jewels as they fall to the ground
Jack Frost nipping at your face
As he weaves his way on a cold winter's day
Snow slowly melting with the promise of spring
Snowdrops and crocuses bursting with new life
Small animals waking from their long sleep
Young lambs skipping and bees-a-buzzing
Summer with its clear blue skies
Long hot days with vibrant sunsets
Autumn with its leaves of red and gold
Falling gently to the ground
Cool evenings as the nights draw in
Misty mornings with dew on the grass
Each season having a beauty of its own.

Doreen Cawley

Thank You

Thank You for the gift of life
Thank You for the simple things in life
Thank You for making me what I am
Thank You for our lovely families
Thank You for the air we breathe
Thank You the joy and any warmth we have
Thank You for being so thoughtful
Thank You for being so cheerful
Thank You for the friends we have
Thank You for the lovely memories we have
Thank You for the feeling of showing love
Thank You for the pleasure of doing something
Thank You for the blessings we've been given
Thank You for the Christian religion
Thank You for capturing the sound of beautiful music
Thank You and honour to Nature's beauty
Thank You for our dedicated doctors and the help we receive
Thank You, for with Your love I made my way
Thank You Lord, my Creator
Thank You Lord for You are timeless and ageless
Thank You Lord, You loved me and always cared
Thank You Lord for helping me to be better
Thank You Lord, You've been so good to me
Thank You Lord for Your treasures on Earth
Thank You Lord for Your Heavenly love
Thank You Lord for all the love You have given me
Thank You Lord for offering help and guidance
Thank You for the faith, hope and trust
Thank You, just smile and be happy and thankful.

Rita Scott

It's A Blessing

Blessings come, all
shapes and sizes
Many come in
all disguises

Some feel good
some feel bad
Some are happy
some are sad

But all are blessings
just the same
When we can see
through love and pain.

It's a blessing

Thelma Roberts

The Gift Of Life

They say that life is precious, yes, of course that's true,
but when I saw you slip away, I was numb and then I felt
the pain tear through me, as I fought to keep my grip on life.

I seemed to walk in shadows, feeling lost and all alone,
while others walked in sunlight, and still had that special person in their life.

I went to say my last goodbye, and as I looked upon her sweet face,
she looked as though she was just sleeping, not gone.
'Let there be Heaven, I whispered, let it all be true,
That my dear mother is with the angels now.'

That special lady who had taught me right from wrong.
Whose gentle smile had always lit up my life.
Her words of encouragement, a hug,
always there when things went wrong, my mother, my guiding light.

All around, people enjoying that beautiful day, winter not far away,
laughter, children at play, couples walking hand in hand,
and then I heard these words, 'Hello, how are you today Mum?'
and the tears slipped gently down my face.

If only I still had that pleasure, to simply say those words,
and see your caring, loving face,
the mother I could no longer embrace.

And then I realised she was right here, in my heart,
a part of me, in me she would live on.
I could not let her down, that
special lady, who had given me the gift of life.

A sudden warmth spread through me, a smile gently touched my lips,
I saw her in my memory, smiling, urging me on.
Yes, life is precious, and once again
I felt the warmth of the sun.

Carole Chignell

Sensations

I hear the croaking ravens and the majesty of the organ
I see the electricity of the heavens and the sparks from my sweater
I taste the sweet marshmallows and the hot tang of ginger.
I smell the seductive scent of roses and the rancid stench of sour milk
I speak words of comfort to the small child fallen from his tricycle
  and curse the driver who forced me into the hedge.
I think of wonders of the world and of its troubles.
I know despair and hope, anger and calm, love and hate.
I know that I am blessed because all things, all emotions are mine.
I know that I am blessed because without pain I cannot know pleasure, without grief I cannot know joy, without anger I cannot know compassion, without love I cannot know God.
Truly I am blessed because I am a human being.

P Wolstenholme

On A Spring Day

On a spring day,
when golden meadows
and
sweet sounds caress
I see in a quiet corner,
the bridge,
where we sheltered
and
stepped through the rain
and mud to kiss.
oten we went there,
the whispered days
of war
and
the parting.

How can I forget
my roundabout thoughts
of a spring day
with golden meadows
and
birds' song?

Ann Eyton Jones

Ode To Spring

The wind bangs down
The raindrops fall
The cold chills my body
Why am I dog-walking at all?

The sky is dull and bleary
I feel tired and weary,
This is winter at its best
Where is spring, still at rest?

Then I spy a glow of colour
Under the hedge and sheltered too,
Snowdrops, a splash of white
Daffodils, a burst of yellow
My heart lifts, life is there
So don't despair, say a prayer!

Leila McLeish

The Extra Mile

Hey there my good friend
Have you done good things today
Did you help all those in trouble
As you passed along the way
When you took a walk down Main Street
Did you wear a great big smile
And for the old, weak and sick
Did you go that extra mile?

When you met a passing stranger
Did you offer friendship's hand
For those with sadness in their eyes
Did you try to understand
For the lonely and the friendless
Did you stop for just a while
And give them what they really need
Time and friendship's smile?

The day my friend is nearly done
Did you do these things today
Did you offer hope and comfort
As you passed along the way?
Remember what they needed most
Was a warm and friendly smile
And to meet someone who cared enough
To go that extra mile.

Howard Atkinson

The Breeze

Stretching and pushing, I must break free,
Free from the earth that's covering me.
Pushing the soil and stones aside,
Into the open I eventually stride.

The ground is damp. From which I have burst,
Helping me grow, halting my thirst.
As I grow, week after week,
Towards the sky I slowly sneak.

With time going by, year after year,
The top of the canopy, I need to be near.
As decades pass, my growth starts to slow,
Aided by rain, and the sun's warm glow.

Brian Williams

Big Brother's Song

Do not think, oh, small and new,
I will not crush
your face for you.
Don't imagine
you have power
crying every darkling hour.
You have stolen
food and love
from the one who
towers above.
You have elbowed me aside,
usurped comfort,
injured pride.
Will I cuddle you?
They smile,
make me love you
with their guile?
I stroke your tiny head
and know
if you cry
I'll rock you so,
hold you to my tiny breast,
Welcome, uninvited guest!

Gill Pomfret

You've Stayed Near

You're not here to hold my hand,
But your grandson does it beautifully.

You're not here to hold me close,
But your granddaughter knows how to cuddle me.

You're not here to be at my side,
But you've left me such gifts of love.

Our children are grown now,
With babes of their own,
Whose blue eyes remind me of you.
But they will never see your fond loving looks,
Or feel the strength of your arms.

But, I'm still here and all on my own,
Still missing your every breath.
Yet comfort and blessings, through these dear little souls,
Tell me daily, your spirit's still here.

Wilma Jayne Gravenor

Living With Memories

Ten years now passed
As I write these words
To be mirrored in my mind
Bringing back to me
The years that used to be
Life's pleasures, now left behind
Her photographs around my room
Bring me brightness every day
I often watch our family films
Since death took my wife away
Sometimes a sadness does appear
To remind me of my grief
Why? The question floods my mind
Making her passing beyond belief
But there is a life still to live
In helping others meet their pain
Discussing joys each shared in life
And those memories that remain
Moments treasured, laughter, fun
Cloud the memory to one's mind
My joy in life, memories of my dear wife
Life's gift for her treasured time.

E L Hannam

You're My Child

You've been my shadow
Since the day you were born
You've spilt paint all over me
And made mud pies out of my lawn

You were sick on my best blouse
And swung off my gold necklace
But I've found it rather beautiful
Seeing that smile on your chubby, little face

A few years on and you have grown
And you are skipping off to school, rather tall
Secretly I'm sad you're slipping through my fingers
And I wonder if you'll ever come back to me at all.

Laura Salmon

Blessings

When I wake each morning
Such a blessing, I'm alive!
When I see the sunrise,
Such a blessing, I have eyes!

When my daughters hug me
Such a blessing, I am loved!
Seems that someone special,
Is watching from above.

Sometimes our lives are hard
And it's difficult to see
Just where the blessings are,
To unlock and find the key.

Daffodils appearing
Tells us spring is on its way.
Such a lovely blessing,
When all is cold and grey.

It is God who gives us blessings,
They are things that are quite free.
He gives them unconditionally,
To be enjoyed by you and me.

Sandra J Walker

Starlit Night

On a starlit night
When the mood is so right
There is always cause to wonder,
About interstellar flight.

A journey to each planet
From there and beyond,
Trekking out to places faraway places,
Where only in our minds
Have we ever gone.

To view the craftwork of Your heavenly hands
On a crisp clear night,
Is our out of this world privilege.

Infinite thanks for the priceless gift,
Of human imagination.

Kevin Welch

Moment

A lifting dream takes me
back to your lab in Kilburn;
back through peeling window frames
watching the trains rush past
to forgotten destinations.
The tracks, the sounds, the hard hat toy-men
in a void of frozen transport.
I see the oak-scratched desk
with diary and name cards waiting;
Same-day Dental Repairs - its lippy logo,
and smell again the acrid clay turning
and rolling, dank, dirt-brown,
the pink wax you shaped into gums
and through the peeling window frames,
the tracks, the trains rushing
to forgotten destinations.
I see the table where you worked,
peaceable in your white laboratory coat,
your stillness in a void of moving things.
Through the lifting dream I sense
our vanished time together,
like diamond prisms, sparkling light;
the smell, the tracks, the trains rushing
to forgotten destinations, lone horn bleeping
in the wind. Is there anything deeper
than the glimpse of this past place,
as the veil of sleep lifts
these disappearing things
into objects more solid
than when we lived in their time?

Gloria Tessler

Springtime

The miracle is happening, the earth is young again.
In garden, glade and orchard, city park and country lane.
The marvel of springtime all wrought anew,
sap has risen in the branches, life has broken through.

Something happens to our hearts when the daffodils appear.
Gaily dancing all around beneath the trees,
it seems to give a lift to our overburdened hearts when the
golden trumpets sound again; we know that spring's the start.

Spring is on the wing, the summer lies ahead.
When the earth is warm and the skies bright and clear,
It's blossom time in England.
The nicest time of year.

D Arnell

Snowdrops and Sorrow

Beside a concrete hydrant
That's opposite the church
A little group of snowdrops live,
You really have to search
Before you find their tiny snouts
Among dead leaves of birch.

My dear mum died one Christmas
And left me all alone.
But the snowdrops are encouragers;
I'm never on my own!
They're at their very brightest
When the winds of winter moan.

So when I feel downhearted
In January's cold air
And think about my mother
And the life we used to share
I only have to rummage in
The grass to find them there

I'm filled with admiration
For their single, pure white flowers
They stand up tall and lovely
Beneath the snowy showers
They amaze me with their courage
And silent, secret powers.

And even in the summer
When their blooms are not on show
I know they're just in hiding
And soon the bulbs will grow
Exactly when I need them
They flower right on cue
Find your own clump of snowdrops
And let them gladden you!

Lesley Robinson

The Coming Spring

Winter is dying and spring is almost here.
The last snowdrops have hung their modest heads,
And pale yellow primrose peep from crimped leaves.
The woods are waking from their careless sleep
as my stiff limbs stir their age-frozen bones
to welcome this, my seventieth spring.

Slowly I climbed the hill whose sharp sides
seem ever steeper each successive year.
I pause, breathlessly, to admire the view
that I have seen in a thousand dreams.
I hear a distant woodpecker hammering
on trees, where long ago, I carved your name.

High upon the summit I feel the southern breeze
bringing back the thick sweet scent of bluebells.
Far away returning swallows will be skimming
over arid lands and white-topped waves.
Soon they will reach Cornwall's welcoming coastline
to rest on high wires like rows of gypsies' pegs.

The sun-warmed meadows will overflow
with delicate daisy and golden buttercup.
Clockwork lambs will leap invisible hurdles
and playful foals will prance on tenuous legs.
Then I will know that spring is here
and my heart will warm with thoughts of you.

John Eccles

Forget Yesterday

There's nothing left to lose
No more to take
I've been born at the wrong time
What a stupid mistake

I've done stuff that was wrong
Said stuff that was wrong
Didn't belong
But I must be strong

Forget yesterday, what's gone before
And I really can't take it any more
Forget nostalgia, I only get upset,
I really can't ever forget.

There's nothing left.

Wendy Day

Counting Blessings

Counting blessings one, two, three
Born into this world
Boundless and free
With skies of blue, seas of green
And a myriad of colours
Fill the earth in-between.

A new year; a new day,
New things to explore
And places to go and play.
People to visit, work to do
Some things are unpleasant
But they must be done too.

Count your blessings one by one
And you will soon see
Life's great, no need to be glum
And with a smile on your face
You'll help to cheer another
Who is locked in a sad place.

There's hunger and drought
And wars being fought
Amongst people full of doubt.
There is sadness and sorrow
In the world, but don't lose faith
Trust in God - it'll be better tomorrow.

Count your blessings lift up your heart
Look toward the light
Set all those problems apart
Then you will surely find
That amid the despair is hope
Which gives purpose to all mankind.

Joan Earle Broad

A Nana's Thoughts

In your eyes . . .
I see the blue of future summers,
In your smile, I rest awhile,
Spirit replenished, basking in such warmth.

Gently, arms enfold you
Holding you close on my lap.
Sleepy, now you take a little nap
Content, I study the contours of your face.

Hearts rhythm begins to race,
At cherished reflections laid bare.
Aware, glimpsed anew - a child now grown
With you loved grandson . . . her very own!

Joanne Manning

Count Your Blessings

'Count your blessings', seems very glib advice
when your world is topsy-turvy
and you feel anything but nice
but stop and rest a moment
in the bustle of the day
take a look around you
and ponder on what they say

Have you eyes to see the beauty of a flower
Have you ears to hear the singing of a bird
Have you feet to carry you where ever
Have you hands that can while away the hours
Have you a home wherein you feel secure
Have you a friend who will always lend an ear
Have you children to fill your days with laughter
Have you a partner who will brush away a tear

If you have health and happiness and friendship
and your cares and worries are but few.
If you can truly count so many blessings
the Lord has indeed been good to you.

Anne Sharples

Think Pleasant Thoughts

Forget the politicians
With their threat of doom and gloom
Forget the eager scientists
With plans for clone and womb
Let industrialists worry
And financial experts moan
Instead try to concentrate
On pleasures of the past
Remembering with gratitude
Dire problems never last
Have faith that in the future
Good times will come once more
Whilst today's PC edicts
Are difficult to ignore
No one can stop us thinking
That lasts for evermore

B Williams

Blessings Abound

You left my life so quickly,
No time to say goodbye.
Whoever thought, one sunny eve,
The next day you would die.
However, through the heartache
And the pain of losing you,
Little bursts of happiness keep breaking through.
The sunlight through the branches,
The birdsong in the trees
As I walk around the garden and feel the gentle breeze.
These are the natural blessings
Sent to cheer the day.
But there are also the steady friends,
Who help along the way,
And the grandchildren who talk of you,
And loved your gentle touch.
So although my life is different,
Those blessings mean so much
And now it's time to gather them,
To realise how great they are.
And however bleak future seems,
They will carry me so far.

Jennie Schofield

Strength

It is with strength,
I will see this through;
The days that lie ahead.
Long days and silent nights,
will comfort me instead.
If I should wake with fear
In my heart;
Fear of being alone.
Tears that fall for yesterday,
Will bring my strength home.

It is with pride,
I'll remember my twin;
A beautiful, gentle face.
Still waters running deep,
A soul engraved with grace.
If I should fall and lose my way;
Strength will persevere,
And fears born of yesterday,
Will show me why I'm here

Jodie Grant

I Still Have Life

Though I am past my three score years and ten,
And lost my dearest only son, three years ago;
I still have many blessings in my life.
The love and comfort that my daughters bring,
Companionship and laughter, joy and fun.
I still can see and hear and smell and speak.
Can see the snowdrops pushing through the wintry earth,
And pale primroses that herald in the spring.
Or hear a blackbird calling from a nearby hedge,
And watch the blue tits flying to and fro
Feeding their fledglings in the cherry tree.
I can still walk on Dartmoor's rocky tors
And hear a buzzard mewing overhead.
Or watch the crashing of the waves upon the beach
And smell the tangy, seaweed-scented air.
I can watch the sunset on a summer's eve
After a family picnic on the sand.
I can hear music, read my books and sing;
Can love our cats and watch our puppy play.
I can still laugh and cry and feel.
I have so many blessings, these are but a few.
I am well blessed, I am content,
I still have life.

Ann Linney

Blessing

Something
That
Makes the
Most of
Mundane
Rhyme,
A ring
Of
Happier
Time,
A group
Of photos
All in
A line,
A blessing.

Nicola Barnes

A New Day

Morning has broken, greet the new day,
Yesterday gone, out of the way.
Whatever it brought, sunshine or tears,
It has joined all the days, amongst all the years.

So open the door, breathe the fresh air,
During the night you have been in God's care.
Look to the sky, with thanks, to say a prayer,
Ask for His guidance and support
As you do the tasks you think you ought.

Wear a smile as you travel each mile,
On your very own road to reach your abode.
To someone in trouble give a helping hand,
They will be pleased, and you will feel grand.

Always let God be your guiding light
Just remember to thank Him
Every day and night
And have faith.

D (Dedman) Huff

In Memory Of My Mother

If I were to die tomorrow, would anyone really care,
Would anyone really miss me with grief too great to bear.
Would anyone say of me gently, she was a loving mother and wife
The world was better for her presence, we were privileged to know her in life.

Or would they say, she was a know all, with a finger in everyone's pie
Her interest anyone's business, she never let a snippet pass by.
Her information was bang up-to-the-minute, she knew who was moving or dead,
Her bush telegraph spread like lightning, but kindly, her heart ruled her head.

Such a one was my dear mother, at fifty-six years old she died,
Taken so suddenly one evening, our tears we could not hide.
Her faith in God was unshaken, each day He gave strength to endure,
The thorns and the cares of everyday life, some that He could not cure.

It is God's will. The people said, what is to be will be.
He only sends enough to bear, a loving Father is he.
At the service they sang her favourite hymn, the same she sang as a bride,
Looking back to the day when she walked down the aisle, to be at her husband's side.

Her home was one of happiness, with two children to love and adore,
Growing together in work and play - who could ask for anything more.
Now she is dead, what a waste of a life, how quickly the years have gone
We knew her in laughter and also in sorrow, her memory will always live on.
Her motto was always try to smile whatever the day may bring,
Help others to climb over life's stile, don't grumble it won't solve a thing,
Today we have learned a lesson, to make good use of every day,
Just remember her life, and what it meant - we think it's the only way.

Olive D Willingale

Grandfather Ben

My grandfather was a tall man
For he could lift me high in his arms
Giving me temporary equality
In the world of adults.

In his hand he held the time of day
So he would listen to my childish tales
And walk his dog and knock in nails
Without concern for seconds lost.

He puffed his pipe and rocked his chair
And drew live pictures with a pencil thick
Of ships and fishes
All things maritime.

The games we played
On much loved shabby boards
Were indispensable
And dominoes and happy hours
Went hand-in-hand
I had to watch him carefully though
Because he winked and cheated oft
And slyly moved his counters so to win
Then I would scold and he would smile
But then we'd laugh and take a break for tea.

My grandfather was a tall man
For he stood tall amongst the others of his kind
He opened countless doors of fun
And made life prickle with delight
Entwining all with his unique companionship.

Norah Mitchell

May

There's a blackbird in my garden.
There's a robin on my lawn.
I was wakened up this morning,
By a chorus around dawn.

As I sit beside my window,
With my toast and cup of tea,
I note the lilac is in bloom,
A wondrous sight to see.

The sounds, perfume and colour
Of May pervade our land,
As once again these blessings fall
From the Great Provider's hand.

Valerie Pestle

A Question Of Appreciation

Does knowing all its Latin name
Add to a rose's matchless form?
A setting sun that sinks in flame
And kindles clouds flushed pink and warm -
Such splendour strewn across the sky
Is not enhanced by knowing why.

Does knowledge of geology
Add majesty to mountains' might?
Does schooling in astronomy
Improve a velvet, starlit night?
Does firing rockets into space
Extend the smile on Moon's white face?

Does knowing caterpillars change
Paint brighter wings on butterflies?
A rainbow's wondrous colour range
Does not depend on being wise.
Does flair to sing a lilting scale
Add magic to the nightingale?

Do changing tints in autumn leaves
Thrill only if we know the tree?
And when the mighty ocean heaves
Or storms stir up an angry sea,
Does understanding tame the roar
Or fail to rouse that sense of awe?

A soft and silent fall of snow
That wraps the hills in perfect white
Is none the purer if we know
What creates this unblemished sight.
And
Can all the learning here on Earth
Surpass the miracle of birth?

Stella Redman

Light

The cold wind wraps around my face
The darkness around my eyes

Waves crash in the distance
White tipped against the blue black night

No birds call in the empty void
Only the moan of the rising gale

Not a sliver of life on land, sea or sky

I'm alone in the bitter gloom

Then like a lamp on the distant horizon
A light - bright and warm - journey's end.

Alasdair Cowie

Come, Fly With Me

Come, fly with me,
Feel as free as a bird.
Come, fly with me,
Don't feel swept away
With the herd.

Come, spread your wings,
Open your heart, your mind.
Come, spread your wings,
To the beauty of life, do
Not be blind.

As the seasons go by,
The wonders they bring.
Do open yourself, to this,
A most beautiful thing.

Autumn leaves flutter down
From the trees,
Winter snow falls without
Much of a breeze,
Spring sees lambs, new life
Is born,
Summer sun's rays are nice
And warm.

So, come fly with me, spread your wings,
Life is full of some wonderful things.
Just open your heart, open your mind,
You never know what magical things
You may find.

Lisa Seeney

Love

Love is for eternity, is it not?
But without it we have nought.
Love, it brings so much pleasure,
But we fail so much to treasure.
Words are sometimes hard to find,
But with love they come and are kind,
Tempers fray and we blow our top.

Suddenly we remember what we forgot,
Our love is best, it's pure and kind,
Hold it steadfast and sweetly smile.
How people wonder why we're always
Happy and smiling.
We remind them then of God's message,
Without love we have nothing.

Gordon E Miles

Life Reflection

Christmas trees are here again.
It seems like only yesterday
We threw the other one away
And swept its needles off the floor,
Then put the lights, I'm not sure where,
I only hope that they're still there.

Life goes by such a pace,
That no one now has got the time
To sit and marvel at the way
That nature changes day by day.
Through summer, autumn, winter, spring,
With all the joy these changes bring.

While almost imperceptibly
The reaper reaps remorselessly,
The child that was a babe in arms
Has grown, and now has children too,
And in the mirror all I see
Is Father gazing back me.

But if it's true, as we've been told,
That in a stable bleak and cold
That Christ was born in Bethlehem
And wise men came to worship Him,
Then in that manger hope was born
That soon a brighter age will dawn.

Gerald Botteley

Niece Talk

Awake most days before the dawn
I have a stretch and then a yawn
Then get ready to face the day
I wonder what ahead may lay
I come downstairs and sit in peace
And await a phone call from my niece
We always chat about this and that
Even talk about Muffin the cat
Discussing problems that we share
Trying to be wise and also fair
Although our health is rather poor
We don't discuss it, for that's a bore
We laugh and make our fun
And see the best in everyone
We talk about the things we eat
And what we eat just for a treat
We regret the pains we share in our back
Say our goodbyes and then shut our trap.

L A G Butler

The Magic Of Spring

What do you think, what do you see?
Everything fresh and new and free,
Birds are singing high in the sky,
Have you ever stopped to wonder why?
God is saying, 'Come on take part'
In a beautiful world and a brand new start.

Your heart will lift, your eyes will shine,
If you look at the beauty and all divine,
Snowdrops raise their delicate heads and
Crocuses burst into sparkling threads
Of gold and purple and white pure as snow,
And all your winter blues will go.

It's a wonderful time, even trees reach out
Their branches, to tell you there is no doubt
That they will be clothed in new array,
Sweet blossoms, green leaves, where ladybirds play,
And birds will sit and flutter their wings,
Chirping and wondering what new life brings.

Suddenly all the fields are green,
And everything wears a bright new sheen.
Little faces from holes appear,
Field mice, hedgehogs and a badger near.
They shuffle around and feel their way,
Revelling in this warm spring day.

It's magic to their beady eyes, and ours too,
With such clear blue skies.
When all the world is wide awake
And beauty surrounds the Earth to make
Us happy, joyous, with living proof
That God surrounds us, with all His truth.

Doreen McDonald Banks

Tenby - Our Silent Shore

So many times over the years
We turn to you with our tears
Loved ones lost at sea or war
All of whom loved you more
Than you will ever know.

But always with your healing hand
You soothe our hearts amid your sand
Your beauty shines upon our face
Helping us proceed, in the human race.

Privileged we see, the last light of the sun
Streaming over Caldey Island
Brimming our silent shore with liquid gold
Our eyes light up with wonder to behold.

The ripples of the water forming
Fragile patterns of cirrus cloud
That are as delicate as filigree
Upon the surface of the gold washed sea.

White gulls float silently
Hushed by your beauty
The ebbing tide creams silently
Upon your ochre sand

God's hand has blessed us,
Who could ask for more
Than we mere suffering man
Could live on this wonderful shore.

Avis Nixon

My Girl

Linda Marie, my dear Linda Marie
I'm so young and you're so old
This is my darling I've been told
But I count my blessings
That you're my sweet girl
For you're the best in the world
And you make my life worth living
And it's you my sweet angel
I long to hold and love
When up to Heaven I'm rising
So please my sweet, loving angel
Let us never, never part
For if we ever did
It would surely break my heart
And leave me crying forever
So let's hold on tightly to one another
Sweet angel of my life.

Donald Tye

The Bond Between A Mother And Her Son

I take my son to the swimming baths as I regularly do.
Attired in his water wings his little arms and legs splashing about
Though not moving far,
The excitement in his eyes the fulfilment in mine.
I love my son.

Then one day he fell, cracking his head on the hard bath floor;
I froze!
My heart leapt, as tears welled up in my eyes . . .
I ran to him quietly.
Picking him up and cuddling him in my arms tightly.

A thousand words, I tried to say all at once, to my son.
Confused and garbled emotions, reigned within my heart and mind,
But one sense making thought prevailed;
I love my son.

Through the often long and painful pregnancy,
the doubts, the fears, at the sickness, and awkwardness of my body
My ever-changing shape that meant constant buying of new clothes.

Then I held him in my arms for the first time
The hard struggle, the pain I had endured through his birth;
All negative and crushing thoughts were soon vanquished,
A distant memory.
As tears of joy welled up in my eyes, only one thought came to me as I looked tenderly at my infant child;
I love my son.

Whatever problems, troubles or strife should assail me during any given day,
Should the world be too hard to face,
my path arduous and seemingly too hopeless to endure,
then one thought above all others radiates a beacon of light into my life:
I love my son.

John Gaze

Aufwiedersehen

Aufwiedersehen my darling, how sad now we're apart,
The loneliness, the emptiness, still ravages my heart.
Almost a year since you passed on, I said my last goodbye,
Why did you have to leave me dear - why did you have to die?

I see you by the window still with composure, full of grace,
I come and kneel beside your chair, and kiss your lovely face.
Why you my love? Why you, oh why? You were the very best,
Why were you called so early to your final place of rest?

Your loving words no longer heard, your smile no longer seen,
A vacuum left within my heart, where you had always been.
Your empty chair, nobody there, no kiss upon my brow,
What would I give? I'd give my all, to have you here right now.

I see you on a photo, now and then and in a while,
And I'm always still enchanted by that captivating smile.
It's still the same as always, when that look you did impart,
A glimpse of that divine, sweet smile, still always melts my heart.

You used to love the simple things, the garden, birds, the sky,
You loved to see and hear the little children running by.
These things meant such a lot to you, in your final days and hours,
The blue tits feeding on the nuts, the gaily coloured flowers.

Your courage and your dignity, made me so proud my dear,
You fought so hard, so brave you were, you hardly shed a tear.
And through all this adversity, you still had thoughts for me,
How can I help? How will he cope when I'm not there to see.

You always did more than your share and did it lovingly,
For me, our son, and others, all within the family.
You were loved by all who knew you, and you held your head up high,
A brave and lovely lady, who did not want to die.

A rowan tree I've planted, in the garden for you dear,
In your memory dearest Christa, and so each and every year,
When its flowers bloom and leaves change colour and then the berries show,
It will bring you close, and once again my heart will be aglow.

Count Our Blessings

I'll see your smile among the blooms, the branches your outstretched arms,
I'll see in the beauty of the tree, the beauty of your charms.
I will think of you each passing phase, of berry, leaf and flower,
Yes darling Chris, I'll reminisce, I'll have my golden hour.

Your three wishes dear, were carried out, we did not let you roam,
We kept you out of hospital, to let you die at home.
I knew how much you loved your home, that's where you wished to be,
In the place you felt secure and safe, at home, indoors with me.

The next wish that you wanted, and on this I have no qualms,
You wished to take your final sleep enfolded in my arms.
As you slipped away, I cuddled you, too hurt, I couldn't cry,
I caressed you dear and said farewell, as in my arms you lie.

Your third wish was, and here I quote, to re-unite with me,
That we would be as one again, when I departed be.
And to this end my darling, to give what you did crave,
A plot has been reserved for me, right by your very grave.

This is your request my dear, and with it I agree,
And then we'll be as one again, for all eternity.
We'll be as close as always, as in the years gone by,
And everlasting nearness as side by side we lie.

The selfless dedication and the love you gave to me,
Will guide and give me courage now, throughout the years to be.
In my mind's eye, all things of you stand tall like massive towers,
A fitting tribute dearest, to a love as deep as ours.

May peace be with you always now, as in the ground you lie,
In countryside you grew to love, beneath the open sky.
Although my heart is breaking, as I pen this through my tears,
I'm an honoured and a grateful man to have known you through these years.

And so aufwiedersehen once more, and now this poem's done,
Yes, rest in peace for evermore, 'neath every setting sun.
And with each new awakening and the lessening of pain,
The strength you've given me will mean, you did not die in vain.

Goodnight, sleep tight, and wait for me,
My thoughts could not be sweeter,
I'll love you till; my final day,
Your ever-loving Peter.

Peter J Sutton

Cure for SAD

(Seasonal Affective Disorder or 'winter blues')

One bone-raw day in December
with summer a memory and spring
a mirage, I watched five starlings
eathing in the middle of a deep,
cold, oily puddle. Birds are not
human, I know, but have they no
feelings? This was the muckiest
murkiest dip for miles.

So there they were, frolicking -
smiling, almost. Well, making
me smile anyway, with their gawky
erratic flapping, straddled
knee-deep, a leg at each corner.

I was in brooding mood before
I saw them. 'Why am I here?'
that stuff. Afterwards I took
flight. I am here to watch the
starlings bathe. That is enough.

Jean Hayes

Blessings Are Precious

Blessings come in many ways,
Some you keep to treasure.
Many fill your heart with love,
And give you so much pleasure.

If you're blessed with family,
That love you . . . come what may.
Feel the Lord has blessed you too,
Thank Him every day.

Many people know *no* love,
Their lives are dull and empty.
So being blessed as you are now,
Deserves your thanks . . . in plenty.

Try and give some happiness,
To someone who has none,
Perhaps you'll be remembered too,
As . . . a person full of fun.

Blessings come in many ways,
I said this at the start,
Remember it forever . . . and
Show love with all your heart.

Joyce Hammond

A Time Of Fresh Hope

Spring will soon, be here again
Ending months, of misery and pain
Gloomy nights, will end once more
We'll welcome spring, through our front door.

The birds will sing, lambs will bleat
No need each day, to turn on the heat
Daffodils will be singing, their own song
To which other flowers, will dance along.

Fragrances will smell, ever so sweet
Make us skip lightly, upon our feet
Fields all around, of a luscious green
We are bedazzled by, the springtime scene.

Buds upon, the boughs of trees
See leaves dance, in a gentle breeze
Rainbows spring forth, from sunshine and rain
And we say goodbye, to winter's pain.

We hear the birds, see the snails
Springtime amazes, it never fails
Bluebells erupting, in the wood
Making us feel, that life is so good.

Our senses soar, to such great heights
Down country lanes, enjoying the delights
Butterflies flutter, between the plants
Such glorious views, they will enhance.

April showers pour forth, from the skies
Nature is ours to share, a wonderful prize
The joy of spring, will ring all around
With delightful pleasure, to be found.

New life found in many nests, fresh air will fill, so many chests
There is one hope to which we cling, that which arrives with each spring.

B W Ballard

Don't Worry, Be Happy!

In this life, many obstacles we face,
Many temptations, we ignore or embrace,
None of us are perfect, we all have our flaws,
We all want excitement, to escape from our chores,
The older you get, the more you regret,
We see our lost opportunities and worry and fret,
But nothing can be done about what's in the past,
So look to the future and don't be downcast.

Christine Nolan

Trampled On, But Not For Long

Perhaps by chance some bird will sing
A joyous tale ne'er heard before,
And fly to heights upon the wing -
There to reveal its truth untold
But measured not with flow'ry tongue:
And with shrill note its tune unsung
Here doth begin with melody:
'Weep not you slaves of agony:
Prick up your ears and list to me.
My song tells naught but victory,
So hearken on the truth and see!

Once by a brook a weed did grow
O'ershadowed by a tree so low
That it did look upon the weed
As serving little use or need
To its Creator, so sublime,
Who seemed but to have squandered time
In tolerating such a dearth
To show its face upon the Earth.

'Show not contempt to me O tree!'
Cried out the weed with joyful glee,
'Unless my life adorned this place
How would'st thou tell the things of grace?''

Roger F de Boer

In Thanksgiving

My faith is the child that's within me still,
I try to use it in adult manner.
My hate is for that which is made to kill.
For the love of God I hold my banner.

My joy is in life that bubbles and flows
In song ascending like a prayer . . .
Willowing, whispering, softly, she goes,
Spreading her radiance into the air.

My heart is in friendship, warm and sincere.
Sharing and caring in kindness and love;
Releasing our demons, casting our fear.
Thanking our Lord, for His gifts from above.

Please be our strength as we pass through this day,
Keep us in love as we go on our way.

P Burdock

The Night Of Christmas Eve

The night of Christmas Eve,
How different from the rest!
So charged with atmospheric love,
How can we not feel blest?

How special is this time?
It's cold and it is late;
But something wonderful is near
For which we all should wait.

Should gentle, falling snow -
So silent in its fall -
Provide a blanket of its flakes
To cover over all

In darkness would it seem
More special than in sun.
This time, this night, brings heartfelt joy
To me and everyone.

For why? Because *this* night,
Which all too soon will *pass,*
Has brought me walking with my Lord,
Home after Midnight Mass.

Frank L Appleyard

Blessings - Count Every One

'All clear,' from cancer is a wonderful thing,
A wedding or new baby to come in the spring,
Birds looking for a new nesting place, to make,
To walk in the countryside, fresh air to intake,
Shrubs and trees, bursting into bud and leaf,
Snowdrops shooting, dark nights going, what a relief.
No snow this winter, that's fine by me,
Hate the stuff, spring is great, fills me with happiness and glee,
Summer to look forward to, with blue sky and sunshine,
Gardens full of flowers, baby birds, fish in the pond, just fine,
Isn't life splendid, sometimes we do find time to stand,
To contemplate if we'd change anything - no I think life is grand.

M Harrott

Woodlands

More lovely are the trees to me
Than all the flowers the rose that's best,
For when the woods are summer dressed
Such is a place of nature blessed.

The woods do have a lovely breath
That fills the air with fragrant scent,
Where light beams down amongst the trees
To gleam on different shades of green.

And at the sides where shadows lie
The woods their secrets keep awhile,
Until the moving beam reveals
The beauty of a woodland flower.

And when the summer season's passed
In autumn's fall of yellow leaves,
There is grandeur in that gold
Amongst the tall and splendid trees.

And when the snow in winter falls
To carpet white the woodland broad,
The trees will wait the winter through
Until the hard Earth yields again.

Then when the spring returns once more
To warm the soil, awake the roots,
And the green buds shoot to leaf the trees
The woods with fragrance breathe again.

Robert William Lockett

Summer Nights

S oft canopy of velvet
U nderpinning the skies
M illions of stars
M oonbeams on fireflies
E vocative perfumes
R oam through the trees.

N ight scented stock
I n a balmy breeze
G irl meeting boy
H eaven is a kiss
T hanks be to God - for
S ummer nights like this.

Jean Mackenzie

Maths, + × ÷ -, Count Our Blessings

Adding up our blessings,
Will multiply our joy,
Do you remember how
To add and multiply
With no computer sitting by?
Praising God for health, home,
Books and music, trees and flowers,
Sharing all these blessings new,
Why - that's division too!
Subtraction?
Take away all grumbles, envy, discontent,
And lack of trust in God's tomorrow -
Think instead of His past goodness
And count again,
Let's count again our blessings -
Count again!

Doris Bannard-Smith

The Comeover

Blown by the wind like an anchorless ship,
Sailing a strangers' sea,
Roofless, abandoned, friendless alone,
The fate of the refugee.

Many years you may live in strangers' land
And work and prosper and thrive;
But never you feel you ever belong,
No matter how hard you strive.

Your roots may float and catch on a tree,
A mountain, a house or a home,
But never you feel you ever belong,
Forever you live quite alone.

Blest are those who live all their life,
Free in the land of their birth,
Surrounded by family and friends of their youth,
With evenings of singing and mirth.

So have pity for those who live in your midst,
But can never adhere to your clan:
And thank God for your luck, if born to belong,
In this beautiful Isle of Man.

Lorna Moffatt

Evening

Golden sun sinks in the west,
Singing birds fly home to rest,
Flowers no tired heads to fall,
Asleep on Mother's breast.

Folded in Mother's wings,
In nests which out of reach clings,
High above among the eaves,
Little birds sleep, while Mother sings.

A child's evening prayer is said,
On Mother's breast pillowed head,
Love light shining in her eyes,
Mother carries her to bed.

B M Kerby

Contemplating Raindrops

I sit and stare through windowpane,
At my garden so green and lush.
Moisture dapples the view obscured,
Sweet rhythm improves the hush.

A single drop, a lonely soul,
Little strength does it command.
When that drop its kin does meet,
Its power must soon be damned.

I look upon the trees so grand,
Leaves bowing deep to every drop.
Puddles grow to stream they start,
When will this downpour stop?

Bounding down the mountains fall,
The gurgling brooks do swell.
Rocky soil they tear and gouge,
Best sound the warning knell.

The mud does slip to glide so slick,
Rocks tumble a race to win.
Aged trees now dance and skate,
From storm clouds did this begin?

I now respect each drop I view,
As I peer beyond my wall.
To look upon the hillside scared,
From which the scene did fall.

Nature will renew itself,
Time will erase the pain.
Each cloud a silver lining has,
Even in the worst of rain.

Ceri D D Griffiths

Hubby

When unemployed, I've heard it said,
There's nowt to do at all,
You might as well just stay in bed,
Sleep, read, or kick a ball.
There's some that do, and some that don't
Just sit down and be idle,
My 'Hubby', bless him, is one that won't
And up to me will sidle . . .

'Er, Honey Dear, you will not mind
If today I have the kitchen
To bake some bread?' I smiled resigned,
'Thanks Love', his eyes bewitchin'.
Outside, when frost and snow is making
Weary travellers slip and slide,
In our kitchen Hubby's baking
Fills my heart with love and pride.

When spring and summer flowers are blooming,
Back and forth, he mows the lawn,
As he does so, quietly singing . . .
Unemployed, but not forlorn.

Doreen Williams

My Living Plant

I have a fantastic green plant
It takes his place at the side of my fireplace
Dark and light green leaves
I look at it every night
When I feel down, the leaves droop
But when I am happy, they perk up.
They are green and healthy, when I feel fine
But go pale and limpid if I'm not well
I cannot move its place as it will die
It loves his place or home
It feels for me, it cries for me
And it's happy for me.
It has a life of its own
I treasure this plant
It knows how I care and how I feel
This plant is real with feelings
Just like me!

Carol Hanney

Zambian Woodland

This woodland, big, and blackened by burning,
With dry stumps and ash next these stumps,
Pushes flowers through the blackened earth
At the driest time - delicate pink and blue
And palest yellow feathery ones
And pale yellow green shoots of new life.
The antelope steps among these,
And when the day is too hot for men to move,
Takes ease amongst the shade of trees.

Just wonder - the strength required
To make palest green from blackened earth -
O the Zambian woods are strong,
Whose tender shoots unfurl unscathed.

Once a mist settled, covering all the land with mist.
It flowed among the trees, softening the leaves,
Blocking the horizons, reducing the world
To intimate smallness. And then it snowed
Out of a black sky. I stood by.
Old timers stood by, muscly miners stood by
Occasionally shuffling on worn out feet
To watch each other in the snow:
To watch Jenny dancing in the snow.
And that morning and the evening that followed
All men as far as I know stood by to see the future given by the hand of God.

John Goulding

A Silver Lining

When the sky is grey, what can you say?
When you feel a little blue, wondering
When the sun will shine again,
When you'll be inspired to sing or shout,
Or write a verse about love
To lift the dark clouds above?

A song to raise the roof,
To proclaim the sky's the limit,
A note of optimism that soars above the daily routines.
When meaning and purpose are somehow obscured,
A silver lining appears around every cloud
And the dullest grey turns to gold!

Cathy Mearman

Come with me and I will show
You gold beyond compare,
There's king cups by the river
And buttercups to share.

Crystals sparkle every time
There wakes a frosty dawn,
And dewy drops on grassy blades
Like pearls, bespatter the lawn.

There's ruby in the sunset
Or wreathed in hawthorn fruit,
And sapphires in a peacock's tail
There's emeralds in spring shoot.

No gems from Cartier's can compare
With nature's diadem
If only we will look around
And be aware of them.

Gwen Place

A Simple Faith Held In Knowledge

We come to 'Our Belief' because we're told,
Because we find it true and, more than these,
Because with our experience it agrees.
Consider what this proposition holds.
For priests, their foremost function, as of old,
Is still to teach the Word, reveal where keys
To faith can still be found. Our modern knees
Do not now bend to cant, however bold!
Where *Learning*, *Will* and *Feeling* all combine,
Belief, expressed in Worship, can endure:
But where minds stand too obdurate to seek
A truth afresh, Belief does not refine.
Our faith sustained in wisdom holds secure.
Our faith upheld in ignorance is weak.

John Beazley

Life

We can live our lives in comfort,
We can live our lives in pain,
If we don't live it,
Then it passes by, just the same.

Sorrow, happiness, darkness or light,
Today is soon tomorrow, then again all is right.

Eveline Nash Gaging

Nature's Blessings

The burned brown land
parched by the summer drought
waits for the blessing
of the quenching rain.

Lands submerged by monsoon
floods wait for the blessings
granted by the draining rivers,
and the heat of the drying sun.

Trees torn and damaged
in wild winter storms wait
for the blessing of the return
of healing spring.

The flowers and the leaves
of spring through lengthening
days bringing the blessing
of the summer's fruits.

And summer in its turn
brings harvest blessings
for all that lives on Earth
fulfilling the blessings

of birth, life, even
death itself that
brings the blessing
of eternal rest.

Rick Storey

I Bless Each Day

I bless each day the sun shines
And at the rising of the moon each night.
For the beauty of this land we live in.
That welcomes my sight as I rise each day.
For the changing seasons,
For the five senses, I still possess.
And the most important fact of all is this.

I am here, now, alive and well,
For all this I am truly blessed and give thanks.

A J Marshall

Legacy For Life

I've known you all my life, 'Dad' you've always been there,
Giving me support, fighting my corner, showing how much you cared,
Sharing my successes, an arm around me when not,
A wry smile, a handshake, knowing I'd given my best shot.
My wild spell. 'Sit right there, I want you to listen to me Son.'
The growing boy. Teaching me the good, excusing the bad I've done.
Fights, that black eye I sported, seeing off the school bully in shame,
Disappointment, in the school Cup Final, after extra time, losing the game.
The girls, my odd drinking night, that look of yours,
It somehow put me right,
Differences? Yes, we had them, driving, savings, pensions,
Out late at night.
The special days together, and those men nights at our local,
Football, how involved you got, so passionately vocal.
I didn't get to say goodbye Dad, it wasn't meant to be,
We were countries apart, when I heard that life had set you free.
I'm a dad, and I still miss you, you were my rock,
My conscience. You left a legacy, my life's dicta.
This poem is my way of telling the world, that I loved you,
As a father, and a dad. I can't better that.

George Carrick

My Prayer

Dear Jesus I would like to say
Of thoughts I have of You each day
I know my faith is very weak
To make it strong, Your love I seek
With all my heart I thank You for
The blessings that on me You pour
Please be with me throughout the day
In all I do and think and say
For people lonely or in pain
Please help them to their faith retain
And let them realise that You
Are always there to help them through.

Joan McQuoid

Wake Up

Do we know our moors and mountains
Are there for us to see?
Just take the time and visit them
There is no entrance fee.

The wonders of the countryside
Are viewed by all these days
Perhaps they know it's under threat
As they sit at home and gaze.

We have the tools to capture
Each fleeting moment when
A dragonfly first spreads its wings
Or an osprey o'er the glen.

So count our blessings as they show
How best to help conserve
Our Flora and our Fauna
That's what it all deserves.

Alan Marten

A Friend

I have a friend
Who's with me till the end
Of time itself
And then beyond.
Though on my own
I never was alone.
Someone with whom I walked
Each day, and often talked.
Silently in my mind
His answers I would find.

His Spirit filled me
Like a living river,
Flowing onwards
Out to others.
Satisfied me ever.

My dear companion,
This, my friend with me
Beyond life's end.
On, on forever,
Through the farthest
Reaches of Eternity.

Diana Morcom

Soft Velvet Wrap

Soft velvet wrap of night encloses
With silken glove as day reposes
On the ruby bed of Miss Sunset;
She rests red hand on horizon west.

Then as nature weaves its magic spell
So old daylight tolls its closing bell
Moon and stars begin to fill the skies
And gossamer maidens veil our eyes.

A land of dreams fills our fertile minds
With old love songs; our favourite lines
Of maple syrup and Mum's jam tart
How the joy of birth gladdens the heart.

Vivid dreams of that first stolen kiss
Being so in love, the endless bliss
Of holding hands on the way to school
And thinking; now this is simply cool.

But dreams like the night come to an end
As must this poem that I have penned
For coming of morning's harsh daylight
Puts our happy dreams once more to flight.

So greet the dawn of a brand new day
Blessing the good Lord when we all pray
For glory of love and warm daylight;
Thank Him for guiding us through this night.

Leslie de la Haye

Showing You Blessings

However bleak the day
We can look back and say
Something good came from yesterday.
We may see it straight away
Or after many a day,
But a blessing is there to stay,
So do not fret about the wrong,
In God's love you can be strong.
He will help you carry on,
Showing you blessings one by one.

Joyce E Pugh

A Smile's Worth

A face robbed of a smile
is not a pleasant thing to see.
A face with a smile
brings hope and comfort to me.

If we count our blessings
a smile should be seen,
no matter what year,
or troubles besetting in-between.

A smile costs nothing
to the giver,
and it conveys friendship
to those who receive.

A smile fosters goodwill
at home, in the workplace, at play.
In short, it enriches all around
come what may.

By giving it (a smile) away,
it makes us none the poorer.
Its magnetic force
easing the stresses of the day.

A smile, we cannot buy, beg, borrow or steal,
from the very soul within it comes,
expressing peace, hope and love,
These virtues, whatever the year, are real.

J Henderson Lightbody

Childhood Recalled

Blazing coal fire, spitting red ember,
Encircled by shining brass fender,
Horse hair sofa; lino cold on bare feet,
Grandfather clock chiming hourly beat.

Black-leaded grate; imposing, grand,
Toasting fork in tremulous old hand,
Housing Gran's home baked bread, golden brown,
Mugs of hot sweet tea to wash it down.

Rain spatters the lace-curtained window
As I sit here snug and protected,
Warmed by the firelights glow,
All memories of my childhood,
So very long ago.

Lilian Bordessa

Count Your Blessings

It isn't easy, counting blessings
Especially when things go wrong
Life, can seem like a long dark road
And you're feeling, far from strong.

But on that road, there might be
Someone, just like you, afraid
All they really need, is just a friend
And together, you'd be no longer one
But two
Then you'd count your blessings
Right to the very end!

Sheila Cummings

Summertime

The nights are lighter, the days are longer,
The air is warm, as the sun gets stronger,
The vibrant colours of the summer flowers,
Give lots of pleasure for many hours,
The trees are clothed in shades of green,
The blue of the sky is a joy to be seen.

The sounds of summer are all around,
As many picnics and barbecues abound,
The jubilant cries from the cricket pitch,
When a ball is caught, and the wickets fall,
The laughter of children playing bat and ball.

Thoughts turn to holidays at home and abroad,
Just pack up and go to where you can afford.
Children love the sands and the sea,
Mums and dads love their deck chairs, and afternoon tea,
Summer's the time to get up and go,
To lawn tennis at Wimbledon, or Chelsea Flower Show.

But however you spend these summer days,
Whether you're active, or just like to laze,
Make the most of each day, summer's so fleeting,
Too soon will be winter, and the rain will be sheeting!

Jean Wood

While You Can

One bite of the cherry is all you get
So while you can don't sit and fret.

Life is short, but very sweet,
I wish I had, so many bleat.

Don't join that band, walk the walk,
Enjoy your space, talk the talk.

Write that book, take that trip,
Seize the moment, don't let it slip.

Now's the time dreams can come true,
Dreams known only to you.

The care and love you've so freely given,
Will probably get you into Heaven.

But until then life's for the brave,
Don't waste this time, there's none to save.

Catherine Hislop

Evanescent Happiness

The warm, wet, shining swimming pool
Has cat's paws where a floating school,
Aspiring fish, with splashing thrills,
The spatial scene contentment fills.

No adolescent shrieking boys
The murmourous air with ghastly noise
Disturbs, but happy children's small alarm
With laughs and smiles their parents charm.

The boy, who on his father's back
Repels imagined foe's attack,
Rides proudly beaming radiance
With pleasure's ever winning lance.
His happiness I'll ne'er forget,
But lost for him in mem'ry's net.

The five-year-old, who dared the chute,
With prancing pride in bathing suit
Tells father and the world her feat,
In happiness her life complete;
My pleasure ne'er will fade away
Although for her it will not stay.

For happiness is lost in part
When noted as a thing apart.

G L Ackers

Life Is What You Make It

When my wife first left me, I was gutted,
Now I would advise every husband to try it.
In a very short time, my life was sublime,
Now I enjoy the peace and the quiet.

When my daughter became a drug addict, I was gutted,
She will only eat things that are sweet.
The future is daunting, her features are haunting,
But at least she is not on the street.

When I lost my job, I was gutted,
It created some worries and fears.
Then with a new lease of life, I had no more strife,
And I look younger than all of my peers.

When my arms and legs dropped off, I was gutted,
I need help to put on my clothes,
But my mind is quite bright, and all through the night,
I type with the end of my nose.

Stephen Haygreen

The Wonders Of Our World

How beautiful it is to see,
Trees, flowers, all around me,
How well our God made these
To give us pleasure I'm sure,
The rain to keep them watered,
The sun for them to flower,
Bulbs come up every year,
For everyone to see.

How do the trees know
When to shed their leaves?
How do bulbs know when to regrow?
These wonders in our world,
For everyone to see.

How do worms live below the soil?
How do birds know where to fly each year?
The stars at night, the sun in the mornings,
These are the wonders of our wonderful world.

J M Drinkhill

The Truth Of Life

As I walk here in the wake of life
Looking at the sky I see the change that takes place
What is life if there is no change or satisfaction?
Do we have to commit ourselves to eternity for life?

What is the pleasure of the heart
If at some stage in our life, we do not take what it desires?
Woman was made for man to sip the pleasures of life,
What can he ask for more,
Should he rot in his own ecstasy?

Can the bull blow his horn?
Can the lark read music?
Take not the thought in scorn for at some stage in life
We think it true or false
Do not the majestic wonders of nature
Mesmerise the human
Or is it reversed so as to humour the buffoon?
Can we live in a world without it
Or do we make-believe that we have committed no sin
Against mankind?
Take only the thought of the lover and you will be glad to seek
That company.

What is love without a lover?
Can we walk in the shadow of life without it?
Can the blackbird sing without a mate?
Do we have to walk in the darkness forever?
If we sit under a tree, do we expect lightning to strike it?
Do we stop and wait for nothing expecting everything?
Can we wonder at the very gifts that come our way
Or do we walk towards the sun without looking for its warmth?
The love that is there for us to have every day,
Should be enough for any man or woman no matter
Who they be.

Peter L Carvell

Memories Of A Loved One

How grey the day
How grey the house
So lonely one doth feel
Inhabitant with glum look face
Silently walking through the place
As silent as a mouse.

Wish you were here
Only you will know
About my inner thoughts
A saddened heart
A faceless smile
Just to light up for a while
My inner feelings grow.

Our days were so happy
How very blessed was I
To have you by my side
Now days are long it seems
Wish you were here and hear you say
I love you more and more each day
But that exists in dreams.

Kathleen Cater

Golden Days

The golden days of summer, are approaching fast,
The evenings will be longer, we will see everything at last.
The birds that sing so sweetly, their song is everywhere,
The little hedgehogs peeping out, want to play if they dare.
The foxes playing in their den, they will come out, but when?
The badgers roaming in the glen, their black and white stripes
Shining in the glen.
The little field mice making their homes on some stalks of wheat,
Making sure they will always have something to eat.
The rabbits shyly peeping from their burrows,
Hope to get a carrot from the farmer's furrows.
The skylarks have already built their nests in fields,
To return to when their song they have yield.
The little bees busy with the flowers,
Collecting pollen to be turned into honey,
Believe me when I tell you, you may see all this,
And you will not need to spend any money.

Zoe French

Monday

Whenever I see a white feather on the ground, I think of Mum.
Needless to say, she crosses my mind often -
With or without this symbol,
Feather or no feather,
Prompted or not . . .

I am not so naïve as to think that this is peculiar to us
Or even deeply 'meaningful'.
After all, to see a white feather on the ground isn't unusual
Nor for it to remind someone of their mum -
(And yet I feel very reassured, when I see a feather,
That, perhaps she's thinking of me too!)

Today, I feel distressed,
Not just because I am having to change offices,
Not only because I am losing this individual old space to share
A new area,
But because I might not fit in
Literally or otherwise.

I look at my things loaded in green crates, piled ominously
And yet at the sad angle of departing crates.
I look at all the files that haven't yet been packed
And my heart feels tired and woolly
So I look at the floor.

Tiny round discs of paper are here and there -
Escapees from the hole punch - and there is
A squashed drawing pin and a few dead paperclips which,
Having fallen from earlier grasps, lie amongst
The un-disconnected cables.

There is something else,
A little, fluffy white feather is on the carpet in my office -
Not a natural resting place, I note, for a feather
Of any persuasion! However must it have come there?
I think of Mum, thinking of me, perhaps . . .

Susan Devlin

Missing You

I stood awhile, and watched the scene,
As the raindrops splashed around.
Pools reflecting the winter sun,
Formed quickly on the ground.
People hurrying on their way,
Collars up against the chill.
Black and spiky leafless branches,
Just showing over the hill.
I wondered what had made me pause,
To take in this seasonal view,
But of course it was on a day like this,
I fell in love with you.
I remember how we ran along,
Avoiding the many puddles,
And sheltering, wherever we could,
Keeping warm with little cuddles.
Time skips by so very fast,
We had taken the highs with the lows,
And through all the good times and the bad,
Our love seemed to grow and grow.
These last few years without you,
Without your love, your warmth, your smile,
Have made me pause so many times,
Memories flood back for a while.
Yet in the end, the day will dawn,
When the good Lord beckons above,
Once again we will walk hand in hand,
Sharing our eternal love.

Ronald Marriott

Sky Alive

That's the anvil-thundercloud
that cracks like iron tumbling in a bucket,
Thor's muscles, arms of steel shining
where lightning lightens a heavy sky.
Birds fly for shelter, they hear, they feel
the peal, hiding in hedges, concealed in trees,
away from bolts of electric snake,
await the ragged rain.

Blue before, where mares' tails flick,
then flecked with tank tracks
for the warrior's chariot -
behold the spear to deal death
till the war ends -
and out they come, those birds
giving a voice to cheer.
Look, that's a mackerel sky.

Barbara Maskens

A Child's Gift

A child can be so very thoughtful,
Bringing small gifts for you,
Brightening up your darkest hour,
In the things they say and do.

Giving a drawing from the classroom,
That was especially done for you,
Rembrandt, he could not paint better,
This picture means the world to you.

To make in school your special cards,
Mother's Day and Christmas too,
It's made so careful and given with love,
A child so proud, and so are you.

A child loves to gather flowers,
A daisy chain to make for you,
To pick a posy of wild flowers,
All these things say 'I love you'.

When you are feeling sad and lonely,
Then a child lights up your day,
With these small gifts so freely given,
I'm now so happy, 'I love you too'.

Caroline Helen Molton

Mum

In the garden of my heart
There is a rose that grew and grew
It's a very special rose as it was
Planted there for you.

Through my eyes I see your love
That was given upon you from above
You supply this love every day
Even throughout hate and dismay.

You never get struck by an angry storm
You'll never turn into an evil form
Always handing out your love and care
Like a lovely, cuddly teddy bear.

You never ever seem down
You never ever show a frown
You're always happy but sometimes sad
Ask me for comfort, I'm not that bad.

Alex Staniforth (11)

Savour The Treasure

Scattered diamonds on velvet leaves
Of lime-green ladies mantle.
Crystal beads on the washing line.
April's store of earth's sweet wine.
Savour the treasure
Before it's gone forever.

Humming bees on campanula blue;
Sunshine at last and warm weather.
The blackbird sings his courtship song;
The garden a patchwork of colour.
Savour the treasure
Before it's gone forever.

Lacy webs on frosty mornings;
Autumn leaves aglow,
Telling us that soon we'll feel
The chilling winds and snow.
Savour the treasure
Before it's gone forever.

Snowflake flowers nodding in the wind,
Green-tipped petals of joy.
Red-breasted robins flying near,
Hunger driving out their fear.
Savour the treasure
Before it's gone forever.

Sue Groom

Holding On

Hold on - hold on - don't let it get you down.
Today's heartache is just tomorrow's frown.

This time next year you'll wonder why you cared.
Don't sigh, don't cry, don't go running scared.

Wise heads - old heads - aching just the same.
Lessons unlearned just come round again.

Hold on - hold on - don't let it get you down.
Today's heartache is just tomorrow's frown.

Sheila Allen

Epiphany

Through darkness gold; three kings go past. The way
Is hard and cold, and still no sign of day.
They journey on. Far in the frozen sky
The vast procession of the stars moves by.

Darkness is fear, the unknown; shadows grow
Across the world, as flooding waters flow
And drown the fields and houses; earth where death
Can blast all beauty with one sudden breath.

Where love itself may fail and die away
Leaving a lonely heart amid the grey
Of shadows of the past . . . and yet, above
Still shines one star, the sign of perfect Love.

Through darkness kings pass by to offer gold,
In winter, fearless of the night and cold;
This is the way to go; humbly to bring
A loving heart to greet the kings' great King.

Through silence singing. Angels from the height
Proclaim with song and trumpet, down the bright
Paths of the stars, to the snow sparkling earth.
God's supreme gift; this miracle of birth.

Diana Momber

Blessings In Disguise

We are blessed when we are born and blessed when we die,
Sometimes we don't seem blessed and wonder why,
When someone dies, our lives fall apart.
But remember they are always in your heart.
Everyone loses someone dear to them some time in their life,
This fills us with emotion, a vacant space, and lots of strife,
We will have memories, sadness, but still life will go on again,
Then someone else comes along and helps to ease our pain.
This is a blessing in disguise and we do not recognise,
Maybe a grandchild, daughter, or son, a friend or whatever,
It will help fill a space we thought gone forever,
It's always hard to lose someone dear,
Whether relative or friend,
You think you are alone, but someone is always there for you
In the end,
Remember no one lives forever, so enjoy life while you may,
All good things come to an end sometime in our life,
So be happy, have memories, long ago and to the day,
Then when the time comes for you to go,
May your blessings be passed to others with love
And a good life and memoirs like you.
Leave some for others and for their friends,
Count all these blessings until your end.

P D Dugdale

Where The Grass Is Greener

I want to go, but I know not where,
And would I know if I were there,
When all around is plenty,
To want I never know,
But still I want to go.

Why should my life feel so empty,
With my cup so full?
Why should life, so pleasant,
To me seem very dull, when all my gains,
They seem to grow - yet still - I want to go.

I want to go, leave all behind,
This way of life that's been so kind -
I wonder why?

Is this to be ungrateful?
Would I regret the day?
Will I, the reason ever know,
Why I should feel this way?
Shall I ever know, the reason why I want to go?

Perhaps when all is left behind,
When this *other life* I find,
All the past I might recall,
And wonder why I left at all,
That *other life* that was so full,
And yet I found so very dull,
Please, someone tell me, why I went,
The reason why I felt so bent?

Gordon West

My Eyes

I thank you Lord who gave me sight,
To see the stars and moon at night,
And then the sunrise in the morn,
The dew that glistens on the lawn.

I see the lovely wild spring flowers,
As I walk in woods for many hours,
The creatures that are in the sky,
A bird, a bee, a butterfly.

A house, a factory, a school,
With children playing as a rule,
Now I know things look just right,
I thank you Lord who gave me sight.

Thomas Dickinson

You - Me, Us - We

Belonging, caring, life sharing words
cannot be separated from the friend
living, breathing, working beside you.

Each breath taken to share power words
from his life, formed but a small part
of what he was and has now left behind.

Penetrating deeply into our minds,
our consciousness, and deeper still
into what we now are and feel.

Moving on he has left us with
a sensitised state of mind that
embodies and is still him.

Part of the mind we should
now all share
as we care and dare.
Teaching - Learning - Exhalting

Loving.

Hugh Webb

The Comforters

Another Christmas Day is past and gone
And like a dead leaf fallen from a tree
It settles down with others of its kind
Part of the history of my short life.

One day a solemn gardener will come,
And tidy up this mess of memories
Then strike a match, and watch the heap dissolve
In smoke and flame, leaving a little ash
To be sown by the wind into the soil.

And now, before the ending of my year,
I seek to bring some order to the pile
Of mingled memories that tease my mind
They take me back to my life's rosy dawn,
And even, as I ponder, half asleep,
Do they include my sojourn in the womb,
Or maybe something even earlier?

If there is something that can be recalled,
Even before the night I was conceived,
Might there not be a bud waiting to break
In a fair garden that I may have known
Before the gardener planted me on Earth?

Michael Darwood

The Right Approach To Happiness

When answers don't come readily to hand,
Ignore frustration; try to understand
Subconscious process soon will see the light.
Rely on common sense to see you right.
Awareness with be sharp, clearly defined
With order, discipline and settled mind.
A happy person's one with time to spare
For calm consideration, gentle care.
An awkward situation need not last -
A lifeline's soon forthcoming from the past.

I've always been a stickler for routine,
It pinpoints the essentials, sets the scene;
Helps concentrate the will for task in hand
Invariably saves time for things you've planned
Routine is never turgid or humdrum
When contemplating pleasures yet to come;
It helps get on with life and heart contents -
And guarantees reward for diligence.

Jack Conway

The Rose

There's a diamond of dew on a sun-kissed rose,
Its heady perfume fills the air.
Flooding my mind with memories sweet,
That will always linger there.
Memories of youth, and days in the sun,
The joyful meetings with friends now gone.
The walks in the country, when summer sun beckoned.
The scent of the briers, with blossoms bedeckoned.

Wild woodbine clambering round rambling hedgerows,
Nature's own decking of ribbons and bows.
Sweet are the thoughts that are brought to mind,
Forgetting the wrath of the winter's wind.
Bumblebees laden with pollen buzz by,
Working so hard, they can hardly fly.
Thanks to the rose with the dew in its heart,
For bringing back memories, so close to my heart.

P E Langton

A Precious Gift

Friendship is precious,
Friends are a must,
A plus,
For the human us.
More precious
Than silver, or gold
We need them still,
To be told
More as we grow old.
Do not lose them,
Or let them slip
Through loving fingers,
So they are lost,
And gone forever
In the myriad throng
Of life,
Pain and strife.
How can one describe
This precious, perfect gift
Of love for one another?
Of loyal friendship,
So great, so wonderful
That always gives
One a lift,
New heart to go on
When all seems black.
A friend who cares,
Who sometimes dares,
But always, always shares
The ups, the downs,
Of life's frenetic merry-go-round.
Helps one to keep
One's feet firmly
On the ground.
A loyal friend,
Who never counts
The cost of friendship
Is really
Indescribable!

Patricia Laing

The Value Of Life

You there in despair
Face sun's bright light.
If you dare.

Where oleanders bloom
In Tuscan shade
I'll be there.

On scented air
The call of the nightjar
Will banish care.

When morning mist
Dusts placid pond
And pines drug the senses rare
You'll be there.

Rose pink temple
Reflect in water
Image eternal
Life everafter.

Crooning the bee
Lulls noon to its sleep
Through long lazy days
Nirvana keep.

Song in the rigging
White foamy wake
Softly is singing
All for your sake.

Balmy the night when
Love comes ahaunting
Secrets a-whispering
Down in the glen.

George Derek Ewer

Untitled

True love is something special,
To cherish and hold dear,
To miss someone when you're apart,
And appreciate when near,
To listen when they're worried,
And try to understand,
To work to build a good life,
Each with a helping hand,
So when this true love comes along,
Your blessings you must count,
This kind of love just can't be bought,
Whatever the amount.

Jan Wickens

Recollections

I brushed the purple thyme
As I weeded in my fair garden.
This was not the scent of damp soil
Always full of promise,
But clinging and fresh and fulfilling to the senses.

And I remembered the Spanish garrigue
Where I wandered alone in January
Before summer's heat scorched everything dry.
At that time were abundant delights
To touch and smell and hear.
In that unspoilt, unknown, natural place
With no one near.
Where was no sound, but birds and the sea's roar.

In this quietude I searched for special things,
In this land at the sea's edge
Where larks soar.
This land, just as nature made it,
A world apart, primitive and wild,
A sanctuary for birds and flowers.
At every step sweet perfumes rose
From treading on all manner of herbs
And fragrant shrubs already in flower.
A perfumier's dream.
And in January,
Miniature daffodils and iris grow
Sway in the wind
Which here always seems to blow.
In this virgin land
Far from the madding crowd,
The mind and heart absorbed
Its sunlit glow.

K M Brown

On The Sky

The youth that bitter taste
Full and blessings and above
Crazy skies oh why? Oh why?
That first time gaze create
Ridge mountains to outshine,
Oh life or chasm erase
To let your voice be heard
And clay in which we lay
Uplifting rolling ends strays
Warming on your way
On what better end the day.

M Trainor

Another Day

Another day of life has come and gone
Lucky are we it goes on and on.
Really, one should never think that way
Just live and be happy, enjoy every day.

Yes, many friends have left this earthly life
Gone, leaving their families, some husband, some wife.
Never dreaming that life would be cut short,
Having to travel alone to that strange port.

To them; you are safe in our Lord's hands
We shall always remember you, through time's sands.
The time you spent with us, here on Earth
More precious than gold, those memories are worth.

Fates joined those two, to share this life
That sad moment when 'those two' were parted.
The times spent together 'really sublime'
If only 'together' finished what they had started.

So understand, life gives no promise or guarantee
So enjoy the moments life has to offer.
Share every moment that each day may bring
You cannot store one's happiness in a coffer.

Just be thankful, for all that you have
Even those times you feel under the weather,
The main thing to remember; lucky you are,
So take life as it comes, being 'together'.

Denis Constance

The Splendour Of A Sunset

The light is slowly fading as the sun sinks low
Depleted now its glory as it slowly weaves behind
Great banks of billowing gilt-edged cloud
Which rearrange formation, fractures reassigned
Chinks where the vermilion sphere peeps through
Of too great luminosity for vision to behold
A round red ball of fire descends to the horizon line
In a fusion of blues and greys and complementing reds and gold.

And now as turquoise pales to graduated orange
A seldom spectacle in transitory mood
As great shafts of yellow light beam skyward
And westward, the sun is even more subdued
Twilight turns to dimness and to dusk
And twinkling lights appear as night draws on
The pattern of the trees dissolve
As darkness envelops and suddenly day is gone.

Elizabeth Love

The Dishcloth

I visited my mother whose sight is slowly failing,
She sits and crochets dishcloths, for other folks who're failing.
A finished square she gave to me with seven corners on it,
I put the cloth upon my head, 'Twill make a lovely bonnet.'
We sat and talked my mum and I discussing this and that,
And very soon forgot about my crochet dishcloth hat.
The bus queue was, as usual full of moans and groans
But they all turned and smiled at me, 'cept those on mobile phones.
The driver with his bus arrived, a sour surly chap,
But not today, he smiled at me and doffed his busman's hat.
All greeted me like long-lost friends, my journey home was bliss.
A young on swaying bicycle cheered and blew a kiss.
A day of joy and happiness, it really must be said,
Even my mirror laughed at me, when it saw what I wore on my head.

D Beaumont

Lose The Blues

Taking down Christmas decorations is a task I've always hated
Following the colour and delight of celebration, it leaves me quite deflated
The cold, dark days of January find me flat, jaded, morose,
I seek the sanctuary of my cosy bed, remain there comatose
But slowly the nights are pulling out, grow increasingly lighter
Improved thought creates an optimistic mood to make outlook brighter
Packets of seeds are in the shops, buy one get one free
Flowers, vegetables, herbs, planning, planting,
I look forward eagerly.
Hello, there's a nice pair of boots, priced at only ten pound
In another store I find music CDs, that are worth a look around
Playing the best of John Denver makes me breathe the pure air
Freedom of wide open spaces, verbal pictures, I feel the wind in my hair
The season of goodwill remains with me, happy moments relived through memory
Exchange of presents, gathering of family around the glittering tree
Bargains in the town help the process of easing back into routine
Spring replaces winter, shrubs and trees are reclothed in green
There are holidays to book, new clothes to replace any past their best
Soon be time to discard top coat, hat, scarves, thermal vest
A chance for pruning to sort items that soon accumulate
With the intention of returning each room to an orderly state
Though grey days are miserable and put patience to the test
Taking a lesson from nature, it offers a chance to recharge and rest
Let's hope the 'season of discontent' gives way to a summer of peace
Whether enjoyed at home, or in Spain, Italy, France or Greece
Every month has good points, we've no need to face any with dread
Simply digest the best bits, savour and flavour our daily bread.

Dennis Overton

Count Your Blessings

When I look into the future
Or gaze back to the past,
I contemplate the pleasure
Of the gifts that really last.
It's not the money value
Or jewels set in gold,
It's not the goods that can be bought,
Nor anything that's sold.
It's love and peace and happiness,
It's friendship, help and trust;
It's freedom from blank loneliness,
And knowing that one just
Has to call on loving friends
When problems come to call,
And that is where the trouble ends -
Is that really all?

Well, what we need to learn from this
Is how to face each scene -
Things are not just hit-and-miss
Nor yet what might have been.
Every single happening
Has a two-fold side
Look first for a cause to sing -
Make sure those tears are dried;
For when you smile, others smile
And say that you are brave
And in a very little while
You'll find that you will have
The strength and vision to perceive
It could have been far worse.
From now on you will believe
That there's a blessing with each curse . . .

Learn your lessons . . .
Count your blessings!

K M Inglis-Taylor

A Poem For My Granddaughter

Let this little girl,
this baby girl be circled
in a ring-a-ring of posies,
tossed with kisses
at her tiny rosy feet,
each gifting its
sweet perfume to
wake her senses slowly,
uniquely as she grows;
daphne, honeysuckle
lily of the valley, jasmine . . .

and colours fabulous
unfold in petals
satin and silk,
the velvet primula
midnight blue and gold,
poppy paper thin scarlet
flowing into purple,
pansies light sky,
orange and black,
deep pink roses
and crimson peonies
soft as her skin,
shining buttercups and neat
white daisies to lace her chin -
everything to wonder at.

And let there be music,
harmony and loving voices,
the whistling wind,
the hushing sea and grasses,
birdsong at dawn and dusk -
and as she falls asleep the
sound of stars celestial,
a trillion triangles,
a million harps from
far, bright constellations,
fading to a universal dark -
simplicity of silence.

Count Our Blessings

Let this little girl tend
her wilderness of dreams
and see them bloom,
love common sense,
give room for learning,
open her heart and mind
to the sun and run
through life with confidence,
gifting all she possesses
to the world's best keeping.

Let this little girl
think outwardly,
feel passionately,
laugh merrily,
mock fears,
dry tears,
pick herself up
when she stumbles,
put hurts
in their place,
find space for
forgetting and forgiving -
herself and others.

Above all let her
grow in peace;
keep faith with life
and hope,
with artlessness sow love
in many hearts -
and in her own sweet heart
know love.

Maggie Goren

Blessings

Blessings all around us lie,
Upon the Earth and in the sky.

The animals and birds entrance,
The trees and plants enhance
Our lives, and it's not by chance.

Blessings all around us live,
In what we take and what we give.

We give and take support and love
Watched over by the precious dove.
Our blessings the sum of one special love.

Ann Dawes-Clifton

To A Grandchild

The path on which we meet in two ways slopes,
To my decline, and upwards
To your hopes.
To tarry here
A little while in bliss
With you my dear
In no wise would I miss.
On paths of time, we walk alone, yet know
I will be with you ever as you go.
Blood of my line has given life
And courses through
The eager strong young heart
And veins of you.
Go on my dear,
And strive to reach your goal.
Leave doubt and fear,
And find what makes you whole,
The love of God
That compasses us all,
And bear the hod
You carry
Standing tall.

C Beach

Our Lovely Friends

Our friends they invited us to share their humble tea
The rain fell fast and through the mast
Guess what I did see?
It was a sight I will recall as I put my pen to paper
The badgers they did come
Yes down they did run and listen to the capers
They played and taunted and ran around
The like you have never seen
By nightfall they had returned
With noses upturned
For their food they were quite keen
They ran on top of the road without stop
And created an animal tournament
By morning they had gone to their homes they had run
What a wonderful adornment,
With white stripes on their heads they scurried along
With food always in sight
I know at times they were naughty
I will always remember the things they did right.

Jessica Temple

What's The Use

What's the use of grumbling,
OK, it's pouring down,
The wind's blowing - gale force
And makes me frown.

The cold makes my fingers ache
But I'm sure it could be worse.
And the wind takes my breath away,
Which makes me want to curse.

But what's the use of grumbling,
We can't control these things,
Might as well ignore them
And see what tomorrow brings.

I try not to grumble,
About things I cannot change,
I'm so thankful to see each day,
Well! *You do at my age.*

Winnie Milnes

My Grandson

My grandson is just six years old,
  With tousled chestnut hair,
And he can be as good as gold -
  But sometimes hard to bear!

His endless questions wear me out,
  And how he lectures me!
Disarmingly his lips soon pout
  If I dare to disagree!

He's innocent and free from guile,
  Impulsive, loveable, true;
His playful antics make me smile:
  His twinkling eyes flash blue.

He loves to whistle, sing and dance,
  Angelic is his face,
And every mischievous side-glance
  Gives life a quicker pace.

He bounces round from morn till night,
  A ball of energy,
A grandson full of fun - and fright!
  Who cheers our family.

He is our blessing, pride and joy,
  So knowing is his head,
Yet he looks such a little boy
  When fast asleep in bed.

Glynfab John

Beauty

I sit beside
My window clear
And view with joy
God's gifts so dear.

In the mirror
Of Nature's fold
His artistry
Is stunning, bold.

Things of beauty,
Joys to treasure,
Lend Life purpose
Without measure.

Gareth D John

Love Comes In Many Forms

Love comes in many forms
Not all of them romance
Some will make you warm inside
Others will make you dance.

The love of a dear mother
Or a newborn babe to hold
To stroke the dear old family pet
All more precious than any gold.

A birthday kiss from your father
A hug from your grown-up son
A husband's bedtime kisses
When the day is almost done.

Story time with Grandma
Children free and wild
A toddler's favourite playthings
Laughing with your child.

Love is not about romance
Stealing kisses in the night
Love is the invisible chord
That fills your life with light.

From the youngest to the oldest
Try to give each day some laughter
Try to add your share of peace and joy
For memories ever after.

Elizabeth Slater Hale

In Praise Of The East Lancs Railway

Crewe Station, circa 1950, food and drink to me!
On the long footbridge, now defunct, notebook and pen in hand,
All summer through I'd join the throng of urchins,
Some from far afield, joy in the daily bustle of the L M R,
Watch mighty engines, many built in our own local works,
Scots, Jubilees, Black Fives, and Stanier's proud pacific breed -
The Coronations, once streamlined, the regal Princess Royals.
We'd watch these mighty beasts haul famous trains -
The Royal and Midday Scots,
The Irish Mail, the Welshman And The Merseyside Express.
How proud we were in 1951, when 'William Shakespeare' of
The new Britannia Class,
Was put on show at Crewe then down to London steamed
To star with Skylon and Discovery's Dome,
At Britain's glorious festival by the Thames.
When ugly, smelly diesels first came on the scene,
We'd greet them with the scorn these hulks deserved,
Soon they, with 'leccies' put steam to the sword,
And drove proud Patriots, 0.8.0s to lingering death
In Woodham's greedy maw.
But thanks to saviours like the E L R,
Some dear old friends still puff along the line:
Bahamas, Ivatt and the Fowler Crab,
A Sunday morning Ramsbottom delight.
The Duke of Gloucester, Black Prince and The Duchess too,
Strut their proud stuff along the Irwell Vale,
And make a man approaching sixty feel again a boy,
Back on Crewe Station in the mists of time.

Alan Swift

Blackthorn

As I walked out early on a March morn
I saw spiny black branches of blackthorn
With starry white blossoms hanging there
Caught the fragrance filling measureless air
Challenging deadness of the dark day,
Glad recognition spring on the way.
Infinite vista of beauty was there
That joy assumed shape of praise and prayer.

Idris Woodfield

The Trials Of A Teenager

As I lie in bed awake
Waiting for morning to break
What will tomorrow bring?
Another teenage uprising
The dos and don'ts of today's youth.
Is that what makes them so uncouth
Forever rebelling against law and order.
Is this why there is so much disorder?
Trying to be free of old rules
Forever trying to make government look like fools
To be young and out of work
My everyday duties I will not shirk
I forever live in hope that I won't
Succumb to dope, who knows
Maybe one day I will get employment
Be able to make ends meet
And pay rent to live my life
Without sorrow who knows
Maybe I won't be a lost cause tomorrow.

A Reilly

Marilyn

On the first of June nineteen-twenty six.
A star was born to work in the pics.
Norma Jean a model so young.
'Love Happy' was one of many parts.
Her stardom shot like a dart.
Fans loved her for her roles.
She didn't spend long on the dole.
Something's got to give.
Ended in tragedy for us fans who liked Marilyn Monroe is dead.
Found in her bed.
In the time of 4/5 August 1962.
Many suspicions arised among her few.
It's sad to lose a star so true.

T S

Let's Live

A pot pourri, kaleidoscope, melange of experience
Eating, drinking, making love passionately, voraciously.
Mundane tasks, too trivial to mention, like dusting,
Watching sparkling motes rise then resettle mischievously
Defrosting the freezer, sweeping crispy leaves
Into piles, bagging them to decay
To blend into crumbling soil enriching
Grass, flowers, trees and so on, ad infinitum.
Waking with bone-cracking yawns, rising, washing,
Cooling sleep-slicked self, inhaling the scent of soap
Eating delicious food with friends in warmth and love,
Snatching food on the hoof when hunger gnaws,
A succulent apple, juice dribbling down the chin.
Reading books of excitement and romance, when by the fire curled
Seeking knowledge or transportation into someone else's world
And there is sadness and loss, agonies of despair,
Anger and frustration when the world is black and cold
All is decay. The sun has gone,
Flowers are dead and flesh grown old.
Fact and fantasy, science, memory and magic fragments
Past and present whirl inside our crystal ball
Each unique. Let us live. Savour each second,
Each taste, whether bitter or sweet.
Let us live them all.

Mary Daulton

Poetry

Browsing through an anthology
Is like living in another world.
From sadness to joy
From heartbreak to happiness,
Everyone has a story to tell,
And that is where words come into their own.
The voice, of course, gives it extra meaning
But reading it like a book
One's picture in the mind may differ.
Every emotion is covered in poetry
From the baby's first rhyme
To a soldier's sad thoughts in war.
There is no subject which cannot be covered in poetry.

Isobel Scarlett

I Am Blind But I Can See

There *is* a life outside this room
Wherein the sounds of silence loom.
A world of shadows from which I long to be free
Yet with beautiful memories to comfort me.

My soul that dwells inside this shell
Keeps telling me that 'all is well'.
For if I listen I'll hear God's voice;
To become a prisoner is my *own* choice.

How I've longed to breathe the cool fresh air,
To walk for miles without a care;
To look upon the fields so green
Scenes that for so long I have not seen.

I try to be grateful, for why despair
When all around me take such care
In looking after my every need . . .
Without them I'd be lost indeed!

But these wonderful people will not let me give in
To this battle I fight, which I'm *going* to win.
I thank the dear Lord for he's shown me the way
To welcome each dawn of every new day.

The voice of my son, so warm and so kind;
His beautiful smile that I see in my mind.
Recognition of voices of those I hold dear;
The sweet songs of birds that I can still hear.

I can still feel the warmth of a gentle kiss;
The touching of hands which I'd certainly miss.
So, although I am *blind,* I really can *see*
That there are *so many folks much worse off than me.*

Vivienne Vale

Metamorphosis

It flew into the studio this morning
A moth of exquisite beauty.
Wings open, colours of orange, red and gold.
Then it rested on the cupboard
Stripes along its underside.
I looked at you in wonder,
My thoughts dwelt on your colours.
How could you have come from such a beginning?

Shirley Ludlow

Look On The Bright Side

I travel in a world of dreams
Where beauty and joy and happiness
Flows the whole day through
And through which I swim and dive and swirl
Enraptured by my life
Then this will end as sudden as it came
And I will plummet into dark unexplored caverns
Of deaths that are never known
Where in every corner lurks a ghost or gremlin
To frighten one
But being steadfast in one's thinking
And hanging on and on
One knows the landscape will change
And these ogres will soon be gone
And sunny dawns and sunlit lakes
And gardens full of flowers
Will once again appear in view
Where we can contemplate and dream for hours.

Paul Gamble

Lucky

When we look around us today
And see the suffering
That goes on every day
Floods and famine everywhere.

To have somewhere
To lay your head
And a roof over your head
Good food in your stomach
Instead of a cup of rice.

Mothers snuggle up to their children
To keep them warm
On a cold winter's night
Just think how lucky
You are and
Thank your lucky stars.

Jessie Moody

The Old Men (For The Young)

In the kingdom of men
There are presidents and ways -
Although you may feel
Empty and dark, these ways are
Tried, tested and true - refined
And loved throughout the
Centuries. You see a man
At rest in his work, looking on -
His hands moving to
Roll his cigarette, or
Purposely over his jaw, whilst
Thinking his gentle thoughts;
Looking to see not his next act
But to see his heart and have
It tell him his next act.
Yes, you see a man in gentle
Conversation with his neighbour -
They are nations and streams,
Both organic and true. You see
A man, older than you, with honour
Struck through his spine like a
Sword, then you can see: there are
Ways and presidents in the Earth
Those men tell to each other
From their hearts to their souls
And back again.

Paul Barron

Welcome Back

Sometimes, a closed door is a blessing,
You're shut out, not welcome inside,
The entry won't open, not even remotely,
No matter how hard it is tried.
You're left hanging, in dying persistence,
Too early for paradise,
In a suspenseful, blank-screen existence
No life flashes before your eyes.
Somehow, power lines start buzzing,
White-coated technicians succeed,
Things are humming and throbbing,
And they have all the bleeping they need.
Slow smiles rekindle to brightness
(One, who was lost, hesitates)
Then a voice, not unworldly, says clearly,
'Welcome back, your carriage awaits.'

Eunice Wyles

Hope

If morning finds you in despair
Uncertainties hang in the air
Just offer up a little prayer
And hope!

If thoughts of work make you depressed,
You'd rather stay at home and rest,
Make the effort, do your best,
Just hope!

When nothing in your life seems clear,
Try to add a little cheer,
Remember you can see and hear
There's hope!

People all around may be
Fighting problems - he, or she,
May want from shackles to break free -
They'll hope!

Look up at the sky above
Hear the cooing of the dove,
Give your morbid fears a shove,
And hope!

Count your blessings, not your loss,
Don't let trauma be your boss,
About the past, don't give a toss,
Just hope!

D Morgan

We Have Survived

We take a lot for granted in what we say and do,
For the flowers we have planted, we hope they will come through,
When things have been difficult, we tend to shy away,
And can't face up to anyone when people try to say,
They know what we are going through and try to give their love,
But it only makes us worse until they give us hugs,
We have our sadness and cope in the way we can,
And give our love and comfort to those who need a hand,
We have come through our sad times and now it's time to give,
We hope you learn a lesson in how to love and live.

June Daniels

Stepping Stones

Many are the stepping stones
We tread on through our lives.
Alighting from the last one
When the time to leave arrives.
Looking back remembering
All the ups and downs,
Recalling all the music
And those romantic sounds.
I picture all the sad days,
And many days of joy;
You were just a little girl,
And me a little boy.
For it was at school I met you
When you walked into the class,
I muttered underneath my breath
'Now that's a bonny lass'
Fate decreed you'd marry me
When we'd reached late teens,
A wife as wonderful as you
Was beyond my wildest dreams.
As gingerly we crossed the stream of
Life, you faltered in your gait,
I watched you being swept away
'Twas then I lost my mate.
Not many stones are left my love
For me to tread upon,
So when I lose my foothold
I'll be joining you . . . *Anon.*

Bill Austin

Angel

Through the clouds emerges an angel
With her wings widespread by her side.
As her eyes are like pearls in the moonlight,
In our troubles we can but confide.

Through the howl of the wind she whispers,
Through the silence she seizes to speak.
As she watchfully gazes upon us,
She has yet to find what we seek.

As she cries the tears of immortals,
As she grieves for our pain from within,
She is brought to a world of destruction,
To a world of sorrow and sin.

An angel that's given us hope,
A saviour that's fought for our plight,
Releases her grasp from our troubles
And departs once again from our sight.

Elena Uteva

Special Delivery

Amy Beth was in a hurry,
Keen to see the world at last.
Put her mother in a flurry
Off to see the midwife . . . fast!
6am, the road was busy
Dad was driving, feeling strong
Rest of family in a tizzy
'Don't worry darling, won't be long.'
Nurse and midwife ready waiting
Soon had Mother into bed;
Found her rapidly dilating,
Before too long . . . the baby's head!
Cries of sheer delight and wonder
'It's a girl,' said Dad with joy
Causing Mum to sigh and ponder
'I'm so happy, girl and boy.
Will our Tommy like his sister?'
'Sure he will,' said Dad with pride
'As she grows, he will assist her,
Always be there by her side.
For I know our Tom won't grumble,
He's big brother, you will see,
Watching her so she won't tumble,
What a pleasure that will be.'
'We've so much to say a prayer for
And we've so much love,' he said
'Gran and Grandad waiting there for
Friends to 'wet the baby's head'
So let us thank God for his blessing
For your safety and your health
These are values worth possessing
Better far than worldly wealth.'

E Martin

A Perfect Yesterday And Tomorrow

Do you remember all our yesterdays
all those smiley faces and special ways?

All those times together full of fun,
there was nothing wrong in what we done.

It never ever went wrong,
for in that love we did belong.

Where all the answers were you and me,
I knew you listened but did you see?

Our love could never have an end,
yet here within a message I send.

This life we live is just a play,
and this scene I write was yesterday.

I see in tomorrow there is a hope,
but a fading star needs a telescope.

All my love for you was free,
as your happiness is ever here with me.

The moon you are looking at is mine,
it will remind us of the next time.

You can see, yet you cannot,
for yesterday is all we have got.

For can you see my Brigadoon,
for you came and yet you left too soon.

Our memories are happy and never sore,
as I try to turn the waves back on the shore.

And on them days I do not see you or call,
it's at that time I love you most of all.

Jim Anderton

Blessings

Have you the eyes to see the raindrops fall
And dance in puddles on the streets and tracks?
The gift of ears to hear the vagrant wind
Shriek in the alleyways and chimney stacks?

And can you smell the perfume of wet grass
Feel dampness on your ankles where you stray?
And are you blessed with voice as you bemoan
'Dear God, it is a truly dreadful day.'

Ann Dempsey

Angels

A pathway to Heaven
Angels show me the way
A pathway to Heaven
Nearer day by day
Open before, before my eyes
All love in Heaven unified.

I am growing old now
Love never will
Love in my memory
Lives with me still
My heart's ever yearning
To be where you are
Listen, listen
Hear the music of the stars.

When my journey's over
On Earth is through
The angels will guide me
Guide me to you
My gentle heart
We've waited so long
Now we are young again
Remember our song.

Beyond Earth's shadow
Way beyond the moon
Choirs of angels sing
Heavenly tunes
Stars all around
Around and above
We dance among the stars
Find our special star,
Our very special star,
Of love.

A King

God's Wonderful World

Who else but God could draw me here
To see the white cloud form tracery
Across a bright blue sky?
Harebells nodding in the breeze
Reflect the colour while I
Draw deep breaths of fragrance
From the wild thyme at my feet
Crushing the plants on the hillside
Up to the old wooden seat
Where I can contemplate
Such a wonderful view
Deeply to appreciate
God's gifts to me and you.
Who else but God could give freely
Such precious gifts of enduring nature
Attracting us to see the wonder
Of His world. Expecting no return
From us except appreciation
Calling to us all to see with adoration
His gifts to you and me.

Betty Gilman

Easter Images

The healing hands of Easter
The fresh new shoots of nature
When the Magdalene met the gardener
And light shone through the door.

A miracle is revealed
In the wakening of furrow and field
Altars ablaze in Roman candles
(Shrines under snowy mantles)
Where the pilgrim picks his way.

Even the sea seems freshly salted
Earth blessed and sweetly anointed
Heaven unrolls her sacred scrolls
(Bearing the names of numberless souls)
Before empires of dust and clay.

The pierced hands of Easter
The gentle way of the Master
When the Magdalene met the gardener
And truth smashed down the door.

Mike Monaghan

The Summer Of '76

If I could keep time in a bubble,
There are memories I'd always keep,
To take out and look at and dream on
In the nights when I just couldn't sleep.

Like the packet of fags on the table
'Just in case we run out' you explained,
Summer days when we lazed in the garden,
And the night when it thundered and rained!

I'll remember that day on the river
In search of the great crested grebe,
And the fun and the laughs and the shiver,
And that rope that you had to retrieve!

Oh, if I could keep time in a bubble,
I'd relive all those kisses we shared,
How *they* are worth all the remembering
As I suddenly realised I cared!

There were times I don't want to remember,
But so much that we've shared and enjoyed,
All those days in the hottest of summers,
When we could have been better employed!

Yes, if I could keep time in a bubble,
Like the herbs that we planted and grew,
All the happiness shared and the laughter,
I would know that I owe it to you.

Mary Thomas

Hebridean Sonnet

A shaft of sun escapes through banks of cloud
To flood the machair strip with sudden light;
The shell-sand pasture early settlers ploughed
Explodes with flowers of purple, yellow, white.

As rain returns and colour disappears,
We count the blessings nature can provide,
Supported by skilled farming over years
And rafts of kelp that stem the swollen tide.

Two centuries ago the burnt ash kelp
Was used to manufacture glass and soap;
The crofters' farms abandoned without help
Left islanders deprived of pride and hope.

Respect for the environment will lift
Our hearts in thanks for giver and the gift.

Angela Butler

Am I Lucky?

I was born in the snow in November twenty-five,
So I guess I am lucky to be alive,
Father worked hard but we were poor,
Mother kept us clothed and fed, we didn't want for more,
We started school when we were five to learn
And left when we were fourteen to start to earn,
I joined The Home Guard when I was sixteen
And was called up for the Royal Navy at eighteen,
When you are young, you dream of romance,
The girl of your dreams, the one who could dance,
I'm in with a chance if I ask her for a dance,
She turns me down, not even a second glance,
Well maybe I'm ugly I don't know,
The mirror broke when I looked in it so who knows,
I can count many blessings for the life I've had,
I've played football, cricket and roller hockey when a lad,
Tennis, table tennis and badminton to name a few,
I've been on holidays abroad but only to Canada I flew,
Photography is my hobby I've printed in the dark room till a few years back
Now I've gone digital printing it's easy, the dark room got the sack,
I'm not rich or famous thank God for that,
I have no credit cards and no debts that's a fact,
I started work at fourteen and retired at sixty-eight,
I live alone and cook, clean and do the washing that's right,
I'm a churchgoer and visit friends each week,
My eyesight is good I still drive after fifty-six years,
I'm very hard of hearing but I walk a mile or two every morning,
So at eighty-one I have very good reason to count my blessings.

Harry Skinn

The Day The Angels Came

I held her hand as she passed away.
As the robin sang at the break of day,
And morning cast a sunbeam on the lawn,
The angels came and she was gone,
But love's still there like the fragrance of a rose,
That never dies or sleeps but only grows.
It's there in evening's mellow hush,
In the sunset's gentle blush,
For oft' in twilight reverie,
My love will come and 'bide with me,
All in beauty as a bride,
Is it an angel by my side?
Then she departs before the dawn,
And casts a sunbeam on the lawn,
A robin sings at the break of day,
I hold her hand as she slips away.

William Smyth

Thoughts To Cheer

When our lives seem cold and drear,
Never forget there are good things near,
Plenty of things to cheer our way,
If we look around us day by day.

In the morn when we open our eyes,
Don't forget to look at the skies,
Sometimes we see a bright red sky,
Or big dark clouds go floating by.

Both may bring us rain today,
Don't let either make us dismay,
A farmer may need this for his crops,
To give us food when we go to shops.

Nature's things cheer dreary hearts,
Beauty of trees in country or parks,
Flowers of all colours bring us cheer,
Changing often throughout the year.

Look at the children so full of fun,
Playing games before school has begun,
Look at a baby, eyes closed tight,
Or smiling, making us feel bright.

Remember happy days you've had,
Even if life now seems so bad,
Be thankful for help you've been given,
Try to help others whose hearts seem riven.

If we are old and cannot go out,
Or lost those hard to live without,
Pray for strength and courage each day,
Then you will have help to cheer your way,
Animal life will cheer us too,
Dogs, cats and birds the whole year through.

Ruby Ling

The Jewel Box

I looked into my box of jewels and saw so little there
I looked around my pantry and I found it rather bare
I looked down at my carpet and it was so threadbare
I looked into my purse that had not a penny to spare.

But when I looked around my home what did I see?
Why the dearest of all treasures, my expanding family
For my children are my jewels, that I don't need to be told
They're sparkling eighteen-carat diamonds with hearts of purest gold.

I can't wear them on my finger, I can't place them round my throat
But we love and care for each other - I really don't mean to gloat
And now I have a bracelet of special priceless pearls
Made up of little grandchildren - happy boys and girls.

Now grandchildren complete my treasure trove
They're the icing on the cake
Even though I can no longer stand in my kitchen to bake
What would I do with diamonds? What would I do with gold?
What would I do with all the pearls now that I'm getting old?

There is no jewel box big enough to hold all my treasure
My family are my everything now that I'm at my leisure
For the pride, the tears, the laughter and all the joy they bring
They make my life complete, they make me want to sing.

Life wasn't always easy, life hasn't always been fair
And when it comes to troubles - of them I've had my share
But each night I take up my rosary and count my blessings too
And hope that such special jewels will come to you and you.

Elizabeth Farrelly

Seaside

Seabird glides above the ocean
Children playing with warm sand
Snake locks dancing in the rock pool
Foamy fingers touch soft land
Where the air is fresh and salty
And the blue sky meets the sea
Colours changing through the daytime
All of nature wild and free
Leave only footprints take home memories
A special gift for you and me.

Pam Hornby

The Anchor And Kite

They are the anchor that tugs my kite.
In all the clever tricks to play
They are the ones that pull from beginning to end.
Those who had nothing gave me so much.
Having lived amongst the less fortunate,
Losing even life itself without dignity.
Knowing that at least there was the chance
To climb up and leave behind the forgotten
That could not. Little did I know.

Only, of course, you don't forget them.
Those who had nothing gave
The gleaming jewel to carry on
Behind an iron mask.

In the ability to fortify himself
With the dignity, ego, vanity and pride,
A persona totally cloaked in an image
In all its absurdities,
The make-up man put on his armour-plated helmet,
Masking inadequacies, living out fantasy in confidence tricks.
The fragile talent only granted by the grace of ability,
Expectancy only by its means.

The kite as mask, masked by life,
Pampered by normality, moaned like a pet.
He remembered those from his past, people who knew
Depression was a luxury they could not afford.
And in the present, noticed those who complained the most
Had the least wrong with them,
And those who complained the least had the most.

So my strength was drawn from the forsaken,
And from those forgotten.
Not from those whose life was so full of expectancy.

In comparison what did I want?
The life of a floating clown, adrift with anchor, had no meaning.
Having the mask of agility, a life granted by the grace of ability.
So dreams become true. Yes. Was the answer instinctively,
As nature is only designed to survive.
Though only the anchor within my heart behind the mask
Really means anything.

Christopher English

God's Blessings To Me

God gave me a happy childhood and loving parents too,
I enjoyed my schooldays as I tried my lessons to do.
At college I found Jesus at the end of a long search,
'Twas such a joy to meet Him, He's never left me in the lurch.
He's showered me with blessings, more than I can say,
I'm happy how I've lived my life and not another way.
He gave me the talent of music, both to teach and to play,
And I hope it blesses others as I use it day by day.
Being single can get lonely but God's given me a treat,
Of a family of twenty pupils who sit on the piano seat.
He's given me a good neighbour who helps me when I've need,
She really understands me through many a really kind deed.
And then there are the poems He so regularly inspires,
They come for every occasion, it seems He never tires.
I also have a family at my church Milton Hall,
And if I am in trouble on anyone I can call.
But above all I have the Lord with me hour by hour,
He is my peace and joy and in trouble a strong tower.
God does little miracles often through the day,
That no one else knows about and I will never say.
So thank you God for blessings unnumbered to the end,
And when I reach the final gate eternal peace please send.

Rita Hardiman

Eilidh

Oh Eilidh with those smiling eyes
And that beguiling look
You know we can't resist you
You read us like a book.

You always life our spirits up
And lots of joy you bring
Every time you visit us
Is like a breath of spring.

Since the day that you were born
And into our life you came
With the gift of love you brought us
Our lives can never be the same.

So as your gran and grandad,
We will your praises sing,
And always say 'We love you'
For all the joys you bring.

We know that life will change you
As the years roll by
But rest assured you'll always be
The apple of our eye.

Ian Russell

High On Pressure

You get that feeling - you know the one . . .
The pit of your stomach has come undone
In front of you is a deep black hole
And on your back is a sack of coal
The pressures of life are all around
There's no solution to be found
You're feeling down and really stressed
You can't look up cos you're so depressed
Now - just think - are things *really* bad?
Or - feeling down makes you sad?
In your mind you've had some good days
They may be distant but they were nice ways
When you felt good and the world was great
Things were fun and your future was fate
Nothing could beat you or get you down
Lines on your face were from laughter - not frown
So think of those days now that you're feeling so dark
Consider all nature, especially the lark
For the more it sings the higher it flies
Never down in the dumps always up in the skies
Let your mind wander over times you've enjoyed
For life is too short to be worried or annoyed.

Alan R Coughlin

Nature's Whisper

Rain tap-dancing against my face,
Wet leather and muscle beneath.
Galloping the surf as home bound we make,
Hoofs pounding on sand we race.

Intoxication of winter's charm,
Flow of energy the sea breakers crash.
Whispers of nature in the wind caught,
Free are my heart and thoughts.

Inhaling the sodden grass and soil,
As through the woods now roam.
Carpet of forna and flora so wild,
Bordering the river that trembles and coils.

Soon the sun swallows the damp,
Through the shivering glow smiling down.
And as Merlin and I complete our ride,
Both fully refreshed and feeling alive.

A A Murphy

Thank God For The Daisies

The deep, dark night
Had been one long fight
Against pain and a delirious brain,
My body was so weary
And thoughts so dreary
That the soft warm bed
Could not soothe my aching head
One way and another I turned -
Not wishing the 'other one' to wake.
I thought myself downstairs I'd take
To crouch upon the couch,
But still sleep eluded me
Despite sleeping pills and tea.
Countless cigarettes I smoked,
Till I coughed and wheezed and choked,
Dear God, give me peace
And from this pain release
My body, and unwind
Too, my troubled mind.
The time dragged wearily
The moon lit the earth eerily,
Impatient for the dawn
I watched the sky, with a yawn -
Still it stayed as dark as ink
Then it seemed that in a twink
Pearly patches quickly spread,
Deepening into rosy red
Then the trill of a blackbird
And chirp of a sparrow I heard -
My spirits began to lift
And depression started to drift
And melt away.
At last the long awaited day was here,
And I shed a thankful tear,
The sun's light banished the shadows eerie
And suddenly I was no longer weary.
My mind cleared and became receptive
And took in sight, deceptive

Count Our Blessings

Of velvet peony buds bejewelled anew
With dancing, glistening dew.
Then, the gladdest sight -
Of daisy petals gathered tight
Their yellow button centres
Seeing that no insect enters.
These are my favourite flowers
Maybe because I spent hours
When a tiny thing,
Making a daisy chain or ring.
Always I'll love their simple faces
And hate the mower when it races
Up and down, slicing off their urchin charm so fair.
Having time to watch them wake gave me a chance to take
Deep breaths of pure cool air,
And thank God with a whispered prayer.

Sylvia Moulds

You Can Make A Difference

You can make a difference
With just a warming smile,
That lightens someone's sombre mood,
For just a little while.

You can make a difference
With just a sympathetic ear,
While someone painfully bares their soul,
Or simply sheds a tear.

You can make a difference
With just a helping hand,
So those that face their darkest hour,
Know you understand.

You can make a difference
With just a comforting word,
Assure another's fragile fears
Their prayers have been heard.

You can make a difference
With just an encouraging sign,
That no matter how the deck is stacked,
Belief will make things fine.

You can make a difference
With just a compassionate touch,
Reinforce we *all* are cherished,
Very, very much.

You can make a difference
That everyone is seeing
And be lauded by 6 billion
As a special human being.

Ray Crutchlow

Thoughts Of Christmas

A little verse for you and yours.
A song of Christmas joy.
To celebrate a special day
And the birth of a Baby Boy.

The shepherds watching o'er their sheep
Beheld a wondrous sight.
As the *angel* of the *Lord* appeared
And the world was filled with light.

Wise men came with riches,
As presents for the Boy.
But wisdom was their greatest gift
And their hearts were filled with joy.

Then came Three Kings from out the East,
They had travelled far and wide,
They laid their gifts beside the crib,
A bright star had been their guide.

Did the first *King* rule the earth and lands,
And the second rule the skies?
The third maybe ruled the hearts of Man
And soothed their mournful cries.

So as we celebrate that glorious day
That happened long ago,
We give presents to our kith and kin
Then off to church we go.

G Hunter Smith

Golden Days

Maybe some day
We'll look back on this one
With a smile in our eye
And say 'Wasn't it lovely?'
We often recall
Some event long ago
And think it was special
Though it didn't seem so
Who knows? But in time
This could be one of those
Picked out for re-living
Given time but who knows?

Terry Grimson

Beacon Light

Within your darkest hour
Into your blackest night
A love will shine for you
Just like a beacon light.

And when your hardest trial
Becomes your toughest fight
A love will shine on through
Just like a beacon light.

Then, when it is over and you can see
You will find love waiting, eternally
Love is nothing, if not for you
Seek out the light to pull you through.

Within your darkest hour
If you cannot see the light
A love is there for you
Seek out the beacon light.

John Michael Scott

Count Our Blessings

Good food on our tables
From shops who have the lot
Let's just count our blessings
As there's plenty who have not

Our health's taken from granted
As we pass throughout our lives
Let's just count our blessings
We've still got kids and wives

Storms, gales and tornadoes
Don't bother us many days
Let's just count our blessings
Our homes don't get blown away

No corrupted evil parliament
Threatening jail if you ever dare
Let's just count our blessings
That we've got Tony Blair!

No real AIDS epidemic
Like somewhere overseas
Let's just count our blessings
For this we should be pleased

Not everyone is as lucky as me
As the daily news normally tells
So I just count my blessings
That it is usually someone else.

Chris Leith

Taken For Granted

When we start wanting more,
We forget what we've got,
All the things staring us in the face,
We're never happy with our lot.
Money can't buy you happiness,
Good things come for free,
Like your lifelong friends,
And the unconditional love of your family,
From the birds in the sky,
To the flowers in bloom,
The good health we keep,
Taken for granted too soon.
The freedom of choice,
The right to choose,
The opportunity and power,
To air our views.
But not everyone is as fortunate as you,
So smile, as this is not to be forgot,
It's not having what you want,
It's wanting what you've got.

Jemma Clare Pinkerton

I Owe You . . .

I was quiet and made no sound
But you gave me voice and I am found

I was confused, had lost my way
But you gave me strength to face the day

I was sinking and unable to swim
But you rescued me and pulled me in

I was trapped and no way out I could see
But you were there and set me free

I was cold, the flame of passion had expired
But you reignited the spark, made me feel desired

I know you are a phase and destined not to stay
But I thank my stars that I met you, every day

Because without you in my life in any way
I think I would have just faded away to grey . . .

J Webb

You Are Part Of Me

Your smile melts my will
And leaves me thinking
Half breathed
Gasping,
Still.

Your eyes fetch my soul
Straight to my heart
Stolen
Majestic,
Cool.

Your walk leads my gaze
Stiff-necked I turn
Enraptured
For your
Ways.

You really do not know
My half-baked love
And blissful
Ignorance
Show.

You . . . are part of me
Real fantasy
Romance
Stifles me
Still.

Mike Morrison

Woman In A Walled Garden

Walled in, not walled up
Hedged around, not hegemony
Heart's home, home-spun
Not homesick, not homogenous.

Still waters, not stagnant
Protected but not cocooned
Reflective but hope not parochial
Flowers bloom here well if fed.

There's life in a walled garden
I want to be a fruitful vine
With tendrils trailing over the wall
Towards the world, writ large.

Helen Dean

Emily, Two Years On

My granddaughter Emily, is now two years old,
And the memories she gave me, I treat them like gold,
They are stored in a place, that I always will find,
For they're safely locked up, in my heart and my mind,
Each laugh and each giggle, she does with great style,
They are stored like an image, along with each smile,
I regard it as precious, each memory I've kept,
Even storing away, every tear she has wept.

Her first words and first steps, they are stored away,
It appears that she learns, something new every day,
And when she says Bampa, and then takes my hand,
She talks in a language, that I can't understand,
But she loves to say hiya, to all that she meets,
And she also says thank you, if you give her some sweets,
When it's time to go home, she will then say bye-bye,
Then she gives me a kiss, with a tear in her eye.

I wish I could show, to the whole human race,
The gleam in her eye, and the smile on her face,
For the pleasure it gives me, if I could pass it round,
Would encourage more friendship, and more love would be found,
And as time goes by, and the years they do pass,
A thousand more memories, I'm sure to amass,
Then my heart and my mind, they will swell up with pride,
And I shall count my blessings, and store them inside.

James Stirrat

If

If you are a disabled man
Count your blessings while you can.
Folk who maybe cannot see
Would really give a lot to be
In a wheelchair, but with sight
Then you could watch the stars at night.

To appreciate the gift of scent
Proves that you were really meant
To inhale the fragrance of a bloom
Like the rose that flowers in June.

If your hearing is still good
Then I think you really should
Listen to the birds at dawn
Or the bees about to swarm.

The whinny from a friendly horse
Might encourage you to take a course
Of lessons from the RDA
To really brighten up your day.

Herdis Churchill

Christmas 2006

What a lovely Christmas,
Full of laughter and goodwill
The family all together
Gladness, our hearts to fill.

The weather rather bleak and wet
But spirits still stayed high
The turkey and the Christmas pud
Then; presents at last we cry.

The day is drawing to a close
The clothes all been tried on
And now I'm feeling rather sad
For Christmas is nearly gone.

But parties to look forward to
I can't wait for mine
Life's very, very hectic,
But I like it, it's just fine.

And when it's truly over
We'll look forward to the spring
The primroses and daisies
The little birds that sing.

So let us all look forward
There's good things still to come
But what we must remember
It's not so good for some.

So spare a thought for others
And say a little prayer
For people not so fortunate
Let's show them that we care.

M Whitehead

Heaven Is . . .

Heaven is new life in spring,
The first light of dawn,
When the birds start to sing.
Heaven is a summer breeze,
Fields of wild flowers,
Butterflies and bees.
Heaven is autumn at her best,
The fruits of the earth, nature yields,
Before she takes a rest.
Heaven is winter fireglow,
Christmas trees, lots of snow.
Heaven is all the wonderful things,
The seasons display,
To cheer us along life's way.

V Taylor

Blessings

If you really counted them
Well the answer would be never.
There are so many blessings
We sadly lose forever.

First we have our lifetime.
However long or short,
Some say I never asked
Others give more thought.

Through life's many happenings,
I've learnt I have great treasure.
My sons were each a blessing,
Given in good measure.

People say God bless you,
When you sneeze,
It helps to keep the Devil out,
Just one big squeeze.

Thinking of my family,
Of Nick and Matt, the girls,
Oliver and Henry,
Their mums give me some twirls.

A blessing is from Heaven
And we must give some thanks,
Life is what you make it,
And cannot be found in banks.

Rosemary Povey

Remembrance

It has become an annual thing for us,
To bow our heads in grief for those who died,
To save us from our enemies and thus,
Enable us to live our lives with pride.
Though sixty, ninety years have passed us by,
Since widespread bloodshed of each major war;
Yet still we find no way to satisfy
Our wish for peace; our aim to fight no more.
Now as we go our self indulgent way,
It's easy to forget the ones who've died,
Who fought the wars of leaders of the day,
Believing right, no matter on which side.
Will ever come the day that dove-like talk
O'ercomes the greed for power of the hawk?

Christopher Head

Look For Me

Look for me in the stillness
Of woodlands in the spring
Where the gentle breeze stirs the topmost branches
Of the trees
Where robins sing

And all is newly mantled
In fresh green elegance
Primroses nestle on mossy banks and violets
Fill the air
With spring fragrance

Look for me on the hilltop
Where buzzards soar and glide
On golden wings. Silent, majestic, beautiful
But ruthless
And eagle-eyed

Look for me in the meadows
Where wild rabbits play
And silvery brooks meander through cool glades
And shady nooks
Along the way

Look for me my dear ones
And you will find me there
In the sweet scent of the honeysuckle
As the breeze
Touches your hair.

Estelle James

Memories

It's six years since he left us - we had to let him go,
But all the memories we have can never lay us low,
So many years of loving and showing that he cared,
Make bittersweet in retrospect the kind of life we shared,
The children growing strong and tall,
Both made their way in life,
They grew up honest, bright and kind,
Proof against stress and strife,
They come and visit often on special days and others,
So that I know for certain I'm the luckiest of mothers.
Their dad, from somewhere, sees them and I'm sure that he is glad,
Breathing, 'Well done, my children, and I beg you don't be sad.'

Janet Bowerman

What's Your Favourite Colour?

When I was a child
My favourite colour was green.
'What's your favourite colour?' we used to ask each other.

When I was a child my favourite food
Was Mum's mince pies.
'What's your favourite food?' we used to ask each other.

When I was a child my favourite time of year
Was autumn because of my birthday.
'What's your favourite time of year?' we used to ask each other.

Later, all grown up, my favourite colour was blue,
I had to learn to like food I could cook for myself or buy,
And my favourite season was spring,
Although the raw smell of new-mown grass cuts into my heart then
With sharp memories of unreturned love . . .
And I'm glad I don't have to go through all that growing up again!

Now I find that the colour my heart calls out for is a strong red,
Not a bright red,
Only a deep, rich, dark, soft, velvet red - like my bedroom curtains -
They're just right.

For favourite foods now I like a good variety:
Bacon, roast chicken, jacket potatoes, interesting salads, chips and so on -
All straightforward, nothing too fancy, nothing out of line with my health or wealth.

My favourite time of year now is summer.
I like the daylight, sunshine, long days, short nights, fine weather,
Going and camping in a field for a week with friends, recharging.

I like the fact that I know who I am now.
Better still, I know who my friends are,
And hope I've learned how to be a friend to them.
Best of all, I know that God has a plan for my life,
Even though I don't know what it is yet.
I can be content in knowing that He knows.

So, what's your favourite colour?
What's your story?

Hilary Mason

Kid Brother

Mum, do not shiver,
Be warm, be warm,
He has closed his tired eyes
And now he sleeps.

He was always your kid brother,
You loved him, you loathed him,
Every mischief and those fights!
But now he sleeps.

You watched him grow so quickly,
Put you through it, the emotions,
Yet he found his way
And one rough diamond shone.

When your loved ones gather,
Laugh! Sing!
He will smile a wry grin
Although he sleeps.

I love you so much Mother,
Remember, remember,
Your kid brother always loved you,
And always will.

Graeme Vine

Amielah My Friend

How time has passed in three short years
Much enjoyment and laughter without tears
No arguments or stress to cause bad feelings
Just fun, appreciation and one's heart reeling.

Often I wanted more from our relationship
But gladly settled for true honest friendship
Now the time grows nigh for your departure
Away to foreign lands for a great adventure.

Will you keep in touch or disappear?
Only you can decide to send good cheer
I wish you well on all your travels
May God be with you whatever India unravels.

Gone are the theatre evenings out in style
Life will not be the same without your smile
But I am so happy that when I am feeling blue
Forever in my heart will be memories of you.

George Alexander

Tomorrow's Yesterdays

The joys of Christmas past have gone and New Year
Left behind.
Old spruce trees dragged to the dump, lying with
Broken toys that have been stuck together with glue or mastic,
Not meant to last.

Tarnished tinsel washed away by winter's rains
Lies blocking drains with soggy leaves and muck
Rotting like unfulfilled dreams in the mire
After the flood, with unused mistle - wasted.

Then the pains of paying sums owing
As the magic plastic bill arrives
The token cost of hope and desire
That dies with the winter's setting sun.

But spring is here . . .
Snowdrops spotting barren soil
Laid by nature's sowings past
Snow pure in the morning dew
Like varnished tears of angels - frozen.
Lie there for all to see.

For lovers walk, hold hands and talk
No lies as spring explodes beneath the sun
Of fire.
We'll feel the heat that warms the heart
As we walk the path of tomorrow
The blood will beat out any sorrow
As we sing or whistle, whatever will be will be.

Terry Davy

The Way To Be

If you can put a smile upon a face that wears a frown,
If you can raise them up, when life has knocked them down,
If you can treat each member of the human race,
With kindness, charity, and hold them in good grace,
Then you are acting as a man,
And - knowing you - I know you can,
If you can take their problems and their pain,
And set them on the road of life again,
You will stand tall, and all the world will know,
This is a man to whom the hurt may go.

Gordon Andrews

Angels

Far above the lark that's trilling,
Pours a song of love that's filling
Aching voids, where love
Once blossomed in my heart.

Mystic sonnet, pure, melodious
Purges mem'ries dark and odious,
Heals my pain, so bringing me
Your joy of life.

He, the Lord who gave me hearing,
Gave you song, that by its healing,
All things that He has created
Shall together work for good.

Thy cascade sweet, has borne my spirit
Our of despond,
And euphoric, now it soars above
The clouds of life's demerits.

God's mercy showing, men have féted
All unknowing, angels.
Perchance, oh feathered friend
Your wings are other than they seem.

We know that hidden hosts surrounding
Fight our fight, God's love abounding.
Blessed tiny angel, out of sight,
Your battle hymn has, my Goliath, slain.

Bill Sutherland

Global Rose

I will name a single rose for you,
Of molten-gold, soft-tinged with apricot.
I will plant your memory in earth
Deep-rooted in this heart of England plot.

You will spring from sharp-thorned crown of briars,
But every bloom from bark-smooth shoots will flame;
From each new rose such perfume will transpire,
That all who pass will wonder whence it came.

Tombs of pharaohs, hanging bowers of kings,
All history perpetuates through you.
The hand of friendship joining Tudor's blooms
Will flower again and fellowship ensue.

I will spin the globe to spread your name.
There is no need to see this rose to know
That while its scent wafts gently round the world
Your care will touch wherever roses blow.

Mary Daniels

Reflection

How can we know when it is time,
To leave this life of yours and mine?
When heart has taken final beat
And time on Earth is then complete.

Passing quick without a warning
In the night before the morning
Is preferable to lingering on
In daily pain when hope is gone.

Whatever time or circumstance
While you're here don't miss a chance
Take the time each single day
To show, your love in every way.

It's always later than you think
Chances pass within a blink
Don't put off another day
The things you really need to say.

Give thanks each day to God above
Because He gave her, you to love
When you're gone the chance is too
To say, 'I've always cherished you.'

So say it daily and don't forget
How it was when you first met
It's the thing that will remain
With her, till you meet again.

Daniel Moore

George Best

Here in Belfast City,
Black mountains climbing tall,
Lies our greatest hero, George Best,
The greatest of them all.

His skills they were like magic,
When he played with Manchester United,
We watched our hearts burst with pride,
Racing with excitement.

A picture of a famous face on a banknote,
Though not in circulation,
Handled carefully with care,
And framed with admiration.

An airport recalls a famous name,
I listen to the drone,
A famous legend rests in peace,
Our George is back home.

Marian McGrath

Alive . . .

A hazy summer's sunset
Stretches flaming fingers across the skies,
A frosty, white winter's morning
Makes me know that I'm alive.

The gentle breeze in the trees
As it plaintively moans and sighs,
The still calm of an August night
Makes me glad that I'm alive.

A raging, uncontrollable tempest
Of wild wind and illuminating lights,
To the cool, cleansing, pure rain
Makes me feel that I'm alive.

The mighty oceans crashing waves
As they roll in with ever-changing tides,
The peaceful trickling mountain stream
Makes me sure that I'm alive.

Translucent mystical moon among
A myriad of stars in the sea of night,
The warm caressing hand of the midday sun
Makes me love that I'm alive.

A favourite song on the radio
Playing again in my head time after time,
The resounding reflection of silence
Makes me believe that I'm alive.

A passionate kiss, a lustful embrace
Losing yourself completely in a lover's eyes,
And an innocent smile from a child
Makes me want to be alive.

Taking each day as it comes
Believing in myself that I am alive,
Whatever life throws in my path,
I know I can always survive . . .

Jo Howson

The Ultimate Blessing!

Every tribe beneath the sky,
Every continent and land
Has discovered its suffused by
Music from their local band.
From the treble, alto, bass,
Melodies reflect devotion,
Tuned to the tenor of their race,
Riffs of truly wild emotion!

Meanwhile oboe, bass guitar
And singers celebrate with joy,
Stanzas writ in tonic sol-fa,
Voiced by each falsetto boy.
String quartets and even more,
The Philharmonic orchestra,
From which each maestro will implore
A symphony or opera.

Perfect pitch or flat tone deaf
Each ear is bathed in cadences
Of such beauty that the hearer's
Nurtured by their covalencies.

Ian Colley

Counting Blessings

Counting blessings is like counting sheep,
Scattered across hill and mountain steep,
And lost between the peak and trough
Of grasses strewn with boulders rough;
It's hard to spot them when you survey -
What's gone before, but now's far away.
Yet when you see the one who's there,
The one who will your burdens share,
The blessings lost come back into sight
With your darkness turning into light:
Then, with more counting, rest does creep
Upon the mind - and you're asleep.

David Radford

A Blessing To Reminisce

The outside display would attract -
If you hadn't the money, you'd be back!
At Christmas, the intermittent rich-coloured lights
Drew in curious shoppers to its sight.

A sweet old lady sat ready to serve,
Rise to open a glass display at a 45-degree curve.
She would reach the toy the boy spied,
Jumping for joy at its acquisition.

Until before home, regretting the decision
When seeing it break, he cried.
The lady would say, 'Is that all, cock?'
Before she sat with dignity, uncreasing her frock.
The husband smoked a pipe,

Emerging from the back room after lunching on tripe.
'That watch will last you a lifetime!'
He would punctuate to a captivated customer,
Knowing they'd return with its guarantee that tomorrow.

Although quality was not its trademark, its passing
Was like an historical tree felled from its bark.
An era that no longer exists,
A part of a culture that I pleasantly reminisce.

Gone just as the rich-coloured lights with no trace,
That welcome distraction and comforting place.
The sweet old lady and her spouse;
Welcomed in a shop that was their house.

Thomas W O'Connell

Empty Nest

You never lose the ones you love.
Their star burns bright
Through endless hours
Of endless days
And dark corners of the night.
You never lose the ones you love.
Although you are apart.
Through sun and rain,
Wind and clouds.
They still remain in the corners of your heart.

Maureen Reynolds

Apple Tree

She stands, proud, fully clothed,
Our neighbour's apple tree,
Heavenly laden, abundantly red,
Apples plenty, beads on a rosary.

The over-hangs on our fence side
My neighbour says are mine,
Picked as much as you can eat
But please, don't damage, or climb.

The lower bough is weighty bent
Straining from fruit overload,
The sturdy trunk takes the weight
Of apples, stuck like fridge magnet.

The only way to say thank you
And it's only proper and right,
To place upon their charitable table
Fruit from their tree, in desert delight.

This sharing between neighbours is a
Blessing, that more of us ought to do,
The fence that partition our gardens
Does not partition the heart of us two.

Philip A McDonnell

Mural Of The Citadel

I see the piece as a beautiful work of art,
There are tropical fish swimming in turquoise waters,
Beautiful fish made of warm glass,
Glass which breathes day and night,
Pulsing life emitting warmth when cold,
And cool when the days and nights are warm,
Ultramarine-blue and scarlet are the colours,
Also gold of the morning sun and again.
More fish in dusky-pink,
In rose-pink smooth waters.
Several mermaids without tails in clear silvery water,
Looking through it all, is
Our lady star of the sea,
In the bluest of gowns.

Pat Seddon

Where Endless Joy Begins

How quietly rest the distant hills, the meadows sleep as well.
Yon valley hushed and bathed in mist like some enchanted dell,
Where age-old trees await the breeze to rouse them from their sleep,
And whispering hedgerows gently doze whilst sheltering the meek,
In twilight's glow before the dawn lost shadows stray with me,
And colours seem of one soft hue midst subtle shades of green.

As I walk on this peaceful way through fields of moistened grass
My memory calls to those I've loved, no more this way to pass.
Yet those who see as my eyes see will dwell in wishful dreams
To realise that the best in life sparkles in babbling streams.
Rare jewels could scarce enrapture me not gold my love ensnare,
For nature's beauty to behold gives wealth beyond compare.

How smooth and deep the lake far reached does steam 'neath summer sky.
What secrets held in unknown depth reflects to steal my eye?
The squeaky grass beneath my feet is crisp and shooting new,
And shy wild flowers bow their heads whilst bathed in morning dew.
A backward glance reveals a path, a path from whence I came,
Yet no firm path I'd set upon or any well-worn lane.

No living soul to share my way as I walk here alone,
The path behind is clearly mine and leads where're I roam.
A far-off glow shows break of day as night gives way to light,
And white clouds edge their silent way . . . the distant sky turns bright,
Then just like magic comes the sun, its warm beams ease the dawn,
To rise above a fresh new day and charm the early morn.

A bird on wing calls to his mate and waterfowl rejoice,
So thankful to survive the night they rise in raucous voice.
The river gently twists and turns in lasting search for rest,
But chuckles as it makes its way, its waters merely jest.
Such wonders that abound from man 'neath never-ending skies
Are freely born, though easy lost through dull unseeing eyes.

Few care to walk this time of day to walk through dew-washed fields,
Or think awhile and offer praise to Earth and all its yields.
This age has made such fools of them, they grasp not what they see
And notice not the butterfly nor the humble honeybee.
They live their lives from day to day with minds on other things
And spurn the beauty of our Earth where endless joy begins.

Keith Hutchins

As We Live It

Tomorrow for you the sun will shine
An extra ray
So count your blessings
While you may
Take a seat there are thousands more
Tragedy has knocked
Very hard on their door.

We see the sun, the moon and stars
Mixed with our lasting jewels
They are His and ours
Comes the spring
The birds will sing
They have been silent
For so long
They lift our hearts
At the dawn
With their chirpy
Little song.

Daffodils not just wakened yet
To set the world aglow
Their nods are sent
From Him above
To show you and me
How much He loves.

There will come a day
Come what may
When our name is wrote
On that book
We will hug and kiss
Not one we will miss
When we meet on that golden shore.

Elizabeth McIntyre

Don't Despair

In dark days of winter
It's easy to despair
We think we are the only one
Have no one, our woes to share.

Misery is catching
So cheer up and get on
With all that life throws at you
Don't dwell on things long gone.

Take a pen and count your blessings
Think of all the folks you know
Would you change your life for their life?
There are days when they feel low.

Peggy Cummins

Sunrise

Sunrise meets me
Rising sun greets me
Aglow with
Iridescent beauty
Clouds frame
Celestial manifestation
That brightens up
An already
Brilliant sky
Setting the tone
For thanks and praise
Which reply
To the standard
From above

S o with all perception of blessing
U ntil mankind gains peace absolute
N ever looking back to war and strife
R emember for the daily struggles of life
I n solitude and meditation
S ow quietude softly speaking volumes
E ngaging yourself and others in peace.

C D Smith

Count Our Blessings

Blessings come in a myriad of ways
- The beauty of a sea of bluebells -
The smell of new-mown hay,
The taste of freshly-made raspberry jam,
The touch of a welcoming handshake,
The sound of a baby's cry at birth.

As a family, sharing the joys and sorrows that come our way,
With a friend who listens, showing no impatience, silently supportive,
In speech, bringing good news,
Telling stories, creating laughter,
In good health, enjoying the freedom of body, mind and spirit.

So much lies before us waiting to be explored by land or sea or air,
How thankful we must be for many blessings to share.

Daphne Florence Murphy

Never Give Up

Never give up hope
When you find yourself on that slippery slope
You will climb again.

Don't give up your dreams
When in despair it seems hopeless
They can come true.

Be a child again, play make-believe
All your fantasies furiously weave
They will materialise.

You must not believe the road is too long
Someone sometime will help you along
They're just out of view.

Stand tall and be strong
For of this world you do belong
Soon light will shine.

Feel part of the plan
Though you don't truly understand
Guidance will find and comfort.

Sharon Beverly-Ruff

Through The Window Of Life

Look through any window, and what can you see?
Faces lit up with joy, or filled with misery
A baby starts crying, a child out to play
To them it is just another day
Shoppers are busy they rush everywhere
Strangers become friends, who live without care
But some faces tell stories, of their lives through the years
Burdened by worries, shackled by fears
The face at the counter, greets you with a smile
Those warm friendly greetings, you get all the while
Someone says 'Hello', and brings a glow to your heart
Friends who meet up, just don't want to part
The young child still plays happily on a swing
Living without worry of what the future might bring
There are tales of joy, toils, worries and strife
It's amazing what you see, through the window of life.

Dave McFadden

Walking On Waves

Treading an upland path,
With glitter of silvery sand,
Walking on waves of turf
As an ocean of moors expand,
I feel my spirit flying free
In the golden air that caresses me,
With siren sounds of a curlew's cry,
And a singing sky.

Surrounding lonely fells
To infinity stride away,
Where shimmering distance
Blurs earth's rim in heaven's wide array.
Beneath hill flowers at my feet
Hug the ground in a dwarfing breeze, and sweet
Their fragrance rising uplifts the soul,
Beyond fear's control.

Born in this atmosphere
Of light, Bronté sisters spring to mind:
In Pennine wilderness
A childhood paradise we find.
Their passion for this airy place
Pervaded days and dreams, and left its trace
In word and song that ever lives and breathes,
So inner joy bequeaths.

Love alike in summer
With its harebells nodding blue and frail,
Filled their hearts in winter
Months when roars aloud an Arctic gale.
The flowering grass of ice
They knew, kiss of endless frosty air,
Snow's embracing silence
Crystal light reflected everywhere.
What troubles came, what pain oppressed,
In alien fields borne unconfessed,
Steadfast a secret vision lit their dreams:
Hills and shining streams.

Elinor Wilson

Generous

Your heart you gave
To this sad, heartless world
And let it pulsate
With life and joy afresh!
You were so great.

Inside the palace of your heart
We were welcomed and loved,
Taken to a dance!
You were so kind.

The splendour of your heart
Rekindled our passion for life,
Inspired us to recast
Destinies and dreams to realise!
You were so bright.

Again and again
You impressed upon us
Your heart was greater
Than this big world!
It opened its gates
To every soul on Earth!
You were so generous.

May your heart,
Whose compassion knew
No bounds,
All follow and crown
To find how to love
And spread hope and delight!

Let your name outlive time
To always be pronounced
With pride and love
'Queen Diana of Hearts,
Queen of all Hearts.'

Lucy Carrington

For I Am Loved

The sun's rays are warming me through,
glowing darts into my skin,
reaching far into my soul,
and only then can I begin
to feel the longed for, gradual melting
of the icy grief within.
For I am loved.

The rain's softness slakes my thirst
and rehydrates each arid feeling
engendered by my inner drought,
the years of waiting for this healing.
In the desert of my life
by nature's altar I am kneeling.
For I am loved.

The wind cools me with its breath,
it speaks to me of love and losses,
of things that even might have been
but never were, as fortune tosses
sticks and stones along life's path.
My burden's cast, no bearing crosses.
For I am loved.

The clouds which float and drift above
enclose me in their secret dreams,
they take the form I want them to,
a world where nothing's as it seems.
I can join them on their journey,
travelling by whatever means.
For I am loved.

Angela R Davies

Tender Tears

Tender tears fall down a tender face
They dwell, then leave and find a place
Time comes along and heals in space
The sorrow flows away to another place
The young hold hands and comfort each other
Just like sisters and brothers
So when the ice crystals fall and cover the earth
They will melt and join a joyous blue sky
And like tender tears
They will fall from your eyes.

Geoffrey Louch

Count Your Blessings

Count your blessings instead of sheep
To guarantee a good night's sleep
So instead of lying worrying and feeling sad
Think of all the happy times you've had.
The memories will come back to you
Then you'll no longer be feeling blue.
Your worries will not just go away
But as they say 'Tomorrow is another day'.
Who knows what your life really has in store
But worrying won't make it less or more.
It'll only make you more depressed
Whereas you might begin to feel you're blessed.
If you are fit and active and really healthy
Who cares whether you are poor or wealthy?
Enough money to live on is all you really need
Excess of it can be a source of greed.
The 'feel good factor' lies in being content
And on how your life is being spent.
So concentrate on counting your blessings instead
As let's face it . . . you'll be a long time dead!

Mary Anne Scott

Real Value

Life is this side of death
The dividing line is so thin
The closer to the line one is
The more precious are
The small - the little things
A raindrop becomes more important than gold
A new day's dawning more than wealth
Each breath eternity
A newborn cry more than mere hope
A smile - a handshake - a kindly word
Give meaning beyond mere existence
What you receive from such things
You can give to others
And that from the old life - comes new
In gratitude give thanks and praise
And know the value of life.

Clive Cornwall

Not Jesus

Jesus he is not
A once great man
Lying on a doorstep of benevolence
Looking for a miracle
Finding little sacrifice
Warmed only by thoughts of his past
Resting against his world
Lost in a life that never was.

Prayer and forgiveness
His only similarity, other than his beard
Disciples, gone, run far from here
Unable to partake in any further contact
Eating daily, his last supper
Drinking from that same cup
Filled but never brimming
Cheap wine, irrelevant but necessary.

Abandoned by all who once believed
Only the brave now come calling
Irregular with visits that last but moments
Feeling uncomfortable inside the gaze of a dropout
Preferring to hide behind their lap of luxury
Limiting contact for fear of embarrassment
Finding many excuses to remain aloof
Monsters that once were true friends.

Slumped by the cross at the end of his journey
Nailed to streets that have become so cruel
Asking his Lord for an end to this madness
Receiving little, taking less
Certain that some place an angel lurks
Ready and willing to end this misery
Staring death in its all out glory
An inevitability that will bring well-earned peace.

Alan Zoltie

I Need . . .

I need to wait
I need to wait and see.

I need to stop.
I need to stop and think.

I need to sit.
I need to sit and be.

I need to be.
I need to be just me.

Clare Todd

The Child

Not long ago, one rainy morn,
The most perfect child ever came to be born.
She arrived in the world all whole and complete,
From her downy head to her tiny feet.
With the bluest of eyes, and not much of a nose,
And half-inch thumbs, and sugar-pink toes.
With tiny dimples, and a soft peachy skin,
Such a wonder we scarce knew where to begin!
From her father and mother there were tears of great joy,
And an ecstatic big sister - glad she wasn't a boy!
But the real miracle is God's wonderful plan,
That's been in operation since Creation began . . .
That somewhere in His world, every day, dusk or dawn,
The most perfect child . . . ever . . . still waits to be born!

G J Outhwaite

Sunset

This is the time of day that I love best -
This hour of stillness, when the sun
Has vanished from the west,
Leaving behind a clear, untroubled sky.
Blazing red is lost in purpling haze
Along the Earth's far rim
And palely glow the dying primrose rays
Beneath the zenith's deepening blue.

Trees stand black and stark
By the still water's edge,
Each branch and twig a stark
Reflection by the sedge.
Waterfowl float lazily to rest
And over all, a crescent gleams afar -
In all the darkening sky
A crescent and the glorious evening star.

Norah Jarvis

Monday - January

My mind pushes upwards away from sleep
The north wind blows, I open one eye
Still dark the day, sun disinclined to shine,
I have the same feeling - so why should I?

I sleep and hide myself in dreams
For I am caressed in sheets of peach
They are my compensation
Which daylight memories cannot reach.

My peach sheets have a gentleness of touch
I look forward to the end of the day
I sink with joy between them
Is that such a sin I pray?

Barbara Robson

Flowers

In my garden I spend many long summer hours
Being amongst most of my favourite flowers,
Like lupins and foxgloves, delphiniums tall,
Asters, French marigolds, mesemphryiums small.

There's a quilt of begonias covers the floor,
Red roses in bloom by the cottage front door,
Forget-me-nots bend from the weight of queen bee,
On the trellis entangled the fragrant sweet pea.

By the white painted gate hollyhocks grow,
In clay chimney pots trailing fuchsias hang low,
Buzy Lizzie and pansy make the borders so bright,
Not forgetting the dahlia, the gardener's delight.

On the dyke of hawthorn the wild roses peek through,
The night-scented air comes from lavender blue,
At the end of each day it's so joyful to be,
In my worn-out old chair with the sunset to see.

Leslie Hogarth

She dips as she flies
That carefree, elegant form

She knows, you know
That the dawn of spring is due

Her plume, her feathers new
Are showy, embraced by morning dew

She dips, as she speedily flies away
But will return to settle at close of day!

Alline Yap-Morris

A Nurse Abroad

(Dedicated to 'Auntie Ruby')

The mirror showed a reflection
Of a woman in her prime
Thirty years behind her
Knowledge in her eyes.

She'd seen the world
Travelled far and wide
Had cried with joy
Celebrated life.

Mourned lost friends
Cried with grief
Known love and hate
Been a rock.

Sun-bleached hair
Framed her face
An image
Of compassion.

She'd found faith
When it was lost
Had given hope
When there was none.

Asked for nothing
In return
To have been there
Was enough.

Felt proud
Was humbled
To be honoured
In this way.

A touch of lipstick
A nervous smile
Her thoughts collected
She was ready.

'We are gathered
Here today
To reward
A dear friend,
For her loyalty
And humanity
Through war
And in famine,
My ladies
And gentlemen
I give you
A remarkable woman.'

Jan Hedger

Nostalgia

The weather's nice today my dear,
come lift your eyes, come wipe your tears.
No time to mourn the sighs of past,
bequeath the lark to sing at last.
Let your sprit touch the sky
raise up your wings and flutter high.
Colours of the world shall shine,
flowers at your feet are thine.

The grass so green upon the hill
with daffodils and falling bells.
Blue are they in summer sun,
I cannot count them one by one.
For if I do my eyes would see
so many cowslips mingling free.

The weather's nice today my dear,
come hold the hand who follows near.
Today come live upon a throne,
reach out your heart to Heaven's home.
Pleasant pastures come with age,
old windmills turn of loves assuage.
'Tis often I would see you smile
if now for only just a while.
Angry were the years I know
where leopards hid beneath the snow.
How lambs they bleat in pastures new,
they bleat of love so young and true.

Nostalgic of the thinking years
remembering such in childhood tears.
Running through the knee-high wild
campions flower, and poppy's child.
Countless prims and cuckoo flower
buttercup play in timeless hour.
Where violets basked in proud esteem
beside the chattering old mill stream.
Comfort then my stolen child,
be comforted, be reconciled.
Come feel the soft and fresh wind blow,
lift up your heart, your gentle soul,
I am of old and ever new,
I come, I wait in thoughts of you.

Michael Massey

The Valley Of Time

We're here but for a while,
To dance, to sing, to love in style.
To worship life and walk the mile
Upon life's road with sheer abandonment,
Surrendered hearts to suffering and enjoyment.

A baby born, a newling at the start,
With open eyes and open heart.
No boundaries, no barriers apart.
She is the world, the world is her.
No evil, good, no power.

Sweet child now as you yearn
To find out more, so much to learn.
This is your life, this is your turn
To touch the light, the stars, the moon,
Th' eternal sky. The world's in tune.

And as you dance this greatest symphony,
From Heaven to Earth now flows the energy.
Your earthly body tasting Eternity.
This planetarium valley of hourly time
Is but a part of life, a taste of bread and wine.

We build a wall, defend the woundedness inside.
We think we're safe, and we can hide
That deepest part, our essence opened wide . . .
Your healing water gushes like a river
Over this war-torn, broken heart . . . I shiver . . .

The fire's out, the phoenix is in flight
And leaves behind the darkness of the night,
Faces the sunshine and the light
Of truth and peace within, integrity,
Heaven and Earth in harmony . . .

Olga Allen

Healthy And Happy

The start of a new year,
The time to reflect:
We make resolutions,
What's right to do next.
But when we grow old,
We're inclined to look back
And relive life's journey,
The joys and the flack.
We've brought up our children,
For them, done our best,
We're healthy and happy,
We surely are blessed!

Corinne Lovell

Marvels For Free

Little things can brighten my days
Lift my heart in many ways.
Waving green of growing corn
Opal sky of glorious dawn.
Lilting voice of happy child
Crash and roar of waves so wild.
Tempting smell of new-baked bread
Book I snugly read in bed.
Spiders' webs and butterflies
Christmas carols, hot mince pies.
Sky at sunset glowing bright
Stars and moon on clearest night.
Clean, fresh washing on the line
Blown in shapes that dry it fine.
Rippling river, sparkling light
Rhythmic beat of ducks in flight.
Pristine snow on winter morn
Glistening diamond frost on lawn.
Puffy clouds in sky so blue
Flowers of earth with myriad hue.
Shades of green in early spring
Dart of swallow on the wing.
Fairy lights on Christmas trees
Busy drone of summer bees.
Lavender, violets, shells and sands
Babies' smiles and tiny hands.
Gentle stream and dipping willows
Open fires and cosy pillows.
All for free and good to know,
Cheer me when I'm feeling low.

Dorothy Leggett

The Weavers

(Dedicated to Jimmy Mahaffy and family)

The weavers had died
And the snow began to fall,
They had said earlier,
'You know, as little girls,
We played marbles
At Dichling, Sussex,
The roundabout and moved
If the horses came: then we
Moved back when they had gone,'
The weavers said, before they died,
And the snow began to fall.

Edmund Saint George Mooney

Mother

Of all the precious words I know there'll never be another
That can compare with a gift of God. A lady known as Mother
Throughout your life when things get rough she'll wipe away your tears
And brighten up your darkest time and soothe those petty fears

If a mother sometimes gets upset and talks to you quite stern
It's because she's teaching you respect for the rules we all must learn
The greatest gift to give her is truth and honesty
To know her child has grown up right will fill her full of glee

As the years roll by she ages and gets a little slower
And the jobs she'll do take longer now for she hasn't got the power
But she proudly goes about her chores content in her company
A jewel in any angel's crown a living symphony

So always think about her love and want she did for you
Make sure she knows she's in your heart and you adore her too
Because that lady is unique you haven't got another
To you she is the queen of souls the saint that's known as Mother

Ray Moore

Count Your Blessings

Count your blessings *one* by *one*
The new year has begun
The old one is laid to rest
Christmas is over, with all the hassle
To prepare, to care for family and friends
So lovely to see them all gathered around the tree
Happy faces of the children full of anticipation
Now the school year has begun and the work for future times
To get good exam results for self-esteem
And make the parents proud
They all have been through it in their time and tried their best
Every day has brought a blessing
Managing something better than yesterday
The future is waiting
And our efforts will be rewarded
Not with a lottery prize
But the knowledge of work - *well done!*

Gusty Cotterell

Lift Up Your Hearts

Some people find the sunshine
  Some people find the rain
Some people find the laughter
  Some people find the pain

Some seek their lot
  Their quest is far and wide
Fools, their quest for fortune lies close by
  Fools, they see it not

Your favourite music fills the air
  Your favourite pie fresh-baked
What treasures lie midst home and garden
  Aye, your happiness 'ere saked

The wise man sees these treasures around
  Enchanted by the birds in the trees
He sees the birds as they build their nests
  Lift up your hearts, 'tis the end of your quest.

John Morrison

Contentment

If your pains are few and problems small
And it seems you have no worries at all,
If you're not bombed, or starved, or shot,
Be satisfied with what you've got.
Don't let a puddle become a lake.
Don't ask for more when you've had your cake.
Accept that when you've had your share,
To ask for more just isn't fair.
Don't be blinded by your own greed.
Be conscious of another's need.
Discontent makes worse your lot,
So be at peace with what you've got.
Concentrate on your life's best
And let the Devil take the rest.

R L Cooper

Eternal Spring

In the depths of winter, when nature is dead
I may long for the spring to arrive
And when everything's stale and my energies fail
I yearn to be fully alive.
And I see:
I must pin my faith in the living God
Since He pins His faith in me.

But the winter is long and I can't see the end
Till the leaves and the snowdrops break through.
Then I very well know, that though progress is slow,
A reward for my labour is due.
And I see:
I must fix my hope on the Son of God
For He fixes His hope in me.

When the spring has come and all nature expands,
Re-creation's an ongoing thing.
Though sometimes it's tough and the going is rough,
Life in Christ is perpetual spring.
And I see:
I must cherish my love for the Holy Ghost,
For He cherishes life in me.

Simon Peterson

My Home

I picture my home
With my mum and dad.

I picture my home
With all the things we had.

I picture my home
Filled with fun and laughter.

I picture my home
With us all going to and fro.

I picture my home
As we children leave one by one.

I picture my home
With only my mum left.

Now she has gone
That home is no longer ours.

Our family home has gone
But we will always hold on to
Those precious and happy memories.

Gwendoline Woodland

I Feel That I Am Blessed

The brilliant morning sunlight
Streams into my room,
Lifting my heart in
The hope of a fair day.
I think of blind people
Who cannot see the morning sunrise
And feel that I am blessed.

My wretched pain seems lighter
I am urged to move
A bit quicker now.
My young grandson arrives
Pokes his head round the door.
His cheeky grin is
The encouragement I need,
A surge of spirit is felt,
I feel that I am blessed.
So many people worse off than me,
I feel that I am blessed.

Gladys Llewellyn

Pennies From Heaven

Each little penny you save,
Is a blessing in disguise.
Ablaze, an orange streaky sunset at dusk,
Charcoal branches, resplendent they stand.
  The gift of sight.

Each and every sound you hear,
Is a blessing in disguise.
Blackbirds merrily sing a chorus each night,
Whilst a woodpecker drums monotonously.
  The gift of sound.

Femininity, a favourite perfume,
Is a blessing in disguise.
Roses, honeysuckle, thyme, fragrance divine,
Smouldering bonfires, sweet mown grass.
  The gift of smell.

Home from school, into the kitchen you dash,
Mum's roly-poly with treacle galore.
Toasted crumpets for supper each Saturday night,
Wagon Wheels, chocolates, just one more.
  The gift of taste.

Diana Frewin

Contentment

I take pleasure in the simple things:
In buttercups and swallows' wings;
In meadow rivulets dimpling by;
And floating cloudlets in the sky;
In crunching leaves and gathered sheaves;
And starlings nesting in the eaves;
A baby smiling its first smile;
And lovers meeting at the style.
Dewdrops nestling in the clover;
The setting sun when day is over;
The dancing flames of a pine-log fire;
Christmas hymns from the cathedral choir;
The hand-clasp of a loving friend;
And toasted crumpets at a journey's end;
The scent of apples, fresh from the tree;
And the sound, in the lock, of my husband's key.

Beryl Wicker

Time Marches On!

Once I was young
Once I was bold
But now I fear
I'm growing old
It's strange 'inside'
One feels the same
A girlish giggle
I still claim.
A sense of humour
Not lost that
Nor have I lost
My superfluous fat!
Can't do press-ups
Stand on my head
But I still sleep
In my own bed.
I cannot *run*
Past house or flat
But I still can walk
Thank God for that.

Esther Hawkins

Memories

The plaintive cry of a seagull
Across a lonely beach
Reminds us of a loved one
Far away and out of reach.
But if we take the time to sit
And close our eyes 'twould seem
That loved one can be nearer
Than we could ever dream.
For all our thoughts and memories
Are special in their way
And as long as we remember them
They'll never go away.
For those we love, who love us too
Will never be apart.
Love is strong and so they'll be
Forever in our hearts.
True love makes the world go round
And even when they're gone
A love so steady, strong and true
Forever will live on.

Ruth Smith

We Lose The Way

Inexplicable, we oft-times 'lose the way'
Whence transpires this shadowy world of grey?
Read a newspaper, matters very sad
Humour too though, things not so bad
Oh! Here's a Van Gogh print 'freebie page'
Fit an ornamental frame, I have, I gauge
An 'Eilleen Donan Castle' print in twin frame I own
Grand, now it will not, in state, hang alone
The castle of true legend, strangely photographs dark any light!
The Van Gogh, painted by a tortured soul, wonderfully bright
I gaze at the pair on the wall, side by side
Realisation as in castle dark I abide
Whether sunshine, rain or snow, I may venture out
Human life's weathered climes vary, no doubt
With faith, I must count my blessings, accept that range
Existing grey darkness, creativity brightens, thus ever to change!

C Harkness

Guardian Angel

(A memorial to my husband, Bill, who died 22nd May 2006)

An angel stood beside me
And was with me every day,
Though cares caused me to stumble,
Made me fall along the way.
I knew my angel was standing there,
My rock, my one true friend,
He was my past, my future,
My beginning and my end.

My angel had no halo
And there wasn't a wing in sight,
There was no harp.
He couldn't sing, nor had the power of flight,
Just two strong arms to hold me
When the going got too tough
And the loving words he told me
When I had had enough.

He was my whole, my everything,
I was glad he was on my side,
My happiness was made complete
When I became his bride.
And loving him as I do
I tell him every day
And count my blessings
One by one, forever and a day.

My angel's no longer here
But his spirit is around
In the million memories
By which our love is bound.

Mary Elizabeth Wigan

Count Our Blessings

Many languages are spoken in this world of ours
Some harsh, like stormy winds, some like soft April showers
Another year has come and gone
And yet we never speak as one
Love comes in, sometimes like a thunderstorm
Other times like the breaking of the dawn
Our lifespan maybe months or years
Sometime finishing with joy, maybe tears
We hope we have brought laughter to many lives
To young children, relatives, husbands, wives
Counting hours, minutes, seconds, means not a lot
Be content with the life that you have got.

Trevor Beach

A Thank-Offering

Do you ever think, while sitting in the comfort of your home,
That, without a doubt, you're rich beyond compare?
Not with wealth that comes from money,
Nor the things that money buys,
But just because the folk around you care.

Do you really see the value of those friendships strong and true
Which are always there and ready to respond?
Which share times of hearty laughter,
Or those moments full of tears,
When the sharing of emotion is the bond.

Do you ever spend a moment thinking of how your life might be
If all those around you didn't give a toss?
And were not prepared to rally round,
Or give a helping hand -
For that is when you'd really know the loss.

So if ever you are sitting in the comfort of your home
And you're tempted to think things have gone awry,
Just pause - and think how rich you are
With love and folk all round -
And then give your praise and thanks to God on high.

And if you really mean that praise and thanks to God on high,
There are ways to show you do, without a doubt.
Don't forget that there are others
Who might need *your* helping hand -
That's what 'love thy neighbour' is really all about.

Angus W MacDonald

Dreams

I sit alone each night and dream
Of all the places that I have seen,
We both enjoyed our wanderings,
Now I am left with such sweet dreams.
I love the long cold winter nights
When the bright embers glow
And the stars shine bright.
So warm and cosy and free from harm
Memories flood back to help keep me warm,
Remembrances of days long gone,
Now that I travel on alone.

Marjorie D Poyner

Our Blessings

I count my blessings every day that God does give to me
The great spirit in every way lives inside of thee.
The air we breathe, the grass so green
The trees that gently sway,
A whisper from the wind, that blows a secret some may say.

The beauty of the Earth, so full of creatures far and wide
The seas, the sky, the cosmos, the picture in our eyes.
The window of the soul, they say, is there for all to see
The energy that pumps our blood, the force that moves in me.

I count my blessings every day, the love from family, the warmth
The peace, the smiles and joy, so great an ancestry.

As night and day pass by so quick and seasons come and go
If only we could learn to live in peace, so love can grow.
With so much pain and sorrow here, all caused my mankind's greed
To reap the seeds that we do sow - a very deadly deed.

Wake up soon the spirit cries and stop your selfish ways
Bring out the light and love inside or soon be end of days.
Stop the pain and suffering,
The wars, the rape, the greed, let's have balance with our lives
And Mother Nature's needs.
Soon our blessings may turn back and bite us all real hard
A lesson we would not forget - just tears of sadness - deep regret.

So stop right now
It's time to act
It starts with you and me
To be the gentle spirit, to set creation free
To count our blessings every day
Have peace and harmony, for we are brothers underneath -
The human family.

Let's learn again a simple life, that only meets our needs
Not our wants or wasteful lives, our gluttonous, evil greed
For at the end, it matters not what wealth you may acquire
'Tis not what you have, but what you are, that we should aspire.

Chris Bampton

One Thing Leads To Another

Birds, bees, dogs, cats, even filthy rats,
Mountains, rivers, valleys, horse 'n' trap,
One's mind, let's focus on a gnat,
Vast blue oceans, mighty trees alive with sap.

Ships that travel the seas, everyone aboard,
Football matches, the winter score,
Beautiful clad ladies, bikini bodies adorned,
Bands, their fans will cheer, then abort.

Singers, actors, talents bonding on stage,
Silly uniforms, gaudy colours a rage,
Running here, running there, laughter to page,
To make audiences laugh the visage.

Thinking about these subjects for poems,
Letting word and verse roam,
This can be done anywhere, even from home,
At times, a subject will cause despair and moan.

Look at your poems, they will inspire,
A song will come when required,
Love song, waltz, tango, ballad, so desired,
'Bristol' studios produces your songs, so desired.

A dot of dust will turn into a song, if required,
Thirty-four songs I have required.

Derrick Charles Anthony Bright

Keeping On Top

No one on the groove
Maybe I ought to move
Mmm, not much love
Flight of the dove
Better off safe up above
Just give the badness a shove
Catch a bus you drove
A walk in an evergreen grove
Children, a treasure trove
Dancing in the cove
Barbecues on the charcoal stove
Hooray, let's be love in a glove
Fit as a fiddle in middle - like in mauve.

Hardeep Singh Leader

Maypole Dancing For A Queen

When I was young and at our school
We had a 'Rose Queen Day'
Only for the youngest girls and just a few young boys
Mothers made our costumes
And came to see our 'Queen'
Who sat upon her flower throne
With 'Rosebud Maids of Honour'
Who held her rosy velvet train
We also had a Maypole
With ribbons gold and green
Dancing round it, in and out
We plaited all the ribbons
And made such a pretty pole
The best you'd ever seen
A memory to hold good fast
When you are old and youth is past!

M M Sleeboom-Derbyshire

My Happiness

Happiness is a sky of blue
The tide ebbing in and out
The stillness of a wood
The ripple of a stream
A golden cornfield
The smell of roses in the summer air
The freshness of everything
After an April shower
Glistening snow over all
Bright sunshine streaming thro' a window
The touch of a hand when I feel low
Moon-glow over the sea
The glow of embers in the grate
The patter of rain on a roof
Finishing a crossword puzzle
And the beaming smile of a loved one, when meeting.

Wendy Andrews Nevard

The Path

There once was a path
I thought would lead me
Through this life
Without trouble, without pain
But I was wrong.
I could never have seen
The storm which struck without warning
Throwing me into chaos
Devastation everywhere
Lost was the path
I was happy to walk.
Through the night I stumbled
Trying to find my way
Not truly knowing where I was going
Until I stumbled from the storm
To the clear skies
I thought I would never see again
And a path to follow once more
A new journey for me to take
A new start, a new way
With discoveries new and dreams of old
And a chance to follow my heart's desire.

Oliver L T Waterer

Ballad Of A Lonely Man

Missed that little house, the smell of the sea,
The feel of your lips roving over me,
So I've left the path that dreamers roam,
I'm a lonely man returning home.

With the weather wet from new-falling snow
And the waves crashing round the rocks below,
I see your face in the soft white foam,
I'm a lonely man returning home.

Love the hills and highways over the land,
But not as much as the touch of your hand,
Seeking silver, I found only chrome,
I'm a lonely man returning home.

Down the path I run to an open door,
A fool who's been looking for something more,
I wanted to fly, wanted to roam,
When all I needed was here at home.

Gerald Hampshire

The Best Things In Life Are Really Free

Seeing rainbows in the heavens
Watching moonlight on a stream
Hearing little children laughing
Life is such a lovely dream.

Stroking shiny, soft fair ringlets
Holding tight a baby's hand
Dimpled fingers fast enclasping -
Or sinking toes in silky sand!

Listening to a cuckoo calling
In the still of April air
Breathing in the springtime's freshness
As new blossoms reappear.

Standing on a lonely cliff top
As the sun sinks in the west
Skies of gold and red enfolding
Could any sight be much more blessed?

Walking 'neath a starlit Heaven
On a frosty moonlit night
A shooting star flies high above us
What a breathless, rapturous sight.

If we would only look and wonder
At the beauteous things we see
We would know each day and moment
The best things in life are really free!

Mollie D Earl

Free

The day I saw a butterfly
I felt uplifted, free,
Because I knew so clearly
It held a message for me.

When flying high, it showed serene
A forward path to take,
The journey took me upwards
And I was more awake.

Then surely I could fly with thee
My spirits soared so high,
Both peace and calm reigned over me
When I saw a butterfly.

Linda Kettle

Live And Learn

Why should I bother to get out of bed
To swallow a pill, to ease the pain in my head?
Why should I bother to wash my hair and face
When I look so ugly and feel out of place?
Why should I bother to eat and drink
When depression is making it hard just to think?

Why should I bother to read or write
When in my black world there can never be light?
Why should I bother to quit drinking, just stop
When I feel like a dirty, rung-out old mop?
Why should I bother to give to the needy
When everyone else is so selfish and greedy?
Why should I bother to be loving and caring
When my heart feels like it's splitting and tearing?
Why should I bother to pretend that I'm sane
When my body is exhausted from mind-numbing pain?

The answer to this is simple but true
So listen and hear to what you have to do.
You must carry on living each day in turn
To struggle and suffer in order to learn.
To learn all you can and teach all you know
So, with knowledge and wisdom, you'll spiritually grow.

Carrie-Ann Hammond

Dainty Butterfly

Butterfly, in gardens, woodlands and meadows you pass,
In summer's looking glass,
You flutter so daintily in flight,
As the warm sun reflects its light,
You dance on air
In each day that's so bright and fair,
You love the colourful, sweet-scented flowers,
Red, blue, white, orange and pink,
From puddles you love to drink,
You flutter in summer's comfort zone,
Your home, sweet home,
You flutter with the dragonfly, your relation,
Such a happy occasion,
Summer's breeze guides you along the way,
In each perfect day.

Joanna Maria John

Friends

What would we do without our friends
To help us along life's way?
Or, if we had no friendly acquaintances
With which to share our day?

Friends are people who lend a hand
When and if, they are needed.
It's a comforting thought, just to know they are there
It's so nice to be befriended.

You may have a lifelong friendship
With the people who live next door.
Or you may have a pet, which is also a friend,
You can take for a walk and meet more.

If we have any worries and need some help,
They are there, with friendly assistance.
They do not press their presence upon one,
But it's a boon to have their thoughtfulness.

We count our blessings when we have friends like this,
Life without friendship is nothing.
Just to know that you are not alone in the world
And their companionship is worth everything.

Judith Herrington

The Spark Within

Count our blessings, that's not hard,
Let's open wide our eyes;
Let's listen to our memories
And that can cause surprise . . .
Maybe our dreams did not come true -
A blessing in disguise?

Our joy is love that we receive
And love that we can give.
There's beauty in this world of ours,
Don't grab, accept, let live!
Life's never trapped within a net,
Praising, we're in the flow,
Creative, joyful, full of fun,
The spark within aglow.

Peter Spurgin

Happy Days

In this happy winter of my days
Happy in so many ways;
Each morn I give thanks and praise
To the Guardian of my days.

For music daily in my home,
For books, both fact and fiction,
Even though I live alone,
Each day's benediction.

The old folks' bus comes to my door
To take me shopping to the store.
Then so much beauty do I see;
Displays of flowers and many a tree.

From memories, eighty years and more
Many memories could be told
And how old hurts which make me sore
Transmuted are to gold.

For family, cousins and friends
And the friends on whom I call
Jesus, best friend of all.
With praise each day begins;
With my thanks each day ends.

Frances Joan Tucker

What If?

What if Eden never happened?
What if Noah never sailed?
What if Wise Men never travelled?
What if Calvary wasn't scaled?
What if the Red Sea never parted?
What if Jericho remained?
What if Sodom and Gomorrah wasn't all that it was claimed?
What if there were no disciples?
What if teachings were not taught?
What if Judas kept his silence?
What if Jesus wasn't caught?
What if Abraham was weaker?
What if his people were not free?
This world, my friend, would be much bleaker,
Then where, *in Hell,* would we all be?

J C Redmond

Little Miss Wonderful

Someone special changed our ways
To brighten up these winter days
Her name is Indiana, what a little treasure
Always with a cheeky smile to see her is a pleasure.

She has three cats and pulls them by their tails
But they don't mind, they run and hide
Behind the chairs and up the stairs
It's always seek and find.

And now she's had her walking shoes
She takes me by the hand
Then points her fingers to the park
Come on Grandad, you understand.

High on the swings
Then down the slide
She smiles and sings and shouts,
Grandad, come on, next it's the roundabout.

Now it's time to head for home
What a laugh we've had
Your mum has had a rest today
But great to see you back.

Now it's nearly four you see
It's Indiana's time for tea
Come on Mam, what have you got?
I'm ready now to eat the lot.

T B Rees

Rotten Corner

(The Spinney)

Today I walked through Rotten Corner
And listened for the Drumming bird.
But alas! He doesn't drum today.

From a nearby Alder, a tiny wren scolds
Me roundly and all around the glade is
Avian song.

Then, *tchick! tchick!* above me on a
Towering beech he sits, in liveried black
And white, with dash of red upon his head.

I withhold my breath, but in just a heartbeat
He has flown and all around the glade is
Avian song.

Today I leave Rotten Corner content, for
In a lofty tree, I spied that elusive
Drumming bird.

Michael Brooks

Coffee Cake For Christmas 2006

Formal logic, metaphysics
Even theology complicate
A pelican in the
Secular Christmas desert.
The philosophical
'It'
Cold depression
This Christmas
Simply blew my brains out.

Angels and saints
Cribs without the baby
Child Freya kiss, kiss, kiss
Everywhere I went
Epiphany of small, medium
And large cribs
Sometimes in unlikely places.

Christ birth is not mere means
Redemption is the 'Ens'.
We frequently get Christmas
Psychologically very wrong,
When we do, or as many,
Wish the season over.
Jesus makes smiles
And thanks
As when Tracy made,
Better than famed Nigella
A coffee cake for me.

Paul Faulkner

Wedding Day Thoughts

From birth to adulthood
We've watched her grow
To independence which we know
Helped her choose the man she would
Want to marry.

We remember our own far-off day
Sacred vows together sworn
A bright, but chilly, Easter morn
New plans and hopes pointing the way
Marriage began.

And life's cycle continues onward
In time they too recall their vow
Reflecting much as we do now
But also, like us, looking forward
With happiness and thanks.

Gerard Chamberlain

The Church Picnic

One family, a day to share.
Children laughing in the rain
For them no thoughts of loss or gain
Just happiness, because they dare.
Warmed with love, confidence and worth
Do they glimpse Heaven here on Earth?

Flowers delicate and rare, God's gift,
For us to protect and share.
Creation is an ever-turning circle,
A continuing miracle of birth,
That keeps on showing us,
Heaven here on Earth.

We walked the lanes together
Then ate and drank and sang our praise.
The cold and rain could not deter
Heaven here on Earth for us today.

For all our days!

Marlene Meilak

Elevated In Worship

I came apart to rest awhile
My body to restore:
To daydream, read and write
By Ards' sunny shore.

My spirit was expectant
But no inspiration came:
So I began to worship,
Praise and ponder Jesus' name.

The miracle began as I let go
Of worry and much fear:
Just as mist and rain had passed,
Inviting sunlit sky and clear.

A stillness touched my soul:
I was on holy ground:
I knew all would be well,
God's provision would abound.

I didn't ask for anything
Tho' my list acute and long:
I simply praised and worshipped,
Now I'm leaving with a song.
Hallelujah!

Shirley Hay

Give And You Will Receive

For every pot, there is a cover,
For every thought, that offers strength,
For every hand, held out in comfort,
There is another, needing you.

For every word, you speak in kindness,
For every deed, you do with love,
For every day, you spend by helping,
For every time, you feel - enough!

There is a person, needing comfort.
There is a person, needing you!
And all the good things, you have offered,
Will hundredfold come back to you.

Then all your clouds find silver linings
And all your troubles will look small;
For in this troubled world of ours
Is still sufficient love for all.

If you are sad, then share your sadness,
Let others help to bring back joy
And see the smile on all those faces.
Be like a child with a new toy.

Take every day, as it is offered.
Give it your all, give it your best
And at the end, you will be able
To find the strength for all the rest.

I wish you joy and love and laughter,
Be it today, or times gone by,
That hold the happiness you're after,
Cheer up and smile - forget to cry.

Helga Dharmpaul

Today

Pull back the shades of night
Embrace the rays of dawning.
Wake to the song of light
Carolling the morning.
Yours is the nascent day
A canvas beyond measure.
Paint the moments richly
With memories to treasure.
Walk down changing years
The future has yet to be.
Take the present in your hand
And let your life run free.

Shirley Johnson

Redeemed

Mine is just a simple faith
It comes from deep within
Because my Saviour died for me
To save my soul from sin
We read within God's Holy Book
How Jesus shed His blood
And upon the Cross at Calvary
He suffered to set me free
Oh, wonderful Redeemer
Help us with the news to tell
How You sacrificed Your life
To save our souls from Hell
We only have to ask our Lord
To lead us day by day
For He promised to be with us
Each step along the way.

Martha Mynott

These Blessings

These blessings, these hallowed benedictions,
Are always desired but ever elusive
And never come at our bidding,
Not for all our frantic searching.

Peering down the muddy road ahead,
Our eyes strain for glory and recognition,
But the way ahead remains empty
And the trees are leafless and stark.

Looking across at the fields,
Soggy with waterlogged grey sheep,
We wonder if blessings are still possible,
Or are they hibernating indefinitely?

Yet when we have forgotten about grace
And stopped asking at all for gifts
And even suspended longing,
Arriving at rueful acceptance.

Then suddenly, magically, out of nowhere
These blessings will leap out before us,
Streaming down the mountainside,
Cascading like a rainbow waterfall.

Suffusing our hearts unexpectedly
With an amazing joy.

Carol Ross

My Angel Loves Me

My angel loves me, Jesus
I can't believe it
I believe my angel loves me
My angel loves me, how exciting is that?
My angel never sleeps
My angel is with me twenty-four hours a day
Is with me for this lifetime and the rest
Has been with me in my lifetimes previous.
You have never turned away from me
When I have turned my back on you.
You have picked me up when I have been pushed down
You catch me when I fall
You protect me from any harm
You mend my broken heart and soul
You cushion my blows in life.
When I am afraid, grieving or unhappy
You surround me in calm, peace and love
You guide me with knowledge, wisdom and insight
Bathe me in God's light.
You glow in and around me with pure light
You show me visions
You take me to Heaven every night
Let me meet with my spirit family.
You were assigned to me at birth
To be with me throughout my lifetime
Through my physical death and into Heaven
To assist me through my life's review
To show me the rights and wrongs
Of my actions, to others
Universe and spirituality.

Jenifer Ellen Austin

Happy Hello

(For Stuart)

Approaching your home today both your hands waved a happy 'Hello',
This demonstration meant more than you could ever know,
Although the warmth I felt I didn't show,
Yet days later I still feel an inner glow.

Such a wonderful sight to see
And to feel that it was just for me,
I was as happy as can be,
When later we sat drinking a cup of tea.

Julie Marie Laura Shearing

Love's Outlook

Just to say those magic words, 'I love you'
The smile in your eyes, the clasp of your hand
The river in my heart overflowing
My darling, I know you understand
The look you gave me in passing
Where I go, what I say and do
Thoughts of our companionship together
I can tell I am one and you are you
Nothing can part our joining together
Death cannot part the words I say
Age cannot lessen, we are one forever
We'll enjoy ourselves, my dearest, for today
You are not far away
Where the ebbing, flowing waters play.

George Camp

'Oh!' Of Wonder

'Oh!' of wonder; 'Ah!' of awe;
Emotions never voiced before.
Tears of happiness are shed
Kneeling tender by the bed.

Picture, music, other art,
Never ever could such heart
Depict, as in this moment where
Man is introduced to heir.

Thus are strong men brought to know
What women intuited long ago.
Life and love are greater than
Macho status of a man.

Spirit quelled and manner mild,
Impact of this newborn child.
Moment when a woman can
Pierce the armour of a man.

Beauty in this creature glows:
Shining eyes and tiny nose,
Little finger, minute nail.
Not one falsely wrought detail.

'Oh!' of wonder; 'Ah!' of awe;
Emotions never voiced before.
Tears of happiness are shed
Kneeling tender by the bed.

Bernard Newton

Love - The World's Light

Those whom love does not choose
Seem not to hear the call
To the true happiness
Some of us still recall -
They turn to poetry
Where they too then see -
Flashes of lightning -
Feel passionate love -
Unquenchable thirst -
But, love, unlike verse
Knows no ending.

Love is constant song
E'en from bleeding wound
With a smiling mouth
For a lost loved one -
Shedding light in heart -
A light which once found
Is to eternity bound -
For love is the will
And purpose of God -
  In Man!
Poetry is just -
The background music!

Daphne Young

Compensations

Our lives are just a mixture of happiness and pain,
We have to face whatever comes and learn to smile again.
When we were devastated by the foolishness of war,
We had to pick the pieces up and go on as before.
My blessings were three little ones, who'd lost a loving dad,
They had to be cared for and not see me looking sad.
I always knew the Lord above was watching us with care
And when my darling daughter died, I knew that He was there.
I found another soulmate and had fifteen happy years,
A loving compensation for the former scalding tears.
But that was many years ago and I'm now ninety-four,
With lots of 'little' blessings from the ones that I once bore.
We have to face the sadness and we have to feel the pain,
So we can count our blessings when all comes right again.

Margaret Violet Hodgson

Memories Are Safe

There is no drowning
In this sea of sorrow; no,
It is a flowing from happiness of being
To something other,
Unsought perhaps,
But full of other mysteries.
It is a different sea
From that of a happy union,
But the unseen presence
Is the same, if we did but know it.
Memories of those we love
Are safe from violation,
Under the lock and key of our hearts.

Oh, why are we so dependent
On eyes and ears and touch,
When deeper sense could show us
That we are not alone?

Margaret Sparshott

Time For Rachel

(Aged four)

At the bottom of the stairs
In the corner shadows,
There is a clock
Which takes the minutes
As they pass and turns
The spun glass of Time
Into life's hours.
The chimes, familiar and sweet,
Are warm and comforting,
And at each measured quarter
Set the soft echoes
Of the house vibrantly ringing.
Rachel listened,
Her small face
Still and wondering,
Then she turned
And gravely said,
'Nanny, your clock
Is singing!'

D M Neu

The Cottage

The track led me back to the cottage, in view,
The home I left, I had other things to do.
Now I am older, my steps bring me near
To recapture the peace I always felt here.
Wild flowers, the meadows and lanes to ramble,
The woods and hills where as kids we would scramble.
There were times for mushrooms, blackberries and nuts,
Christmas holly carted on frozen ruts
With frosts that made a postcard scene
In those happy days, where we all had been.
I remember the wind whistling round the old place
With gusts down the chimney, leaving smuts on our face.
Under the doors the draught would creep,
Strange rattles to fright as we went to sleep.
A coldness, a hush, an eerie white light
Snowfall transformed to a magical sight.
The lavatory was down the garden path,
Bizarre memories, but, now we can laugh.
An old copper we stoked, the clothes to boil,
For our harassed mum a long day of toil,
A cooking range, with black lead to shine,
Being the eldest, the job usually mine.
Come the summer, the sun and long, leisured days
Of a different life with warm, pleasured ways.
Rounders and picnics, haymaking fun,
Happiness, laughter and much to be done,
Enjoyed by us all helping along,
Now I feel sad those days are gone.
We have to move on in life, come what may
Holding on to our memories, just like today.

Patricia Evans

Just Passing

I may pop in and see you
When I'm up in my balloon,
I'll try to give a shout
As I'm passing by the moon,

I hope you'll be around
Near the pinkest fluffy cloud,
I don't know if you'll hear me
So I'll shout it very loud,

Darling Jim, I love you,
Are you listening my dear?
Please send a brilliant rainbow
To show me you are near.

Margery Crabtree

The Hourglass Of Life

The hourglass of life is now counting down
And so time on Earth swiftly passes by.
Over the years that have brought laughter and tears,
I have been blessed, so do not cry.

What happiness my family has brought,
Born to parents whose love I possessed.
With a brother and sister, what fun we had,
When time stood still and life was blessed.

The church bells rang out on my wedding day,
I continued the journey through time
Soon we were three when our daughter was born
And then everything seemed sublime.

Joy and sadness has filled my long life,
But I have been blessed with loving friends
And two grandchildren that bring me such delight,
Will comfort me as my journey ends.

My life has been kind in so many ways,
With happy memories of days gone by.
That I spent with those I loved so dearly,
Who gave me joy so I did not cry.

As time goes on enjoy it whilst you can,
When I have departed, do not feel sad.
My guardian angel will take care of me,
Just remember good times that we've had.

Remember self-pity destroys the soul,
So spread a little sunshine on your way.
Then smile through your tears when you're feeling low
And count your blessings every day.

Doreen M Bowers

To Love Somebody

Loving you brings happiness untold
And memories so beautiful to cherish
Your kindness gives me pleasure and contentment
And starts each day with wonderful feelings to share.

Since meeting you I have learnt many precious things
The beauty of our life enfolding
I try to give you the love you so richly deserve
And wish you happiness for the future.

Every birthday makes me feel so special
And loving gestures bring a multitude of beautiful gifts
As I continue to make the most of each day
I know that you will remain in my thoughts forever.

Marjory Price

Brighter Days

Soft winds rippling through golden ears of corn;
Silver salmon leaping their way upstream.
Lambs and calves in the green fields being born;
Pure white swans on a sliding river seen.

Solitary robin, the gardener's friend;
Honeysuckle scenting the air around.
Blushing skies as the busy sun descends;
Rosy-cheeked apples in our orchards found.

Laughter of children in the winter snow;
Squirrels sleeping till warmer days return.
Crisp autumn leaves with colours all aglow;
Blackbird listening for the tunnelling worm.

The rowan tree proud of its bright red hair;
Diamond stars gleaming in infinite skies.
The hedgehog, badger, the foal and the mare;
New life replacing the old life that dies.

Robert Corrigan

Magnolia Fantasia

Hadleigh Salvation adherents breathtaking visit to Wisley,
240 acres of beautiful gardens
Lovingly cultured blooms in the orchid house.

Lose oneself in the alpine meadow and rock garden
Rhododendron, azalea, heather, pine trum aroetirm,
Fruit field, perennial mixed borders.

Wander, extantically over rose and herb land,
Wonder at the Chinese Pavilion
Glorious magnolia tree 'Charles Dickens' variety.

Unbelievable water lilies, various colours lie on a magnificent lake,
Ingenious mobility vehicle, stops, security controlled,
Refreshments at Conservatory orchid terrace coffee, cafes
Inspirational horticultural books, innovate gifts purchased at shop.

All displays are numbered with name of plants
A well-planned plant shop encourages the amateur,
The intense hot weather, children in shorts, hats.

The beauty everywhere, awesome.
Relaxing, eating high quality, inspiring dishes,
Smell the luscious scents, artful fruits,
Nature, a gracious grandeur.

Patricia Turpin

Past Present And Future

These days after Christmas seem so cold and bleak,
But glancing at photos, what a pleasure to see
Happy faces of children, all aglow,
Building a snowman in deepest snow,
Sheltered by a slender, frosty fir tree.

And from the window, how lovely to view
A cheeky robin in full song;
And to glimpse in the garden the very first bloom,
A pure white camellia, to fight off the gloom.
In my memory these treasures will always belong.

Now a look to the future, forgetting past years,
Breathing new life into long-lost ideas.
A trip to the theatre, holidays to review,
A bunch of flowers, a lost friendship to renew.
No one knows just what is in store
But I'll try making this year the best year of all.

Joan Mathers

Blink Of An Eye

To the world I say, enjoy each day
Just as if it were your last,
Try not to dwell on bad times
That you have suffered in the past,
When you awake each morning
Count your blessings you're alive,
But you all know life's precious.
So be strong, and you'll survive,
And there's so much beauty in the world to see
So make time to look around,
Forget life's silly rat race,
God left such beauty to be found,
Now if there are days when you are sad
And you feel life's let you down,
Share your troubles with a friend
Then your mountain's just a mound,
Shakespeare said, 'All the world is a stage
But you can't rehearse this one,
So smile, don't frown, then take a bow
For when life's gone, it's gone.'

Shirley Jones Dwyer

The Wheel Of Love

Friends and family are a gift
A gift that we must cherish
Neglect, dishonour or hurt them
Their love for you could perish

Take care to nurture all
Their kindness to you
And even though at times they falter
Always let your love shine through

To be loved is to be rich indeed
You blossom, like a flower
With care, with such unselfishness
We shine from hour to hour

When times are hard, they will be there for you
Willingly and then
The wheel of love and friendship
Spins around again and again.

Elizabeth Mackinnon

Remembrance

If you've known someone good and kind
Who lived his life to please
Then you know you've been blessed.

You'll always have a memory
To make you smile when low
Just put it to the test.

It isn't brains or beauty rare
That builds your spirit up
As well you'll find.

It's just the simple, kindly acts
Recalled, of loved ones gone
That lift those left behind.

We owe it to them not to grieve
But smile with happy thoughts
Remembering the past.

We've much to thank our Maker for
We've known a real good friend
And that will last.

Joan Hammond

Creation's Liturgy

Swift as the hare,
Birds flowing on air
Praise grace of God:
Rays' light and shade
Which sharpen and fade
Praise fun of God:
Peaks' panorama
Dry walls of hill farmer
Praise beauty of God:
Tenderly breezes
Shy softly whisper
Praise cooling of God

Spring trees in blossom
From top to bottom
Praise freshening of God:
Summer's dark greens
Polished gloss scenes
Praise ripening of God:
Autumns that fall
In golden-brown thrall
Praise seasoning of God:
White years' blanket end
By killing germs, friend
Praise curing of God

First light of the day
Has led us to pray
Thanksgiving to God:
I will never suspect
Each mark of respect
But give thanks to God:
Whoever shows care
Helps me to declare
Thanksgiving to God:
When in human story
The brilliance of glory
Thanks be to God

When what nature is giving
Enhances our living
Thanks be to God:
A Heaven designed show
Of Christ here below
Thanks be to God:
You who have frowned
Walk celestial ground
Thanksgiving to God:
With one voice give vent
To Earth's sacrament
Thanks be to God.

David Speed

I Can't Wait Until The Spring

I can't wait until the spring
To see the buds begin to swell,
To see the catkins on the waking trees
As Nature casts her spell.

The warmer weather creeping up,
The howling wind suppressed
And little sparrows gathering twigs
To build their hedgerow nests.

I want to see the rising sun
Shine colours through the rain,
Clouds disappear and clearing skies
Grow high and blue again.

I want to see the tiny shoots
Where dormant earth has been
And watch the spring-heeled lambs
Jump high in meadows green.

I can't wait to see the blossom
Spread on the cherry tree,
So I can gather flowers
To bring spring home with me.

Helen E Langstone

Moods Of The Sea - Like You And Me

I often sit beside the sea
And watch with great intensity
Its angry, black and rolling waves -
Then sometimes all is quite serene.
I think of life in similar tones
When all is black and lashing waves
A loved one's taken to an early grave
The heavy rolling waves roll in
They crash upon our life within
But! - life goes on - and all is calm
Until another crisis forms
The sea is ruthless - as is life
But we move on - that too is life
We watch the sea in all its moods
The anger - wrath - the churning foam
All we can do is ride the storms.

Janet Mary Kirkland

The Joy Of Grandchildren

You love your children with a love so sublime,
But somehow there is never enough quality time.
Working so hard to provide a quality life,
You leave a lot of the caring to your wife.

As you get older and the pace calms down,
There are a lot more smiles and less of a frown.
More time to relax and pass on what we've learned,
The experience to appear quite unconcerned.

Your grandchildren add an exciting new dimension,
Loving and caring without all the tension.
Each one has their own unique personality,
They need handling differently without banality.

I look forward to daily hugs and kisses,
They love us enormously, me and my missus.
They can twist us round their little fingers,
When they are away, they always ring us.

I know that I would be really sad,
If I never heard the word 'Grandad'.
I know that Charley, Bonnie and young Georgie,
Will always mean the whole world to me.

David Ian Muncaster

Find Happiness In Giving

Give of yourself to those in need,
Give of your time and then proceed
To give what is precious,
Your compassion, your strength,
And go to any length
To give of yourself in their hour of need,
Whatever their race, colour or creed.
Cook them a meal, or hold a hand,
And always a smile, while you stand
And do the chores, a job worthwhile,
You know that it will make someone smile.
Your reward will be the love that you get
From the people that you met
Along the way, and as you go from day-to-day
Thank the Lord for your health
And He will give you a wealth
Of happiness all your days,
And that in itself is enough praise.

H J Palmer

Accentuate The Penultimate

Anon, anon, the sexton to his task.
How long before that doleful bell shall toll?
More frequently that question one might ask
As youthful nonchalance strips from the soul.
Some time will lapse 'twixt final bonk and bell
And so that noise I will not even heed.
That's for the living, Hemmingway did tell,
To make them ponder where their lives might lead.
All maudlin thoughts begone - fade evanescent
To be replaced by some I think more clever.
The future doesn't exist till it comes present;
Until it does my life goes on forever!
 Take cheer, old hearties - life more slow is fun;
 Time, still, for love and laughter. Broach the tun.

Frank W A Sutton

A Bright Side Awaits

In life there is always a bright side
Should things look forbiddingly grim.
Though mud mars the scene at the ebb tide,
With the high tide, the sea flows back in.

When clouds in the grey skies are bursting
Till torrents of rain cascade down,
Before long the sun will shine brightly
And a rainbow will arch o'er our town.

After chilling winds bite us in winter
And a cold, nippy air strokes our face,
Spring's warmth will envelop the bare land
Which her carpet of flowers will embrace.

Should we enter a tunnel incessant
With darkness and gloom end to end,
As blindly we worm our way through it
A chink of light creeps round the bend.

So even though grim seems the outlook
A bright side awaits to appear.
Just give it a chance to take over
And put the dark side to the rear.

Joan Zambelli

Thoughts

Every cloud has a silver lining
Every trouble has an end
When your world seems torn to pieces
Remember time will always mend.

The sun will not hide forever
From your life in this domain
Dark clouds disperse and so reveal
What you thought lost was but another gain.

To understand and love your treasures
You must travel through life's darkest night
To appreciate the truth of beauty
You must gaze upon the ugly sight.

Without the contrast, how can you know
The value of life's measures?
Without some sadness in your life
You cannot appreciate the pleasures.

Danny Pyle

Reason For Living

I'm still alive despite everything,
Why? Because she is with me,
She lights up my day and night.
I'm totally committed to her; because I love her.
She turns night into day and day into night.
She has become my reason for living.
There are so many fools in this world;
A tightrope between sanity and madness,
But she keeps me together.
A vision of beauty in the morning dew.
I need you tonight and forever;
Let me shipwreck in your thighs,
Let me die in your arms,
Let me drown in your tears,
Her laughter makes me smile,
A smile that turns her on and on and on!
The touch of her skin against mine;
The smell of her skin is nectar to my nostrils.
She is my whole life; death cannot be contemplated,
Not in our lifetime!
She inspires my very being.

Brian Denton

Daydreaming - Whilst Away

Lying here thinking, *where would I rather be?*
Stretched on a beach, being lapped by the sea,
Or maybe by a riverbank shaded with trees
Smelling the grass and resting at ease.
Standing tall on a hilltop, feeling the wind
Getting up early to hear the birds sing.
Or the rain on my face as I walk a mile
The happiness of children, that makes me smile.
Meeting with friends, chatting aloud,
Enjoying the laughter, hiding the cloud.
Deep down wondering, *can time break the spell?*
Maybe I'll hear the words - that all is well.
But when all's said and done, the best place for me,
Is at home, in my chair, with a good cup of tea!

Alice Turner

The Ring

So long it stayed upon her hand,
The ring that formed a golden band,
Within its circle flowed her life,
The loving mother, the caring wife.

It felt her pulsing, beating heart,
But when her world, it fell apart,
It felt the flow within its circle ebb,
Her earthly cares she now had shed.

I held her close and clasped her hand,
My tears flowed down upon that golden band,
The ring of gold it seemed to glow,
With all the love that in its circle flowed.

I slipped the ring gently from her hand,
My mother's plain, but precious band,
I knew her spirit would survive,
Within the ring I would wear with pride.

It now feels my pulsing, beating heart
And though the two of us are far apart,
Through its circle I feel her love,
It flows through my body to my heart above.

Oh, precious band, I will treasure you,
With memories of my mother, kind and true,
Though placed on another's hand when I am gone,
The love in your circle will still flow on.

Rita Maher

Count Your Blessings

Count your blessings is an age-old saying, known my many, if not all,
Whether you are young, old, rich, poor, fat, thin, short or tall.
I wonder how many people really do count their blessings one by one,
Or take them for granted, like the rising and setting of the moon and sun.

A young mother caresses her newborn baby with tired delight,
While her husband counts his blessings and views with pride
Their new arrival, what a wonderful sight.

A young man is saved from a sinking ship in heavy seas,
His mother counts his blessings and dances with glee.

An elderly couple celebrate their golden wedding with their family
And friends at a grand party
And count their blessings that they are still feeling fit and hearty.
So, if you're the reader of this poem, have a reason to be grateful
For certain experiences in your life, maybe happy, beneficial
Or a problem solved that was very pressing,
So, don't forget that age-old saying and count your blessings.

Peter Guy Towner

Friendships

There's always been so many friends around me;
From childhood pals, right to the present day.
So many folks I think of constantly.

The years were free from animosity
Give and take has always been the way
There's always been so many friends round me.

Love without conditions is the key
Though over time, many have passed away
So many folks I think of constantly.

Over the years, many I seldom see
In moving on, that is the price to pay
There have always been so many friends round me.

Though far apart, I know we all agree
That in our thoughts our friends will always stay
So many folks I think of constantly.

Our memories and thoughts always fly free
Friendship is always faithful, come what may
There have always been so many friends round me
So many folks I think of constantly.

Ida Shewan

Count Your Blessings

If I can see the sky -
Grey cloud or dome of blue,
If I can see the sun
Setting fire to the dew;

If I can feel the wind -
Wild storm or gentlest breeze
And listen to the music
Of raindrops through the trees;

If I can count the wingéd hours,
Filled with sunshine - bright with flowers
And breathe the scent of new-mown hay -
Golden swathes - in neat array;

If I can watch the birds
And listen to their song,
Hear the hum of bees
And the laughing brook
Dancing merrily along;

If I can taste the fruit
Plucked fresh from off the bough,
Appease my hunger, quench my thirst,
Savour the bountiful gifts of the earth;

If I can fill my days
And trust they lead
Through pleasant ways;

If, all around, I feel God's care -
Find beauty, joy and love to share,
Then whatsoever else betide
I am content . . . and satisfied.

So count your blessings
And to yourself be true,
Giving thanks for the wondrous world
The Lord has created . . . for you.

Elizabeth Amy Johns

Wishing On A Rainbow

A rainbow spreads its arc across the sky,
The swallows cannot reach it, nor can I.
If I could catch that rainbow
And hold it in my hand,
See the colours glow,
Make three wishes and
How happy I would be,
I'd put it in a box
And keep it, just for me.

Doris Mary Miller

Solace

When you struggle to cope
With your deep despair,
Exhausted as the day begins.
Alone in a sanctuary
Where self-loathing causes a desire
To harm yourself.
Wild dreams about drowning
Send you close to the edge,
Losing control.
I will take these traumatic memories
And turn them into narrative ones,
Bringing them into the open,
Making them lose their emotional power.
Together we will find a faith
That brings you solace.
Feel that sense of expectancy
And that strange sense of peace.
I will persevere with you
Through these dark years.
Sometimes you may lose your way,
But always you can believe in me.
For I love you more than life itself.
Find your solace in me.

Beverly Maiden

Simple Pleasures

The greatest of pleasures are the simple ones

A walk through a wood or a leafy lane
The scent of roses on a summer's day
The sight of a butterfly as it flies away

After the winter, when we're weary of snow
We notice the snowdrops have started to grow
We hear the songbirds starting to sing

With a song they are hoping to welcome the spring
These simple pleasures are here for all to share
For these wonderful things are everywhere.

Barbara Smith

Our Pleasures

If opening the curtains on a bright sunny morning
Gives me so much pleasure,
So does closing the curtains on a dark, miserable evening.
Yes, the clock has gone forward and I think we are off Greenwich Mean Time.
So life goes on and the birds and the bees
Come out later in the warmth, to feed and dance and mime,
Like the magpies do in pairs.
One for sorrow, two for joy,
Three for a girl and four for a boy.
I wonder what the background of that saying is?
There are often words of wisdom in rhymes, in their beginnings
My grandma would say, 'Don't cast your clout till May is out'
It took me an age to realise that a clout was a vest
And that May meant May blossom-time.
It was to keep warm, as the best way to keep the doctor away
And that an apple a day also keeps the doctor away.
Remember that was the time when one had to pay the doctor,
Now we just grumble about the NHS!
And how long we have to wait to go to see the doctor.
Yes, this generation does grumble to excess.
Our health service is the best in the world.
If one had an accident on the road, at once
There's a paramedic and a policeman speeding to save your life
And a hospital bed, if required, ready for your comfort and care.
Let's praise life and all its goodness,
In our beautiful place called England.
Let's welcome the rain to bring on the crops.
We have forgotten how to live in thankfulness
And how to find each day a pleasure.

ABC

Summer - Haiku

Humming honeybees,
perfume of English gardens
on a southern breeze.

David Hancock

Jack Frost

I woke to a beautiful day
Frost had come in the night
Gone were the greens and golds
Of the world outside my window
Transforming it to pure white
Touched by the wings of an angel
When the sun caught crystals of light
As a child I loved my window
I awoke to shiver and shake
The cold taking my breath away
But there in all its beauty
Was Jack Frost covering my windows
The fragile gems of diamonds and stars
Its glories I remember still
Now, I have heat in my house
Jack never comes to touch my window
He stays well away
I do miss his visits
But enjoy him better from afar.

M Roe

The Silver Lining

I wonder what the future holds,
As we stand upon its brink?
New birth, new death, new happiness,
New sorrow, do you think?
Whatever life throws at us,
Resilient we must be,
And do the very best we can
For others, then we'll see
That God helps those who help themselves,
We know this to be true,
And, if you look around, you'll see
Other folk much worse than you.
Every day there's a chance to give
Your time and service too,
To other people in despair,
And this will benefit *you!*
So, 'pick yourself up, dust yourself down',
Look for the silver lining,
Which sits behind the darkest cloud,
And where the sun is always shining!

Jasmine Grace Geddes

Diamond Blessings

Oh those wonderful, wonderful years
When we were young and free.
Before the changing hand of time
Cast shadows of days to be.

So long as memory lasts, we keep
The joy of those far-off times
To keep us glad when days are hard
Like mountains steep to climb.

We remember the children round our feet
As we walked the sunlit ways.
Their shining eyes and joyous laughter
Like music to gladden our days.

It seems there were no cloudy skies,
And few were the drops of rain
That fell upon the paths we trod
And long to tread again.

No life is known to be free from pain;
Later sad times were ours.
Our lives are short, we grow and bloom
Then wither like the flowers.

But sixty years wed is no mean thing
To remember and celebrate
That God has given our love to last
Till we come to the Heavenly Gate.

Mary Johnson-Riley

Four

Washing and ironing and dusting too
Can wait, I've better things to do.
My little grandson's only four
And he's waiting by the kitchen door.

He'll play in the sandpit with bucket and spade
And build the best castle that ever was made.
He's sand in his pockets and sand in his hair,
He's the picture of innocence standing there.

He asks lots of questions about many things,
Like, 'Who paints the colour on a butterfly's wings?'
I'll give him an answer (though I really don't know)
About fairies and magic and how all things grow.

He will believe me because in his eyes
I'm the fount of all knowledge and ever so wise.
He'll grow up, of course and learn more and more,
But to me, in my heart, he will always be four.

Daphne Hanson

New House

News arrives, you've got the house,
Need boxes for packing, even the mouse.
Keys in ignition, go into overdrive,
Hoping this manic pressure, you'll survive.

Papers to sign and understand,
Lists to make, do we need this pan?
Numbers to ring and ladders to climb,
Dashing to change address and dine!

Doctors to change, a headache in itself,
After all this graft, will my figure be svelte?
Things to throw away or charity bag,
Nothing goes smooth, mustn't lose my rag!

Unpacking, where will everything go?
Box upon box to empty and throw.
Not enough space, some things are redundant,
We brought too much, things over-abundant.

At last we see light at the end of the tunnel,
Finished unpacking, what to do with this funnel?
Everything neat, tidy and in place,
Now I can slow down and go at a snail's pace!

Joan Lister

The Spring Garden

I love my garden in the spring,
There's a contented joy in everything.
Cherry, hawthorn and rowan tree,
Competing in splendour for all to see.

Blackbird, thrush, chaffinch and robin,
Building their nests. The air is throbbing
With joyous toil - never stopping,
Until their chick on the grass is hopping.

Daffodils, tulips, narcissi and wallflower,
Such radiant colour enhances my bower.
Unseen and silent while winter was here,
Now in such brilliance, their colours so clear.

After the day when the evening will fall,
I listen, entranced, to the blackbird call.
The song of the thrush so fine and true,
Such sweetness is there for me and you.

These little souls bring joy to life,
How bereft we would be in this world of strife,
Without the simple, innocent thing,
Which beauty and peace of mind still bring.

Dorothy Hill Bradshaw

His Work

(Jesus said 'I must work the works of Him that sent me, while it is yet day', part of John 9;4)

Our Lord has something special
For each of us to do
Maybe the gift of singing
Of Jesus' love for you
To some the gift of preaching
To sinners near or far
Seeking 'the lost' for Jesus
To bring them to His care.
Or to give a helping hand
To some who've gone astray
Leading them back to Jesus
For He's the narrow way.
Oh may we seek to serve Him
In this new year ahead
In the quiet place of prayer
And, through God's daily bread.

Beth Stewart

Sir Liontooth

What is happiness? Ask Sir Liontooth -
But what is his answer and who is he?

A magical knight from Camelot
Who spurred his horse to Avalon?
Did he fight crusades in Palestine,
Hiding the Holy Grail at far Rosslyn?
Perhaps he isn't fierce at all,
His name a modern, psychic blind -
Yet I sense his medieval spirit
Guiding us on the safe, causeway path
To St Quiricus and Julietta,
Whose honeyed stones glow in winter sunsets.

And in May the peace and grace of the place
Where cow parsley waves above reed-lined rhynes -
Were these green-soaked fields his manor lands
Now grazed by sheep and prancing lambs?
This is our happiness today,
As we walk with children and explore -
What can Sir Liontooth have to add
Tomorrow when the moment has passed?

S A Mottram

Storm Winds

Storm winds blow all the leaves away,
In twirling showers they tumble down.
Green-cladded trees, more bare each day,
Have shed turned coats of gold and brown.

Bare skeletons of wood, they stand
Four square against the winter's gales;
But come the spring they greet the land
With fresh new life, to grace our vales.

So we, ourselves, may face fierce winds,
Which beat upon us, raise our fears;
But later, when the storm unwinds,
God gives new hope for later years.

And so, a special wish for you;
Your tree of life be clothed again.
As fresh green buds burst forth anew,
God's rainbow arc outshines the rain.

Ron Shettle

The Father's Love

So deep, so high, so wide
Yet so personal and gentle
So warm and comforting
Making us feel special
As His spirit hovers around us
Touching softly and lightly
Like the wings of a dove
Showering blessing upon blessing
Filled with tenderness and love
Going before us to prepare the way
Wonderfully holding us every day
There is no end to the depth
Of His love for you and me
He proved that by Jesus
Dying on a Cross at Calvary
So let us put on the full armour
Each and every one
Stand firm, be counted for Jesus
God's precious Son.

I Mcdonald

The Grandchildren - Christ-Child's Love

Their smiles lead us
To Heaven
In our hearts
And all around,
They open doors
To all wonders
To be found.

Out and in sail ships
With treasures of gold
And yet again is
Christmas story told.

Their tears wash
Our eyes clean
So we can see
Through this foggy scene
With the eyes
Of a newborn child.

B E Pattie

Looking To The Future

A new year has just started!
I have seen eighty-one so far.
Those historical days departed!
No longer driving my car!
Looking forward to the days ahead!
What pleasures will they bring?
The first sign of the flower head
And then I will know it is spring!
I will see Lewis, my great grandson
And maybe Emma too!
With the rest of my lovely family,
There is oh, so much to do!
Each cloud has a silver lining!
Lovely birds and all the bees!
No time to sit just whining,
Take a walk amongst the trees!
Just count your blessings and look around!
Think of the many, each day are house-bound!
The blind, who rely on the eyes of the dog!
I count my blessings and I say thank God!
I am so lucky to live in this wonderful place!
With no ambition to join the race into space!
But to carry on sharing this steady old life!
With my family and Betty, my wonderful wife!

A E Powell

My Blessings

I count my blessings day by day
For all the good things that have come my way
I am getting old and rather deaf
But hopefully I will live for a long time yet
I still work in the Oxfam shop twice a week
And I have lovely friends who each week I meet
With a cosy little flat and good things to eat
These are all blessings I enjoy each day
As I continue along life's way.
On days I don't feel quite so well
I think of others worse off than me
Some without limbs and some who cannot see
And some who are poor and do not have enough to eat
And unlike me, they never get a treat
Then I think of my blessings and how lucky I am
With family, friends and a lovely little home
From which I do not often roam.
I may not be so nimble now and sometimes ride a scooter
But I get out and about and am blessed with good sight
To enjoy all the different season's delights
My blessings help to brighten each day
And I hope things continue to go on this way.

S C Talmadge

Blessed

When we're tired and lonely
Or feeling 'out of sorts' and blue,
That's when we need to lift our heads
And fix our eyes on You.

For You have promised peace of mind
To those who look to You,
And this promise covers everyone
Not just the chosen few.

We'll always have troubles in this world
And some can be hard to bear,
But we never have to be alone
Because, Jesus, You're always there.

So when we wait on You, Lord
Our strength You've promised to renew,
You lift the heavy burdens
And we are truly blessed by You.

Dawn Armstrong

Portrait Of Love

The lovely face looks back at me
From within the golden frame
Beguiling eyes, a winsome smile
Alice is her name
Perhaps her hair belies her age
She's neither young nor old
As I take a closer look, I see
Silver threads among the gold

Throughout my youth and childhood
We were always side by side
My best friend and philosopher
Protector and my guide
Whenever trouble troubled me
And when at times oppressed
No wiser, worldly counsellor
That's when I loved her best

Time came when I reached womanhood
Little more than twenty-one
God saw she had suffered more than enough
My most precious gift was gone

There's a secret place within my heart
For which there is no other
I will always
Love her until I die
Who else, my own dear *mother.*

Joy D Richardson

Touch

Touch is action,
Touching is soft -
Touch is the baby talk of love.

Touch is teaching;
Touching guides -
Touching steadies the rough rides.

Touching echoes
Friendships true -
Touch conveys 'I love you'.

Geoff Gaskill

Enough Sun For A Rainbow

It's raining, it's raining,
The lowering clouds
Are obscuring the mountains from view.
The birds sing, it's spring,
But the blossoms drip low
On boughs recently laden with snow.

The sludge underfoot
Makes each sliding step slow
And the dogs spatter mud on the grass.
The insects are hiding,
The wind's disappeared,
Each drain sings a song as you pass.

You look at the sky,
Expecting dull grey,
But your spirits are lifted to find
That a ray from the sun
Has burst through the clouds
And a rainbow has suddenly formed.

It doesn't last long,
Dissolves as you watch,
But the warmth that it wraps round your heart
Brings a smile to your lips
And a spring to your step
As it tells you the rain will not last.

Jeanette E Burden

Julia Strong

Julia, blaze of colours so rich,
Fantasia girl and lover of kitsch,
Dismantler of kitchens with practical flair,
A partner fulfilling and extraordinaire.
You've galvanised everything, stirred me to change
And helped all my thinking to rearrange!
Our future is golden, a glory life long,
A couple conjoined who truly belong,
So let us go forward, like lambs in the spring,
Me with my princess and you with your king.

John Birkett

Nature's Holy Place

One morning by the River Sow
On sunny autumn day,
We two strolled on its tree-filled banks
Quite close to Stafford way.

There, willows in abundance grew
Some in the water trailed,
Their grey-green leaves had yellow tips
And down the river sailed.

For fun, we walked 'neath curtain thick
The very air was green,
It seemed this was a sacred spot
Like special church unseen.

The cave-like shape was shadowy
No grass was on the ground,
Just carpet thick from last year's leaves
A soft and rustling sound.

The sun half-twinkled from outside
As branches moved in breeze,
Created just for private prayer
For us alone to please.

How safe we felt beneath that tree
In our protected space,
We knew no harm could come to us
In nature's holy place.

Mary Lefebvre

A Special Blessing

Blessings galore have been given to me
Four sons, their twelve offspring for all to see
Followed by 'greats' one, two and three
The latest of these is Sage.

Sage was born in November
A bouncing boy of Canadian birth
One to remember
Numbers one and two were a boy and a girl
Numbers four and five will soon arrive.

All bring love and joy to our lives
All blessings on which our existence survives
Great blessings for which I thank God each day.

Dolly Harmer

New Year Blessings

'Tis our privilege when fit and well to
Welcome this new year
A chance to change our course of life
Whatever may occur
We all remember moments when we spoke
Without much thought
Times we were far away when a wise
Counsellor was sought

To bridge a gap or heal a wound requires
Frankincense, myrrh and gold
The Wise Men thought of your every need
With warmth they, you, enfold
Let rest the year gone by
We all are wiser now
Be strong and grasp fresh hope with each
Inspired vow

A golden thread has held us strong
Nigh on 2,000 years
Some trials won, some prayers refused
Our lives refreshed with tears
Grasp this golden thread woven o'er the years
To unite with all our brothers as new millennium heirs.

Olive Bedford

My Joy Is Blue And Gold

I walked along the shore one day,
  The sea was blue,
  The sand was gold
And I was just a child
Laughing, as the lacy foam
Splashed round my ankles, cool and fresh;
  My joy was blue and gold.

Each springtime, as the garden bloomed,
  The sky was blue,
  The tree was gold,
When I was just a girl
And the laburnum, which I loved,
Shone gold against the clear, clear sky;
  My joy was blue and gold.

He waited by the altar there,
  My flowers were blue,
  My flowers were gold,
As I walked down the aisle
He smiled at me as he looked round
Upon that well-remembered day,
  Signed with a ring of gold.

Margaret Ballard

Colours Of Our Lives

Life is such a mixture,
Pain and pleasure, sorrow, joy,
Light and shadow, hopes and fears
Follow us across the years.
A patchwork of experience
Lined with laughter, sewn in tears.

Each day brings its moments
For gratitude and praise,
The darkest clouds may mar the view,
Yet they will let the sun shine through,
The blackest night gives way to dawn,
As birdsong greets a new day born.

If we look about us
There is much to cheer the heart,
Green shoots of hope in winter,
Fragrant blossom in the spring,
Brilliant blue, the skies of summer,
Autumn days aflame with gold.

If we but gaze in wonder
As the seasons come and go,
Colours of our lives in every shade and hue
Will enrich our days with blessing
As we contemplate anew
The world within our view.

Carol Mansfield

Missed Blessings

I count these blessings, one by one:
Someone's daughter, someone's son
Lying there, in close array
Then one by one, they pass away.
Hospice children - nothing more can be done
We are sorry, someone's son.
We do our best, day by day.
How long now? We really cannot say.
All these dear ones will go into the light
If you wish, you could stay overnight
We firmly believe that life goes on
For someone's daughter, someone's son.

Joyce Le Vicount

See The Good In Me

Mother
Do you see
Me
For who
I really am?
This gentle
Loving person
Willing to
Do all
That I can.
Do you see
The beauty
That people
Say I have?
Do you see
The honesty
That runs
Through me?
Or
The laughter
I bring
To your
Boring home?
Do you see
Me
Cooking, cleaning
Doing the chores?
That's before
I leave
To go
To school.
Then in
The evening
It's back
To the shop
To buy
Your fags
And paper
I never stop . . .

Count Our Blessings

Do you see
The good
In me?
Or
Do you just
Choose not?
I've never
Brought you
Trouble
In any kind
Of way.
So
See the good
In me
And I'll
Never walk
Away.

Sharon Lambley Dzus

Count My Blessings

Count my blessings
Count my blessings
For we know You are true
For all our blessings come from You
And I know my wife
Has gone home to You
And she also was true
And she was a blessing too
And the memories are blessings too, of my wife
And the memories of my dad, they are blessings too
And my mum is a blessing too
And I thank You for my life, which is a blessing too
Without, I would not know these blessings . . .
And the best blessing is knowing You
For You are love
Which is true
The greatest blessing is knowing You
Thank You, my Saviour, Jesus
For You are true.

Stanley John Moore

A Simple Thank You

Two small words that mean a lot
Just for the friendship we've got
A rare commodity that we should respect
No matter who it may affect
A neighbour who gives a helping hand
Or a family member who will understand
Your worries and problems that might exist
More comfort and courage they may enlist

We can count our blessings every day
And give thanks in a special way
Look forward to the days ahead
With luck it won't be all gloom and dread
There is always someone at the door
To do a few errands or more
At the end of our day we may get on our knees
With friends and family we needn't say please!

Joseph Broadley

Blessings

I have the sun to shine by day
To keep me warm and light my day.

And when in bed at night I sleep
The moon and stars their watch to keep.

I have the showers and summer breeze
The golden crops and leafy trees.

A garden for my leisure hours
The country lanes and wayside flowers.

Amazing creatures, small and great
Far too many to contemplate.

Changing seasons guaranteed
Food to satisfy my need.

Loving friends, their help to give
A comfy home in which to live.

God's creation all around
Wonders, blessings that abound.

Every day my thanks I give
For the gifts that I receive.

Though a sinner self-confessed
With what wonders I am blessed.

Janet Cavill

Mother's Day

It just didn't happen,
I've never been a mum,
Never had a daughter,
Never had a son.
Never even minded,
Been busy as a bee,
A husband and spaniels
Have been my family.

I've tall, handsome stepsons,
Godchildren too,
All very anxious,
To teach me something new.
There's a wacky warehouse
Where kids size up and play,
I'm a tad too old to go in free,
But I can't keep away!

We have hours of simple fun,
But it's easy to lose the knack,
Adulthood is tricky
And there's no turning back.

On a special afternoon,
I was quite overcome,
With chocolates and a lovely card
From my goddaughter and godson.
A very happy Mother's Day
They were wishing me,
And I was thrilled and tickled to bits
As I could ever be!

Gloria Thorne

It Is A Wonderful Life

A touch on the hand is so grand
It's nice to know that someone does care
And when you smile to say hello
It's another kindness you know
It's nice to know there's someone around
Remember when in despair
That there is someone there to give you a hand
And help you put your feet back on the ground

There are many blessings Heaven-sent
Especially for you they could be meant
So if you have someone look after you
It means their friendship is true
So fill the day with love and laughter
And you will be loved for ever after
Remember it's a blessing sent
And many happy hours are all well spent

Tomorrow may be a brighter day
You may hear someone say
They want you for friendship or love
So thank you lucky stars above
There is always something nice could happen for you
Life is beautiful, it's true
It's nice to see animals and hear birds sing
It's just another wonderful thing
Whether or not you have a husband or wife
Remember it's a wonderful life
It's full of change and not all strife
It is a wonderful life.

John Walker

Remember

Do you remember the seat under the trees at the villa in Sorrento
Overlooking the lavender haze over the bay
Where we sat for a fleeting moment or so
With dappled sunlight through the trees in the heat of the day?

Did the gentle ladies of yesteryear
Read Keats, Tasso and Browning
Perhaps in their eye a tear?
Did they hear Caruso or Gigli
In the beauty of a warm night
Rustling shirts and stoles gently ruffled by warm breezes
While listening with great feeling and delight?

Perhaps we were there in another world far away
Maybe that's why the yearning
It might show us the way
To our perpetual urge for returning.

Joan Gladys Cashford

Stillness

Stillness prevails
As I sit on the balcony
Only a flutter of birds' wings
A robin, chaffinch, sparrow and blackbird too
They come and they go
Or they twitter and sing
But they wait for darkness to be still.

Quietness descends on all around
Broken only by song of night birds
Invaded by low-flying planes
Imposed by the train in the valley
Sending its *tat-a-tat* through the air
Then the horn to warn of its coming
Or maybe the car in the bends of the hills.

Peace descends at last
And a feeling of well-being and well done
A mind in a state of peace
Peace and tranquillity all around
The heavens above drop stillness and peace
All is accepting that peace from above
Man with creation
Sharing at last peace all around.

A V R Cracknell

Retiring?

Another day - it's getting light,
The papers come - I think I might
Go down and make a cup of tea
And bring the paper back with me.
What bliss to settle back in bed
A comfy pillow at my head
Here comes the sun - it's going to be
Another lovely day I see.
What fun I have now I am old
No more venturing into the cold
Altho' I do go out each day
For exercise, fresh air and play.
I find all sorts of things to do
Which might seem quite mundane to you
But they keep me happy, good as gold
If this is retirement then I am sold.

J Johnson

Count Each Blessing

Bring in the New Year 2007
Laughter lines;
Double chin,
Broken nails,
Craggy teeth.
Cellulite around my being
Belly button protruding
Bottom dropped.
Legs like logs
Hair sparse
Laughter lines
Double chin
Life, love, happiness
Joy, life: lives here.
Come on in and enjoy
Happy New Year
Let the blessings begin.

Porché Pink Poet

Blessings

My philosophy of life tells me
To help someone each day,
To use my brain to keep it fit
And use my body the same way.

I count my blessings
When I go to bed at night,
The love my family gives me
Though they may be out of sight.

But just a phone call would bring them
To be with me, each one,
They bring me joy and happiness
Which never will be gone.

I'm thankful that I wake each morn
To sun, or wind, or rain,
I can greet my friends and my cat
And spend another day.

So many little things make up my life
And I'm thankful for them all.

Joan M E Gray

Delights

As the Christmas bells loud; ring out
Bringing together the devout
Through the side streets and the alley
'Cross the high hill and the valley

Musical notes: a singing sound
Across town and village resound
The birds will awake from the dark
Sleeping done, throughout fields and park

From their beaks, all of them singing
Into my ears it is ringing
The robin among the foremost
Flitting through trees, like a ghost

A parting loved one's goodbye kiss
Enjoy thus, this moment of bliss
With arms that are all enfolding
Thrill to the charms, that they're holding

All of these make my heart to fill
With love that is never still
Always seeking for new delights
Like a full moon on winter's nights

A blue sea on a sun-washed beach
Gulls calling, flying out of reach
Of children as they chase them away
This will always make a happy day.

Len Beddow

The Ties That Bind

For birdsong in the morning,
For ponies by the brig,
For work the circling seasons bring
In kale yard, field and rig.

For moonlight on the lochan,
The sweet, sad song of seal,
The piercing call of otter,
Brief summer's bright mareel.

For knitting by the peat fire
When all the doors are fast
And howling round about the lum
Is the furious winter's blast.

For ancient peace and heather moors,
Each peaty pool and burn -
If I was gone from Shetland
For these my heart would yearn.

Stella Shepherd

Count Your Blessings

We walked in the woods
My dear one and I
On a beautiful day in spring,
And a wonderful sight
There came to our eyes
Of the wild flowers blossoming.
Violets and primrose, anemones too
Such beauty was ours to adore
With the sun shining through
And the skies oh so blue
What could we ask for more?

Just one thing was wrong
On that glorious day
Our country was waging war
And soon came the time
For my love to leave
As others had gone before
The days seemed long
As the war went on
But at last there came a day
When my prayers were answered!
What joy was ours!
He was home at last to stay!

Now life could begin.
Soon our children were born
We were a family at last
Living and loving and
Thanking our God
For His guidance through all of the past.

Now the years have flown,
We are growing old,
Our blessings we count day by day,
And we thank our Lord
As we look back on life,
He is still our Friend and our Stay.

Gladys E Cooper

Blessings At 76

I have so many blessings,
It's hard to pick and choose
Which one I most appreciate
And least would like to lose.

My senses enrich life so much
Through hearing, sight and smell,
Ability to taste and touch;
These all have served me well.

The gift of recognising
The things I hear and see,
Learning and memorising,
Are all blessings to me.

One blessing that I treasure
Is my mobility;
Its worth I cannot measure,
It daily sets me free

To rise and dress, prepare myself
For all the day may bring;
To reach what's in cupboard or shelf,
Clean house, do gardening.

Since I can move, sit, stand and walk,
I may go where I will,
Do shopping, meet a friend and talk,
Or even climb a hill!

I may no longer move as fast
Or far, as once I could,
But while mobility shall last
I'll praise God, life is good!

Nancy Solly

Wake Me Tomorrow

Within each morn when I awake
A warm cup of tea - I go to make
Then as I dress and watch the news
From start to end it's political views
I know things happen within the day
Life, I believe, is an emotional play
Either the sunshine makes you smile
Wearing attire in an elegant style
Or defiant winds that just won't settle
Straight to the kitchen - switch on the kettle
Whatever the decision in which we decide
About love and life that grows ever wide
Remember within each day that leaves
That it's time to roll up our sleeves
And start to accept that the past has gone
A loving family can live has a happy one
But I still hold ideals that will forever last
And grab each day as a new beginning
Then breathe again, knowing that I am winning.

Lee Connor

Pass Me Another Pillow

The hours I work bring me pain
And every morning starts again
Never a chance to say 'bye' to those I love
Makes me wonder what I was dreaming of
Why do bad things happen to the best?
Is that a way to break us in every test?
Tears flow like rain into every ocean
As feelings are dismissed like a passive emotion
Half-past midnight; watching minutes tick by
Never getting closer to learning *why?*
Every day; dawn never seems to arrive
But still we face the battle to survive
For no other plight do we know
Sat watching the rain fall into the snow
Taking my thoughts with me - no place for release
Maybe one day I'll find eternal peace
But till that day comes around
I shall listen for laughter in every new sound.

Graham Connor

By The Sea

Gold-crested waves climb and topple
Into spreading foam.
Effervescent bubbles melt to cool green
Gems of dazzling beauty.
People chat and laugh, gesticulate
And smile.
They nod and wave and peer and gaze.
Engines roar as swift demons surge
Through watery hillocks.
Clouds scud, jostle and overtake
Reflected in the glazed surface beneath.
Towels flutter and shake themselves
Into insensibility.
Shiny bodies lie beneath the golden shafts
Soaking up the penetrating warmth
To brownish tones.
People gaze and stare
Locked within themselves
And shut off from the world.
And as I meditate amidst this loveliness
My being is concerned
With thoughts of you
And happiness prevails.

Nina Woolf

Zombies In The 21st Century

I sometimes wonder if life is real
Or is it just a phase
Or do we live in a parallel world
Where every saint is a slave?

And when at the end of a long life
The preacher comes to call,
You have become a burden on the state,
There's no room at the inn,
You have left it far too late.

Yet when I sit and meditate and wonder
Why a person should think they can dictate
Imposing their will upon another,
For seen naked
They look no different than each other.

So when I am old and grey
And life's spark is almost out
I'll gather daisies on the hill
Shout with my last remaining breath,
'Is this what life is all about?'

Rosaleen Clarke

Feelings

(This poem is in memory of my wife, Meg)

I sit while I am all alone
And try to fathom out,
The deepness of your love for me
And how it came about.

I very often wonder
What you saw in me,
I never fail to wonder
Just what it could be.

I lie awake and think of you
And wonder what you're doing now,
I miss you very much, you see
If you were here, I'd know and how!

It's really just the little things
That to me mean so much,
A smile across the room -
The gentleness of your touch.

I toss and turn every night
Wishing you were here,
But then, while I'm fast asleep
It's good to feel you near.

You have a special way of adding
Joy to living,
You have a most unselfish way
Of love and cheerful giving.

You also have a thoughtful way
Of showing that you care,
You're always understanding
When skies are dark or fair.

As I look out of the window
Just thinking about you,
It seems as though part of me is missing
And there's nothing I can do.

Count Our Blessings

I have all I need when I look upon your face
I have all I need should we go from place to place,
You are all I want should I look both far and wide
I'll always love you and need you by my side.

To me our love is beyond compare
And I know it's something rare,
It's not often that you see this kind
I find you're always on my mind.

I'm really content when you're around
And I always listen for the sound of you,
Coming through the door,
Each day I seem to love you more.

I suppose you also think of me,
At least I hope you do,
Because things aren't quite the same
When not shared with you.

So, dearest Meg, please excuse me if I boast,
Because to me you are the 'most',
Thank you for letting me share your life
Thank you, my darling, for being my wife.

Edward Brookes

Counting Spoons And Blessings

TS Eliot counting his spoons,
one for each season of life.
The iris and the lily smiled.
A street corner flew into spring.
Dylan Thomas penned thoughts,
saying technically we are all dead
Be thankful for the joy and warmth of life.
Byron lay down his cloak
at the volcano's foot.
We need no salesman,
those slick destroyer of words.
Poets survive to capture the absurd,
Jesus was not betrayed by Judas
He was betrayed by men,
so blessed by Sylvia Plath's oven smile.

Collin Rossini

The Power Of Music

(Dedicated to Bob Gillman - died 1st February 2007)

Music is such a wonderful thing -
It can turn any winter into spring.
In everyone's life it plays such a part -
Soothes the soul, lifts the heart.
Music is there throughout your life,
From baby to child, student, husband or wife.
The man in the pub with a tear in his eye
Remembers rocking a newborn with a calm lullaby.
The worldly-wise boss in private admits
He collects Baroque and classical hits!
Songs can go with you, inside your head;
Anywhere - shopping, to work, even to bed.
Harmonies mix with melodies sweet
People whistle or tap their feet.

But stop awhile and quietly stand . . .
Hear the silence that goes hand in hand
With the lilting tunes and rhythmic sound.
Music truly does make the world go round.

Be calm and still in body and mind.
Let music flood in - leave sorrows behind.

Phyllis Yeoman

Past Year, New Year

Thank God for the past year, for all He's done for you
For all the times that you've been blessed and for each new day too
For all that He's provided and blessed you with each day
Yes, count your many blessings and thank Him when you pray
For a year of ups and downs, I'm sure it will have been
Where through the good and bad days, God's love you will have seen
His faithfulness, forgiveness and the love He's given you
All this you'll see again, through the new year it is true
So thank God for the past year, for all His blessings too
Then thank Him for a new year and each day He gives to you
For His faithfulness, forgiveness and the love He's giving you
For all that He's providing, and all His blessings too
A year of ups and downs, again it's sure to
Where through the good and bad days, God's love for you you'll see
The same yesterday, today, forever it is true
Each day, each week, each month, each year God will bless you.

Royston Davies

Getting On With It

We must never give in
We must always go on
With a positive outlook, everyone
As we live our life, it goes forward and on
We cannot live backwards, no, not one
Do not dwell on the past, be it bad or good
We know it is right, we know what we should
Then shake yourself up
Look forward and on
To the good things in life
That are to come
Always be positive, a ray of sun
And be a good example to everyone.

Evelyn A Evans

Joanne

My granddaughter, Jo, is a smashing girl
Her head is on straight and not in a whirl.

'Hello Nan, how are you?'
Her smile that would melt the ice in the freezer,

I answer back, 'OK!' just to please her
Now she has grown into a teenager,

My, how the time has flown these last few years
It seems not very long since I wiped away her tears,

From the day she was born, she shone like a jewel
I guess our Joanne is nobody's fool.

I wonder how she will cope in her life
I reckon she'll make someone a good wife,

I wish I could see into the future
Or be around at least just to help her.

This is my poem to our Joanne
I have written just as much as I can,

I love you, my darling - goodbye and good luck
And try to remember me by reading my book.

Sheila Moore

Moments

Golden moments of long ago
Embers of fires yet still glow
Distant thoughts always near
Visions timeless, forever clear.

Melody haunting, a constant refrain
Words once spoken heard again
Long those days of never end
Oh! To have anew pretend.

Wooded path to secret place
Time bygone, the fond embrace
Yesteryear of blithe and bliss
Linger still that tender kiss.

Many joys alas were swift
Sea of reminiscence upon to drift
One remembered so enchanting
Golden moments everlasting.

Harold Taylor

Remember

(This poem is dedicated to my parents, Derek & Sylvia Pritchard who passed away December 2006. God bless, rest in peace together)

How do we count our blessings
When our world seems so bleak and empty?
How do we count our blessings
When our loved ones have just departed?
How do we count our blessings
When our days are full of tears and sadness?
How do we count our blessings
When our world has just fallen apart?
The only way we can count our blessings
In the fullness of time is,
By remembering the rich tapestries of memories
Our loved ones have left behind,
By remembering their love for us
Their laughter and joy,
By remembering their smiles
With gladness not pain,
By remembering our loved ones
Are never really departed,
While we hold them so dear in our hearts,
By remembering to give thanks
For the special love that we had
And the joy and happiness they brought to our lives;
And to count all our blessings
And keep them close in our hearts.
For blessings we have
Even though we are apart.

Zandra Collisson

Redeemed To Life

The colours of the spring
Speak to your heart
The colours so bright, so clear

The blue of the sky
The yellow of the sun
O yes says my heart
  Paint my heart like the blossom I see
  Paint my heart to be like Thee
  Sweet Saviour of the world
O how I love Thee . . .
As I look at the blossom
That blossoms for Thee

Red, yellow, white and blue -
Painted, painted for me and you
Yes, says the Easter that springs to life

Saved and redeemed

Redeemed to life.

Val Backs

Thoughts To Treasure

If a dark cloud hovers overhead
And your path seems strewn with gates
That bar your way
Gaze around you even though your footsteps
Feel like lead
Resolve that tomorrow is another day

The sun is shining, lighting up the gloom
Of a winter day, a warmth is there
With promises, however faint
That things can change
And help you on your way

Cast your mind on all the things of beauty that you know
Shared joys in nature, friendships, fun you had
However long ago
These blessings stay with us forever, come what may
Treasures, pearls beyond price keep in memory
The loves and joys of yesterday.

Mary McGuigan

Count Our Blessings

In the aftermath of Christmas and season of goodwill,
Do your troubles overwhelm you?
Is your life lonely and grim?
As the years reflect our sadness
And the awesome brevity of life,
Do you see that spark of hope
In the beauty of the universe?
Or feel God's touch and gentle presence
Among clouds of doubt and hopelessness?
Count our blessings, for with Him none are too small.
Look up to Him - not down in despair!
Lift all your troubles to Him in prayer,
He'll comfort and strengthen you, giving you hope.
Lifting your spirit and revealing His plans
For a future that's inclined to His will.
If only we'll trust Him and humbly obey.
So let's count our blessings, list them one by one,
You will be surprised what the Lord has done.

Sylvia Williams

Count Your Blessings

With not a care in the world I strolled down the street
It was rather unfortunate I had to meet
A man full of woe and all the ailments there were,
I listened politely as his life he laid bare.

One hour later and decidedly jaded,
My thoughts of a stroll had mysteriously faded.
So I headed for home, with faltering step,
As I pondered how sad some people could get.

How much happier that man would be,
If only the chink in the clouds he could see,
What happiness lies behind is for all,
So count your blessings, no matter how small.

Face each day with a smile and a prayer
Then your worries will fade and your aches disappear.
You'll feel so much brighter and be more aware,
That people are friendly and really do care.

Grace Edna Tomes

Different Colour

Hold the fire
Do not rant and rage
Or bang the cage
Do not stamp your feet
At those who you meet
Hold the fire
Who made you so mad
By treating you so bad?
Man, woman, girl or lad
Hold the fire
Stay calm and quiet
It is no time for a riot
Stay above all that
Wear your happy hat
Hold the fire
Put a smile on your face
Make this a cheerful place
Put your troubles behind you
Better to be happy than blue.

Graeme Doherty

Simple Pleasures

There is a lot of misery in the world today
But there is much to cheer us,
At the start of a new day.

The glory of the morning
When the sunlight gilds the sky.
The cheerful song of the blackbird
Perched in the tree nearby.
The graceful flight of the buzzard
As he soars up in the air
And the sound of children's voices
As they sing at morning prayer.
Friends and family round us
As we travel on life's way
And moon and stars to guide us
At the ending of the day.

Christine Youd

Smugs And Me

My darling wife had passed away,
I was lost and in the wilderness of grief.
Then, you were there, Smugs, my lovely girl,
With coal-black, laughing eyes and smiley face.

You, too, had sadness in your loving heart,
But we were meant to meet and laugh and love.
And laugh and love we did, for all those lovely years,
Back to happiness and joy for you and I.

That little car of yours, took us so many miles,
To sit on sun-bleached, sea-washed benches.
Drinking wine and laughing like children,
Your dark locks of hair, blowing in the breeze.

Springtime walks in Oxford's glorious streets,
Summer strolls on Bournemouth's golden sands.
Autumn ambles in Stratford's special places,
Winter at Christmastime, in Canterbury's Cathedral.

Not a day passed, when we did not laugh and sing,
Or hold each other's hand and walk with joy.
I am so glad we met, dear Smugs, I loved you then,
I love you now and always will, my lovely.

You too, Smugs, have been taken from me now,
Far too young and I am sad, but not dark.
For every day I find myself smiling with joy,
At things we said and did and loved, my dear.

Glyn Davies

Room Inside

Solemn sister holds her breath
Silent, cheek to cheek with this tiny brother
Who seeks the softness of her skin.

The eldest strokes his head
His will is to embrace as an equal
  But touch lightly, hold easily
    He is not yet grown enough
To join safely in a brother's game.

Now we look as one, eye to eye
  And I read there that it is
An unexpected pleasure that we meet
And so my heart is opened yet once again.

Yvonne Slagt-Fordham

Ninety-Five Not Out

I have been a nonagenarian for six years I have been told
For other generations it means, truly, I am quite old
The change begins when you have survived for nine and eighty years
Be sure whatever your station in life with all the joy there will also be tears
Tears when you think life is unfair
Remembering hours you are alone, looking at vacant chairs
Joy, rejoicing the safe arrival of a second son
Tears when you stand by his graveside, life has to go on
Ninety-five years growing older and older, shorter in wind but in memory long
Memories, memories, I am singing that old school song
Greatest wealth is content with a little, a quotation I once read
No silver linings in the twenties, grateful for a handout of soup and bread
Then time changed so quickly for me, much better times ahead
The love of a wife and family, a humble home, a job and money to spend
'Tempus Fugit' retirement, an era had come to an end
Retirement without a partner, a happening for which I had not prepared
The things we had planned to do, remembering the problems we shared
Thirty-four years of retirement, accepting change, getting old will bring
Coping with health adversities, still able to sing
'Count your many blessings, name them one by one'
With hindsight was there better things I could have done?
Wishful thinking will not help me now, ninety-five is rather late
Whatever happens tomorrow, is often described as fate
Today I am very happy, I'll give thanks for the blessings I've had
Greetings from children, grandchildren, great-grandchildren tomorrow I'll not be sad
The dawn brings another today, in this rich creation we share
Thank you, Lord Jesus, for me the words You've given, in Your gracious love and care
That my pen has spread a little pleasure
In these multiple years above the allotted three score years and ten
Dear Lord, my gratitude I cannot measure.

F G Norgrove

To Byzantium

I drift, as in a dream and come before
The iron stains that streak the studded door.
It creaks and groans and inward swings to show
A wide and dim-lit hall of candle glow.
A whirl of snow drives in to carpet stone,
Till boom of door - shut signals me, alone.
This ancient mansion, filled with frosty airs,
What lives or lies beyond the darkened stairs?

Deep dust betrays the floor not trod for years,
But mutterings and whispers fill my ears,
While fitful sconces dance the panelled walls
That hold old secrets: scandals, glitt'ring balls.
I upwards glide, by rich-carved newel posts
Of sleeping nymphs, led on by ghostly hosts
That form as wraiths and then as quickly fade,
To come alive as beauties, fine arrayed

In sapphired gowns and rubies, a dazz'ling sight,
A swirl of wealth and life by candlelight
As faded tapestries come live again
To fife and drum that beat a lost refrain.
The Lords and Ladies gay, old servants grey,
They smile and nod in turn and point my way,
Till down the long perspective looms a door,
Where I, uneasy, stand and wait before

The legend, scripted fine in glowing gold:
'Avaunt thou Time, for here We break thy hold'.
I pause and enter and float in mighty space
Of thinning clouds in fast and teeming race
Through deepest blue, whilst ever in my ears,
A mystic music sounds that stills my fears.
And She now comes, as up the shining stairs,
In clearing mist, She takes my hand in Hers.

Epilogue

And as we speed through starlit wastes, we come,
Barefoot, in Love, before Byzantium.

Brian MacDonald

Reflections

Count your blessings - reminisce
The findings of each day
A crescent moon I saw last night
A snowdrop bud today
Reluctant to open while cold winds blow
The beauty within this small flower will show
Such pleasure I'll get when this miracle takes place
As with patience I wait to see that small face.

Count your blessings in this changing world
They will be memories to keep or unfurl
For blessings are not in material things
Compared to new life a baby can bring.

Blessings are in the seasons of change every year
The treasures you find to remind you bring tears
But look for the sunrise, vivid in colour so bright
Or a sunset as beautiful on a cold, frosty night
Webs woven by spiders, an intricate delight
Count your blessings for they are all there
They can be yours and are free for us all
Created by love with hands unseen as leaves fall
Take time to look around, it's all there to see
Before science and Man weald the axe to destroy
The summer sun is yet to shine in time
As I pray new life and hope will shine.

Irene Siviour

Blue Hyacinth

Stars fall
from its thick stem,
its scent
assaults the walls.

Six-petalled
variegated bells
cluster into a poem,
a tumble of perfume

from a bulb
planted in dark autumn.
In its thin layers
circle secrets.

Sue Moules

The Changing Scene

Standing, looking out of my window
Such an expanse to see,
The Earth in her morning finery
One of nature's mysteries.

But all around the peaceful scene is changing
As machinery comes into play
Turning over field and hedgerow
Making way, as roads are now being converted into motorways.

And houses also taking precedence on land
For sale.
Gone are the animals' natural habitats
Where's home going to be for them?

And with the increasing rise in pollution
No one seems to be doing anything
There are lots of conversations, but no solutions
As it's affecting everything
Even our weather has taken a bad turn.

How can we make resolutions?
For they're awful hard to keep
Living in this troubled world
That's full of selfishness and greed.

But still we count our blessings
Though small they seem to be
And as each new day develops
With strength of mind we'll see it through.

Valerie Thompson

Photograph - Circa 1942

The four of us, in summer wear,
My brother there, with Brylcreemed hair,
And sisters three, with winning smiles,
In the middle of a war.
Why was it shot, this picture rare?
Dressed so smart and tidy hair,
Peg's wedding or her 21st?
She can't remember, nor can I,
Captured by the camera's eye,
The four of us, in black and white,
We smile for all eternity,
Until the children throw it out!

Sheila Seabourne

The Gardener's Hope

Last year I could not call a year of grace
Waiting for spring, its soft breath on my cheek
Instead each day brought darkness, cold, so bleak
The wind round every corner slapped my face.

I tried to walk with friends upon the way
Umbrellas up, their movement stiff against the rain
We could but give the slightest nod that day
To stand for long the sleetish winds did pain.

Homeward-bound with discontent to stoke the fire
Boil yet another kettle - hug the hearth
I even dreamt of India, saw the funeral pyre
Golden heat the sun's rays throughout the Earth
Flames leaping, refining all to gold.

Now sense must come - 'tis summer in a while
The garden shows the filtering sun so bold
The blossom and the bloom is set on trial
To come however ill the months may seem.

Behatted, coated and bewildered round each border in a dream
Numbed fingers plucking flowers in their bed
Another month pass on and to the future look ahead.

Bear with nature and its provoking way
Summer must surely come in radiance to stay
Long enough for aching bones to nourish flesh to bare
Bring love to all the things put in our care.

God alone decides how to misplace
His to wither any vine without a trace
All in a trice our minds and hearts are clear
We greet the sun with upturned hands and face
Forget the days which nearly did not grace.

Pamela Estelle Gibson

Ageing

Old age is something that comes to us all,
The healthy, weak, small and the tall,
It's like life's ups and downs,
That miss none of us,
So look forward to it without a grudge.
For when we reach that stage,
We should never misjudge,
As a lifetime we've had to learn wisdom and trust,
Like all human beings, there is sometimes a flaw,
If we look close enough, that flaw's in us all,
As nobody is perfect,
Most of us know,
So look forward to old age with a little more glow.

P Ashcroft

Harborne Walkway

Hissing, spitting traveller
Steaming thro' the culvert
Blackened iron monster
With its belly on fire
Track and wheels in
A hurried hot flirtation
Grumbling thro' to Harborne
From the city spire

Puffing, groaning, gasping
Swearing at the incline
Bursting at the buffers
With its people-packed cars
Barristers and butchers
Men from 'The Prudential'
Hurry home to suppers
Or their favourite bars

Dusty 'Brum' commuters
Quickly to-ing, fro-ing
Weary heads a-nodding
O'er the 'Evening Mail'
Eternal tussling
Over open windows
Tired, triumphant females
Retreating from 'The Sales'

Beeching's cruel axes
Chopping up the railways
Harborne flier falling
To the senseless blade
Rusting rail lines
Tripping up the rabbits
Running thro' to nowhere
While the memories fade

Bless preservation
What a lovely notion
Open up the rail route
For a walking way
Sunday lovers
Strolling where the lines went

Count Our Blessings

Breathe sweet honeysuckle
Where the squirrels play

Dusky bluebell carpet
Fitted where the train roared
Clovers white and purple
Brush meandering feet
Yarrow and cuckoo flowers
Blue germander speedwell
Lazily in splendour
Match Man's best ever feat

'We were here before you'
Dandelion to engine
'Blow your whistle elsewhere
Where the people rush'
Locomotive lovers
Miss the hiss of progress
Forget-me-not lovers
Hear the sweet, sweet hush

Blighted elm tree benches
Blending with the vista
Resting, questing amblers
Watch the sun swing low
Lovers and ramblers
All who love the sweet life
Walk home with a smiling heart
Reach home with a glow.

Pamela James

Dancing Conductor

He dances:
legs, feet, hands, arms, shoulders, head;
in his brain
he is dancing;
in the brains of the audience
there is dancing;
the players' feet are tapping;
in their brains
they are dancing too;
the conductor dances -
hips, waist, chest, back,
every part of him

Outside the concert hall
is the whole world
not dancing?

Neville Davis

Count Your Blessings

It's easy enough to say we should count our blessings
Not so easy, perhaps
When you lose sight of what those blessings are
So perhaps these lines may help us to see how rich we really are

Riches are the sounds of life as each new day is born
Two ears hear and two eyes to see the morning dawn
Warm clothes to wear and two legs firm and strong
Riches are a loved one there to kiss you when you go
A friendly neighbour at the gate, who waves and shouts, 'Hello!'
A sure and steady job in life so you can pay your way
And pleasant folk to smile at you and work with every day
Riches are a free land, where you're not afraid to speak
People with a conscience where the strong will aid the weak
A land where justice is the right of all and not the few
Where children have a chance to grow up strong
And straight and true
Riches are the things we have, but never think about
The precious gifts other nations have to do without
Won for us in times gone past by men long dead and gone
They fought for us so we should count our riches, one by one.

Matilda Phoebe Fishwick

Count Our Blessings

Count our blessings, every one,
From the food on your plate,
To the food in your tum,
To your kids in school,
Plus your dad and mum,
Your neighbour in the yard,
Where birds and bees hum,
Your cousin, who's a sailor
But minus his rum!
For health and wealth,
To make you less dumb,
For peace and happiness,
By gum!
Tickling a baby's tum,
Whistling a tune,
Or even a hum,
All these make up a tidy sum.
Let's count our blessings, every one.

Gill Mainwaring

Stop Awhile

If you are feeling down and low,
Not knowing which way to turn or go,
Just stop awhile and look around,
At all the beauty that can be found.

Try taking a walk down a country lane,
Or in a forest after rain,
Go into town, sit on a seat,
Where other lonely people you may meet.

With your eyes you have the power,
To see all there is to see,
The colours of the rainbow,
Flowers that bloom, birds and all the trees.

Then your hands, they can be busy,
As each day comes along
And be thankful for the air you breathe,
That helps to keep you strong.

Be thankful too, for the legs you have,
So that you can walk, run, or even play,
For your heart that keeps you going,
And the love that comes your way.

Then there is the sun and moon,
Beautiful starry nights, and
All the beauty that's abound,
To fill you with delight.

So, with all these gifts around you,
You have riches by the score,
Just forget all your troubles
And find happiness once more.

Maud Eleanor Hobbs

Musical Interludes

Throughout life spirits need lifting
When dark days and thoughts surround us.
In times of war, musicians have
Taken great risks with their lives
To entertain and boost morale
Of battle-weary, homesick troops.
In World War II civilians
Attended works' canteen concerts
And dinner hour performances
To relax from armaments work.

To stirring tunes of all nations,
Military bands and soldiers
Keep time and march in formation,
Giving observers much pleasure.

Churches resound with hymn-singing.
Often messages touch us
And lighten the load we carried
When we entered our Lord's own place.

But what of my own remedies
For my gloom and pits of despair?
Circumstances of my lifestyle
Are not what I would have chosen,
Though like many other persons
I have to make the best of them.
Vocal and orchestral music
Have long been nearest to my heart.
Listening to Classic FM,
Tapes, CDs, practising singing,
Watching Prom concerts on TV,
Bring me back to serenity.

E Joan Knight

Best Described In A Song

Emotions are best described in a song,
Listen good, listen hard, listen long.
Our feelings we have aren't right or wrong
Remember the words in your favourite song.
Songs with special words can be healing
Because after all we generate our own feeling.

Anthony Bernard Harper

Forward Planning

Though Adam's creation was perfect indeed
he heeded the Devil who planted a seed,
its root was rebellion and hating and sin
which grows like a weed and rampages within.

Another creation was 'Jesus the Christ,
most holy and perfect, the lamb sacrificed,
to come to the Earth to atone for all sin' -
believe and He sows you a new seed to win.

Its fruit will be righteous and loving and true,
a gift from the Father to me and to you.
His planting will flourish, accomplish His plan -
a harvest of love from this one righteous man.

Though Christ was begotten as God's only Son,
this plan was created to save everyone,
rebellion and hate simply fading away
in every believer when God has His way.

Winnie Pat Lee

God's Blessings

The sun is out, there's been no snow around,
And the birds are merrily singing,
There's been much wind and breezes abound,
Trees' branches they've been flinging.

The squirrels are running along the fence,
Looking for acorns and nuts,
They've even been sitting on the bench
And eating the birds' peanuts.

I sit at my window and watch all the happenings,
The scenes are ever-changing,
The birds playing games in and out the ivy,
From bird bath to table, their space far ranging.

There's a blue sky and cotton wool clouds
And dappled sunlight across the lawn,
The sparrows, doves, pigeons and crows,
Awaiting for their chorus at dawn.

I have friends all around me
And God's nature outside,
Let me count my blessings
And live and love with pride.

Maureen Williams

Count Your Assets

'Count your assets, one by one,'
Advice came from Joe's friend
'Evil has to you been done,
But your trade must not end.'
Counting assets in his store,
Joe was in deep despair,
'Empty shelves and damaged door,
Fittings beyond repair!'
'Surely, one thing you have missed,
Very important still.
You omitted from your list,
The asset of goodwill.
Well your corner shop is known,
As is your friendly face.
Firmly has your business grown
And blessed has been this place.
Many know you have been kind,
Food for them you reserved,
Shut-ins, groceries would find,
Beyond your duty served.'
Compensation to Joe poured
Eased from his bitter pill,
Joe and business were restored,
Because of his goodwill.
Faithful is God's servant, true
And is no longer stressed,
God's goodwill he seeks to do,
By this great asset blessed.

D J Price

Morning Sky Over Suburbia

I stare with wonder at a flame-wrinkled sky
set on a canvas of light blue
stretching all across commuter land
as motorists entombed in steel shells
vex about when the lights will change,
the sight like a wounded snake.
A mist rolls softly across the park
as birds majestically glide
and lights still shine in distant streets
as if they were fallen stars.

Then the mutable clouds turn yellow
as the sun peers over the horizon
but nature's magic has caressed my mind
before the boredom of the daily grind.

Guy Fletcher

Look Around You

If you're feeling in despair
Count your blessings, they're everywhere.
Look around you have some shares
Of all God's blessings, not only cares.
The little bird up in the tree
Singing his heart out for you and me
Buds on the flowers bursting out you see
Soon to be brilliant and buzzing with the bee.
After the storms look up to the sky
Bright blue with fluffy white clouds drifting by.
Sun shining warm on the world from on high
Bringing back life where sleeping plants lie.
Put a spring in your step as nature has done
Walk tall and smile, make your life fun
Count your blessings again - break into a run
Say a kind word as you go, feel the warm sun.
See a baby smile as you go on your way
It sets the whole face aglow and it will make your day.
Don't look back on your life, look forward with hope
Think of these things then know you will cope.

Betty R Lloyd

Special Inspiration

My thoughts are with this lady, lying lonely on her bed,
This is her life of sanctuary, for her, each day to dread,
Her joints, her bones disjointed, her frame has withered so,
It makes me cross she's stricken . . . will this arthritis ever go?
A murmur you hear not never, as she lies there looking round,
For her too late, she prays I know, a cure that might be found,
Her life, a window outward view onto the garden lawn,
For months, for years and weeks and hours her life is so forlorn,
Smile, determination for each day has seen her through this pain
Those childhood thoughts are happy ones, please bring them back again,
She's inspiration to us all, her strength to conquer this,
But next time when you come around, 'Please give my aunt a miss,'
Rid her please, of paining joints, it's no life for my aunt,
To see her suffer without fuss, I feel helpless, *help I can't,*
I count my blessings day to day for what life gives to me,
But my dear aunt knows nothing else to be just plain, pain free,
My thoughts are with her daily in the quietness of her room,
I wish God's miracle would happen and make her well quite soon.

Caroline Bone

Time Gone By

You still play around all the time,
Even though you have now reached nine,
Where have all the years gone,
Since you were my baby, little one?

Laughing, joking, having fun,
You will always be my number one son,
Speeding here, there and everywhere on your bike,
Not a moment to lose, you have a goal in sight,
To meet your friends and have a good time,
I have to let you go and be independent and that's fine,
But remember everything we have taught you,
Be polite and kind, like you know you ought to.

When you come home and go to bed,
You don't have to tell me everything that has been said,
Sometimes there is no need for me to know,
You can be sure I'm here, if you ever feel low,
That's what mums are for, to help when needed,
Then I know your dad and I have succeeded.

Then when you have grown up and we are old,
You will be there to make decisions and be bold.
Look after us son, like we love and look after you
And I promise you one day you will be rewarded true.

Jill K Gilbert

A Celebration

Hip hip hooray, for this very special day
Ten years ago they opened the door
To this quite special place
If only the building could talk
Of wondrous things being done
By so many kind people
A haven of rest to so many folk
Who need help in many ways
Today we have a beautiful cake
Made for the occasion
Stirred by each and everyone present
Created by our lovely cook
With fun and laughter from all
And surely making us ponder
And think, how lucky we are
To have our lovely day centre
Here in Hungerford
May it continue forever
With Richard around
To keep us all in order.

J Nicoll

Sweet Memories

Looking back on fading years,
Years of happiness and tears,
I get to thinking of the days,
When mothers struggled with their stays.

The morning cups of hot sweet sop,
'Runs' down the street with whip and top,
The noisy games of 'put and take',
Mam's aromatic seeded cake.

My sister gaily blowing bubbles,
The copper boilers wash day troubles,
Bradman and Larwood in cigarette packets,
Flat pieces of wood were our Wimbledon rackets.

On the chalked hopscotch squares my memory doth linger,
The thrill and the dare of 'knocking up ginger'
The grand prix of the streets was a race with your hoop,
The noise from the cock in Dad's chicken coop.

The fuss and the mess to kill that old sinner,
Red, white limed walls foreran Christmas dinner,
A stout-handled club to hit high my catti,
New white Whitsun shoes, soon tarred and quite tatty.

Street games we'd play for hours and hours,
Whilst Mother embroidered her silk leaves and flowers,
Dad cut and rubbed his smelly thick twist,
Uncles and aunts called around to play whist.

Black pea soup with simmering ham bone
And forecasting rain by consulting our fir cone,
The trips to the beach by horse and trap,
Baby enfolded on Mam's ample lap.

Rob Wilton we'd clap from high in the 'Gods'
And the weekend objections to boiled senna pods,
Oh, memories sweet, they come and they go,
Mine give a lift when I'm feeling low.

Fred Davies

Blessings

B is for blessings large and small
L is for love we give and receive from all
E is for excitement when friends come to call
S is for sharing, it's not hard to do
S is for smiling at everyone we see
I is for interest in this world of ours
N is for positive thinking without no
G is for God the Maker of all
S is for Saviour who loves us so.

Rachel Ritchie

The Makin' Green *

(For Joan Eardley, RSA, 1921-1963)

Catterline Bay
curves like a sickle
around the sea-lashed shore
where snell nor'easters stab like knives.

Under the floating ghost
of a pale winter sun, a straggle
of low cottages coories doon
into the gale, hugging the wrenched cliff top.

The arc between the Watch House and the Creel
you made your own, immortalised, unravelling
the drying salmon nets, interpreting the barley stooks,
identifying with the blood-red clay.

Here, on the makin' green, you set up your easel
and, like Turner, in a clash of pigment,
confronted wild, unbroken walls of water,
the boiling waves still spinning over rocks,

the gurling storm. Here at douce harvest time,
on golden days, you painted poppies,
cornfields, sunsets, hives of bees,
the jade-green moon in a slate-blue sky.

And here, to the wailing wave, the tempest's rack,
mourned by the curlew's melancholy keen,
so briefly borrowed you were given back,
your ashes scattered on the lonesome makin' green.

*(*A flat area on the shore at Catterline
where nets were woven and mended.)*

Norman Bissett

Present For The Future

We grow with acts of kindness,
Now knowing what we are weaving
Into the cloth of life,
Multicoloured strands of interwoven
Lives,
Each being part of a greater design,
Our life's long actions add to the whole
Design,
Further generations, we hope enhancing
The design,
With the multicoloured strands of action,
For greater good of whole Earth.

Brian Tallowin

My Friend Janice - Sixty Years Young

As we travel through our lives
There are people all around
With some of them we will collide
Off some we will rebound

As we reach this time in our lives
Perhaps with fear and trepidation
It is in fact a time for looking back
And yet a time for preparation

Preparing for our time to come
Looking forward, but at this age
We are older and much wiser
Not locked in a 'PC' cage

As you celebrate this birthday
What's important, we all know
Is not what you've amassed in the bank
Where on holiday you go

Not how big your house is
Not your make of car
These are not the kind of things
That makes us who we are

We can measure our success in life
Not with money, following trends
But on who we can rely on
The old chestnut of 'good friends'

Janice is the birthday girl
The first sixty of the year
And if she's counting her success
She has nothing at all to fear

For her birthday, what she wanted
Was to spend the time with friends
But if she asked them all to come
The list would never end

What stands out about this friendship
Is that it stood the test of time
The distance in-between us
Could be a hill to climb

But there has never been a time
When we've not been welcomed in
No matter how long in-between
And there's usually quite a din

We can talk and laugh and sing
We can argue till we're blue
Because I know that nothing will change
My friend will still be you.

Ann Tyas

Count Our Blessings

Whether fortunes may rise or fall,
As through life we make our steppings,
Always in future we must all,
Remember to count our blessings.

No matter where our paths may lead,
Whatever shape our dwellings,
We must try to temper our speed,
Leaving time to count our blessings.

Who knows where life leads day by day,
Given our comings and goings,
Allow some time along life's way,
To stop and just count our blessings.

The speed of life just gathers pace,
We vary our clothes and dressings,
Yet through it all we find a place,
Just to pause and count our blessings.

We struggle with all our beliefs,
Many mistakes in our guessings,
Let us then ponder with relief,
That we can still count our blessings!

David Spanton

Wistful Thinking

Postcard from Dordogne
Evoking family holidays.

Lunch preparing clatter
Through doors wide to sunflower fields,
Butterfly grandchildren prostate
Beneath an afternoon sheet.
Spider-Man salamanders on a hot lintel.
Bric-a-brac stalls
Where antique prices were asked for junk
And haggling never failed.
Escaping a zenith sun
In the sepulchral cool of a cavernous church.
Lizette's estaminet
When earthbound stars sliced night
And long evenings were too short;
(We stopped counting after three bottles!)

Pity about our health,
Wish we were there.
But memories linger.

John Harwood

Count Your Blessings

A blessing in disguise uplifts the weary spirit,
When we are troubled with anxiety,
Just look at all the opportunities around,
At nature's wondrous unlimited bounty,

When we are blessed with a unique body and mind,
When others less fortunate than ourselves,
Have a multitude of handicaps,
That make our troubles seem so small and insignificant,

So hold on to the message of love and hope
And bless others profoundly who have no home,
No future, the weak and vulnerable,
Who walk the troubled streets alone,

By helping others, we are helping ourselves,
To bring achievement, hope and glory,
To a beautiful universe and world,
That chance meeting full of smiles,

When the heart is noble and true,
When we change our perspective,
Anything is achievable and possible,
When we show appreciation to others,

When we are respectful and kind,
We can all become role models,
To the young, adult and old,
Who may have lost their way, for whatever reason,

With compassion and understanding,
With the magic of wisdom and sincerity,
With no mask or trick,
We can all accomplish beautiful miracles,

When love finally champions through,
With dedication and determination,
Perseverance will follow you,
To the ends of the Earth when we say thank you,

And the universe will listen to that truthful whisper inside,
For a blessing that was meant for you,
For helping others out of a dilemma,
For God was listening too.

James Stephen Cameron

Countryside Delight

We walk the fields together each day
Me and my pup, Taffy
And as we look around us
It's amazing what we see
A deer rushes through the hedge
It's gone back to the wood
The bluebells flowering on the bank
They really do look good
The buzzard sitting on its nest
High up in the ash tree
The wild ducks swimming on the pond
Oblivious to my dog and me
People driving their cars from morning till night
Not for me the motorways
The countryside is just right.

R J Moulton

The Best Things In Life Are Free - Happiness

Happiness
Is being surrounded by myriad books,
And all the time in the world
To read them.

Happiness
Is for words to appear
From nowhere into my mind
And form into an epic poem
That I have written.

Happiness
Is spending time together,
Going for a drive,
Admiring the countryside
And everything else we see,
Sitting in companionable silence
Just looking; together.

Sarah Robinson

Thankful For Life

I count my blessing for everyone
For all that I have
And all that I've done
I treasure each minute of the day
Each hour I have
Each hour that I stay
I live for the memory of my life
For all what it is
And to be a wife
These are the memories I love to keep
Share comfort to all
And for friends to seek
I cannot wish for more than what's true
I have more than some
That's out of the blue
I have everything I'm thankful for
I count my blessings
And the world I tour.

Margaret Burtenshaw-Haines

Fifty Years Of Blessings

It was fifty years ago I wed
I don't regret the vows I said
We've had our trials and our joys
Blessed we were with two healthy boys

Of grandchildren we now have four
They're a blessing, that's for sure
We have a roof over our head
Warm nourishing food and a comfy bed

Friends who love, friends who share
People who show they really care
Yes, there's been sickness, pain and tears
But so many blessings in fifty years

We're not rich but then we're not poor
We have so much to be thankful for
So as we walk along life's way
We count our blessings every day.

Mary Shepherd

Why Blessings Should Be Counted

Take some time to count
Your blessings every day.
Then you realise
That love has come your way.
For love is the real reason
Why blessings do take place.
Love is the reason why
Our hearts feel full of grace.

When we realise we are blessed
We value all life around.
Each emotion we feel and try
Keeps feet firmly on the ground.
Blessings are to be cherished
They cause such joy and hope.
Pure warmth is felt by many
And blessings help you cope.
They shine and smile in lives
Surely easing the way ahead.
Blessings are gently presented
So souls and spirits will be fed.

Nichola J Keel

Cloudy Night

Cloudy night
Not much in sight
Soft orange tinge
The street light singe
A peaceful haze
Disrupts my gaze
Of occasional twinkle
The starlight sprinkle
Cloud forms sail
The earthly veil
Holds in the warm
Until early morn
Temperature fall
Songbirds will call
Out for the dew
A morning of new
Start the new day
In a positive way!

F Ian Tiso

Frost

Scampering faces in the thickets
Disappear at the crackle of a twig,
And where a cobweb hangs, I see
The tattered diamonds steal along
The fragile threads.

A puff of air breaks the line,
The shimmering beads fall down,
And all are dashed to pieces
Against the decaying leaves.

Like tears the wet patches traverse
The path through the wood,
Where a million broken jewels
Lie beneath our wandering feet.

Soon they will freeze
Into white crystals
And a great blanket will
Hide a million jewels
From the tossing stars.

Robert Lambert

Son

God blessed me with a bundle of joy
A beautiful bouncing baby boy
In my arms I held him
Close towards my heart
For now his life's beginning
And we will never part.

I'll be your strength
As you are mine
I'll give you love now
And for all time.

You're just so special, son
You see
And I thank the Lord
For sending thee.

Dominica Kelly

Just A Moment

Just a moment, could I borrow a few seconds of your time?
To explain to you your journey in life
Is exactly the same as mine.

You see, we walk by faith not by daylight
And try to do our best in things which are right.
But life can be hard and throughout the years
We both encounter stress, darkness and fears.

Yet throughout this world of ours
And through all types of defeats,
There's a glorious ray of hope with new friends we get to meet.
You see, there's always this other person . . .
Who will say the things we've just wanted to hear
And isn't it peculiar they can take away that fear,
It's because they've walked in your shoes
They've been exactly down your way,
So . . . never feel lonely, you see, this friend's journey
  is really part of *your* day.

Just a moment, could you spare a few more seconds of your time?
So I can tell you of a peace I've found, and where it is to find
My peace I will leave with you, not a peace the world can give
That perfect peace deep in your heart that helps you as you live.

You see these words can be said in one moment,
These words are for you my good friend
There from Jesus, with love and comfort,
Just ask and he'll send a new friend . . . so

Thank you for giving me these moments
Time is so precious you see
Now we're not just good friends . . . but companions,
In the good fellowship,
With him . . . and you . . . and me.

Les Campbell

The Farmer

Feast thine eyes if thou wilt,
Upon this wondrous patchwork quilt.
From barren land by the farmer's hand,
Crops are sown thus crops are grown,
Here grow seeds to meet our needs,
Without the farmer 'twould be just weeds.

He toils through sun and wind and rain,
To bring us eggs and milk and grain.
He mends the pens and feeds the hens,
Milks the cows and farrows the sows,
He bails the hay all through the day,
Our praise and thanks must go his way.

Maryrose Walmsley

Count Your Blessings

A new day dawns; shine with the sun!
Fresh time is offered, let's have fun.
Birds are singing; have you no voice?
Make others happy, it's your choice.

A smile remembered like that photograph,
A touch, a word, can make you laugh.
New starts may frighten; fear thou not!
Others share the same tight knot.

A parent, sibling first helped you out.
Look up and over when there's none about.
Your hairs are filed no sparrow falls . . .
Without some care; notice the walls!

Have you no treasure? Can't you eat?
Then drink in pleasure from your seat.
You cannot move? Then blink an eye
For someone soon is coming by.

Rejoice this day, there's no other way
To face the future come what may.
Clouds may soon hide the sun
Give thanks while the day is run.

Peter M Ashforth

Lovely Things

I know of many lovely things
In which I can rejoice.
Listening to Mother as she sings
In her melodious voice.

Looking at beauteous countryside,
Watching small children play,
Opening cards at Christmastide,
Singing a joyful lay.

Dancing a quickstep at the ball,
Wearing a gorgeous dress,
Reading a book and best of all,
Seeing God's loveliness.

Jillian Mounter

Spring

The curtains of winter
Are being pulled back
We will see the daffodils
Again.

The sun has put its
Hat on
As the sun proclaims
It's coming out to play
Suddenly it's May.

The goddess lights the soul
We're no longer peasants
We drink clear water
From the well.

They try to brainwash
Us to war
But we had it all before
A moment lost in time
Ends my little rhyme.

Thomas E Murphy

Blessings

I count my blessings each and every day
For all good things which come my way
My family, friends who share laughter and fun
Refreshing rain, the warmth of the sun
A bed to sleep in, food on my table
Health and strength to make me able
I do at least one good daily deed
Helping others in their time of need
Beautiful sunrises, sunsets too
Or just to enjoy a beautiful view
When it's hard to keep going when life is tough
If days are dark and the road is rough
I count my blessings, I am not on my own
With Jesus beside me, I am not alone
So, today, tomorrow and every day
I'll keep counting the blessings which come my way.

W Barrett

Love Is . . .

And love is the manger
And love is the star
And love is the fusion
Be it near or afar.
And love is the promise
In constancy given.
And love is the palette
That bursts from the prism.
And love is the seed
And love is the birth
And love is the fruit
From the root of dry earth.
And love is the gift
Beyond price and yet free.
And love is the candle
And love is the tree.
And love is the question
And love the reply
The gift born in Heaven
That never can die.
And love never changes
In three, yet the whole.
And love is the vision
Of mind, heart and soul.
And love is the leper
And love is the Lord
And love is the action
Made flesh by the word.
And love is the rose
And love is the thorn
And love is the nail
And love is the crown.
And love is the alpha
The beginning and end
And there in the midst
God chose me - a friend.

Pamela M Leaf

Here And Now

I need to say thank you for eighty-five years,
Of ups and downs with laughter and tears,
For a journey of a lifetime I give my thanks,
To a God who never fails to fill in the blanks.

When I need a friend, He finds ways to provide,
I still do my best with His hand to guide,
I accept many changes that are meant to be,
I learn to adjust when they are clear to me.

God's peace and love are our innermost needs,
We can have these in a crowd or alone on a beach,
When we let go of self-doubts and really believe,
We see we are in God's plan and He will achieve.

I see so much beauty in God's created world,
Autumn tints - spring flowers - the seasons' colours unfurl,
In new life all around us, of this we are a part,
With God's love and blessings to enrich every heart.

Kathleen McBurney

Happiness

It's like the butterfly
That settled on my hand
One sunny afternoon
Not so long ago.

Your heart may sing
With delight
At the flight
Of the butterfly.

Or your mood may swing
To the depths of gloom
At the thought of winter
And what it may bring.

But your spirits may soar,
You feel happy once more
At the thought of spring and the butterfly.

Catch happiness whenever you can,
Young man!

Christina Stowell

Springtime Walk

The May blossom white,
A wonderful sight,
A paean of praise
For the chilly spring days.

The buttercups gold,
Their glories unfold,
Reflect here below,
The sun's golden glow.

The woodland pathway
Shows the best of the day,
The breathtaking view
Of a carpet of blue.

Daphne Wilkinson

A Hand Will Guide You

Communication can strengthen
Your hand. Conversation is a
Gift it will help you to understand.
Temptation should be resisted
And rejected out of hand.
A trail should be just a beginning.
Its purpose maybe not, a passage
To your freedom. Little
Things could mean a lot.
Trespass you will not.
A hand will guide you.
A light will show you the way.
Some things are created others will
Grow. Time won't change it.
No one may want to know.
You can live your life a stranger.
Get stuck in the past.
Life is what you make it.
Simple or not, a little bit of sympathy
Is better than none at all.
It should be appreciated no
Matter how small.

Richard Mahoney

Mustn't Grumble

When I wake up in the morning
And my eyes have power to see
With arms that can embrace you
My limbs . . . strong, walking free

With ears the power to listen
To each lovely birdsong trills
My soul gives thanks - 'tis blessed indeed
My heart with gladness fills

There's so much to be thankful for
These gifts . . . direct from Heaven
I grumble . . . *not!* but praise each day
True riches I've been given.

Elizabeth Joyce Walker

Blessed

Blessed are those who are forgiven -
May that include us all.
Blessed, those who kick the gossip habit,
Who do not judge and do not rabbit.
Blessed, too, are those who work
To help others and do not shirk.
Blessed are the druggies who succeed
In breaking free from ganja weed.
Blessed are those who help them do it
So they won't live their life to rue it.
Blessed are those whose crimes were many -
Oft leaving their victims without a penny -
Blessed, because they broke away
From sin and crime for a better way.
Blessed be the poor immigrant
Who safety and a home may want,
Blessed be government's kindly acts
That help them share our island pax.
Blessed are those who live for others
Knowing we are all sisters and brothers.
Blessed be the human race
That learns to live at God's slower pace.
Blessed all those who are forgiven.
Blessed be God indeed.

Jo Allen

Count Our Blessings

We moan and moan the weather's foul
The bus is late, packed and full -
Such rudeness from all British Rail
And all one's friends too busy to call.
It's much too hot or far too cold
And TV shows are crude - or worse -
Signs in the high street I've been told
To hold on tightly to my purse.
Hoodies and the metal face
Threaten me without a cause -
And now I feel right out of place
Always rushing - never pause.
But once I'm home I shift my gaze
To photographs of family dear -
To a warm home with chairs to laze
And my dear husband ever near. I
Count my blessings every day
I still have health and food to eat -
And spare a thought or start to pray
For those who have no name or street.
For those without a family name
Who walk the streets with hunger strong -
For all the weak and sick and lame
Give them the hope - let them belong.
Count your blessings - one by one
Pick up the phone and send some light -
And when the deed is promptly done
Sleep soundly in your bed tonight.

Valerie Cubitt

Memories

My sister and I sat quietly on the old rag mat
Mother reading aloud while knitting a hat
Waiting in lamplight for Dad to return home
Back from World War I, never again to roam.

Remember these words my mother would say
I still remember them to this very day
Now you count your blessings - name them one by one -
You will be surprised what God has done.

Eileen Witt-Way

The Club Walk

Come flaming June or chill December,
One day each month, ours to remember,
Remember for a dozen reasons,
The intrigue of the changing seasons.

Green spring, when magic's in the air,
Warm summer - colour everywhere,
The autumn when there's gold to spare,
And winter when it's all laid bare.

Yet we are never short of treasure.
Ours is wealth of no mean measure,
Invested in our company,
Is boundless, buoyant bonhomie.

The prospectus, as you may surmise,
An enterprise of exercise,
Our wanderlust to gratify,
Our souls and senses satisfy.

Pilgrims, we try to understand,
The beauty of our native land,
The country parks, the ancient towns,
The tangled woods and chalky downs.

There on a hilltop, pause to rest
And with a wondrous view be blessed,
Or, lost in awe we'll simply stare,
As if spellbound by legends there.

So lightly tread, as you pass by,
That breath of wind may be a sigh,
Of some fair maid or gallant knight,
Who linger yet, just out of sight.

In ones and twos, romantics dream,
The groups will chat on any theme
And where the time goes, Heaven knows,
Another walk draws to a close.

Tired, but content, at journey's end,
We may find time and funds to spend,
Upon a lunch and glass of beer,
Before a homeward course we steer.

If life's rich tapestry seems pale,
The air you breathe fumy and stale,
Maybe it's time to go and talk,
With people who enjoy to walk.

R Bowhill

Remember

A baby's hand, gripping my finger,
Tuneful song, sung by good singer.
The beauty of a baby's large clear eyes,
A dazzling, sparkling sunrise.
A glowing, wonderful sunset,
The colours I'll never forget.
The heat of God's sun on my face
My grandmother crocheting lace.
Welcome rain, after long drought,
Cheerful noise of children - they shout.
Gorgeous rainbow, over God's green fold
The sun going behind a cloud - so cold.
Rays of light, when sun shines through
A radiant sun, in a sky of blue.
Drifting clouds' shadows, on sunlit fields,
Floating clouds act as real heat shields.
So peaceful - a stroll in the park,
Stars that shine, when it is dark.
A day out, at the seaside,
All 'kids' enjoy a donkey ride.
The 'grown-ups' splodging in the sea
Trousers and dresses held up, on head a 'hanky'.
Sand in sandwiches and jugs of tea,
People watching and laughing at Punch and Judy.
Skylark's song in spring,
Cuckoo on the wing.
This is what I remember
From January to December.

Alfred Smirk

Spring

There is no other sound that gives
Such instant sweet delight,
Like the springtime song of happy birds
So tuneful, clear and bright.

Woodpecker drums upon a tree
Resounding through the wood.
Blackbird and robin sing for joy
Winter's past and life is good.

Little wrens flit to and fro,
Their high notes pure and true.
And moorhens dabble in the stream,
As we gaze for a flash of blue.

No kingfisher is seen today,
But tit and finch abound.
And the countryside is wondrously filled
With a glorious harmony of sound.

Christine Saunders

The Vision

I closed my eyes and there did see
A garden fair and a white blossom tree.
I looked again and standing there
Head bowed low, as if in prayer
A figure dressed in white was she
Standing under a white blossom tree.

I watched there in silence
Then just like a snowstorm
The blossoms all fell
Around the still form
In this garden so fair,
All this I could see
I could still see the figure
Under the white blossom tree.

Then it all faded
But who did I see
Perhaps the Mother of my God
Oh, I hope it was she
Who stood with bowed head
Under the white blossom tree.

Monica Guiry

Look Beyond

When you've only yourself to rely on
And nobody's shoulder to cry on,
When there's no one to say
'Are you all right today?'
And all those you knew have passed on;

When you're sitting there fretting and crying
And all of life's problems seem trying,
When you're wondering why
Life is passing you by
And you find yourself sobbing and sighing;

Things mostly come right in the end
There's hope and there's joy round the bend
If you give life a chance
You could probably glance
At a face you will know as a friend!

J Unsworth

Land Of Promise

Smell the sweet rose
gaze on a stout oak,
tread a castle keep
built of granite stone,
walk in a climate
fickle as nature's own
breath, wander through
fields glowing a
painter's hue, add
to all this a folk,
staunch, hearty and
brave, where freedom
is unfettered by guilt;
then ask of me
where is this place
having these gifts
which seem like
a bounteous dream?
The answer is simple,
its fame is unique;
the whole world
envies its shores.
Go, go, stand firmly
on England's rich soil,
close your eyes
and breathe deeply
keen air of the free,
then awake and savour the dream.

Harold Brawn-Meek

Blessings

Be as pure as the lily
Gentle and true as a dove
May you grow strong and stalwart as the oak
Fill your hearts with love.
Ever honest in word and deed
Be kind and tolerant towards your fellow men
Regardless of colour or creed;
Lend a sympathetic ear to the sick
And be forever true to yourselves.
To these codes of living you must try to stick
Let these be your goals and heritage.

Gwyneth Elizabeth Scott

We Are Brothers Of This, Our Fragile Earth

This Earth does not belong to us, but to all who visit
Its beauty and spiritual harmony, whether we
Are white or of a coloured skin, be we human or animal
Be we strong or weak, we all have a place on this planet.

Young or old, some wise in thoughts and words or innocent in youth,
We are here to go through time to visit its mountains tall and topped
With snow, cascades of white in waterfalls,
Or simple trickles of streams
That spread to rivers and then to oceans,
That precious giver of life - water.

The pink of another day with the rays of the morning sun's
Warmth to make the trees and flowers grow and blossom, for us and
Animals too, food for sustenance and then to give us cover from the
Chill of the night, where shadows dance and creatures of this
Time come out to feed, play and explore their Earth.

We are as harvesters, we sow the seed of life upon this Earth
And watch it grow, we cut and pick when it is ripe and in turn
Give thanks to the Earth for its goodness, sun, wind and water all
Harness their powers to help us in this our daily toil.

The fragile beauty of this our Mother Earth was given to us to love
And protect, this gentle but strong planet of ours, we are forever in
Its debt, it was made for us to cherish, for we are the brothers
Of this, our fragile Earth.

Carol List

Educated Musical Mind

Educated musical mind
Came from an early age
Of becoming disabled
It took centre stage
Also thinking life
Putting money back
Wake up morning singing
So music not of lack
Soul, Motown, pop and Reggae
Now jazz with classical
Above all else, now opera
See, one has matured.

Michael D Bedford

Nature's Blessings

There is no charge for rainbows
And birdsong is quite free.
You pay nothing for the summer breeze,
Or the gentle hum of the bee.

The twinkling stars and moonlight,
Flowers bathed in dew.
The sunrise and the sunset,
Each a blessing just for you.

The honeysuckle's perfume,
A cloudless sky of blue.
All are part of nature's gifts
And they're given freely too.

Even in nature's bleakest hour
You'll find a blessing there.
Every snowflake is unique
And snowdrops wait to stir.

There's an endless stream of blessings
So just think of one each day
Then your burden will seem less heavy
And hope will light your way.

Carole Revell

Blessings Remembered

I count my blessings one by one
Most of all the ones now gone,
Sadly look back down long years
Excuse me please if I shed tears.

As a young girl, lived through the war
Was blessed to survive, but left a scar,
Mother and Father loved me so dearly
This helped through life, still see them clearly.

Now I am living through the winter of life
Enjoy nature's glory, relax without strife,
Sunrise, sunset, each season changing
Birds high in trees, sweet choirs singing.

Photos in rows of son and family
These also my blessings, smiling so happily,
There's still one blessing, before it's too late
This world lives in peace, this blessing create.

Muriel Rodgers

White Down

Today we walked on White Down for butterflies and flowers
The sun was hot, the wind was light, we could have stayed for hours.
We found the clustered bellflower and violet helleborine,
Water-pepper and centaury, just waiting to be seen.
Basil, marjoram, viper's bugloss and scarlet pimpernel,
Ploughman's spikenard, yellow-wort and dainty little harebell.

We came across a grassy bank where scented flowers grew
And glimpsed the silver spotted skipper and the chalk hill blue.
The meadow brown and gatekeeper were dancing everywhere
And pretty little common blue joined in without a care.
We chased the clouded yellow, his colour very bright,
He flew into the chalk pit and disappeared from sight.

Then further on, on bramble hedge, sat delicate painted lady,
With comma, peacock, admiral and silver wash fritillary.
Time was quickly passing by and so we wandered back,
Just in time to see a deer standing in his track.
A marsh tit feeding, caught our eye, our walk was now complete
But we'll return again next year, for nature's little treat.

Jan Shorter

Suddenly, It's Spring

Exclusive fragrant fitted carpets
when bluebells stir covering mossy glades
offbeat springtime colour, carpets all shades blue
mingled velvet patches with violet purple blending
compliment the woodland view.

From nearby, cuckoo calling note, sounds the news
bitter winter cold, icy frost dismayed
sun-like reflection, daffodil crowds in bloom
broadcast chorus, the news by trumpets, gold conveyed.

Keenly, gardener's green lawns mow
dandelions capitulate, daisy days cut short over
honeybees' frantic, madly buzzing search
plentiful yesterday, nectar-filled flowering clover.

Spring fever spreads, the housewife sent
cobweb duster shaking crazy, flashing pails mops
hunting clutter hoards, in hiding, housebound kept
somewhere a busy kettle sings, all and everything stops.

Man about the house in action too
outside, inside maintenance, decorating, painting
annual motivation, blue sky contemplation and thank Heaven
suddenly, it's spring!

Mildred F Barney

Hawthorn Blossom

My bows are bent beneath my branches
Filled with blossom - heavily, of a beautiful cream.
A perfect flower spread so neatly
Upon the binding arms of a hawthorn tree.

A warm breeze whispers through my twisted finger
To release a fragrance so mellow and sweet.
What a fine reminder that it is midsummer and the bumblebees
Sip the nectar quite pleasantly -

While sitting on the hawthorn blossom
Like a perfect majestic seat.

Carole Morris

Priorities

Opened a can and
broke a nail

got the bread out -
it was stale

lost my purse on
the bus to town -
left my brolly, so
the rain came down

when I got home, I'd
locked myself out -
(keys on the table
without a doubt)

I forced a window through
a tiny chink

tripped on the ledge and
fell in the sink!

After all that, I needed
some tea - flopped in the
chair to watch TV

watching the news that
appeared on the screen,
children were starving -

a hellish scene

all of my problems dissolved
into air and I felt myself
thinking, *thank God I'm not
there!*

Jennifer D Wootton

The Flower In My Heart

The flower in my heart, it shines so bright,
The flower in my heart, it fills my soul with delight.

The flower in my heart, makes me sing a song,
About where I've been and where I belong.

The flower in my heart, never lets me feel blue,
It showers my body with a love that's oh, so true.

The flower in my heart, makes me feel so humble,
With this sweet, sweet flower, tell me how could I grumble.

The flower in my heart, makes me want to shout out loud,
Whether there is or is no crowd.

The flower in my heart, came from God that's for sure,
It protects me for ever, if I'm rich or if I'm poor.

The flower in my heart, makes me thank my lucky stars,
It helps me cope with all my hurts and all my scars.

Thank you Lord, for this special, sweet flower,
For it really does comfort me, each and every hour.

Garry Mitchell

The Simple Things In Life

I spied a daisy in flower today,
A dreary day, all cloudy and grey.
Out of season, alone in the grass,
Bright and wide open where I had to pass.
My spirits lifted, I went on my way,
A glimpse of summer on a winter's day.

These early days of the year seem long,
But the birds start singing their love song.
And new life is stirring all around,
As bulbs send their shoots above the ground.
When sunshine comes to pierce the gloom,
They all will be bursting into bloom.

Just the little things in life will cheer,
A helping hand, a listening ear.
A friendly word, a smile in the street,
Can lighten the hearts of those we meet.
It's the simple things that mean so much
And convey to us all God's healing touch.

Beryl R Daintree

In A Breath It's Gone

A grain of sand through fingers falls
Blows gently in the breeze.
In my heart a loved one calls
Words lost . . . upon the seas.

How complete, the unison, of sea and sand
Secrets and passions to keep.
Will Man it *keep* . . . or to its bosom
Death to bring . . . eternal . . . sleep!

As the spider weaves a silken web
Dew draped upon its threads.
This fragile Earth and all it holds
When oceans roar . . . *destruction* . . . spreads.

Waves crash and churn upon the shore
Taking all within its path.
Cleansing, to its inner core
Oblivious! Whether . . . rich or poor.

How gently now it laps my feet
Soft, as a rippling stream.
Provoked by Man it can erupt
To shatter all . . . one's dreams.

Gently, now it slumbers
Humming a gentle song.
How fragile life and all it holds
In a breath . . . and then . . . it's gone!

Sylvia Connor

Seasons

Autumn leaves floating down
Making slippery pavements all around,
A stormy day, washing can't dry
Winter has come, snowflakes fall
Covering the bulbs that wait for spring
When new life pops up everywhere
Lambs are born and my heart is glad to hear
The blackbird sing, twittering
Splashing in the birdbath
Take care of the soil, then flowers will bloom
Transforming the garden into nature's colourful wonderland
Contentment comes in the silent air
We see nature's beauty everywhere.

Joan M Waller

Only A Bird

It was one of those days,
You know the sort -
Dull, overcast, rain,
A peep of sun, a suggestion so short
Maybe a mistake, or maybe for fun
Just to tease and then to run.
Why show your face on such a day?
Hide behind a cloud, keep out of the way.

'Not so,' sang the robin, in my neighbour's tree,
'Let's cheer things up, we can - you will see.'
He gazed down from his perch and opened wide his beak,
His song was so sweet, I could not speak.
The sun came out, the clouds drifted away,
He was only a bird, but he brightened the day.

N M Beddoes

Friends

I have a friend who's calling round and popping in to see me,
We will have a good old natter, over a cup of tea.
We'll talk about the old days, when we were at different schools
And I'll tell her about the times, I was always breaking the rules,
I think my friend was good, when she was a girl,
I was the one for mischief and always in a twirl,
But now we are grown with families and have come to no real harm,
I think I have changed a lot, but my friend is still full of charm,
We have been through a lot together, over the years,
Lots of fun and laughter and a few tears,
But I hope we will stay friends forever,
For good friends are hard to find,
If we stay friends till we are old, I'll say that life has been kind,
So, in she will come for her tea, it won't take long to make,
We will forget the diets we've been on and have a piece of cake,
We won't tell each other we're not losing weight,
We don't care if we've got figures of eight,
We won't say we are getting fat anymore,
Because that's what good friends are really for.

Stephanie Harvey

Gifts From Spirit

Sit in the garden
And see how many things
There are in it.
Just as these fruits,
Vegetables, flowers ripen
And blossom and provide their
Gifts of pleasure and food.

So we in the garden of life
Give our particular gifts
That can ripen and perfect
And be given to others
For pleasure and provision.

Just as we sit and watch
Our gardens growing,
So Spirit watch the garden
Of life growing.
They see the many gifts ripening
And the blossoming to perfection.

Then they, like you, choose
The ripe fruit from that garden of life
To use them for the channelling
Of the gifts of love and friendship,
Understanding and compassion
To the rest of mankind.

Ripened and perfect gifts of the fruit of life,
Of beauty, comfort, happiness, peace,
Plucked from the garden of the world.

Irene DiMascio

The Fundamental

Forget those woes should they betide
Drive them far, dispel its chide.
If signals herald cheat and gloom
Sweep out the grit which fosters doom.
Savour a joy and radiant shine
A lilt melodious of linnets fine.
Transcend a whispering wind discreet
As life bubbles in spheres begin to meet.
Blessings are though seldom seen
Along a buff of clouds between
Their skips and turns like rope of play
When schoolgirls count in skittish way.
Be they winners with team at school
The test behoves that grip of rule.

Tom Cabin

Pressed Flowers And Hours

Long ago, in Lichfield near a cathedral house,
I did see - a pressed book of flowers.
Like butterflies' wings, thin and unreal,
As the delicate rings of many summers spread.

Some mauve, faded pink and pale -
Green leaves, blue pimpernel and speedwell.
Forget-me-nots, simple messages that spoke
Of God's love tied in little knots, love for our sake.

In the above sky, life and doves circled around
Sandwiches laid on a table in a café,
Waiting to be ate, burbling televisions in
A wayside shop, living close to others
That in a motionless string seemed endlessly
Passed in a moment,
Music that played the Dancing Queen
Of long ago, Abba voices, songs of the angel voices.

Longings and preferences of streets, lanes,
Hedges and meadowsweets - winding
In times like little white lilies and the
Third and fourth Heaven of pressed flowers and hours.

Doreen R Sylvester

May

Oh!
What a lovely month is May
With signs of summer on the way
Casting caution on one side
Her colour scheme revealed with pride
Trees and hedges turning green
Blossomed boughs besiege the scene
Bluebells carpeting the ground
Violets in our hedgerows found
Cowslips greet us with surprise
Reward enough for watchful eyes
Abounding beauty everywhere
Anticipation fills the air
With songs of birds from early dawn
Welcoming a world reborn
Gardens suddenly ablaze
Human hearts filled full with praise
Faith and hope seem born anew
Amazing what a month can do
With grateful hearts once more we pray
Enchanted by the month of May.

Cecil John Lewis

Blessings

Memories are photographs in the mind
If you keep them there, you will find
There's many a blessing in your life
And you'll forget all the trouble and strife.

There are friends and neighbours too
All around, to welcome you
So never think that you're alone
Count your blessings, don't sit and moan.

In everyone's life, there is something good
If only one looks around
Then you will find,
Many blessings abound.

E Hoy

The Meeting

A slim, lonely figure
Viewed through
Lattice windows.

The mountain descent
Through thick mist
Into clear blue.

The door being opened,
The figure welcomed,
Her rucksack placed inside.

The mountain lost to mist
The valley sparkling in colour.

There was the smile,
The comforting suggestion
Of finding the housekeeper.

She noticed the rough beard,
Untidy hair, patched trousers
But was hungry for kindness.

The mountain, out of sight,
Seemed another world as
The figures walked from view.

Godfrey Dodds

Jordana, So Special And Precious

Her smile is heart-warming
Her laugh is heart-warming
When you're down she lifts you
Just to see her beautiful face
To see that beautiful smile
Yes, my special, precious girl
I live day by day and get along
But the day and days I see
My girl, Jordana
I am all cheered up
I am happier, yes happier
She certainly put the sun
Into sunshine
When I am around her
I am on a high, just really happy
It's always sad to leave her
But the thought of seeing her again
Keeps me going
Yes, until the days and days
I see her beautiful heart-warming smile
Hear her heart-warming laugh
Yes, see my princess Jordana
My special, precious girl
I love her loads
She loves me
We just have a very special relationship
We just know we love each other to bits
Yes, she is my special, precious girl
Her smile, her laugh, her ways
Just everything about her is special
Just so heart-warming
Just so, so special
My special, precious princess
My girl, Jordana.

David J Hall

Finding A Blessing

A storm was raging, gale force winds and driving rain
As I opened the door, I saw a glimmer of sun
Then a rainbow begun
Its beauty quickly spread across the sky above
Giving a promise of hope and love

Next morning was miserable, cold and wet - and yet
As dawn broke, some little birds burst into song
My thoughts were, *things can't be all wrong*

Spring is just around the corner, with its beauty money cannot buy
The bulbs are peeping through, soon to be a carpet of colour
To cheer the heart and delight the eye
Always remember God is in His Heaven and He cares for you and I.

Marion Henderson

Count Your Blessings

Count your blessings
When you are feeling blue.
If you write them down
It will become obvious,
You have quite a few.
Draw on those blessings
When trouble
Comes your way.
Counting your many blessings
Will help take sorrow and sadness away.
With whatever comes your way.
Life is generally good.
To counter balance
Any bad.
Enjoy the many blessings,
Making your life
Enriched and happy.
Also well balanced,
Because in actual fact,
It is the only life
You will ever have.

Sheila Booth

Life's Memories

Memories are treasures of heart and mind,
Which the past and present closely bind.
Recalling many times and places,
Happenings and beloved faces.

The heart remembers, how can it forget?
Those in whose company we were so blest,
Whose lives touched ours in so many ways,
Whose loving and caring enriched our days.

In remembering we recall the past,
Love and friendships that deepen and last.
Times of joy and laughter, sadness and tears,
Meetings and partings throughout the years.

Memories are like the petals that fall
From flowers whose beauty we recall.
When gathered up within the heart,
Sweet is the fragrance they still impart.

Edith Stell

Tomorrow

Tomorrow is the horizon
Beyond which we cannot see
As we set sail into life
Through many a calm and stormy sea

Tomorrow is the destination
On which one day, we hope to land
But winds of fate can change our course
And lead to a change of plan

Tomorrow is a voyage
With many a port of call
Sometimes we will be welcome
Other times, not at all

Tomorrow is never quite what we thought
It may come as a bad surprise
Leaving us pondering the saying
Better to travel than to arrive

So why not just enjoy the journey
Listen to words of the wise
You may not be there tomorrow
When the sun begins to rise.

Kenneth Benoy

Blessings

Count our blessings one by one -
When we are well and feeling good
To count them is a joy
When we are ill or really sad
To count them is so very hard.

Count our blessings one by one -
For the people we remember all our life
For the children who keep us young
For the old folk who give us so much love
For the friends we could not live without.

Count our blessings one by one -
For the warmth of the sun and summer breeze
For the winter snow changing our world with its icy magic
For the mystery of the unknown, the spirit of God
For God is in Heaven - all's right with the world.

Jean Ferguson

Maybeck Musings

Untrodden paths, where sedges grow,
Footholds unsure, banks sharp and steep;
Far from familiar ways below,
Where woods inviolate secrets keep.

Here solitary hawthorn bush
Is crowned in summer's glorious sheen,
White petals touched with crimson flush
Like satin robe to deck a queen.

No voice profane or harsh tone heard
The waking silence here offends,
Only the note of woodland bird
As soft accompaniment attends.

Then speak, sage spirits of the grove,
Hear me, you Dryads of the trees -
Teach this sad wight no more to rove
But in such place to find heart's ease.

Barrie Williams

Out Of The Blue

We both saw the battered sign -
Motor Museum
Continued driving along the straight, empty road
Soon decided to go back
Easily done in this remote part of Australia
No other cars, no people -
Just the dusty, red earth . . . the eucalyptus trees . . .
The God who put the blue in the sky.
At the sign we turned off
Followed a long, stony track
Arrived at an isolated house, small and white
Around it what looked like
Large, corrugated iron shacks.
No sign of life, just silence and stillness -
No other visitors.
We stopped the car, saw him sitting by the house
An elderly man, checked shirt, braces, an old cap
We smiled, said hello, he walked slowly towards us -
Gladly opened all doors
Showed us, free of charge, his private collection
Vintage cars, a 1915 T-Type Ford, a 1929 Chevrolet
And more, also a BSA motorbike.
Petrol pumps, posters, garage forecourt signs -
He had accumulated in his museum
Things from the past, anything, everything.
Odd washing machines, invalid chairs
Sewing machines, tools of all kinds, kitchen utensils
Rusty farming implements.
On a phonograph he played an old record
Showed us paintings he had made - he was talented.
Inside the house he had a pianola
Sitting in front of it, he made it play a tune
With the man on the pianola, we sang . . .
A timeless song.

Claire-Lyse Sylvester

Innocence

I see them still,
Two small girls dancing
In a green bay.
They laughed with the joy
Of being one
And embraced;
Their faces
Mirrored in each other's eyes.

They stood
Upon the bank,
Side by side, holding hands.
Then fell backwards
With a merry shriek
Into a shallow pool
To rise amid a burst
Of sunlit water drops.

They ran through
Woods made green
By vernal springs,
Flowers cushioned
Their bare and delicate feet.
With voices pure
They sang their songs
Of innocence.

Across the burning sands
Of the Kalahari,
Over the grassy savannas
Of the Okefenokee,
Down the swift-flowing waters
Of the Orinoco,
Up the garden path
And safely home.

P G Williams

Looking Forward

The winter winds are howling round
And rain is scattered on the ground.
Don't be disheartened with it all,
For spring will soon receive her call,
Then little seeds of hope will grow,
And lots of pretty flowers show.
We cannot wait to ease our gloom,
With sunny skies, we'll be in *bloom*.

Heather Overfield

Think Positive

Oh, what joy it is to be alive
Especially as it was thought I would not survive
For I was such a weakling when I was born
That nobody thought I would last very long.

Yet here I am at ninety-six
Still full of fun and life and tricks,
Oh, yes I've had my ups and downs
With many a smile and many a frown.

Ten years ago I had cancer of the throat
Now, when I sing, it sounds like an old nanny goat.
I then had a paralysis and could not walk
But at least I was able to laugh and talk.

I now have a pacemaker to help the old heart
And my eyes are dimming, but that is just part
Of growing old, or so I've been told,
But at least I can hear and am not shut out in the cold.

To look on the bright side, is what I try to do
This way is one way to see things through,
When you are in trouble or distress
Think positive and your life will be blessed.

Phyllis Ing

The Hug That Heals

There are many kinds of hugs in life
Each one meaning a different thing.
The hug of pleasure and of joy
The hug that makes you sing.

There's the hug of comfort at a loss
Or the hug that is earned in praise,
The hug of passion and of love
Shown in many different ways.

There's the hug of sorrow when you part
Or the hug when again you meet.
There's the hug of celebration
Showing that life is sweet.

But the greatest of all hugs
When given by someone sincere,
Is the hug that heals the spirit
And helps your problems disappear.

Joan Gallen

The Persistence Of Memory

Outside the Berlin Hotel
Strains
Of dance music

I saw your face
Gaunt and ghost-like
You beckoned
Gloved fingers in the air

I'd never had a car
Tramlines
Dwindling into the distance

Perspective

I heard your voice ring
Out
With bell-like clarity
You are my choice

Are deco
Choker around your neck
Chiffon
Scarf upon your head

All our yesterdays

So long ago before
The war
September 1936

And yet
The Persistence Of Memory . . .

Rupert Smith

Kind People

It would be nice if we could be
Thro' our lives act graciously.
Trying to be polite and kind
Not always easy with some in mind.

Smiles proffered, a frown reply
Is something in life passing them by?
Perhaps the person's way ahead
Is full of gloom and tears to shed.

If we can help, going on our way
Giving good cheer, lifting clouds of grey.
Things in life will be worthwhile
If we can change a frown to a smile.

Ivy E Baker

Minx

Bewitched by your minx allure
I succumbed, e'en tho' there's no known cure
For your smoky eye, tongue tipped lip pouting attraction,
Your provocative, sensual, rumba weaving action,
Egotistically I flaunt my pride,
At being the focus of this aside,
I hold you in dance embrace
Eye locked eye, expressive face,
I fantasise, till I believe
You are mine to receive.
Then, I realise with deep despair
That you are a *minx,* my dear,
Pert, mischievous, coquette, a jade
A bold, flirtatious woman, as displayed.
Yet, I would have no other, my dear
A pitched stump, a fondled hand, so near.
My pert, smiling, flirtatious minx, my delight,
My fond memory, till I sleep in grave's long night
I'll think of you
(Escape).

Andy Quinn

June's Garden

The fresh cut grass shines in the stead
Of that which mown, went on ahead
And now lies heaped behind the shed.

The tortoise lazily surveys
Where dandelions stood in former days
That added colour to its graze.

The blackbird twists and strains its head
Tugs the worm from earthy bed
For youngsters waiting to be fed.

The sun, now at its height, displays
Subliminal splendour in its rays,
Enfolding all in restful haze.

May balmy thoughts of sunny days
Persist in years ahead.
And help outweigh the gloom and grey
Of days when tears were shed.

Del Isaacs

Dawning Of A New Day

I woke up this morning
To the sound of birds singing
While the frost laid upon the ground
The sun popped out to say hello

Because this is a dawning of a new year
And beginning of a new day

I see trees that started budding
Their buds on the tiny branches
And growing their fresh green leaves
After the harsh winter as they start to appear
While the flowers gently unfold
Their delicate petals to soak up the loving sun's rays of light
While birds flitter to and fro
Feeding from my tree

Because this is the dawning of a new year
A beginning of a new day

Rabbits poke their tiny heads out of the burrows
To sniff the cold, frosty air
While they scurry to and fro to get away
From the cold, chilly wind that swirls around all day long
Poppies sway in the vast swirling wind up on the hillside

Because this is the dawning of a new year
And a beginning of a new day

So here I am writing this poem
Just for you to read
Bringing in the new year
Because I have come of a new age myself
As I look to the future
Like we all do

Because this is the dawning of a new year
And a beginning of our first new day.

Samantha Rose Whitworth

Precious Gifts

My life is filled with blessings,
Too many to recall,
Love, laughter, friendship, beauty, faith,
I'm grateful for them all.
For Mother Nature's bounty,
First daffodil in spring,
The colours of the sunset,
A butterfly's soft wing.
Returning drenched from pouring rain,
Deep puddles round me glisten,
A songbird's tuning up again
And I must pause to listen.
Warm human contacts mean so much,
Good family and friends,
A smile of recognition,
Loving care that never ends.
Faith truly is a blessing,
Firm belief in our Dear Lord,
Who lives with and within us,
Through His own spirit poured.
I'm growing old and now look back
On ninety years and more,
My feeble limbs no longer do
What they could do before.
Those grandiose schemes of ardent youth,
My present frailty shatters,
But now I'm blessed with calm content,
So rich in all that matters.

V E Godfrey

Snow On Trees

Swirling, silent, flakes of snow,
Drifting downwards, fast, then slow.
Settling softly on each tree,
A white, gold shape of filigree.
Each tree a jewel in its own right,
Retains its beauty through the night.
That master craftsman, morning sun,
Highlights each jewel, one by one.
Nature's mantle, soft and white,
Transforms each tree for our delight.

John David Robertson

Touch

What is it about *touch*, Lord,
That is so special?
Bringing comfort and blessing
In so many ways.

The velvetiness of new cords
A close haircut
Magnolia buds
A bulrush spike and pussy willow.

The smoothness of pebbles
Rounded and shaped
By the pounding of waves on the beach.
Of polished wood
Acorns, conkers and hazelnuts.
The fur of a cat, a rabbit
And feathers.

The softness of new holly leaves
Of pine and fir needles
Of *teddies* and rose petals.
The springy crispness of a newly cut hedge
Of tight dark curls of Afro hair
And sprigs of heather.

The roughness of tree trunks
Of rocks and river stones
Of slatted fences
And dry sea sand.

'These are a few of my favourite things!'

Mary-Joan Lloyd

The Day An Angel Came

I thought the angel came to stay,
Until, after comforting me, she went away.
Her wings did me enfold with love,
Oh! How I wish she had not returned above.
But she was needed elsewhere that day
So I thanked her as she left, then knelt to pray.

Marjorie Busby

A Touch Of Frost

Only the late roses bloom, in fretting beds,
Showering the lawn with petal drooping heads;
Autumnal reds
And aching yellow petals
Mix tenderly with greys and browns
Of failing older plants.
The leaning fence still battles
With some wayward wind
Which whistles from the east
To pipe its echo down the pallid street.

Each house disclaims its roots
By tree or bush.
And what a hush
When frost begin to paint the grass
In virgin white and teases crispness
Of each fallen leaf.
The berries glow like winter flames
And thrush and blackbird
Fill their maws
With stolen fruits
And fluff their feathers against the cold.

Double glazing keeps at bay
The frozen breath;
And central heating warms the way
Into the house. No shivers now
From creaking draughts which slid
Their icy fingers down one's back;
And brought red noses from the snuffling colds.
The winter holds
No bitter, clawing blight
Except on carol night
When all the black frowned sky
A-glaze with stars
Grips tight around one's ears,
Reminding that the dead of winter's night
Is but a touch.

L McIntosh

Love Is

Love is
A soft-blossomed cheek
Against my face
Warmth and love
This special time
Is mine.

Love is
When tiny hands reach out
To feel me near
It could be Grandad's ear
Or her cuddly dog and teddy bear.

Love is
To snuggle up close
And close those sleepy eyes
Deep sleep
And contented sighs.

No wealth could take the place
Of this cherub face
Wealth is in her touch
And twinkling eyes
Wealth in her giggles
Wealth in her sighs.

A baby, to grown-up girl
A precious gift from God
My granddaughter.

Frederick Seymour

First Frost

A shiver of ice
whispers across the puddle tops
to glaze the moonlit windows
of a secret nether world.

Gossamer panes of spangled ice
scumble the branches mirrored in a pond
and feathered crystals plume the bracken fronds
to conjure an enchanted land
from yesterday's banality.

Freda Bunce

A Garden Alphabet

A sters,
B luebells,
C elandines,
D andelions too.
E very
F lower
G arlanded with diamond drops of dew.
H oneysuckle
I ntertwined with
J asmine's starry showers
K indly
L arkspur
M arching
N ext to
O pening
P oppy flowers.
Q uintessential
R oses
S leeping in the sun.
T ime slowly
U nfolding, till
V elvet evening's come
W eary weeping willows
X eranthemums, sweet peas
Y earning for the murmur of summer's
Z ephyr breeze.

My garden is an alphabet of nature's bounteous care
A place of joy and peacefulness for everyone to share.

Geraldine Bowden

Iraq 2004

I long for the nights, when safe in his bed
I believed that a benign force looked down.
Before time ambushed my dreams to shreds
In the heat and flies of Al Amarah town.

Now mothers in Iraq, who curse my name,
Grieving at a dusty grave for a mangled son,
Rejoice that my hero lives with guilt and shame.
And his mother wishes his bloody duty undone.

They slapped his back, called him lion-hearted.
But ignored his unease with a victor's pride
In having no choice in ending lives just started.
He cried within, for heroes must be dry-eyed.

Protect our blessings - never justify war.
Learn from a nameless victim who smiles no more.

Anon

Neighbours

Every day, I can say
Thank you Lord, come what may
For without a single doubt
(And trying not to sound devout)
God will bless me with something good
From those around my neighbourhood.

A tap on my window or door
Brings a smile from number four
Bob, from further down the road
Does my shopping, to ease my load
Visits from the vicar brings me peace
While the nurse helps my pain decrease.

All in all, my journey's light
Thanks to friends who ease my plight
Housebound and sick, they make me humble
Knowing they care, when I feel so feeble
And each evening when day is done
I count my blessings, one by one.

Jean Everest

Old Faithful

The other day we went for a lovely drive along a country lane
But when your amber light came on inside, your power did wane
We have been on such enjoyable rides before this day together
Driving the boys to school and uni (and back!) whatever the weather

Well the garage man said you weren't worth the trouble to do
I nearly cried down the phone at him and I defended you!
Chattering along the long windy roads we often sped
Your engine churning along making a comforting quiet sound

The garage man in the end, at last, saw some sense
He fixed your problems and he fixed your lights
So I am happy again, you are back on my drive
I hope in the next few years you'll continue to survive

I know your shiny red coat has somewhat faded
But you have been a blessing to us for nearly a decade
Yes, your sunroof has gone a bit green round the edges
You're not the latest model, but worth it, cos we're friends!

Sheila Cheesman

My Love For Grandma

I remember ninety years ago,
When I was seven years old.
Pushing Grandma's garden gates
'Wide open'
Then scampering along the path
And climbing big white steps,
That lead to her front door.
I rang the bell
In seconds the door was opened
The excitement filled the air,
As there, beside those big wide stairs
Stood an 'Xmas tree' that reached to the ceiling.
It was laden from the floor, right to the top,
With glittering baubles, tinsel, sweets and pop
And gifts for all the family.
Xmas Day couldn't come fast enough.
'Well, time does pass,' so all were dressed in their best.
Mums, dads, children and friends arrive
Then, all seated around a large table
Eating, drinking, chatting and laughing
'Celebrating Xmas'.

(Those bygone days will never fade
Or be forgotten) for its warmth and
Lasting love. Grandma was like a
'Guardian Angel', happiest when she
Was with her family and 'her
Grandchildren' she doted over them.

Peggy Johnson

Life's Real Riches

A happy home, a few close friends,
Some favourite records, odds and ends,
Well-loved books upon a shelf
Reflecting something of yourself.

Someone to share these little things,
To speed life's years on gentle wings,
Thankful for blessings from above,
The promise of eternal love.

Olive Miller

Mother Said

Just count your blessings, my mother said
At night, when I was put to bed
Under army coats, these were my cover
All I knew was, I loved my mother
Yes, count your blessings, my mother said
As she scraped jam upon my bread
Hot tea came in a blue striped mug
Got from the 'rag man' as was the rug
Now count your blessings, mother said
Over and over, until at work she dropped down dead
She passed so soon, only aged fifty-two
I was so young, distraught, what would I do?
I strove myself to be a good and guiding mum
Three beautiful children, mine had become
But, count your blessings, I heard myself say
When their father upped and went away
We had no luxuries, money was real tight
But I could hug you close at night
My blessings counted, I could see
That you were all my luxury
I awake in the morning with a job in hand
Looking after the aged and infirm, you understand?
Count your blessings, I hear colleagues say
That may be you in need, one of these days.
Well, my role of Grandma arrived, you see
I was blessed with grandchildren, three
But count your blessings, I still hear myself say
As my daughter struggles with her rent to pay
Times can still be hard, when work is short
But my darling, love, it cannot be bought
So, count your blessings, as my mother said
As you pull up their duvet on their bed
That smile, the giggle, the hug so tight
The 'I love you, Mum,' as you say goodnight
Count your blessings, not your strife
There is nothing richer than the gift of life.

Jacky Dale

Sixty-Five Roses

Upon learning that my four-year-old son
Richard, has cystic fibrosis,
I was in shock, then I mourned.
Finally I became furious and fought back.
Frantically every night I would call everywhere
Looking for help; there was none.
One night after several long and agonising
Phone calls pleading for help,
Richard came into the room
And said, 'Mommy I know who you work for.'
With some trepidation
I posed the question back to him, 'Who, Richard?'
'Sixty-five roses,' he said with a smile.
I went to him and tenderly pressed his tiny body
To mine, so he couldn't see
The tears running down my cheeks.
I was amazed since I had never told him
That he had advanced liver cancer.
Then as I hugged him, I realised
He couldn't pronounce cystic fibrosis,
Now every time, for the past thirty-eight years,
As I visit Richard, I smile and cry
As I gaze on a seven-year-old's gravestone
That reads 'sixty-five roses'.

Richard, it has been thirty-eight years
That's why we placed sixty-five roses
On your grave today
Then got on our knees and silently prayed,
No, not for you our sweetie
For we know you're safe in Heaven
But for us whose hearts have never mended.
We want to thank you Richard and need to apologise,
We stood by your grave today and told you our reasons why.
Sixty-five roses lay beautifully on your grave
To signify the illness that took your life away.
We always knew this was the place
Where in your youth you'd lay
And all we asked and wanted was for it to be maintained.

Count Our Blessings

Many people loved you and many heard our plea,
For each time we come to visit
We find things placed anonymously:
Sixty-five roses
We placed there today
Sixty-five roses is what took you away.

The children are so young that they are unable to pronounce
Cystic fibrosis, so say sixty-five roses -
This moved us,
Enough to support us to finding a cure
And tell you about the disease our little boy heard as
Sixty-five roses - cystic fibrosis.
Easy to say as 'sixty-five roses',
Difficult to cure as 'cystic fibrosis'.

John Faucett

The Day We Felt Such Anger

We feel for the folks who live in Dunblane,
For we know what it's like to feel such pain.
On the day of those killings, just a few hours before,
Mark, our grandson, was murdered on a far distant shore.
Stabbed through the heart and left to die
In Lanzarote, we ask ourselves, 'Why?'

What sort of person can harm little ones
Or end the life of a beloved son?
Mark's Mum and Dad mourn him dreadfully,
As do the rest of the family,
What sort of world do we live in today,
Where children aren't safe, either at work, or at play?

But Mark loved children and we'd like to feel,
That the day of the murders wasn't for real.
That he gathered the little ones close, for protection
And guided them forward on the Highway to Heaven.
And in Heaven they'll stay, till we meet again,
Our Mark and the children who lived in Dunblane.

Olive Smith

Driving Down To Derry Town

I'm driving down to Derry town
Where the Foyle is fast and flowing;
I'm driving down to Derry town
And I know the road I'm going.
I'm driving through Dungiven town
And the weather, sure it's raining;
But I'm cosy in my speeding car
With its wooden dashboard shining.
I'm driving past old Claudy town
While my sweetheart waits and wonders;
It's been so long, my heart cries sore
So tiresome are my blunders.
Through Drumahoe with Derry nigh
A cloudy teardrop fogs my eye;
I'm nearly there in Derry town
Are my hopeless expectations high?
I'm here at last in Derry town
All my apprehensions roaring;
I'm here my love, at last I'm home
My drive to Derry town is done.

John F McCartney

Hell

Escape: Such a fruitless endeavour
From the demons of love and of trust
Redeem me, O Lord: Ease my torture
Lest my dreams burn away in the dust

While the wind's cryin' out Bloody Mary
And the whores ply their trade on the street
Where the fallen, the wrecked
And the crucified men
Are embroiled in their constant retreat

There's no chance: Not a hope or a prospect
Resurrection is out of our hands
Beneath marble halls failed and dying
The price social order demands

So come all ye derelict failures
You poets and drunkards and bums
Sit down for a drink alongside me
We'll rejoice when our judgement day comes

We'll stumble to Hell in good company
But at least we can say we were free

John Robinson

New Beginnings

I listen to the winds of time
As the old year passes into the shadows of yesterday
A gentle breeze pure and untarnished
Carrying the hidden secrets of tomorrow
Sends a ripple through my soul
Leaving behind the pains and sorrows
In the history already written
We now can reach out for a new beginning
To watch the breaking of a new dawn
As the night breaks into day
Casts its crimson reflection of hope
Over the Earth's face
As life awakens to a new era
Looking to the distant horizon
A new journey before you to take
With each step, a new task
To fulfil the challenges of today
Moving into the unknown of the future
New lessons to be learnt
A new memory
To take and hold deep within our mind
To learn new ways
To understand our destiny
For we have the power
To place a new trust into the hearts of others
To bring the gift of peace
That has been lost in the darkness of time

Susan Russell-Smith

A Precious Gift

We have waited many years for you,
Too many for us to count.
But today we heard the news,
In a few months, you'll be about.
The anticipation is mounting,
Time is flying by.
How can we contain ourselves?
It makes us want to cry.
The time is here, the waiting done,
The precious gift from Heaven, has turned into a son.

Marion Lee

Rainbows In The Mist!

Lucid pearls of morning dew entrapped
in the spider's web,
Cast a shimmering kaleidoscope of colours
on each silken thread,
Gossamer strands amongst the dancing stems
of Wattle trees,
Each, vibrating in unison, with the breath
of autumn's breeze,
The spider lazily, even gently languishing
in her gossamer bed,
Taking succour from these lucid pearls
entrapped within her web,
As Nature's lips might well have kissed
rainbows in the mist.

Nicholas Maughan

Ode To Passion

Caught by the abandoned beauty in the mourner's wail and weep,
Purity of emotion, innocent, broken, fresh and loud.
Sweet fear, desperation, frenzied rapture of given grief,
Remembered passion through carnal hysterics in the bonfire's crowd.
Empty chairs at a table, walls hollow, paradox gone, night looms,
No jaws to howl, dead without feeling, in bare and empty rooms.

Concealed mystery of man, to open the soul and laugh and moan,
Not only ecstasy of desperation, frailty in pain and loss we all embrace and own.
Details irrelevant to the swelling of the heart in ambivalence, fear or pain,
Relive past emotions well to ensure profundity not revealed in vain.
Passion lives on in the bonfire glow and the firework adrenalin squeal,
Although streamed out through laughter, still beauty, humbling and real.

Overwhelming to the psyche, outward signs of pain,
Yet the source of instinct sees fingerprints in the dancing of the flame,
Imagine the static in the air on that day of loss and shame.
Sweat, blood and tears.

Remember the fifth of November not for rhymed triviality,
Take away the fear on the streets, the desperate willingness to die,
It disrespects those who felt the air and corrupts the true humanity,
Turning souls into stereotypes makes all men gone a lie.
To understand the past, remember the reason's why and positively cope,
Fill the next generation with logic, laughter and love, to detour our repressive slope.

Remember, remember the fifth of November, blood, sweat and tears,
The static lives on, in the fire, dance and song, that're let loose every year.

Denise Delaney

Our Blessings

Do we ever stop awhile
In life's long busy day
And all God's blessings count
That God has given away?

Do we ever stop and look around
At all the things we own?
Do we thank God for our health
When we wake at dawn?

Do we look at our families
Growing up healthy and strong,
And thank God for His many blessings
As we go along?

Do we look at the sun by day,
As it ripens the fruit and the grain,
The moon and stars shining at night
Or a welcome shower of rain?

God sends us blessings every day,
If we'd only pause to see -
Our home, our food and family,
How thankful we should be.

When we take a walk outside,
What beauty is around -
The flowers, birds and the trees,
What blessings to be found.

What joy, a little child can bring,
With such bright shining eyes;
And in her little hand tightly held
For you a posy to surprise.

Let's think of someone alone and old;
Their loved ones far away.
We could show them that we care,
And with them God's blessings share.

Betty Morris

Perseverance

The winter winds were blowing strongly
The dark clouds in the sky were menacing and low
Threatening the frozen land beneath them
With a heavy blanket of snow.

The tired traveller trudged onward
His head held down against the gale
His clothes were dripping with moisture
His skin was icy cold and pale.

Now the large white flakes were falling
The traveller pulled his collar high
The road ahead seemed never-ending
Causing him to utter one long sigh.

Slipping and stumbling he forged ahead
His world was nothing but swirling snow
He had walked many difficult miles
But there was still some way to go.

Chilled to the bone and feeling faint
He suddenly saw in the distance a light
And as he reached the brow of a hill
His destination came in sight.

His spirits lifted as he thought of his wife
Who would be waiting with freshly cooked food
And he thought of his children
Which lifted his dark, gloomy mood.

Although our paths often feel lonely
To stop and give up we cannot afford
We must persevere and continue on our way
In order to receive our rightful award.

Denise Castellani

Blessings Acknowledged

Today has been a bad time, so many things gone wrong,
So frustrating and annoying, oh how for peace we long.
Because so many problems, are encountered every day,
Sometimes in frustration, we think everything goes astray.
But relax and then consider all the blessings that we hold.
Have we food enough to eat, and a shelter from the cold?
Clothing in abundance, and shoes upon our feet?
Do we drive a motorcar, have utilities in our street?
Are we sound of wind and limb, can we see and can we hear?
In freedom can we roam, or persecution do we fear?
Are we envious of another, or do we aspire to hate?
Does the good outweigh the bad, are we resentful of our state?
To always think of self, leads down a tortuous path.
Soon hedonism thrives, with trouble the aftermath.
In every walk of life, tribulations will arise.
The solution how to cope should come as no surprise!
How special *you* are to God, yes *you* who read these lines.
In this world there is much beauty, there are so many signs.
A baby newly born, emitting a healthy cry.
Flowers with great colours, sunset streaked across the sky.
A smile to light the face, when someone's feeling low,
Realising you are loved, unconditionally . . . 'tis so!
If the question is just why dreadful things arise,
None can ever tell us, e'en the wisest of the wise.
The answer lies with Christ, He cares indeed for all,
In our heartaches and our trials . . . if only Jesus we would call.
The comfort that He gives, surpasses human aid,
So to seek Him out in prayer, please do not be afraid.

Cecilia Skudder

Blessed With Treasure

I have gold when the day has begun
And still more with the bright setting sun
Silver that gleams for my dreams
Diamonds whose scattered light streams
Sapphires in the deepest blue sea
Emerald grass throne just for me
Rubies in roses that grow
Multi-hued gem-flowers on show
Crystal notes as the birds fly above
Sparkling rainbows in my treasure trove.

Ida Jones

Life Is Worthwhile

'I want you, I need you.'
What more can I say?
My heart fills with love
for you every day.

I wake up each morning
beside you, so snug.
I just have to turn
and give you a hug.

Slowly you turn
and give me a smile.
Now I know
why life is worthwhile.

J Brown

Countless Blessings

I have a multitude of blessings
On the path I take each day.
They come from all the passers-by
That I meet along the way.
I oft stumble and I fumble,
Stick dropping to the floor.
'Tis then I meet someone who helps me,
Who does my stick and balance restore.
Sometimes I'm just plain weary,
Shoulders droop, I feel alone.
A passer-by then takes my elbow,
For those last few steps to home,
Oh, sometimes I wallow in a puddle,
Self-pity is its name.
Mentally I retrace my steps
Till I don't quite feel the same.
Did not a lady smile at me?
Someone else called me sweetheart.
I then begin to count my blessings,
So many, where to start?
Oh yes, sometimes I am weary,
But I can sit quietly and take a rest.
All things are bright and beautiful,
O Dear Lord, how I am blest,
Thank you . . .

Rosie Hues

God's Petworth Out-Station

(A poem specially composed and dedicated to Petworth United Reformed Church and its members to add to their celebrations on its 150th birthday on 25th October 2005)

From this poet's biased research
The United Reformed Church
On Golden Square in Petworth town
Is the gem in the Sussex crown
That glorifies God's creation.

In psalm one hundred and fifty
King David's great lines are thrifty
Yet call for crashing paeans of praise
All voices or instruments can raise
To thank God for our salvation.

Now we know of God's ancient plan
That brought Christ to be born as man -
And share our daily jokes and tears
For thirty-three amazing years
Then die for our recreation.

This third time, from the sacred ground
Of this fold where Christ's love abounds
Hear the jubilee ram's horn sound
For His flock whose faith knows few bounds
To bless God's Petworth out-station.

Ronald Rodger Caseby

Skin-Deep

Beauty can be that lovely face
or a smile, sincere and warm.
Beauty can be the comfort given,
to someone afraid in a storm.

Beauty can be the countenance
but not just the face you see.
Beauty can be the prayer you say,
for a troubled mind to be free.

Beauty can be the newborn child,
who may be dark or fair of the skin.
Beauty is all the love you can feel,
as true beauty comes from within.

Ann Potkins

Burbage Common In Winter

Early morning sun awakens,
Lights 'The Common' with a glow,
Shimmers o'er the frozen wasteland,
Penetrates the fallen snow,
On, through woodland's wintry slumber,
Laden branches, bending low,
Cobwebs hang in lacy splendour;
Frosted gowns of dazzling snow,
A passing flock of Fieldfare, swooping,
Strip bare the hawthorn bushes, red,
And, as if in sheer defiance,
Sings the Robin overhead,
And as his clear, strong notes resound
Across the fields, where drifting snow
Hides the promise of the Springtime;
Lifts the heart and makes it glow.
Dappled sunshine, gently resting,
Smokes the melting, rutted ground,
Children's feet, the puddles testing,
Shrieking, squealing, happy sounds,
And as this wintry landscape glistens,
As children, we return again.
Remembering with joyful gladness,
Times long past and winters gone.
Who could fail to be enchanted?
By this intricate design,
Who, but God, could ever fashion
Such a landscape so divine!

Linda J Bodicoat

Remember This

When you are sad and feeling low
Remember this
A sigh is like a prayer
A tear will wash away despair
Reflect and count your blessings
And hope will fill your heart.

Helen Dick

New Life Begins

Spring, new life begins
I wander in the meadow and the lea
Each bud I see upon the tree
I listen to birds' harmony

Peace I feel within my soul
I see the creatures large and small
Hurrying here, scurrying there
About their business everywhere

For new homes they must prepare
In her gown edged with green
I watch the snowdrops dance
Worn like a crown, spring's queen

Purple-yellow crocuses
Join in the dance of spring
Birds sing welcoming new climes
As frosty icicles drip crystal drops

Worms turn beneath the leaves
That warmed them from harsh winter
As they slept without a sound
Yes, new life abounds

Life song is sung amongst the breeze
As we see new buds and leaves
Warming beneath a winter sun
As new year is now begun.

Anne Marshall

Eternal Love

What will I find that marks the changing day?
What lights the way as evening comes to pass?
What will I find when darkness me surrounds?
The Love of God!

What waits for me beyond this earthly plane?
What shall I find among the heavenly hosts?
What will I see before me in that place?
The Love of God!

What will my eyes, now dim, hope there to see?
What will these ears, though dull, hope there to hear?
What will my soul, repentant, hope to find?
The Eternal Love of God!

Graeme Leslie Jennens

A Garnish Of Joy

I was born in war's arms,
endowing the depleted world
with new infancy,
rocking in destruction's cradle,
growing strong on freedom's diet.

In the glow of parental care
I blossomed in spring's youth,
absorbed nature's freshness,
dressed in wisdom's knowledge,
matured in adult seasoning.

Partnered in nuptial harmony
I was blest with future's child.
Life's challenges flavoured my days.
Experience's hand designed
my judgement.

I have travelled into maturity
in love's heart,
reliving youthful days
in the boundless energy
of generation's children.

As I hold hands with the passing years,
and drift into memory's dreams,
life's panorama will be perceived
as special moments in time,
garnished with joy.

Angela Bradley

And each day I wish
That I had something remarkable to tell you,
Something, which will change your life,
Or better still, keep you safe,
But try as I might
Most of time is ordinary,
And soon spent,
Yet because of our love
It is time Heaven sent,
Heaven sent.

Peter Butterworth

Count Your Blessings!

My life began at four-pound weight
A twin discovered very late.
In 1930s there was no scan
Given fourteen days, my lifespan.

Health was poor over twenty years
I puffed and wheezed, lips blue by then.
I prayed for death at seventeen
Could not face life anymore.

There were no inhalers, just tablet 'F'
Eight hours to work, then loss of weight,
Count your blessings, you healthy ones
Tablets destroy your learning, dull your brain.

Today, just sixty-seven years on
I feel a lot better than I did then,
My life did have its ups and downs
Made redundant twice - a blessing!

By changing jobs I met people
People I never knew,
Now friends who still support me
In work and charity too.

I count my life a blessing
For my mother is ninety-four,
I am still alive to support her
Hoping for many years more.

Thomas Wylie

Count Your Blessings

You've heard folk say that life is short
Maybe you don't think it's true.
But think of all there is to see
And all there is to do.
Think of travelling . . . Think of people
That you've yet to meet.
Think of summers in the sun
And all those Christmas treats.
What about that special person
And all that you could share.
So count your blessings you're alive
And have the time to care.
For of all the things that come in life
And there are quite a few,
No blessing is more precious
Than the love that's given to you.

Joyce Hudspith

Dear Theo. May 1889

You would love this garden.
I sit in this secret corner
where there is much darkness;
but hope and light in the distant horizon
though the path is long.

The twisted olive trees are my companions.
Admire their knotted trunks,
contorted dancers craving applause -
I weep at their distortion,
but relish their certain fruitfulness.

Yesterday, I chanced upon a strange moth,
well-hidden amongst the greenness.
I sketched it hurriedly,
its stillness death-like.
Such astonishing colours, vibrant greens;
so vulnerable I could not disturb it.

I am now content in these quiet places.
St Remy in spring is a pageant
of colour; vast fields disappearing
into the purple hills,
where pale clouds swirl and linger.

Darkness has its own power.
This ivy, gloriously alive, if left
to flourish, will strangle smaller plants.
There is much brittle life here.
I am driven to magnify its state.
To dress its existence with light,
in blazing layers
as for a carnival.

E Mary Wilce

Hope

B eauty opens the new winter door
L ife - precious stillness - offers much more
E vergreens elegant against a frosty morn
S ecrets of the night transposing into dawn
S pringtime beckons - rejuvenates the earth
I mages of grandchild's miracle birth
'N eighbourhood Watch', an essence of care
G lorious praise for His love everywhere.

Janet Collinson

The Best Things In Life Are Free

That's how this world seems to me
The things that bring us greatest pleasure
Are all around, for us to treasure
Winter, spring, summer and autumn
The countryside is moresome
A walk down the lane
On a fresh spring morning
The air is fresh, new life awakes
Birds sing in bush and tree
All are there for us to see
Newborn lambs, life begins anew
As all the flowers are breaking through
April rain, and summer sun
The world is bright, days are fun
Children laugh with glee, everything is bright
Streams, and water, are a delight, ducks on ponds
There for everyone, autumn brings pure delight
Changing colours, from green, to red and gold
Leaves fall on the ground, all these things are heaven-sent
And free there for us to share, log fires, winter snow
Ice on ponds, where once ducks swam
Every day life is a pleasure, if only we can see the treasure
Yes, I believe, the best things in life are free
If we open our eyes, and hearts, we will discover
All around is hidden treasure
Heaven-sent for our world by pleasure.

Irene Corbett

Living For . . .

Life is but a wonderful mystery
Through the ages it's been asked what could it be?
What purpose is the human race?
Why here? Why now? This common place
We struggle, we strive, we try
Still we hear each other cry
What is our existence for?
It's for the living of, no more!

Jean McDonnell

Count Your Blessings

In the stillness of the Sunday morning
I heard singing,
As I turned the corner a delightful picture emerged.

Walking down the street was an African family.
The children, holding hands
As they headed for the beach, were singing.
Their childish voices echoing in the quietness.

They were from Ghana,
Associated with a local church.
Six bonny children,
Boys and girls with gentle angelic faces
Showing caring for their siblings.

I decided I must take a picture
To capture this loving family,
Just to remember the joy I felt.

I found them on the beach
Holding hands in a circle with their parents
Thanking God for all their blessings.

Surely an inspiration to us all
Who take so much for granted.

May 'God Bless' this humble little family
Though in their humbleness were quite impressive.
Amen.

Rhoda Glanville

God's Gift Of A Son

In December nineteen hundred and ninety-nine,
Three days short of Christmas Day
At 2.23pm little Callum,
Into this world made his way.
His star-struck father, Jason,
Gazed down with relief and pure joy,
As Tammy cradled in her arms
This wondrous infant boy.
For them a truly magical time,
A memory they never will forget,
A very special Christmas present
And first grandchild for Colette.

E Bowen

Our Son

Welcome to our little boy
Welcome to our son
We gaze on him with pride and joy
A new life just begun

Tiny fingers, tiny toes
A treasure to behold
A tiny little turned-up nose
More precious to us than gold

We will watch him grow into a man
We will teach him all things good
Always be there when we can
Just like good parents should

Welcome to our darling boy
Each day for him we'll pray
That he will know both love and joy
As he grows stronger every day.

Grace Wallace

Grace

Thank you for the joy you bring
Thank you for the songs you sing
Thank you for your tears and laughter
Thank you for being my granddaughter

Hugs and kisses by the score
Inspirational, 'Je t'adore'
Stars and moon bow down before you
Heaven's angels all adore you

Thank you for your eyes of blue
Thank you for my knowing you
Thank you for your magic chuckle
Thank you for your mum who suckled

Innocent, but older yet
With your smile I can't forget
Wise, beyond your childish ways
Remember; the whole world is your stage

Thank you for the joy you bring
Thank you for the songs you sing
Thank you for your tears and laughter
Thank you for being my granddaughter.

Elizabeth Boultwood

Family Portrait

There is a photograph I treasure,
The value of which I can't measure,
Of a group of us three bright sparks,
Sitting cross-legged in a field in Central Park.

The one in the middle was me at the age of three,
My brother Alfred was nine years older than me,
And Hubert about seven or so years ahead,
It was at a time in our lives when we knew no dread.

When we hadn't too many problems to surmount,
And we had lots of blessings we could count,
Before Adolph Hitler came knocking on every door,
Or incendiary bombs fell down chimneys to make us poor.

And you can see us smiling without a care,
With me and my doll and a ribbon in my hair,
My two brothers grin at either side not knowing,
That one day they would go forth a flying.

Or fight the Hun on the home front,
ARP and NFS what a stunt!
Who could guess what they would become?
And little Audrey, that's me, looks so overcome.

She has no idea that she would go on a train far from home,
A little evacuee who never wanted to roam,
But the photo captures a moment in time,
When everything seemed quite sublime.

And now as I look back to that sweet moment,
When someone captured it on camera to become a monument,
But now my mind has taken focus on the wondrous art,
Of how we three survived it all till now though far apart.

And the picture tells a simple truth,
How those once really close in youth,
Are never really so very far from home,
For home is where the heart is no matter where we roam.

A providential hand lays on our lives,
And brings us through the darkest times,
Renews us as we trust his love to comfort and sustain,
And that one moment in time will always the same remain.

Audrey Hogan

Love Waits

O God, you are my secret garden,
You are that very special place,
Where I would wish to dare to creep
Through low and hidden entrance
There to meet, in glad surprise,
My sunshine and my friend.

You say You have been waiting
With longing for my coming,
Now here I am, I've come at last,
Though how to lift my eyes!
Tongue-tied, timid, at a loss,
I bow in Your great Presence.

You are the perfume of the rose,
Rich velvet shades of crimson,
Glory of the dawn, the sunset's glow,
The life, the home I long to reach.

Yours is the voice that speaks so low
I have to bend, not just my head,
But all of me - my proud
And self-sufficient self,
And bending low I then might see
The many minute treasures
You've spread around my feet.

Yes, bending low I come to know
A little of the pain You felt,
The weight of man-made rough-hewn Cross
You bore with love and suffering joy.

Such love as waits
And waits and waits
With patience never-ending
For the one who seeks
But hesitates
To give her all, to Love.

Oonagh Twomey

Beauty

Oh how beautiful it is to watch the flowers grow
Daffodils, tulips, the crocuses peeping through the snow
Oh how beautiful to see the sunrise from afar
The crescent of the moon and the twinkle of a star

The rivers that flow on their way on the sea
The sight of the leaves as they grow on a tree
Oh how lucky we are to be part of this charade
To see the hills, the valleys, the light and the shade

How beautiful it is to hear the church bells ring
And to listen to the choirboys as they sing
To see the little babies, so soft and so sweet
With curly little fingers and dainty little feet

There is so much beauty for us to behold
Let us count our blessings whether young or old
There is beauty in kindness and beauty in thought
Let us do as we should and do as we ought

There's beauty in loving, there's beauty in giving,
Let us bear this in mind while we are living.

Marjorie Tateson

Shattered

We all go through agonising periods in our life.
Life suddenly shattered when we lose husband or wife.
Maybe your mother or a child, it rocks our foundation
We lose our stability, heartbreaking in that situation.

Our life completely changed, circumstances adrift.
Loneliness and isolation, only one solution uplifts.
We must count our blessings day by day.
Our weeping will one day go far away.

Deep down in our hearts they will always be there.
Your memories of them no one can compare.
The laughter and the good times you had.
You forget the sad times, don't think of the bad.

God's resources will contribute to our provision.
In our difficulties He will create a diversion . . .
Communion with the Lord is the only way to heal.
It happened to me, so I know how you must feel.

We must live out our lives giving our love to all.
Getting ready for Paradise when we answer His call.
God promises that we will all meet again.
If we believe in His Son, and with Him we will reign.

Sylvia Harbert

Little Eden

Today it seems the world's gone mad
As switching on the news
I hear of violence and hate
Such pessimistic views

We seldom learn of pleasant things
To lighten up our day
Of jobs well done, or kindly deeds
We meet along the way

But through the window then, I see
Amidst the murky gloom
My winter jasmine growing there
A mass of golden bloom

A taste of garden joys to come
Of blossom pink and white
With frogs returning to the pond
Their spawn a welcome sight

Mother Nature never fails
When things seem most depressing
To spread her beauty all around
Each month by month progressing

So with the lengthening days ahead
I'll rest and gaze in wonder
Enjoying fragrance in the air
Just sit and plan and ponder.

Sheila Leheup

So Many To Count

It's never too soon
it's never too late
to find it's a boon
to appreciate . . .
the meanderings
the panderings
the condescence then
the transcendence . . .
all those wondrous times
all those wondrous scenes
ring out all the chimes
for God's good blessings . . .

Bill Chapman

The Chrysalis

Watch the beautiful butterflies,
Studying in earnest their very short lives.
There is so much to learn from them,
As they flutter from flower to stem.

The larvae hatch from tiny eggs,
Then turn into caterpillars with tiny legs.
But soon the caterpillar begins to change,
Its body structure starts to rearrange.

Turning into a chrysalis, but watch, there is more to this,
We call this change metamorphosis.
Chrysalis will rest there till the spring,
But another change nature will bring.

Soon the chrysalis will start to move,
Nature is about to slowly prove.
That the sunshine of the spring,
Will bring forth a beautiful thing.

The cocoon skin is starting to split,
A beautiful butterfly starts to emerge a little bit.
First the pretty wings, which are still wet,
Then the body, but it won't fly yet.

Pretty little creature will stand and rest,
And will just dry out, now comes the best.
It starts to move its painted wings,
Suddenly flies off, in the warmth of the spring.

Just like butterflies throughout our lives,
We go through the motions and say our goodbyes.
Constantly changing from year to year,
Before we know it, old age is here.

Our bodies will die, we become a chrysalis,
It's not the finish, just listen to this.
For out of the chrysalis will emerge a golden being,
Perfect in every way, worth waiting for, and seeing.

Josie Smith

Glad To Be Alive

When you hold your first grandchild
And give thanks for their life,
You hope and pray for health and happiness
With not too much sorrow or strife.

I count my many blessings
Every day that I'm given,
Never taking for granted
The joy in just living.

Blessings come in many ways,
The sun on your face,
With the warmth of its rays.
Birds singing in the trees
With wind rustling all their leaves.

To have family and friends,
A warm home and no debt.
The cat sleeping in the armchair,
A well-pampered pet.

A home full of love
Nothing tainted by hate,
Overcoming greed, petty quarrelling,
It's never too late.

Be thankful you're alive
And enjoy all you see,
Thank God up above
For taking care of thee.

P Stennett

All The Days

Stephen Hawking said that one day we will know the mind of God.
I knew the mind of God one day - for one second.

So long ago, before my world began.
Waiting in a small, quiet room to sign away a life.

It wasn't difficult.
Three signatures - mine and two doctors.
They were easy to get.

After all, it wasn't really a life.
No one had smiled or cried or even breathed.
I signed, they signed. It wasn't difficult.

And then a mind that was not mine intervened for one second.
Apologising for wasting their time, searching for the door through stinging tears,
Then knowing my own mind again, wanting to go back - but too late.

And now my darling, all the days later,
I know that the best decision of my life was not made by me.
I see the past and the future in your eyes
And although I have had no contact with Him before or since,
For just one second I knew the mind of God.

Pam Ellis

Brighter Days Are Coming

January days can be dark and dreary
Making us all feel tired and weary
Alas, soon the snowdrops and daffodils
Will be starting to shoot up and cheer us
Crocuses, yellow, mauve and white are fearless.
Jack Frost on the lawn is white and shiny
Glistening dewdrops off leaves are tiny
Sun is getting warmer, spring is on its way
Soon more flowers will be coming into bud
Birds will be nesting for their young
Once Valentine's Day has been and gone
Robin's bright redbreast shines in the sun
Blue tits, blue and gold, chase each other for fun
Finding titbits people put out for them
Nature is lovely really, when we
Get the time to relax, watching TV
Doing jigsaws or crossword puzzles
Or hobbies like we do
Nothing is nicer than when I think of you.

Marian Clark

I Count My Blessings

As I rise this morning to a brand new day
I count my blessings as I kneel down to pray

I am so fortunate for my good health
My heart is rich in spiritual love and wealth
To renew my mind and change my heart
A daily challenge; I have made a start!

I aim to improve myself today in every single way
Everything I did before is now past and yesterday
Trying to live my life as the Lord Jesus Christ
Loving, giving, forgiving with hope of an afterlife!

Thinking of all the gifts I truly do possess
I realise how much I am so truly blessed

I have a mind, soul and body, I was given a free will
My heart is light, and full of joy, when at peace and still
I have my lungs I was given, a spirit and my breath
My heart is light, for I have life and not death!

I have my legs, with which I can run and walk
My heart is light, for I can sing with my voice and talk
I have my arms, with which I can reach out and hold
My heart is light, with warmth and affection not cold!

I have my ears, with which I can listen and hear
My heart is light, unburdened, no longer a prisoner to fear
I have my vision, and the scriptures, and I can see
My heart is light, knowing the Saviour set me free!

Kateryna Mazelan

Hope

Though conflict rages right across the globe,
And terror hides behind disarming smiles,
Yet blossom will return to gladden trees
And bluebells ring the chimes of mankind's hope.

So long as hope survives in human hearts
Mankind may learn to live in harmony
If tolerance is spread across the faiths,
As nature's rhythms promise to endure.

Pat Barfoot

The Sparrow

I saw a little sparrow,
A handsome, lively bird,
Bobbing through cars and shoppers,
Totally unperturbed.

He pecked at things I couldn't see,
On the pavement and the ground,
Oblivious to the mayhem
That was all around.

He had no thought of worries,
No chaff of mortal sin,
An unblemished little spirit,
Who lived with kith and kin.

He looked to me an anomaly,
Amidst this world of strife,
He had the air that showed no care,
About this thing called life.

He didn't strive for riches,
His needs? His daily bread,
No worries or frustrations
Cluttered that bird-brained head.

Little sparrow, you're a lucky chap,
You may not have a lot,
Unlike us, you seem content
With the little that you've got.

Stephen G Cox

Happiness Within

I count my blessings every day,
I am so blessed in many ways.
My granddaughter who is two years old,
Gives me a smile and I'm richer than gold.

In the garden I can see
The crocus, the daffodil just budding,
I count my blessings as I can see
The signs of spring approaching.

I've learned to appreciate what I've been given
And to take one day at a time
And to count my blessings every day,
Especially when I'm feeling down.

For there's always someone worse off than me,
And I know as the years roll on,
If I count my blessings every day,
Then I can be happy in every way.

Margaret Donaghy

Shadows Around The Moon

The old house is asleep at night,
No sound of children or birds,
No music playing,
Just the sound of the breeze
Like a purring cat.

Trees, tall, pointed fingers,
Reach towards the sky.
Moonlight breaks through
The dancing clouds
Shining her light onto
The barren ground below.

As many times before
I stand at this window
Watching the patterns made
By the clouds around the moon.
I watch and ponder the mystery of
This gentle friend who has been
There forever, keeping silent guard.

She has seen human happiness,
Despair, wars, senseless crimes
And all the time we laughed, loved,
Warred and fought she has been
Mankind's companion,
Our everlasting friend.

Lelia Grant

Faith And Hope

We have two good friends,
Who are with us night and day,
And if you believe in them,
They will never go away,
They help us through our worries,
Our troubles and our strife,
Keep us on an even keel,
On the bumpy road of life,
Their names are Faith and Hope,
Our blessings from above,
God has given them to us,
They are His gifts of love.

Stephen L Freeman

A Good Innings

In my time of life,
When the knees creak
Oh! The trouble and strife!
And the flesh is weak.

I'll sprint for the bus
Like before without fuss,
But with that blood rush
The puffed lungs feel bust.

You're as young as you feel
And age before beauty,
Will I be trim and nifty
By the time that I am fifty?

I think the head's screwed on,
It's a shame I crossed the thread,
And half the hair's all gone
So I'll wear a hat instead.

Must I now consider the denture,
Just a memory away from dementia?
Will I be able to keep my humour
When they come and lance the tumour?

So when I reach half century
Am I wise and join the gentry?
Do I embrace the coming years,
The ups and downs, the laughs and tears?

I can see the party on the day,
Jolly balloons and hurrah! hooray!
Jokes and beers, green jelly and canapé,
Rocking music, disco bubbles, Wah ha hey!

Family and friends, slaps on the back,
It's not so bad and not so black.
Now I've arrived at Halfway House
I should be a man and not a mouse!

So now it's chin up and stride out the door,
It's magnificent to be ten and two score!
There's so much to do just like before,
Look out, I'm gonna beat my chest and roar!

Trevor R Sizeland

Lamledra

From the top of Lamledra Hill
climb the stile and walk down.
The footbath passes cattle
soberly grazing on the mound.

Betwixt the headland of Dodman
and the jagged rocks of the Manese,
lies a peaceful shell-covered cove,
Vault Beach not reached with ease.

The sapphire ocean calm and deep,
reflected from the cloudless sky.
Gentle waves lap the strand,
a place no mortal could pass by

without reflecting on the scene.
A picture to hold within the mind,
an image of beauty to remember
and bring forth in a quiet time.

How blessed to hear the waves below,
feel the gentle breeze upon the face,
enjoy the smell of fauna and grass,
this is surely my favourite place.

To reach the shore and sea below
by foot trek down the steep incline.
When on the rocks just rest awhile
and dwell upon the return climb.

Rita Pedrick

Joan

While I wanted to scream
Your voice on the phone
Eased anger's steam
You made me realise
I could still dream
Though I have shed many a tear
I found the gift of your friendship
Through the wreckage of this year.

Bernadette O'Reilly

A Baby's Smile

My heart's been broken many times
In early years I was full of joy
I used to walk the beaches - tread the sea
But now that has all changed for me.

A lump keeps whelming in my throat
I choke back tears 'cause now I can't walk
But then while out in my wheelchair
I see a baby look at me - his little hand he tries to raise.

His big brown eyes look up and down
He blesses me with a great big smile
I want to hold him in my arms
But my arms are weak, I just grip my hands.

I've gone through pain in body, mind
Now told I'll just get worse
My loved one takes me out to Milton Keynes
Amongst the people so loving and caring.

If it wasn't for the blessing of the babies' smiles
I'm sure I'd want to fade away
God gave me more than I could hope for
When He sends the babies out in prams.

They all look and smile at me though so young
A baby's smile is my miracle blessing
I feel I've something to live for
The babies' smiles and little hands.

Rosina Drury

The Ties That Bind

Through all the years
Mid joy and tears
There is a bond
Of which we're fond
The family ties that bind

In times of sorrow
With no hope of tomorrow
Much love shines through
Because we knew
The family ties that bind

Always the good in loved ones we see
Together forever we will be
Side by side our thoughts we seal
Proving how unconditional we feel
The family ties that bind.

Shirley Davis

Light Of Love

A storehouse of blessings from high above
lighting up the sky with eternal love.
Sparkling starlight in the darkness of the night,
and daytime glory with sunshine so bright.
Sunrise and sunset - a beautiful treasure.
The wonder of colours in such great measure.
Love in the songs of the birds and the buzz of the bees,
and the gentle caress of a scented summer breeze,
The earth adorned with plants of every hue,
producing seeds to grow anew.
Trees climbing to majestic height,
reaching out to the heavenly light.
The waters of the springs, the rivers and the sea
- all gifts of love - given free.
But the greatest blessing is the lifeline of prayer
that leads a lost soul out of deepest despair,
to bring out a smile from behind sadness and sorrow,
and finds the way to a better tomorrow.
The guiding light of love - the saving grace -
is the warmest, comforting embrace.

Irena Bunce

Awakened Memories

There they sit, by illness trapped
So many thoughts in memories wrapped
Suddenly a familiar tune they hear
And recollection becomes quite clear
The words they sing with emotions deep
Sometimes they may even weep
They talk of events now long past
Their blessing is the memories last
Sometimes, with imagination embroidered
By a mind which seems disordered
But, perhaps our loving God did plan
This blessing of memory for a stricken man
No longer mobile, strong and fit
Destined long hours there to sit
When visiting, these little sparks of memory shine
Perhaps infused by a love divine
They shine like points upon a star
They're a special blessing, truly they are
So we thank our God in Heaven above
For these shared blessings, shared with love.

Brenda Hughes

I'm Happy Being Me!

I like to be quiet
I like to think
I like to meditate
I like to be solitary
I'm happy being me

I like to walk
I like to stroll
I like a life of rural surroundings
I like to walk for miles and miles
I'm happy being me

I like to be in the kitchen
I like to be at the stove
I like to create my recipes
I like to be at home
I'm happy being me

I like to be in the garden
I like to dig with a spade
I like to run the Flymo over the lawns
I like to keep the garden nurtured
I'm happy being me

I like to go on a holiday
By car or coach or train or plane
I like to discover the heart of a place
Whether Stratford, Cwmbran, Moffatt or Paree
I'm happy being me

I like to be with my children
I like to be with my family
I like to be in their presence
And to give them presents, gifts and treats
I'm happy being me.

Margaret Bennett

Sunlight Of Your Smile

The sunlight of your smile lit a beacon in my heart:
It welcomed me without precondition
For pure love ignores status, achievement means nothing to you.
I'm so blessed to have the untouched love of a child.

Damien Plummer

The Dawn

The dawn it rises from the ground,
And blankets all the earth around,
With soft grey clouds all moist with mist.
And jewels of liquid cobwebs kissed,
A ghostly sheen upon the sheep, cause shivers as they rise from sleep,
To eat the grass and drink the dew,
Then scratch themselves against the yew.
The mushrooms through the grass do steal,
The pale white orbs almost unreal,
To rise and die throughout the dawn,
Then reappear as though reborn.
A worthy crop with fleshly hoods,
Mmmm! With egg and bacon does taste good.
The birth of this, an autumn day,
When God's creation makes its way,
From dark to light in shifting shades,
O'er fields and woods and forest glades.
Begins this . . . an autumn day.

Daniel Callaghan

The Gathering

In the stillness of the sterile room
I urge her to stay a while
As siblings struggle through the fog
To reach her one last time.

Now fear and pain have left her
And at last she is at peace
We are joined together
United in our grief.

As we watch the new dawn rising
We catch up on the years
The paths our lives have taken
The laughter and the tears.

It's so good to be together
And remember our strong bonds
To laugh at childhood memories
Those far-off carefree days.

The world is getting smaller
There's really no excuse
Not to meet to toast her memory
In Australia, Spain and Greece.

Rosemary Jennings

Sometimes

Sometimes a pleasant surprise comes along
When things go wrong
When the wind cuts and freezes the air
And snatches your words away
When you want to say something that matters
You battle through icy waters
Till only a stillness remains.

The winter cherry is flowering
A crisp white rose is smiling
You can curl up in the arms of your chair
With a book of verse
Just think how lucky you are
Things could be worse.

Sometimes a pleasant surprise comes along
A hedgehog crossing the lawn
A buttermilk cat asleep in the sun
When the church bells chime
You think of childhood Sundays
Life is bitter-sweet.

When the church bells chime
Sometimes mother and daughter meet
To remember the power of prayer
And how we survived the journey
Through the years.

Beth Izatt Anderson

Wonderland

Have you seen the heather when purple is its hue,
Or the far-off lochans so wonderful to view?
Have you walked through leafy glades then paused and stood,
To see the flowers that blossom in a bluebell wood?

Have you seen the tall pines swaying in the breeze,
Sensed the heady perfume from cones among the trees?
Hear the song of wild birds, melodies from high,
See the setting sun in a western sky.

Stand now in a highland glen when all is quiet and still,
Hear the murmur of the water in a nearby rill,
See the wavelets lapping on a sandy shore,
Landscape ever changing, lasting evermore.

Walk again among the ferns as autumn leaves now fall,
Marvel at the beauty of nature overall,
Take once more a journey, see treasures as you go,
From summer, spring and autumn to winter's falling snow.

Alister Thomson

Chaos Theory

The precious, silent haunting of the new birth's precious lair,
Lives in winter's solitude and summer's lack of care:
The sharp sweetness of spring still clings
To the blues without the orange sky,
As winter scarred its loss on forward
To be seen and felt by a new sun's eye.
As though it remembers, somewhere inside, what it was like to die.

The pink shoots creep out cautiously,
Great boughs, pregnant, grasp up, away;
Tenaciously gripping such a tenuous hold
On the delicate, small heart that the forest will lay.
A beautiful ballet:
Where nature gives birth and kills every day.

In every way the vulnerable seed
Is weak 'n' fresh and a sacred thing,
A chaotic force of life unleashed
Ensures the future small things bring.
In the sun's heat - then the leaves brown -
Land busy 'n' rich in food, fight and sound;
And in the later cold, darkness where . . . nothing is found,
It seems a pretender is crowned . . .

Then as a noble prince returns to sire his father's throne,
Infectious raw energy bursts through to claim spring as its own.

In the harsh alone of winter, life looks within and chooses spring.

Denise Delaney

Death

No, I shall not bother to think about it.
What's the point?
It's there. Untouched, unchanged -
Like a rheumaticy joint.

Why should I bother about it?
Come it will.
If a thousand thoughts I give it,
It will not change the drill.

It will not change the slipping away,
The polka down the tunnel.
I just hope someone stray
Will open the gate
And let out a blast on the funnel!

Dorothy J Russell

My Eternal Love

My love for you will always be
Higher than the mountains
And deeper than the sea.
Whenever I needed someone to care
You were the one who was always there.
All my life I depended on you,
You were my friend so loyal and true.
Now time and space will not keep us apart
I will love you always with all of my heart.
Two soulmates who shared one life
Brought together as husband and wife.
You are my future, you are my past
You are my beginning, you are my last.
And that's the way it will always be
As we drift along to eternity.
On and on until the end of time
I am yours and you are mine.
You were to me a gift from above
And you will always be
My eternal love.

Robert Beach

A Grandchild's Questions

'Is this holiday sand
In my hand?'
With sincerity Suzie asks.
'Will it be here
When I come back next year
So I can play
Like I have done today?'
The sand is so vast
And the sea flows so fast,
She thinks it will take her away,
Imagination alive
For our little
Suzie
Is only just
Five!

Kathleen Harper

The Wind-Blown Rose

(My cousin Ray died on 4th September 2006.
This poem is dedicated to his family)

The beauty of Rye entranced Ray and I
Our last together, he and I.
The food was simple
The laughter long
The sky was blue
The wind not strong.
We mooched and poked,
We talked and joked.
The buildings so white
Never saw such a sight,
The beauty of Rye
So entranced Ray and I
The day flying by
As a wind-blown rose.

Flowing tears now drench my eye,
As I remember, at Christmas,
That day in Rye.

Looking back - I wonder
Looking back - I ponder
Ray - sweet - gentle Ray
Did he 'know' that upon that day in Rye
We would say our last 'Goodbye'

Cynthia Taylor

The Wonderful World

Spring is here, small shoots appear everywhere
One cannot deny to look around and find something new
I can add quite a few
The red-breasted robin who takes over the garden, possessive I think
To gather sweet scraps, chirps and away he goes
To a mound in the hedge away from his foes
Then a little wren, his tail stands straight at the end
Loves insects on plants and trees you can depend
The sea is not so far away
Welsh marshland a delight for breeding curlews
Such a sight, terns, oystercatchers, snipe, background
Of cliffs and rocks all have their say
One cannot withhold that the small things in life count
No end of searching can bring peace of mind
Than to look around at nature's wonders
Sunshine, wind and rain where, where can one find?

Mabel E Nickholds

The Snow Fairy

Beyond a winter sky the setting sun
Sank behind a line of forest firs,
And in the foreground danced a soaring pine
Outlined in delight against a veil

Of crimson merging into violet blue.
We were in a dusk-enchanted fairyland;
And yet this was about to form the backdrop
To a drama never seen before

Amidst these snow-clad meadows, fields and woods.
For soon the snowmen rushed out in their legions,
Lining up in ranks upon the ice;
And through the crystal trees another host

Poured forth to meet them on the sloping plain
Below the pine. Both sides now whipped out swords
Of jagged ice; and as they faced each other,
Panting hard, their noses fighting-red,

A snow fairy emerged from woods of white
As frozen boughs dissolved to let her through.
'Peace! Put back your swords!' she cried in haste.
'The greatest virtues are to be content

With what we have, and to forgive all wrongs.
Life is precious: blood must not be shed.'
The snowmen stood irresolute, some poised
For combat, others ready to give in;

But as they froze, the snow began to melt;
For sunshine caused the glistening ice to thaw.
And now the red-nosed snowmen disappeared
As Spring restored white fields to golden-brown;

And where the snow fairy had stood, a silver birch
Now danced against new forest foliage.
And yet, amongst those leaves of laurel green,
We still seemed to see her radiant smile -

That truest expression of sacred love
Flowing from her Master's throne above.

Robert D Hayward

The Lane

On hawthorn hedgerows woodbine trails
And climbs up towards the sky,
Spreading forth a fragrance sweet,
Its blushing blooms awry.
Soft green moss grows under fronds
Of bracken stiff and high.
Birdsong sounds now here, now there,
While drowsy bees drone by -
Heavily laden - from the hill
With heather's rich supply.
From hazel branches overhead
Brown ripened nuts drop nigh.
A squirrel scurries swiftly down
To hide its loot nearby.
The sun's rays filter through the trees
Their coolness to defy.
Near brambles bearing lush black fruit,
In dappled dell I lie.
The peace of my best-loved retreat
Few people could deny.

Joan-Pamela Moore

You Laughing

A sense of you waiting for me
Around the corner. Dodging, laughing.
'Recognise me,' you say. Touch me.
And I begin to think of myself
In many teasing bodies. Only this early
Sad awakening spreads its dim light.
Perhaps I have been absent. Feeling these changes;
My body responding to the
Subtle quivers of cells
Dancing their mischief, who or what
Am I then?
Did I change during the night?
Did my soul and yours swap places?
I think perhaps we must learn to look
At ourselves differently
In this slanting light, this change of mood.
Another recumbence, another dawn,
Another pair of eyes seeing what mine never will.
It's a question, perhaps,
Only of being empty; dodging each other
Between the park's green tentacles.
They grasp you as the children
Gurgle their thrilled, evasive laughter,
And distantly, my father sings to me.
His photograph waving in the air.

Gloria Tessler

Memories

I sit here in the darkness
Ensconced in my armchair
I watch the firelight flicker
And see the pictures there
As I watch the glowing embers
Shadows dance upon the wall
And I am back in memory
To days when I was small
Those happy golden yesterdays
When all the world seemed gay
No troubles then to fret about
In happy childhood days
I know that I was loved a lot
By parents good and kind
I've lost them now but still can keep
The love they left behind
I hope that I can also give
To children of my own
The love and care that came to me
Before I too am gone
There are so many pictures
To take me through the years
I've had my share of happiness
Of sadness love and tears
I don't know what tomorrow brings
To what the fates conspire
But meanwhile I am happy
With my pictures in the fire.

Lydia Barnett

Living In A Drive

The last house, near a stream at the end of a drive,
  Faces another house whose master has gone.
They've left two widows with memories still alive,
  But my family's here, though the other's the only one.
Yet further up the road are others alone.
  No friendship is forceful, but all would help each other
When lonely, or needing help - and there's always the phone!
  There are children further up with father and mother;
There's a cat which wanders across the street to roam
  In other gardens, but walks on the top of my fence
Because of the dog, which is sure he is ruler at home,
  So the cat thinks it's wiser to walk higher up. That makes sense!
I admit I don't know all who live in the drive,
  But we wave with a smile when I pass - and they know I'm alive.

Mabel Underwood

Each New Day

Some people feel so lonely,
They also feel so sad,
But just think of what's around us,
Then things don't seem so bad.

As the daylight dawns upon us,
With the start of each new day,
We can think of things that we can do,
To pass our time away.

Like watching flowers growing in the garden,
Or birds flying in the sky,
Or the children playing in the park,
And the people walking by.

There are friends we have to turn to,
When things just get us down,
The world is full of surprises,
So wear a smile, don't frown.

Glennis Ecclestone

Forever Friends

(Dedicated to Sally, Sarah, Elfed, Vi, Thomas, Keith, Karen, Dai, Eirian, Charlotte, Val, Margs, Olwen, Harold, Tom, Ivor, Walley, Valley, Roy, Ron, Sue)

Ethereal world's birth
Intangible from earth.
Guardian angel chimes
Recall special times.

Remember your life's eye,
Always sense true-mind's sigh.
Your laughs, cries echo by,
Reborn free butterfly.

Beautiful serene face
Transformed, full of grace,
Loyal hearts feel no fear
Haven's peace is love's sphere.

Emerge earth's chrysalis.
Feel Heaven's healing kiss.
Memories rest behind.
Life's cameos rewind.

Forever cloud-words walk.
Relive linked-arms hug talk.
You always beside me
Through our eternity.

Hilary Ann Morris

Wander

O fishes, would you welcome me,
If I fell into your deep, deep sea?
And if swim my arms could do not well,
Would you me where to rest at night so tell?
And eagles as they soar so high,
My friends be, if but I could fly?
Then if my legs be not too strong,
To carry me more miles along,
Would the grass that grows e'er 'neath my feet.
Provide me with a noonday seat?
Would that mountain up in the sky,
Let me it climb, and with my eyes try
To see what'er had been unseen,
And look back at where I had been?
Through the sun and rain and clouds
That run their race,
It isn't such a bad old place!

Alistair McLean

Had It All

And with a heavy heart
I open my eyes
And it's sometimes so hard
To see the silver lining

Ever since I've been left without you
My skies are mostly troubled
And it pains my heart to know
I'll never share your time again

But the memories of us
They shall never fade
I can get through tomorrow
By remembering our yesterdays

And thoughts of you ease my pain
The love we shared, always a comfort
I can smile at times
Knowing I had it all.

Elaine Donaldson

The Cycle Of Life - For Cameron

The tiny fingers, pink and chubby,
Lay still and peaceful on the quilt,
The soft, and gentle sounds of breathing
Stirred the heart, and raced the pulse.
Blonding strands of fine hair framed
The perfect face, so fresh and young,
And little dreams made all his features
Smile and warm, and my heart sang.

For was this not a grandchild dear
Of only days, and yet already
A special member of our dynasty?
A surging, overwhelming love
Rose within my heart, and stirred
Up all the memories of years gone by,
When his mummy lay aside,
And snuffled, smiled and looked so mild.

In a twinkling, all the years
Rushed past in tumult.
Days of worry when illness struck,
Teenage problems, boyfriend sorrows,
But - before the slightest melancholy lingered
Came the joys, the moments, ne'er repeated,
Of first words, and hugs and talk.
And now, the cycle starts again, in the most amazing way
When a life is shared among the members, old and grey,
Oh! what joy, what love, what laughter
With this new life, we start again.

Elizabeth M Sudder

Riga Park

Fallen leaves from tortured trees
Whose branches have witnessed so much
The gentle breeze that blows with ease
The softest Eastern touch

The skies a grey on this melodic day
The sound of the river flowing
An understated wealth of health
A morbidity that is glowing.

Darren Simon

Count Your Blessings

Faraway places beyond tumultuous oceans
Have heard and seen the anger of the heavens,
God strived to bring the wicked down
From their pedestals of wooden heads of idols
And sought the green lands, so lush, with a noise of crying ravens,

He is in control, the world is His, with miracles sublime,
Still striving to keep the wickedness of Man
Away from the peaceful followers of honesty and love,
To stroll through the green lands, climb the mountains
Without fear or hatred in one's lifespan.

The wonderful colours of the flowers of spring,
The birds, and trees majestic and strong,
The fish in the rivers, a fisherman's joy,
All made by God's hand for peace and love,
Wherever there are green lands that's where we belong.

The sun shines through my window, a new year's just begun,
The birds are on the wing, tho' early days for them,
We hope this year brings happiness to young and old alike,
The Lord will take their fears away from future years to come,
With love to enter every heart, so ends the great A-men.

Eileen Chamberlain

The Path

From the cradle to the classroom, to the things that make us free,
To the struggles and the strivings, such is life on family tree.
For the tree has many branches, and the leaves are rich in vein,
So life's pathway will be varied, and the treading marked with pain.

As our crossroads can be many, and the signs in number dearth,
Yet it seems a hand's directing, while we tread this mothered Earth.
Like the way our bread is kneaded, and the loaves in ovens bake,
Thus our lives mature in wisdom, with experience, our wake.

Just as sunlight and the moonlight shed their beams across the land,
There is hope that springs eternal, for the future may be planned.
See the way the cookies crumble, note the way all things are made,
Watch as oceans' waves in tumble - such our lives before they fade.

But the tree on which we started, and the leaves that grew profuse,
Bear the fruits of good or poison, some in clusters; some diffuse.
Thus one's deeds will so develop into things that light the mind,
Or they'll spawn and just envelop all and sundry, unrefined.

William Mack

Life Goes On

Yes, sadness has reared in every life,
We all have to struggle to cope.
But sunshine usually follows rain,
To help and heal with hope.

We will never know how or why,
The veil of sorrows will be lifted,
To reveal the new road ahead,
And sands of gloom now shifted.

There are many blessings in this world,
These help us when we are down.
We must savour these gifts bestowed,
And absorb the happiness around.

New life, healing, the beauty of our world,
The sun, moon and stars.
Family, pets and friends we make,
All these pleasures and treasures are ours.

Sometimes we weep, sometimes we smile,
Happiness will win in the end.
Count your blessings as life goes on,
Find riches around each bend.

Gwyneth Cleworth

Replace And Renew

Plant some quiet in your corner and allow
Your soul to drift. Don't let troubles spoil
Your peace as, though life's seeds you sift,
Use your rake to gather badness and put it
In the bin. Replace it with just one good
Thought and plant it cleanly without sin.
Keep that thought within your heart as
Daily hurts appear.
Glance back to your corner, you'll find a
Garden full of goodness that you can harvest
Year by year.
Re-clasp the buckle of your life
Think of goodness, not of strife.

J W Whiteacre

The Ultimate

Bliss exists for almost all on land;
one deep, one incomparable balm
compensates for imperfection,
misgivings of philosophers;
faith's unfortunate rejection;
from Man's disillusionment a calm;
music's singularity, occurs.

Listening, hysteria ignored,
the pulsing evil wills employed,
repeated here, Godlessly on Earth,
no truer blessing souls enslave,
by praying, we realise its worth.
On wistful wings I flew, enjoyed
sequestered note my Maker gave.

To adversary should I disclose
my tryst with tone or might he jeer?
A shield of beauty then exudes,
forbids all influence of pain
as, unperturbed, a string excudes,
such loveliness I shed a tear,
uncertainty's harassment vain.

Volumes stimulate the mind, enthral,
and lectures feed the intellect
but orchestration hoists me high,
empties the heart of grief and ache
as in my lonely bed I lie;
with each classic chord I may expect
in dreaming still to be awake.

Ruth Daviat

The Sweet Shop

I dream of candyfloss
and sugar pops
and things to eat
I love my sweets
at the corner shop.

But don't you know
it's not far to go
it's just across the street
where I'm hot on my feet
for the paper for my dad
who gives me 3p
for a lucky bag
yes, you get some sweets
and a toy
so that I will enjoy.

Deborah Storey

Forever

No feather ever touched its whispered way
More gentle than your hand touching my face.
No fragrant flower ever scented
More subtle than your breath upon my lips.
No heavenly sound broke a silence
More than your voice of raptured love.
No hand, no matter how distant away,
Touched my body as the thought of you.
No stars lit the velvet sky -
No breeze searched the features of my face -
No sun brushed the tips of Elysium waves
To make the diamonds of your tears
Than my love for you.
Touch -
Hold -
Keep
My memory
For in my silent years
You will always be there.

Peter Wait

Depend On It

A feeling of despair
No hope to cope
No path to find the way
No guiding rope.

An urge just to obey
Sleep and forget
But on the longest day
The sun will set.

The wind blows living seed
The earth will spin
Despair will go in time
Peace will come in.

Somewhere the lamp is lit
Depend on it.

Alan Dickson

The Gift Of Water

The life-sustaining mountain streams flow down,
At times in haste, towards the distant sea,
Cascading into shining waterfalls,
In rapid rhythm, liquid melody,
Like song and laughter tinkling over stones,
Conveying joy to those who may pass by.
Upon the plains the pace becomes more slow,
In gentle rivers, pools and twinkling lakes,
And there is water lodging underground:
Deep cooling wells to quench each creature's thirst;
So in the winter when the world is grey,
With many storm clouds darkening the sky,
Let us give thanks for purifying rain
That fills the reservoirs to meet our needs.
It cleans the grime away, makes fresh again
And even on the gloomiest of days,
When raindrops hang from every bare-branched tree,
They, bright as jewels, shimmer beads of light.

Anne Greenhow

How Blessed Am I

Walking down the High Street on a wet and windy day,
The banks were full, the shops were full,
Not far from Christmas Day;
I was feeling so unhappy, totally depressed,
I looked up to the heavens, feeling totally un-blessed;
I really felt ashamed with my attitude to life,
A lovely home, a lovely dog, an even lovelier wife!
There were tramps among the doorways trying hard to beg,
A man came past on crutches, he only had one leg;
I asked myself the question, 'Has the world gone mad?'
He was looking happy: I was feeling sad!
God spoke to me that moment, 'The world is in a state,'
Chronic alcoholics leaving it too late.
Suicides increasing, people whom we know,
People giving up on life, nowhere else to go;
Pregnant daughters, drug-crazed sons, I feel I want to cry,
And then I pause and realise, how very blessed am I;
We need to count our blessings as we travel on life's way,
And thank God for all His goodness, on each and every day.

William J Bartram

Hope

The onslaught is fierce and sharp-bladed bringing
Fear and black-winged terror, sable night
Without the pale sparkles of stars. Forces
Unknown, shadowing into something
Ill-defined and merging, for transient
Seconds, into a known but blank character
And, just as quickly, de-forming into
Black chaos, into waves of uncontrollable
And bitter, dispassionate seas: my being
Overwhelmed. But then a fragmentary light,
Reflecting a previously experienced joy,
Tugging at memory in the watery trough, and again,
Deep emotion is stirred and lightens the fear and
Hope begins to shape. The formless clay of
Darkness is moulded into the conviction
That the future is good and I am blessed.

Roger Bellamy

Count My Blessings?

Count my blessings? Well, here's one
Nearly 88, but not yet done!
Thank God for my parents
Christians through and through
Brought us kids up properly
Our wonderful blessings two.
Successful schooldays: worked, that's me
Won scholarships - blessing three,
We all five survived the war
John and Ken got married - blessings four
We three missed death by yards in Devon
Blessings five, six and seven.
Hobbies? Performing music's mine
Choir, organ/piano, that's eight and nine.
My job in bank I loved, and then
Thirty years' pension so far - blessing ten
Fifty-seven foreign holidays - take 'slides' - that's eleven
And twelve, having poems in print - that's Heaven!

Dorothy M Parker

Disappearing World

Jungle trees
Are calling me;
I hear - oh so near
A hungry jackal howl,
And the hoot of an owl.
I know
Just where to go
To see the tigers roam,
And find the eagle's home.

Birds! Beasts!
Snakes that hiss
Insects! Lizards!
All of this
God-given joy
Mankind will destroy,
And in its place
He will replace
Motorway and street,
Bingo hall, pubs, brick and concrete.

Weep! for lack of human foresight.
Weep! for the destruction of our birthright.
Bulldozers churn; forests burn -
Man will never learn.
Pray! as our green-world disappears;
God help us -
There'll be nothing left but tears.

J Castel-Nuovo

The First One

A memory as strong as steel
Everlasting as the green trees
Where we sheltered laughing
As young pleasure rained down
Before the storm of change
When life meant life infinite
Not a big empty vacuum
Her lips and smile stay with us
An umbrella of the past
A shield with many holes
That reality drips through
It's not even today we can
Wipe our emotions dry
As I stand at the same bus stop
She put soul, rain and sun
Into my world.

John Ball

The Blessings We All Possess

The search for the feeling of blessedness
From which hope, eternal, often springs,
Is the wonderful transformation
To delight, from despair, that it brings.

In this troubled world that we live in
Problems, many, are clouding our brow,
We search for a simple remedy
But at times we know not how.

As our hopes and dreams begin to fade
Without them we flounder on, in vain,
We need to count all of our blessings
To cope with the immeasurable pain.

We struggle on with private emotion,
Often battles rage within each mind,
Then with the need for quiet pleasure
We can savour the peace that we find.

Maybe it's because we're not conscious
Of the blessings we always possess,
The beauty that's apparent throughout our lives
We fail to treasure, to caress.

The springtime in all of its beauty
With new life that appears all around,
Roundelays of musical songsters,
Bright colours of glory to astound.

A vivid rainbow after a shower
Where the sun's dazzling colours shine through,
The excitement of laughing children
For them, troubles in life seem so few.

The smell of grass that's newly mown,
Pleasant perfume from a scented flower,
God's gifts for all to appreciate
As we treasure each happy hour.

As we count our blessings, one by one,
Feelings of happiness linger on.

Irene Grahame

Give A Little Love

The kind of thing that makes people sad
Is the way that animals are treated so bad,
Cruelty, does anyone care? From cats and dogs,
To seals and bear.
It breaks our hearts when we see,
The injuries people cause,
Surely there should be a lot more stricter laws.
Our little pets don't ask for much,
Food and warmth, a gentle touch,
Some of these atrocious injuries the
Animals have to endure, very often are so bad
That there's sometimes no cure.
These animals trust us to help them survive
So we must help all we can to keep them alive.
After all, every creature has the right to live
So they will need all the love that each of us can give.

Sheila Buckingham

Friendship Is A Blessing

There are miles and miles o' rivers,
There are miles and miles o' sea,
This world has many problems,
On that we all agree.

But we won't heed the problems,
Nor winter's cold, cold blast,
For we have lasting friendships,
Friendships that do last.

Friendship is a blessing,
That we can give each day,
Money comes and money goes,
It's never here to stay.

So let us 'treasure blessings',
Forgetting all those fears,
Blessings are such 'precious things'
That last throughout the years.

There's miles and miles o' deserts,
There are miles and miles o' sand,
Countless people in our world,
That need a helping hand.

Jimmy Sinclair

Count Our Blessings

Our minds go back to younger days
With many blessings there
And there were many hardships
That families would share.

The pace of life was different
From how we live today,
And then we had no 'Nanny State'
To help us on our way!

There was just news in the papers
And much less aggro, too,
When people paid for what they had,
If they couldn't, they made do.

But, there were a lot of blessings
And, with most, a sense of pride,
And the special day was Sunday,
One special, set aside.

My memories go back, my friend,
To over eighty years,
And there were so many blessings
But still a lot of tears.

But now, in New Labour's Britain,
Standards have dropped so low
And crime is now so prevalent
That the prisons overflow.

You can really 'count your blessings'
If you're in Government,
With an admirable pension
You can really feel content.

So, 'count our blessings' in our minds,
They're blessing in the past,
But if we get 'New Labour' out
Blessings can start at last.

Laurence Cooper

Blessings

Lord, where shall I begin, and where to end?
So many are the blessings which You send.
Even bad things You can turn to final good,
And this, the world has scarcely understood.

But I have eyes to see Your constant care.
Look where I may, and You are always there.
Sorrow or joy, great triumph or defeat,
I bring them all and lay them at Your feet.

You never fail my needs to understand;
Gladness or grief, allowed by Your good hand.
My every circumstance controlled by You
Becomes a step towards the goal in view.

May I be always with this grace endowed,
Seeing the rainbow rather than the cloud.
Finding Your constant presence a delight,
Till blind faith's trusting end's in glorious sight.

Mary Pledge

Dreaming

Can you imagine the splendour
Of a ballroom in Heaven above?
The clouds with the colour from sunsets -
The light from the stars and the moon.

The glow from the brightness at dawning
And a chorus of angels in song,
Music from harps; and the breezes
From wings of a heavenly throng.

The life of a loved one helping
To bring to a world full of fear;
The hopes and the dreams we all cherish -
The loved ones we long to be near.

To dance on in dreams
Must be better by far
Than the battles and heartaches of war
Happiness as the theme of dreaming,
For evermore.

Peggy Morrill

Elsina's Centenary

(In memoriam: Elsie Muriel, née O'Connor, later Richards, then Hamilton Davies; 27.6.1907 - 8.8.2002)

She came into a world in which the pace of life was slow -
A baby born by Mersey's shore a century ago;
This year would bring her 100th birthday, were she still alive -
What changes, though, she must have seen till she was 95!
Apparently a pretty child, she could recall being seen
To head the May Procession as the chosen May Day Queen;
Her childhood was a simple one, she grew up by the sea
And played with friends and siblings, on the beach, quite safe and free;
There must have been some sorrow, times when everybody cried
As in a tragic accident, her youngest sister died,
Then with her other sisters (only infants, little more)
She watched her only brother as he proudly went to war -
He'd thought there'd be excitement and he went with bated breath
But all he got was poisonous gas and an untimely death.
(That was the first of two World Wars that changed the world for good
But little Elsie, at the time, could not have understood.)
Born to a world of horse and carts, she saw the car arrive
And did, in fact, astonish people when she learned to drive,
For she remembered crowds of shoppers who would stare and squeal
To see a girl of sixteen summers sitting at the wheel!
She learned to be a gentlewoman - jobs were for the men,
Careers were for the gentlemen (that was the thinking then).
They taught her ballroom dancing, flower arranging, what to say
To interest the eligible men who came her way,
So married twice and widowed twice, an asset as a wife,
Devoted to her children and their children all her life,
She earned a reputation as a hostess of the best
And travelled widely through the world before she came to rest;
A commonplace event, you think? A birth like any other?
Not me - the baby born that day grew up to be my mother!

Rosemary Vandeldt

Field At Sunnyside

(For George and Florence Kent, beloved grandparents passed)

The freezing fog made it raw,
Hanging in the air
A starched white sheet.
The fire crackled as if to beckon
A sanctuary by the hearth.
My fingers and toes numb,
Watching semi-invisible bovine forms
Plod wearily over crispy grass.
Each step creaking slightly.
Sweet grassy breath, billowing from damp nostrils.
I expected you to be there, both of you.
Rusty collander of cabbage leaves,
Now a distant memory,
For a second a frozen tear
Then a fireside chair for tea and cake.

Sarah Kent

Contentment

Curtains drawn back to maximise light
Windows opened at the end of the night
Tea and toast to start the day right
Clothes chosen for comfort, not too tight

A friend to ring to arrange to meet
A gentle walk before the day's heat
A few spaces made on the store shelves
Soda farls with blueberry jam to treat myself
Unpack the shopping, custard creams and coffee
A few chores are done before any hobby

A gentle breeze, plenty of shade
In this park in the garden that I have made
To read a good book in and eat a nice roll
The afternoon TV play was good for the soul
My watercolour painting is coming along
The sparrows and blackbirds are singing their song

Salmon for dinner, croquette potatoes too
The medics say fish is good for you
My doctor's appointment is postponed
Aches and pains are on hold
Tomorrow is another day
For a bit more of the same I shall pray.

Sylvia Shafto

Beached On Sunday

The beach roasted in the sun.
A determined sea pounded the
Steep pebbled shore.
A green flag strained on its post.

Pink children by the score
Played in the ribbon strip
Disputed by the sea,
A group close by were sharing food
To cries of 'that's not fair' and 'have some more'.

There were sunshades, windbreaks
And folding chairs,
There were legs waxed clean as morning air
And those still covered in Neanderthal hair.

Many backsides too,
One could hardly keep abreast
Of all the shapes and varying hues.
A few were brown,
Most paler than a harvest moon,
Some twice as large
And nearly quite as round.

As the day turned
A red flag took the place of green,
We drifted weary to the town,
Waited each in line for cod and chips;
They were more than fine.
It seemed that on the whole
Most chips got swallowed whole.

The journey driving home
Was a tranquil affair.
A boy snoring in the back
Had salted, sanded hair, his day
Spent fighting with the sea.
He stopped its flow,
Turned it back.

Alex Laird

Blessings

I knelt in prayer one morning -
to thank You for this day.
Counting all the blessings -
bestowed along life's way.

The path has not been easy -
so many hills to climb.
I carried on relentlessly
until You showed me a sign.

You spoke to me of treasures -
that lay along life's way.
No gold or silver would I need,
if I took time to pray.

The dark clouds seemed to part,
as the golden sun shone through.
You changed my life completely -
as I was born anew.

When the brightness of the day -
meets the darkness of the night,
I count my blessings, once again -
for I have seen the light.

Nina Graham

Blessings

The geese in formation overhead fly
Dark shapes against the evening sky.
Looking upwards I watch them flying by
Honking their praise-song and I wonder why?

What have they to say that I have not?
Or was I too busy and so forgot
To say thank You for all these wonders I see
And to ask for a blessing on me?

I will ask a blessing for my family
For all the many times You have blessed me
I thank You for your daily care for me
Your blessings are so very personal You see.

Blessings fall on us from above
Part of the measure of God's love.
Freely He gives us and we receive
All that He offers for our needs.

Diana Mackenzie Blench

She Was Only 7 Years Old . . .

My daughter asked me one starlit night
'Is that my daddy in the sky?'
She pointed to a gleaming star
I said, 'Yes, that's where you go when you die . . .'

She asked if I would join him
End up a star next to her dad
I felt a rip across my heart
Which made me very sad . . .

It stirred a lot of feelings
I had never felt for a while
I kissed her and I hugged her
And said, 'I love you,' with a tender smile . . .

She then asked who would look after her
If I was to die too
I told her, 'Your big sisters
They would always look after you . . .'

I never had a fear of death
Before she asked this question that night
But now I never want to leave her side
I will hold on to life so tight . . .

Some take life for granted
They just don't care what they do
But if your child asked you that question
I think it would change your whole life too . . .

Janet Brook

A Blessed Wife

I keep all your cards and letters to me
And bless the day that we two met
A sign of our wonderful life together
Those happy memories I can't forget
So many years we had together
Working and laughing, with just a few tears
Blessed with love and understanding
Facing together our hopes and fears
But our handsome sons and beautiful daughters
That mean far more than earthly things
Are blessings you left, beyond compare
Just seeing them, and my heart sings
So even though you are gone, my love
There's no regret for our past life
I can only thank our God above
That I was a truly blessed wife.

June Davies

Balance And Contrasts

On the occasions when you feel down
And depression hurts you like a pain
Remember that nothing lasts forever
The clouds will lift and you'll smile again.

Nature has a basic rule which says
That every coin must have two sides.
You can't have one without the other
Whatever your inner-self decides.

The sun sets and the moon takes its place
To let you rest your weary eyes
When you awake a new day has dawned
And the sun's rays will light the skies.

The tide comes in and then it retreats
Rain and floods will soon counter drought
Through all this your heart still beats
But to take a breath you must first breathe out.

How can you understand what love means
If you've only encountered hate
Or know the sheer pleasure of giving
If you've never experienced that state?

The people you've known and things you've done
Will have left their imprint on your life;
So gather together the joy and fun
And forget all the tears and the strife

Then on the bad days you'll have your store
Of delights to recall from the past
To sustain you till a brighter time comes
When the minutes will tick away too fast.

Betty Nevell

Find The Good In Life

As we travel the pathway along life's way
We must make decisions day after day
Sometimes we make a mistake in life
It causes us to have trouble and strife
We must put this behind us and learn as we go
Each lesson will teach us what we should know
Living each day, trying our best
To get through each hour and pass the test
For life itself is a test we must take
It changes each day with every turn we make
It challenges us with what is wrong or right
When we make the right choice we can sleep at night
So many things in life can go wrong
But we have been given laughter, music and song
To balance our lives in so many ways
With the sun chasing the clouds, sending down its warm rays
Uplifting our spirits, helping to lighten the load
Putting us on a happier road
Life is hard but we have a wonderful world too
With birds and flowers in colours of every hue
It's the nature of life to have dark and light
We must have them both to have the balance right
So take a hold of life, enjoy being alive
Find the good things around you and you will survive.

Glenys Hannon

In The Garden

Fruit from the boughs hung clustered.
The garden green and still,
Birds in the sky flew gaily,
To all of Heaven fill.
The sun, with golden brightness,
Lit up this magic scene,
Serene in all its glory,
The garden still and green.

I sat and thought with pleasure,
So happy in that scene,
Fruit from the boughs hung clustered,
And all at once it seemed,
That joy had filled my senses,
And all of Heaven sang,
Tumultuous my emotions,
The bells of Heaven rang.

Mary Hughes

The Attic

The attic room
May be small
But the views
Will enthral

The eye is drawn
Toward the fells
The rolling hills
The dips and dells

To the stand of trees
And beyond
Where Mother Nature
Works and bonds

In the village
Time has stood still
Sheltered from
The world's ills

Woodsmoke drifts
In the air
As churchgoers walk
To evening prayer

From here I see
The stars on high
Orion sparkles
In the winter sky

Thank you landlord
For the attic room
Where well-being
And persona bloom.

Myra D Walker

Riding Into Spring

Riding through barren fields of snowy furrows,
where small trimmed hedges once flourished,
now covered in powdery, shimmering snow.
Glancing at snow-capped glistening hills.
Heavy hooves submerged in pristine whiteness,
we jump bubbling, foaming brooks.
Splash in frosty, snow-lined streams,
no escape from the raw, frosty air.
Slithering and slipping, sun descends.
A few rays of precious sunlight escape,
highlighting the new birth of growth,
buds are thickening, snowdrops appearing
everywhere, glimpses of new green life emerging.
From the depth of winter comes spring,
bringing hope of a new beginning.
This is my nirvana.

Patricia Helsby

Open Your Eyes And See

The wonderment on a child's face at their first pantomime,
Delicate butterflies' wings as soft as a baby bird's feather,
A kiss as gentle as a snowflake as it slowly falls to earth,
Happiness, the birth of a grandchild,
Perhaps the one you thought you would never have,
Warm sunshine as it falls upon your face,
The first word a mother hears her child say, like a baby's first step,
The one you nearly missed,
The smell of a garden full of beautiful flowers,
Or as you walk along the beach the tang of the sea,
The feel of a baby kitten's fur as delicate as a silk scarf,
Love given freely, without asking anything in return,
The gentleness of a lover as he takes his lover's hand,
A smell of newly baked bread the one you can't resist,
Or when you make a Christmas cake that you can't wait to eat,
A babbling brook, gurgling over stones as it goes,
Colours of greenfinches as they fly to rest upon a fence,
Pureness of the first fall of snow where no man has trodden,
A gentle summer breeze as it ruffles a young girl's hair,
The wagging of a dog's tail pleased to see you home,
A feeling of pride when at your offspring you look,
First buds upon the trees letting you know spring is coming,
Cry of a newborn baby letting you know they are there,
Kindness of a stranger, who you never saw again,
Many things and blessings are free
As long as you don't forget to see.

H Dormand

Making The Best . . .

She thought it was as well
she'd bought an extra light bulb
when one plinked out
leaving her in the darkest bathroom.
Familiar objects vanished.

'It's well my hearing's good,
although my eyes are dim these days.
I'd know if anybody called,
I'd hear the knock for sure, that is,
when someone calls.'

It was as well she could imagine things:
herself, submerged into an underwater sea,
a universe, The sound of waters make
a special ringing, singing
all at one pitch and
fish of many shades and stripes,
coral, sand and rock, and best of all,
sea anemones which wave and clutch
in colour whenever she lies down
surrendering to tinnitus. It's much too much
to contemplate against a pillow. 'Another world,'
she smiled, 'and such are for the looking.'

Her cat became a tiger for a while,
pounding, feinting with a piece of string
as if it were a meal to be.
How good it is to love a pet, she thought,
to feel his fur against my hand
and let the rumblings of his purr
vibrate throughout my arm and chest!
How good it is, even in little ways
to be appreciated!

Diane Burrow

God's Blessings

Blessings surround us in so many ways,
Even on the darkest and most dismal of days,
Give thanks to God that you wake up each morn,
He's given us breath since the day we were born.
If you are healthy and can see and hear,
Then you have blessings beyond compare.
So many things in this life are free,
The sunshine, rain, flowers and trees.
The great outdoors, the spacious seas,
The changing seasons - blessings indeed.
Trust in God, His promises are true
Just remember, He is always blessing you.

Vera Hankins

The Letter

(After the painting by Vermeer)

The letter is opened with care
As if unfolding time itself, each corner
Representing where it was sealed;
Fingers now enter to break, to peel.
The breath is held - suspended of rhythm,
Delicious in anticipation, not released
Until the drift is caught. The heart opens
To its compliment yet appreciates
The slightest nuance. A world might stop
For this and ambiguity
Would have it held forever!
That lifting eye, the gaze, the wonder
Has the rest of time to ponder.
These unfolding words as paper live
For this brief space yet give
A pleasure greater than their artifice.

William Birtwistle

My Blessings Personified

The first of my blessings is to wake each day
Thrilled in the knowledge I've not passed away.
The next welcome blessing, I'm blessed with good health
The next is enjoying a comforting wealth.
I don't mean I'm rich, I'm far from that,
I don't own a mansion or a Mayfair flat.
I have enough money to keep me from worry,
If a household appliance should suddenly break,
I can replace it in a hurry.
Another great blessing with which I'm endowed,
My friends and relations, a wonderful crowd.
I live amongst neighbours both caring and kind,
A more friendly group you would struggle to find.
The jewel in my crown of blessings,
That serves to perfect my already sweet life,
It's Ann, my lifelong companion, my best friend
And loving wife.

Geoffrey Alan Chapman

Have You Noticed

The world is becoming beautiful,
Have you noticed this?
In the way people hug,
In the way people kiss.
Have you noticed
How the world is getting better?
In the book,
In the letter.
Have you noticed,
How the world is improving?
In the way people talk,
In the way people sing.
Have you noticed how people everywhere
Are taking care of the land?
Isn't that lovely,
Isn't that grand.
Have you noticed
How the world is becoming one mind?
How people are getting
So soft and kind.
The world is becoming full of bliss
Have you noticed this?
It's something you could not miss,
Have you noticed?
Have you really noticed?

Joe Staunton

A New Day

A new day is born, what can we expect?
Just open your heart and take a deep breath.
Ah! That's better, you're able to say,
For your eyes will be able to take in the day.
If it is fair and bright, one immediately feels good,
If dull and dreary or pouring with rain,
Just hope it will clear and the sun shine again.
For we cannot change the weather,
It may affect our mood
But put the bad thoughts behind us
And think of the good.
Amazing how much better one feels,
When looking on the bright side.
It really is much better
And a smile with a cheery good morning
May help another as well, to perk up
And have a good day after all.

Phyllis Wright

A Bundle Of Blessings

Blessings come to us in so many ways,
Like one is to experience the beginning of a day,
Blessings are a gift for all of us,
How you see those blessings, in you, have trust.

A shared smile with a stranger feels good, so new,
It's something that can be shared by one and all,
Like an embrace from your lover, then, at times alone,
To be part of a family, in a loving home.

To be healthy in body, mind and soul,
With peace of mind, allows us to feel contentedly whole,
News of a birth of a baby, so new and fresh,
For couples who've been trying, it's a beautiful wish.

All around us are blessings like a rainbow above,
Whether you're young or old, see them positively with love,
To be able to watch your children grow and come to no harm,
To experience a sunset, while the sea is calm.

Mother Nature is beautiful, full of blessings to give,
It allows our lives to be more bountiful, plus wonderful to live,
So when in times of sorrow, grief or despair,
Just allow yourself some blessings, then see if life is unfair.

P Deakin

Ann Joy

A remarkable woman, you had a heart of gold,
Cherished memories I possess, are what I now lovingly hold,
You had an aura that only your being was blessed with,
Your closest think of you often as the years pass by,
You are still sadly missed, more than words can adequately express.
It's as if yesterday still existed, my recollections ever fresh,
Whenever the sun shines, I see your smiling face,
Your presence I feel, when its rays deflect your once grace,
I view the months and seasons like the passing time it is,
Deep in my memory, I still picture you as my wonderful sis,
Yes, you were my sister, my friend, most importantly an endearing treasure,
The love and closeness of a brother and sister no one could ever measure,
I miss your warm friendship, companionship and kind ways,
Without you, my life has been a chasm, that is what my emptiness says,
You mourned the passing of your beautiful daughter, Linda, a heartrending blow,
Little did I realise a few years later I would lose you also,
We rarely talked about your painful loss, it was too much to bear,
Whenever we did, tears welled in our eyes, our heart strings it would tear.
Often I reflect upon both your lives, the memorable times we shared
Such intimacy bound us together, though nothing else compared,
Tenderly put, your existence will not be forgotten by family, especially Roy,
Ann and Linda Coldicott, very much you were an inspirational Joy.

Roy Fisher

Life

God made us all to live our lives in sunshine and the rain
To feel the laughter and the joy or sadness and the pain
Each day we must try to learn which path we have to follow
And keep our feet on the path looking forward to tomorrow

Some days we have our ups and downs, there's sunshine
and there's showers
If it wasn't for the rainy days, we would not have the flowers
Just think of all the happy times and the miracle of birth
So try to make the most of life we have to share on Earth

Each of us has a time, our burden big or small
If we can share each other's load, it's not so hard at all
At times the path is rocky, the hill is very steep
But every day I say thank you before I go to sleep.

Evelyn Ingram

Lucy

Her tiny fingers clasp my hand as she greets us at the door
And leads us to her land of toys covering the floor

She makes us both an imaginary cup of tea
Looking for approval which of course she'll get from me

Her smile illuminates the room as we play
And her mother bids bye-bye as it's her working day

At eighteen months she is unaware
Her crisp clean clothes and happy life not all little children share

But all such knowledge in good time
As these moments with our grandchild remain sublime.

Sam Spruce

Hands

Hands are for holding: a pencil to write;
A lamp or a candle to see by at night;
A needle for sewing; the garment to mend,
But mostly for holding the hand of a friend.

Hands are for feeling: the way in the dark;
A kitten's soft fur; an oak tree's rough bark;
The tug of a kite string when trees bow and bend
Or the warmth in the touch of the hand of a friend.

Hands are for gesturing: pointing the way;
Waving goodbye at the end of the day.
Held out in welcome at a long journey's end
In the gentle embrace of the hands of a friend.

Frances Stubbs

Life Is What You Make Of It!

I may not have much money
Or an expensive flashy car,
I may not have a big house
Or get to travel far;
But I do have lots of friends
And an extra special son!
I have a very close family
Who to me are number one!

I may not be a model
Or a wife of a king,
I may not be a famous person
Or wear a diamond ring;
But I do have all I need
Of that there is no doubt!
I make the most of all I have
If not, I go without!

I may not get a real wage
Or work each day till late,
I may not be a pop star
Or go out on special dates;
But I do have a rewarding job
And I do the best I can!
I look after my son Joshua
Who I call 'my little man'.

I may not have the very best
Or everything I'd like,
I may not get to fly a plane
Or own a brand new bike;
But I am as happy as can be
And that is not a lie!
Your life is what you make of it
Until the day you die!

Patricia Daly

Counting Blessings

Waking up each morning, what do I see?
The sky above with clouds or sun shining on me.
Sounds that I truly love most to hear
Are the songs of birds, so full of cheer.
At the start of each new day
Can be heard the humdrum of the motorway
Children rushing past on their way to school
Not to be late must be the rule.
A stroll in the park with dogs walking
Folks are seen, laughing and talking.
As evening comes with the setting sun,
How has the day been for everyone?
It is time now for us to rest,
Looking around at nature, I do not jest,
How pleased am I, that I am possessing,
The ability to count my every blessing.
In prayer to earnestly thank God above,
For the many things created with His love.

June Allum

The Search For Silver And Gold (True Alchemy)

True gold is your voice on the phone
When the days are long
When I haven't seen you in a while.
Treasured memories of the past
All we have said and done and seen together
Through the years.

True silver is the shine in your hair
The glance of those green eyes
With the hint of mirth
That always lurks beneath the surface
The raised dark eyebrows
Questioning, frowning, conveying puzzlement
Needing to enlighten my errant thoughts and ways
A beloved face
Never far from my questing gaze.

In the presence of my loved ones
Is my search truly rewarded.

Beryl Johnson

The Optimist

When love, sometimes, goes out of the window
And he finds himself lovelorn, all alone
Instead of sobbing, sad as a willow
Honing his pain on the bitterness stone
He looks forward to the next dance
Hoping to meet love and romance
Swapping the bad for the good in his stride
He always sees, of the coin, the bright side.

In winter when dark nights curtail daylight
When cold has undressed most trees of their leaves
He sees in the smallest glimmer, delight
A ray of hope with fervour he perceives
He looks forward to spring; the scents
The colours, the sap that ascends
Regarding life as a great adventure
He awaits with curious eyes the future.

He celebrates life as it comes his way
But never envies what others possess
He knows material desires pave the way,
Leaving the mind frustrated, for distress
Why waste time 'Ars longa, vita brevis'
'Omnia vincit amor de profundis'
He washes all bad memories with the soap
Of forgiveness to reveal rosy hope.

Negative people see futilities
Nothing else in life, they can't be impressed
So they fail to seize opportunities
They survive in gloom and doom, self-oppressed
They find the bottle of wine half empty
He sees it half full, of good quality
Of his own life he is the catalyst
He's forever a confirmed optimist.

J-C Chandenier

Brave Jane

Jane Tomlinson is Yorkshire's pride
Completing her epic bike ride
Cycling from Rome to Leeds
Fighting cancer with her deeds
Big in heart, yet small in frame
This heroine has climbed to fame
Cycling on despite the pain
Withstanding both hot sun and rain
Now that Jane has passed the test
She deserves a well-earned rest.

Terence Leslie Iceton

Counting Our Blessings

If our blessings we now count
We find what our life is really about
If we admit to having none
This means our life can't be much fun
Then we're really a negative soul
And finding more blessings must be our goal.
Benefiting from someone's foresight
Should be appreciated with all our might.
Soft summer rain after a drought
Pushes depressive misery out.
Finding new skills in which to take part,
Increasing our knowledge is an art.
Giving a smile to all around
Or having a laugh, lovely sound.
If our life causes us to moan
We find ourselves really alone.
No one likes us if we complain
On summing it up it becomes quite plain.
If our blessings we now count
We find what our life is really about.

Ruby Lawrence

Quality Of Life

Blessed am I to be alive
Healthy in mind and body
Imagination on increase
Memories not started to recede.
With fading eyes I still view
The world in awe and wonder
My sense of smell still inhales
All of nature's bounty.
Hearing is not impaired
To slightest sound alerted
Teeth and taste buds
Stood test of time
I eat what's recommended.
Exercise keeps limbs supple
Blessed then am I
With extra muscle.
The will to live life to the full
Triumphs over every trial.

Robert Fallon

Red Poppies Bloom

Oh blessed Earth where love survives
There are people with a rainbow in their eyes
Like a sign from God for His broken child
There are people who will smile on a lonely street
Warming your heart on a misty, cold winter's day.
There are people like the brightest stars above
Shedding light on your path in the darkest of nights
There are people who speak and sow seeds of hope
And red poppies bloom under darkest clouds.
There are people who pray for your soul to blossom
Like an oasis in the desert of a dry barren land
There are people who see the black Madonna's tears
And are carried to Heaven in chariots of gold.
There are people who sing a precious new song
Like the purest holy angels before the throne.
There are people with the face of the whitest dove
Who bring blessed peace from realms above.
There are people who will drop words of silver pearls
Into your troubled mind of velvet cushion in black despair
There are people like the healing fruitful trees
Whose loving autumn leaves are blown on all humanity.
There are people who run through sun-kissed fields of wheat
Like Mary in joy, dance and laugh at the Master's feet.
A yellow butterfly circles and draws a jewelled halo
Around my sweet mother's graceful blessed head.
There are people who flame like a comet in the sky
Over planet Earth, light up ten million minds
There are people who see the amazing beauty in life
And give thanks to God and His Son, Jesus Christ.

Thomas Hull

Life's Blessings

A summer breeze with gentle flow
A rainbow after a storm
Soft falling snow
A crisp frosty morn
The innocence in a child's smile
An infant newborn; a lover's kiss
All the joys in living
Within a shrinking world:
Count your blessings
For life is as fleeting
As a breath of wind.

Arthur Pickles

My Blessings

I look in the mirror expecting a change in some miraculous way
But nothing is different - I still look the same although it's my birthday today!
It seems a good time to look back on a life which was blessed from the start,
Born to parents who wanted and loved me - I still treasure them in my heart.
My childhood was happy in spite of the fact that I was an 'only one'.
How could I be lonely when my mother was mother to everyone?
And during the dark hungry days of the war when so many fine men were killed,
My uncles were spared and returned home when the noises of war were stilled.
God blessed me in another way, for I was one of only three
To gain a scholarship to the high school, lucky, lucky me!
He blessed me too in music - I had always been able to sing
And now, with hard work and tuition, my voice began to take wing!
Operas, oratorios, folk songs . . . I sang in many guises . . .
I competed in festivals all over the land and I won my prizes.
Because my voice was a gift from God, I used it to glorify Him
And still sing in my church choir and praise Him in psalm and hymn.
What a blessing I received in '54 when Ted and I said 'I do',
We've happily shared almost 53 years and a love that's strong and true.
And the greatest blessing God could give, which gave us endless joy,
Was of course our long-awaited son, our precious little boy.
And then to make our lives complete He blessed us once more
With our beautiful daughter, Elizabeth, whom we both adore.
There cannot be many more blessed than me with friends whose love I treasure,
Old friends and new and that includes you, for knowing you is my pleasure.
So today, I look back over 77 years filled with music, laughter and love,
I thank my family, I thank my friends and I thank my God above.

Elizabeth Brown

Life's Blessings

To have a spring in your step as you go through the day,
Brings to mind the blessings we can have on the way.

To have an eye to see the beauty of a tree,
Flowers, nature, as it's meant to be.

The family, a smile on a grandchild's face
Brings happiness to outdo any pace.

To win that ambition, so important to youth,
Does it really matter who wins it on foot?

To look to the heavens, the cumuli in the sky,
Fills one with pleasure and joy for that sky.

When one is young and ambition draws near
These things are forgotten, such I pity I fear.

But when one is old, ambition is spent,
So count your blessings and feel content.

Elsie Woodward

Comfort

The Lord is with you,
As long as you remain with Him.
His divine presence
Can never be dim.
Through the darkest clouds in life
Our God will come shining through,
With the redemption, salvation and glory,
Reserved in Heaven for you.
Have you received Him?
The Lord it is at hand.
Have you received Him?
Do we understand?
All can be forgiven
A new life ahead,
A life worth the living
His arms are outspread.
The Lord can be with you
For He is the way,
What love and devotion
Accept Him today.

Elsie G B Horrocks

The Discovery

By dawn's light, the fresh snow glistened like diamonds
Crunching underfoot as I walked through the village lanes
Morning slipped from night's hold.
Impacted ice had frozen solid from the previous night
Tho' I was sure-footed in my sturdy boots.
I pulled my coat tight as cold air pinched my inward breath
And my outward breath resembled large puffs of smoke.
Thin watery sunshine forced her way through spidery black branches
I was in a world of black and white.
As I turned the corner it was then I noticed
A splash of colour under the brittle hedge
Gold and purple buds were pushing their way through the snow
I bent down, eagerly brushing away the powder, gasping with wonder
As I removed a glove I thought I felt a surge of warmth
Throbbing through the tightly closed tips, I smiled.
Welcome harbingers of spring, my first crocuses of the new year!

Theresa Carrier

Look Beyond

When you lose a loved one
You've been with for many years
And you feel your world has ended
Try smiling through the tears.

Everyone has memories
Of things they used to share
Think of these when you are sad
And feel a presence there.

Try looking to the future
You won't always be alone
Accept the help that's offered
Welcome people to your home.

There will be times when you feel down
And even in despair
Seek comfort in the Lord above
And say a little prayer.

Barbara Welsby

Like The Cheshire Cat

She took her world by the hand,
wiped its face and sent it out to play
in the garden of her life.

There were no weeds in that garden,
only flowers; flowers of love,
flowers of humour, flowers of wisdom,
flowers of comforting,
nurtured by the radiance of her smile.

With no warning, dark clouds gathered
and she began gradually to fade away
like the Cheshire cat in the story.

Every day,
through the growing transparency
of her being,
could be seen glimpses of the past -
her beloved mountains
in their white wedding dresses,
echoing with happy laughter,
and the raucous seagulls,
wheeling and swooping
over bright clear water.

Then, like the Cheshire cat,
she was gone,
leaving only her smile,
graven on our hearts.

Ken Angus

The Darkest Days Before The Dawn Of Spring

While walking in the woods today
Amongst the leaves, brown, crisp and dry
With little light to lift the sky
The darkest days before the dawn of spring
But in the gloom my eyes can see
Bright green shoots are pushing through
Promising a fine display of bluebells
And the celandine - with her tiny golden face
Will bring back beauty to this place
And with these thoughts of new life born
My heart begins to sing
On this dark day before the dawn of spring.

Cynthia Shum

Thoughts For The Day

Count your blessings, is what they say
When you are feeling low.
What makes you laugh or makes you glow
What gives life to your day.

Open your eyes and see the way
Your world is going on
Look at the sky, the trees, the grass
Feel the warmth of the sun.

Hear the sounds, the birds, the wind
The rustle of the leaves
Smell the perfume of the flowers
Touch the web the spider weaves.

Take the hands of the ones you love
Hold them in your arms
Give the love you have to give
Don't let them feel alone.

Attracta Wheeler

Count Your Blessings

When days are short and nights are long
It's good to sing a little song
It's wise a neighbour to invite
And when at last your neighbour's gone
You count your blessings one by one.

David Sheasby

The Grand Design

I look at walls,
Each stone or brick carefully laid
And I see the work of many hands.

I gaze at the hills
And the mountains beyond
And I see the work of One Hand.

I look at planes,
A thousand components to each
And I see the work of many hands.

I watch the birds,
Effortlessly crossing the air
And I see the work of One Hand.

I observe tractors, ploughs and harvesters,
Each labouring on the fields
And I see the work of many hands.

I consider the soil, seed and rain,
A simple formula
And I see the work of One Hand.

Colin Padgett

The Smile

'Oh, what a lovely smile.'
'Ah yeas, but selectively bestowed,'
He said with quiet sadness.
'I take it you've not been favoured,'
She looked at him thoughtfully.
'No.'
'And it hurts?' she probed.
'A little . . . damn, a lot.'
'Have you asked yourself why?'
She will not leave well alone.
'I know why.'
'Are you doing something about it?'
She persists.
'I would give my right arm to, but how?'
'You leave it to me.'
And we parted after our brief
Encounter with *the smile.*

Scholastica Bennin-Sam

How To Cope With Winter

At this time of the year many people suffer the winter blues
And they often feel like going on a winter cruise
Some people say there is nothing enjoyable to do
For a small number of people this can be true
These are people who suffer in health because of daylight
Living at this time of year for them can be a big fight
Their friends and not just medical staff
Should make an effort to make them smile and have a laugh.

At this time of the year many people just stay where they live
They can find plenty to do or say and to each other give
Many as they start in their life to face another year
Feel good to know their loved ones are healthy and near
The basic essentials are more important than a winter treat
These would be clothing or food and also heat
Also people should be thankful for a roof over their head
And know that every night they can peacefully go to bed.

At this time of the year many people do not go out a lot
They do not know for them what the world has got
A person could go out with a friend for a walk
Both could admire the winter scenery as they have a talk
People should go for walks for a good reason
Everybody eats too much food over the festive season
Remember, no matter what time of the year it may be
There will always be something good to do or see.

Robert Doherty

Countless Wonders

Sometimes, when walking at my ease
By green and lovely country ways,
I feel at one with all around,
Wrapped in the mystic summer haze.

Conveyed to unfamiliar heights,
A tiny speck in one great whole,
I clasp the beauty to my heart,
I feel the magic in my soul.

An age-old longing fills my head
Yearning to know from where and why,
This tantalising hidden truth
To understand before I die.

Perhaps, enthralled by nature's wealth
To dig too deep we should not strive,
The Earth with countless wonders teems -
Let it suffice that I'm alive!

Molly Read

Stop And Think

Life can be long or maybe too short
With ups and downs along life's way
But within your heart you may well know
You have been fortunate in this world to stay.

Growing old with abundant memories so full
With heartfelt love for all that's around
But for those that life was cut too short
Sincerely leaving behind sweet memories abound.

Stop and smell, feel and hear our wondrous life
In all its glory in our daily life
Give help and love to all those about
And count your blessings instead to belie.

We are given these once in a lifetime views
Of unimaginable wonders in our world
Thank God and feel humble at being selected
In His arms and being a disciple in His rainbow shroud.

Valerie Marshall

With Different Eyes

I meant to do so much;
A lifetime's not enough
For all the promises I made;
And of late
The colours more intense;
Like fields of rape
That burst upon the eye,
And am surprised by red sun
Going down
And red sun rising.
The wind-whipped grass
A blue-green revelation;
The scent of hawthorn after rain
Stopping me in my tracks,
As if a new sensation -
Taking my breath away . . .
And I relish it.

Catherine Reay

Blessings

Blessings come in different ways
First in waking to brand new days
Pleasures in many things we gain
In families and the friends we attain.

Cuddles of our children and grandchildren too
That shows of a love so pure and true
Little things they say to make us smile
Why, it makes everything worthwhile.

The lovely scene of a babbling brook
So much beauty wherever we look
Multicoloured sunsets, wonderful array
Are some of the blessings along life's way.

Rainbow's beautiful arc is seen
Shining stars and silvery moonbeam
Warmth of the sun in a clear blue sky
How delightful to see the butterfly.

Varied trees, they give us shade
When walking through the glade
Peace in the garden and pretty flowers
For them to survive God sends the showers.

The splendour of the countryside
Green fields stretching far and wide
Horses, cows, goats and sheep so content
While from the bank comes violets' sweet scent.

The dawn chorus that gives us great pleasure
A wealth of musical sound to treasure
We should enjoy each moment that we live
Our free gift from God, all of His to give.

Elizabeth Mary Dowler

Holding On

Keep holding on to the lifeline of hope
When you're tossed on life's angry sea.
Keep holding on, never let go
No matter how desperate you be.
You plead 'no more', but the angry waves roar
As they crash on the cliffs, relentless,
You feel for sure you can take no more
You're alone, afraid and defenceless,
But you keep holding on, with a faith that is strong
No current can beat or divide,
Holding on to the lifeline of hope
Safely carried in shore with the tide.

Betty Willeard

The Joy Of Nature

I sit and hear a bird on high
My eyes look up towards the sky
To see the sun just shining there
A wonderful world I do declare.

In the garden I look around
To see the plants there in the ground
The colour of the shrubs and trees
And leaves go floating in the breeze.

The bird table stands to their delight
The food upon is quite a sight
A dish of water standing there
They all turn up without a care.

The spider's web just hanging there
To lure a fly into her lair
And in the morning there so still
The mist that makes the world stand still.

Under rocks there is still small life
An ant so small works with all its might
The centipede goes marching by
On these small insects we rely.

This world of nature for you to see
That we may share in time of need
And look upon all living things
This joy of life that they may bring.

R Claxton

Lucky Star

A lucky star - that's what she said
Had hovered high above my head
When I was born - dear Gran, a dream . . .
A hope . . . desire . . . was all she'd seen.

But strangely through the years I've clung
To what she said when I was young
My star - the one that guides me through
The unlit path - the road that's new.

The one that helps to make me strong
When things in life go badly wrong
The one that always helps me take
Decisions that perhaps can't wait.

Now life's half gone and Gran long dead
But still I cling - a star she'd said
The star of hope - the light to see
Must still be watching over me.

Jo Lewis

Counting My Blessings

On Monday I woke rather early
With ideas spinning round in my head;
I worked out what I'd do through the week,
'Thanks for my thoughts, Lord,' I said.
On Tuesday I went out strolling
And lots of my friends did I meet;
We were all taking a constitutional
And I thanked God for my feet.
On Wednesday I went to the library
To change the books I had read;
They'd transported me to places unknown.
'Thanks, God, for my eyes,' I said.
On Thursday I went to choir practice.
Of songs there's a wonderful choice
To lift up the heart from depression;
I thanked the Lord for my voice.
On Friday to the wireless I listened,
The comedy had me in tears.
I laughed till I cried at 'The Huddlines'
And thanked the Lord for my ears.
Saturday I took the grandchildren
To play for a time on the sands.
With buckets and spades we made castles
And I thanked the Lord for my hands.
On Sunday I rose feeling happy;
The day got off to a good start
So I thanked God for all of His blessings
From the bottom of my heart.

Margaret Collins

Sonnet To Pat

On your birthday I bid you well,
Another year has just gone by.
Friendship flourishes, we can tell;
Thus proving that it is no lie
That thoughtful words and caring smile
Show so clearly, just as the eye
Reveals to all no trace of guile;
True friendship lives, indeed for aye.
How greatly valued by this soul
The feeling you alone do give
To bolster downcast spirits foul
And help make such a human live.
The muse if back, much thanks to you
This verse just proves that this is true.

David Oliver

God's Blessings

When I say we are blessed
People say, 'Oh no, not me,' and start to moan their lot
But I say stop awhile and look at what we've got
A home that's warm, fresh and bright
A bed that's comfy to sleep in at night
Enough to eat, I know I'm well fed
The knowledge and pleasure from the books I have read
Our children's love, so precious to have
Hugs and comfort when we are sad
God's love around us gives us hope to go on
When the days are weary and things go wrong
And I know how lucky I am to be free
In this beautiful world for all to see
Sunshine and showers, birds' song and flowers
Lakes and trees, mountains and glens
The joy in our lives of kindness and friends
The knowledge we gain as we grow old
Warm clothes to wear as the weather grows cold
Yes, we are blessed, can you not see?
In this wonderful world God gives you and me.

Christine Corby

Faithful Feelings

Faces now look down from Heaven,
Glowing brightly on the ground.
For the souls of loved ones live on,
Sending peace and love around.
Hands of angels guard God's people,
Of each colour, faith and race.
For they are outstretched to welcome -
Every saved soul to that place.

Warmth and glory, now are beaming -
Down upon each person here.
For the people, who have passed on,
Streaming joy on souls, so dear.
For now loved ones live forever -
In that heavenly blessed land,
And they, now, are helping others -
With the touch of God's own hand.

Souls of sorrow, pain and suffering,
With our hearts are truly healed.
For our loved ones send God's blessings,
And so tear-filled eyes are sealed.
Oh what bliss and heavenly glory -
Now pours down upon each soul,
Who believes that there's a Heaven,
Which can help make wounded whole.

Julie Colleen Duffy

The Face In The Mirror

I look in the mirror and what do I see?
This wrinkled old woman, that cannot be me.
The hair that was glossy is all thin and streaky
And the face that was bonny now looks downright peaky.

I had legs that were straight and a body so curvy
That boys used to say to me, 'My, but you're lovely.'
And truck drivers' whistles would ring in my ear,
Now they just honk me to make their path clear
As I try to make haste but the legs won't respond
And the looks that I get are far from being fond.

But life has a way of letting you know
That the only wise way is to go with the flow.
You do lose your looks which makes you feel pained
But hold on a minute, just look what you've gained.
I have my dear family and heaps of good friends
And I'm still slim enough to follow the trends,
The fullness of time has produced even more,
Four grandchildren, yes, to spoil and adore.

So don't be downcast for life can be fun
And I love to take part, just don't ask me to run!

Nada Mooney

Countless Blessings

For every bird that ever flew
For every breeze that ever blew
For every flower that ever grew
  I praise and thank You.

Every baby laughing
Every man striving
Every woman dancing
Can make the music and silence of time
Echo Your silence and word
  Holy Trinity.

Through the hands that break Earth's crust
And crush her wine to feed each
And all with Your living bread
  We praise and thank You
  Risen Lord.

Angela Cutrale Matheson

In The Countryside

How I love to stroll through the countryside
Where shy and elusive wildlife does dwell
Where magnificent birds of prey freely glide
And wild flowers dispense their fragrant smell.

Where the songbirds nest high in the tall trees
And sing their melodies so sweet and so clear
Where different scents drift heady in the breeze
And the loud buzz and hue of insects you can hear.

Where the wild rabbits you can often see
Out in the fields nibbling the lush green grass
And the squirrels foraging in a tall beech tree
And shy deer grazing in a clearing as you pass.

Where colourful butterflies so delicate on the wing
In search of nectar they visit each wild flower
And where nature is truly such a wondrous thing
Where you can wander entranced for many an hour.

Yes, the countryside to me is such a wonderful place
Where I can wander among true nature and feel free
So free for a while from the rest of the human race
Where everything lives together in perfect harmony.

A V Carlin

Count Your Blessings

Count your blessings
One by one
If you have a good family
Good friends
Somewhere to live
Food on the table.

Count your blessings
If you can hear the birds singing
Dogs barking, cats miaowing
Count your blessings.

If you can see and hear the trees blowing
The blue sky, seasons changing
Just sit back and count your blessings
There are so many things to be grateful for
So just sit back and look around when you feel down
And think of others that are not so fortunate
Just count your blessings.

Doreen Hall

Wrap Yourself In A Rainbow

Wrap yourself in a rainbow
of beautiful coloured thought.
Fill your heart with the light of love
and walk on cushioned air.
Dance your way through a busy day
to secret music of the spheres.
Light the day with friendship's
glow sprinkled with a touch of mirth.

Let today be a white canvas
on which you can display
your purples, blues and splashes
of gold and every hue and tint
to colour the scene you paint
with your palette of love.
Wrap yourself in a rainbow today
with colour from head to toe,
feel complete - at one with all -
this mirrors the rainbow of God.

Edna Holford

Life

Life is for living
Life is today
Vibrant, the colours of the rainbow
The sun setting on a summer's eve
Big, red, unbelievable.

My life is now
My every day a journey
Full of exhilaration
Setting out in expectation
Not knowing where I go
Delighting in the voyage
And the company.

In my life
You are a force
You bring contentment -
Resentment has ńo place
As long as you are there.

You in my life
Is all I ask
You bring me joy - just to be with you
To drink in your smile
Know that you are happy.

I've love enough for two
It's all for you.

Peter Meredith

Friendship

Friendship is a feeling of contentment and ease
To call on the other in their time of need.
To tell of a problem and know you are heard,
That help is at hand without saying a word.

Someone to laugh with and share in the fun
To part for a while without feeling you're shunned.

It could be with someone way back from the past
And the feeling of joy when you meet them at last.
The years in-between do not matter a bit
That's the meaning of true and sincere friendship.

Anne Baker

A Smile, A Precious Gift

When my son was in an RTA
The sunshine around us turned to grey
For his recovery I would sit and pray
That he would be given strength each day.

His little body was cut and grazed
At his recovery I am amazed
We are lucky his sight was saved
The bad by good was outweighed.

Slowly his smile started to come back
Even though some days seemed really black
Day and night with him we sat
He really is a lucky chap.

The worst of it we have overcome
What's been done is done
Against the pain and hurt he has won
To see him smile again
I am a very proud mum.

Carol Paxton

Abbie

I met a lady on a hot summer's day
With Harley, her dog, on a Cotswold way.
We've corresponded every week
By letters, notelets, it makes you think!
She's filled a big gap in my life
By love and friendship, ridding strife.
So Abbie I'd like to say a big thank you
'Twas a God-incidence - that's true.

Marian Bythel

Magic In The Sky

Mine eyes beheld a flock of sparrows
Pierce the sky like golden arrows.
Against the sun these dots of fire
Adorned the sky with strange attire.
Beyond transparent backcloth clouds
Delicate lacy snow-white shrouds
Gliding beauties, no sound, no noise,
Graceful dancers, regal, poise.
Darted arrows flying high
Breathless beauty silhouette sky.
Wandering eyes can never tire
Scanning sky as birds fly higher.
Mine eyes beheld this flock of sparrows
Pierce the sky like golden arrows.

Shula Bailey

Harmony

Thank God for the rising sun and the morning light
For a crimson sky and the gift of sight,
For the charming dawn chorus as daybreak nears
Bringing joy untold to all our ears.

It is so rewarding to walk mid the flowers
All dewy and scented in the early hours,
A carpet of gorse all bright and yellow
Stimulating, pure, invigorating and mellow.

As nature seems at its very best
With birds happily building their nests,
How blessed to roam by the gurgling stream
Just to sit, reflect, muse and even dream.

What a joy it is to feel God's goodness all around
His wondrous creation never ceases to astound,
To be in tune with the environment and to keep it green
So that the air we breathe will always be clean.

In the face of adversity, natural disasters and war
Let's extend the hand of friendship to lessen the jar,
Though our contribution be small, it is better than none at all
Let's count our blessings and include one and all.

Mary Ryder

Magpies And Rainbows

On our way to the woods a magpie
Rose up from the road reluctantly
Leaving behind a mangled meal.
We walked between banks of bracken,
Limp rags in a sea of tangled undergrowth
Fluttering like russet prayer flags,
And past gossamer-spangled clumps of wiry heather.
Half-buried branches lay forgotten
In a battlefield of rotten sawn-off stumps
And the ruffled silk of storm-filled pools
Spilled over with tiny fish-scale ripples.
We heard the muffled voices of the trees
By the track, gleaming silver where touched
By a wintry sun. Then we were back again
Beneath smiling clouds and colours
Bright with the flush of recent rain,
To where the shade of the wood gives way
To an open landscape of brush and scrub.
A rainbow appeared, and a second one
To form two complete arcs in a vivid cascade
Of every hue from gold to indigo blue
And I wondered as I stood and watched them fade
If that night I would dream in black and white
Of a solitary magpie flying by,
Or of two rainbows slung across the sky?

Rosina Winiarski

Calls Of Nature

Try to cup the silence
With memory -
The field and valley
So supreme -
I pass familiar faces,
See those fountains of antiquity.
Early summer restoration
With flowers that flourish
And furnish the landscape
With prisms of colour.
The original summer
That watchful eye,
That rests in spring -
And winter's wake
Calls of nature.

Roger Thornton

A Celebration

On such a day:
Hope is in the awakening hedgerows;
In the new green coat of the Downs;
The sparkle of the sea beyond the cliff edge;
The mournful contradiction of the gulls' cries
As they perform magical pirouettes,
Balanced on a breeze
And their joy in living.

On such a day:
I walk with a spring in my step
That I thought had been lost to my years
And I know that Heaven is here and now
And visible -
Not buried in the damp mud of a graveyard
Nor seared by the flames of the crematorium,
Man's imitation of Hell.

On such a day:
The Earth sings with the small birds
From the top twigs of the greening copse
To tell us that the men in black,
Who inscribed grim warnings
In their books of mediaeval doom,
Were wrong to tell us to burn candles now
For a putative life hereafter.

On such a day:
There is no mystery,
No fear of the world to come,
Nor need of terror and cowering
At the onward march of death.
Each hour is a reward to the spirit,
Each minute a jewelled vision
Of all there is and all there need be.

Ted Harriott

Buttercups

Thousands of buttercups caught my eye
In dozens of fields as I passed by
The shining yellow glittered in the noonday sun
As I went on a coach trip
For an afternoon run
Just like a carpet they were spread
Or maybe a bedcover someone said
So cheerful and bright and pretty to see
How contented and happy those buttercups made me.

Violetta Ferguson

What A Wonderful World

Just take a minute to look up into the sky,
Watch fluffy clouds rolling on by.
Some lined with silver, some almost pink
Stand in amazement, it makes you think.
Out in the garden, breathe the fresh air,
Take a good look at what's going on there.
Birds in the treetops singing their song,
Look and you'll find them all the day long.

In the springtime everything seems so much greener,
The air that we breathe is fresher and cleaner.
Bulbs are emerging from wintry ground,
Snowdrops, crocuses and aconites around.
As days go on the bluebells appear,
Telling us all that summer is near.
Forget all the noise and the toxic fumes,
Admire the flowers with colourful plumes.

Still the birds sing a lively refrain,
Waiting for a summery shower of rain.
As summer wanes, autumn is nigh,
The clouds move much faster in windy sky.
Time now to harvest all that we've grown,
The bounty we get from the seeds we have sown.
Leaf colours turning orange, brown, yellow,
Autumn, the season when things start to mellow.

Then winter comes with plants still flowering,
Rain is much colder when it comes showering.
Still birds are singing, the blackbird and robin,
Perched atop seedheads in the wind bobbin'.
A whole year of wonderment, a year of surprise,
It's all there for you, just open your eyes.
Make the most of your days; we're not here forever,
You can still take a look whatever the weather.

It's a wonderful world if you just care to look,
Just like the pictures you see in a book.
You don't have to travel far; it's all around,
There's colour and beauty waiting to be found.
Don't walk around sad and depressed,
The trees and the plants will soon get dressed
With leaves and flowers all unfurled,
Just make the most of our wonderful world.

Dorothy Fuller

Blessings From The Lord

Blessings in abundance
The Lord has given to me
Since I learned to trust Him
With childlike simplicity.

I take to Him my problems
I take to Him my cares
He stills the fiercest tempest
And wipes away my tears.

He's a friend to share your heartaches
And be with you through the years
In widowhood you are lonely
So just talk to Him in prayer.

Money cannot buy these blessings
They're all given so freely
By God who gave His only Son
To die on Calvary.

For the most precious blessing
A soul can ever know
Is to have your sins forgiven
And a heart made white as snow.

The promise of a heavenly home
The hope of eternal bliss
One day to see the Saviour
And our loved ones whom we miss.

Seek God to know these blessings
And then as day by day you go
You'll be a blessing to others
And your life will overflow.

Doreen Reeves

There's Always One

There is always a grape that is squashed in the bunch
or the sauce still to get when you sit down to lunch,
the two eggs you need when the shopping's not done
and one has gone bad - but 'there is always one'.

On a night out the drinker who goes to the loo -
the moment that he knows that his round is due,
the one joke you tell, you can't recall more,
but 'there is always one' that has heard it before.

You're driving along midst more cars - at a pace,
you know the road's narrow so you keep your place,
the next thing you know, is a *vroom* and he's gone -
oh - he's there in the ditch, yes, 'there is always one'.

It's your birthday, the postman has been to the door,
it feels great to see envelopes over the floor,
the day's started well, so you plan having fun
but there's one from the tax man - 'there has to be one'.

Your world is all mixed up, you're right round the bend,
the problems keep mounting, there just seems no end,
you are all on your own - so just what can be done -
just look to your friends and you'll find more than one.

Jim Pritchard

Inevitable

A perfect man with a perfect woman, perfect in every way
Feelings riding high, very hard to keep at bay
Let it run its course, there's no time left to waste
The destination's clear, keep watching this space

Trying to hold back feelings is very hard to do
When the inevitable happens it's still long overdue
The most natural thing in the world, that's how it feels
Moving further forward - wheels with wheels

No shame of what's been done this time
It just had to happen, it really is no crime
A quick hello, a card, a telephone call, all there to enhance
A warm, heartfelt deep feeling from a passing glance

A secret between two people, it remains to behold
Details held in two closed hearts never to be told
Closer than close, if the distance wasn't so great
We could have pooled our resources and then we could create

You only come here once, make the most before you breathe your last
Think of all the good times, reflect on a wonderful past
I was the joy, always there, in bad times and in laughter
From this day forward, always close by and in the ever after

Leigh Smart

Life at times can get so tough
That some may feel they've had enough
But try, stay strong and don't despair
Trust me, I know cos I've been there.

The death of loved ones, young and old
Maybe no shelter from the cold
Addiction, lonely, short of cash
Confidence that's had a bash.

Now listen to me, people care
There's lots of help for you out there
So seek them out and play your part
It really helps to make a start.

A little hug, a friendly smile
Things you've missed for quite a while
Problems shared, don't feel alone
Just pick up the telephone.

Take things easy, don't rush in
Happiness comes from deep within
Each day try a simple task
It helps to lift that gloomy mask.

If memories just bring you pain
Wash them away like distant rain
Think of things you'd like to do
The future's really up to you!

So close your eyes and dream awhile
A lovely view, a young child's smile
Golden sands and deep blue seas
Autumn trees with golden leaves.

Life is usually what you make
Good things are there for you to take
So on the days when you feel blue
Try happy thoughts, you will get through.

A grey sky turns to bright sunshine
Maybe at last you're feeling fine
Things won't change just overnight
But better days may be in sight.

Clare Andrews

Blessings From Above

The blessings which God has bestowed on Man
Are countless as the grains of sand
Taken for granted, of this I'm sure
Perhaps it's time to find a cure
Man's selfishness needs to be amended
Just look around you, is commended
You will see others with so much less
Struggling to cope, their life in a mess
Their purse may be empty, their table bare
While others have plenty, with more to spare
Stylish clothes and possessions galore
Yet, for most, the norm is to want more and more.
The remedy lies in God's Holy Book
Please stop and take time to look
From His word flows endless grace
Free to all the human race
Priceless teachings for Man are given
To think of others as you prepare for Heaven
Show forth His love in caring ways
Serving Him the rest of your days
We are reminded in a hymn
To seek none of self, but all of Him
Blessings you will know more and more
Sent from God's abundant store.

Nancy Cowie

The Four-Leaf Clover

The seven ancient wonders of the world
A lighthouse of white marble in Alexandria
The Colossus of Rhodes was gradually unfurled
Mausoleum of Halicarnassus commemorated by Queen Artemisia.

The Statue of Zeus 433BC worshipped in Olympia
A Temple of Artemis with treasures overflowing
The Walls and Hanging Gardens of Babylonia
Egypt's greatest pyramid during King Rhufus ruling.

All man-made and quite breathtaking
Seen no doubt by millions of onlookers
Hast thou beheld a humble clover containing
A blessing of four leaves for believers?

Jenny Wren

Is This Spring?

The sky is dark and grey
Sparkling white seagulls pass this way
What is something trying to say?
Is this spring?

The winter weather came at last
Snow that melted very fast
It's not like winter in the past
Is this spring?

The winds so very hard they blow
Trees shake, which way to go?
No one really seems to know
Is this spring?

Global warming is the cause
Brought on by Man with iron horse
Factories, smoke, chemicals the source
Is this spring?

Perhaps if we used the power given
The wind, the sea, not atoms riven
The word that to us by nature given
Then it would be spring.

Politicians are all talking
The people are out walking
The birds are all squawking
Sun shining, *now it is spring!*

Angela Robinson

Pure Joy

Pure joy hidden;
extend the tentacles
and touch the pain of others,
and empathize: and there
it lies forgotten.

Pure joy, welcome to
my place, welcome
to my heart.

I expected nothing
but without ceremony
you entered to stay,
to fill my life.

Marie McCarthy

Little Flower

In life's darkest, wintriest hour
When despair booms the knell;
Little hope for Earth's smallest flower;
Despondent dreams of life in Hell

Slowly, surely, snow's ice melts
Little flower reaches out its root
And embraces dear Mother Earth;
Fondling and nurturing each little foot.

Red robin redbreast's tweeting shrill
Beckons little flower to rise
Answering nature's call, to wake
Little flower, stretches to the skies.

Darkened skies shed their gloom
And scatter despair on the wind
Padded foot the rabbit's hind
Leaves cares and tears, behind.

To greet little flower, padded foot
Stands proud, to show the way
Tentatively rising little flower follows suit
And opens its eyes, to brand new day.

Red robin's rusty coat now stirring
Ruffled feathers spread, inviting wind;
Inspired flight, soaring high above
Dispersing fears, sinful gloom.

Bright sun's healing rays, shine
On padded foot and little flower;
Red robin sails on trusted wing,
Born bright, the beautiful spring!

Kenneth Cutts

Fiona

(The love of my life who died 27/02/2006)

Your smile dies with the night's fading sun
And the creeping darkness takes you away.
To a needed, peaceful, deep, deep sleep
Where that smile for eternity stays . . .
As you live where finally all life meets
Only to be awakened again by the rise of that sun
With eyes blue as the endless sky . . .
Your smile warming as the summer sun.

John Liberkowski

Question Be

A vision of a world set apart
Our lives and loves are near to heart.
Bringing with them their own refrain
I will walk in peace throughout the rain
With God's help, I'm not alone
This Earth for me has all but shown
That we are one, though many have sought
To leave and let for what they ought.
Brings to me visions of what can seem
A life in sunshine, may ever so deem
To drift in time, a second long
Through my generation where I belong
I must use it wisely my mind may say
Can one see what's coming, there of today
A hazard be, it may seem blight
But best I will to do what's right
Take and console a person alone
And keep them to your heart
To show that lives can be much more
If getting a fresh-made start
No hindsight of happenings, however have we
For life can be its own
We don't know what will come today
Much lesser than what's known
If a help I get I'll ne'er forget
Of your kindness through it all
And second time around will plan
To have what's best install
Take it with you, this brand new day.

Hugh Campbell

Blessings To Count On

B lessings to count on
L ove from relatives and friends
E xceptional kindness that is
S hown to us at times of need
S miles that lighten our hearts and
I lluminate our lives when we feel down
N ature with all its extraordinary
G lory as each different
S eason brings magnificent beauty.

Margaret Cutler

At Sea

We crossed the Pacific Ocean
When I was away at sea
With water all around us
As far as the eye could see.

With dolphins on the port side
It was a sight to see
As they leapt from the water
In splendid majesty.

The albatross he followed
As we crossed the mighty sea
Through the Hawaiian islands
And on past Waikiki.

As we headed on our course
Towards the land of the rising sun
Flying fish would skip and run
What a sight, it sure was fun.

Frank P Martin

Wedding Day Thoughts

The Bride

Thank God for Joanna, what more can I say?
For thirty-five years it's been always that way,
It's that magic word 'daughter'; it's that heavenly tie,
That delightful entrapment, from that very first cry
When the words, 'It's a daughter,' enveloped my heart
And a bond was perfected that nothing can part.

But, 'You're losing your daughter,' I hear you all say,
'You've just handed her over, she is going away,'
'She'll belong to another,' says your voice in my head,
'She'll be his now, you've lost her, just believe what we've said.'

Then my heart says, 'Joanna' and hers says, 'Yes Dad,'
And my head fills with memories and I know I'll be glad,
For although there'll be changes in life that's for sure,
There will be no departing, the bond is secure.
All this gaining and losing, just a silly old rhyme,
She's my daughter, *my daughter*, thank God for all time.

The Groom

Thank God it is Colin, what more need be said?
He can make her eyes sparkle; he can light up her head,
He can make her heart quicken and her spirits ascend,
Seems to me a good mixture for a fairy-tale end.

Myself

I've no fear about losing, no despair to dispel,
Just a satisfied feeling that all will be well.

Robert McIlveen

The Candle And The Light

The candle and the light
Were burning happily bright
Heydays were surely implored
Unaware of the dangers in sight

The light said to the candle,
'Hand in hand we shall handle
Any impediments in our way
Together we shall mangle.'

Unexpectedly, that very day
A gust of wind blew the light away
Left the poor candle all alone
And the candle started to decay.

The candle asked a wise old sage
Told him of his horror and rage,
'Why it left me amid the darkness?
Upon this loathesome worldly stage.'

The sage replied, 'In this case
Darkness prevails at the lamp's base
Learn to accept the facts of life
Alas! At least put on a brave face.'

Hamza Ismail

A Prayer At Bedtime

Lord, thank You for another day,
For smiles and laughter on the way,
For loving wife and friends sincere,
For children far and children near.

And thank You, Lord, for board and bed,
For blessings poured upon my head;
For beast and bird and things that crawl,
And flowers bright and trees so tall.

Dear Lord, for some I intercede -
The lonely, poor and those in need -
Give me Your grace to find the strength
To succour them in love at length.

Forgive me, Lord, the wrongs I do,
And draw me closer still to You,
And as this old day slips away
Grant me the gift of sleep, I pray.

Raymond Holley

A Good Time To Be Living

Step out into the early morning garden after rain
When sun has bejewelled grass spikes with ruby, sapphire, amethyst,
Snowdrop bows to crocus, blackbird sings on rich-perfuming purple-blooming lilac,
To see, to hear such simple riches -
This is spring - a good time to be living.

Here is warm sweet-scented air across the strawberry field.
Walk carefully across the crisp cream straw, gently parting dark green leaves,
Now discover the glistening dew-blessed, red-dressed berries.
To see, to savour such simple riches -
This is summer - a good time to be living.

Scuffle feet across the red-gold crunch of leaves.
See the last swinging, skimming flight of swallows seeking south.
Scent of apples and berries across the corn-cream, hazy-dream crispness,
To see, to touch such simple riches -
This is autumn - a good time to be living.

Tracery of frost now sparkles on leaves and hedgerows,
Stillness signifying soft white snow hastening from dust-grey sky.
Silhouettes of birch and oak create a simple-boughed, nature-proud sculpture.
To see, to be part of such riches -
This is winter - a good time to be living.

Ivy Gallagher

Silver Linings

We watch the television news or read our daily papers
With their negative reporting every day.
Behind the gloom and doom it is sometimes hard to find
The lovely things that lift us on our way.

A rainbow bright with colours as the sun shines through a shower
That bathes us with its own refracted light
Small birds doing belly-flops who've yet to get the hang
Of this peculiar motion known as flight.

Kittens pouncing sideways on imaginary prey
And chasing things that dare to move about
Those kindly folk who care about their neighbours and their friends
And are always standing ready to help out.

Nature does her best in spite of all this Earth's pollution
Buds and flowers still come pushing through
We may have caused her sometimes to get the timing wrong
So we must be thinking now of what to do.

We have a kind Creator who loves what He has made
Even us, with all our foolish ways
He still sends down His blessings, but we have to be tuned in
To the wavelength which is opened up by praise.

Kay Kisby

Blessings In Disguise

They say, count your blessings,
Yes, each and every one
Think of all you may possess
And be thankful when each day is done
Thinking, walking, listening, talking
Laughing, eating, crying, loving
Blessings that we may not realise
But take too much for granted
And there they are before our very eyes
But we don't notice even if we wanted
Friends, neighbours, workmates, family
All at times help us on our way
Sons, daughters, grandchildren, baby
They are all blessings in their own way
Moon, stars, sun, rain, rainbow
Yes, all are blessings we should know
Lover, wife, husband, best friend
They're all our blessings to the very end
So we should *stop*, appreciate these wonderful things
And pause, remember to count our blessings.

Charles A Jones

Ghosts Of Time

Time flickers like the turbulence of fragile moments
Caught in heartfelt loveless whispers
Or a mother's kiss on the cheek
The cauldron of despair swings intermittently
Like the pendulum of life's journey
Through the vortex of childhood dreams
Which are often not realised
In this melancholy reflection of maturity
But when one contemplates hope
It is but a precious thing
Not to be dispelled in the icy darkness
Of a cold winter's night
For spring is but a breath away
And thoughts of yesteryear
Haunt the unsuspecting
Ghosts of time.

Finnan Boyle

Reflections

(Inspired by Father Derek)

Life is so good if we allow it to be
So much to enjoy, such beauty to see.
The pleasure of wine tantalising the tongue
The sound of a hymn beautifully sung.
The clutch at your heart to hear a baby's first cry
The thrill of the eagle soaring high.
The company of friends, the memories we share
Or the concern of a stranger to prove that they care.
To look out from the mountain and see God's world at your feet
Where its beauty's unrivalled till Heaven and Earth meet.
The feel of the wind or the sun on your face
The love and hope we have for the whole human race.
If only they could understand so their cares could be cured
God gave us this life to be enjoyed not endured.

Pamela Matthews

A Lonely Heart, Whole

When life is difficult
And kindness on vacation
A smile is an antidote
To cruel desperation.

A smile lights up the face
Can show utter compassion
Is wonderful to share
In those times of depression.

A simple action to perform
Which begins in the heart
Flies forward to the receiver
Like a swift winning dart.

Do not try to prevent them
Give freedom to your soul
A smile, a worthy prescription
To make a lonely heart whole.

Maureen Westwood O'Hara

Viewpoint

The angle at which you view life
has a photographic feel.
Absorbing technicalities
you go for what is real.
Correctly capturing the essence
of the moment of the day.
There is no rational explanation,
you by instinct know the way.

You know the way to get things done,
you know the way to make it happen.
From conjuring up a super meal
to freely sharing your compassion.
There is a wealth of experience
way beyond the years.
Handling the daily cut and thrust,
suppressing all the fears.

All the fears but one perhaps,
and that to which you're prone.
All around it's full of people,
that doesn't make you less alone.
You see it in the daytime,
you feel it most at night,
you feel it shouldn't be there,
you know it can't be right.

But there's a different view on this,
not rejection but another's loss.
It's surprising the response you get
when they feel you wear an indifferent gloss.
Take on board this good advice,
there is something you can do.
Form a clear space in-between,
let them come to you.

Press down firmly on the hurt,
do it once again.
Tell them what they ought to hear,
how can they complain?
Black is white -
it's sunshine in the rain.
Tell them what they want to hear,
you can still explain.

Maurice Western

September Song

There's nothing the matter with me
I'm as healthy and fit as can be
Of course, I've arthritis in my left knee
My BP's too high and my hair's growing thin
But I'm wonderfully well for the state that I'm in.

Now when I was young in dress kit blue
I could dance and would flirt the long night through
I could run many miles with pack without fuss
But today I'm reluctant to run for the bus
To walk with my dog I get puffed the way home
And the state of my feet would make a saint groan
But there's nothing the matter with me.

The moral is this as my tale I unfold
For soldiers like me who are growing too old
It is better to tell them 'I'm fine' with a grin
Than to tell them the truth, what a mess I am in
So there's nothing the matter with me
And I'm long past 83, still I'm as fit as a flea.

How does one tell when youth is all spent?
When your 'get up and go' has all got up and went
Old soldiers don't mind when they think with a grin
Of all the good places their 'get-ups' have been
Though memory's fading with head in a spin
I'm wonderfully well for the way that I'm in.

So life is still good with lots to do
I go to the races and visit the zoo
And I can share with our youngsters too
The fun that we had, the things we've done
In the far-off lands of tropical sun
In the golden years when we were young.

Perhaps they too will seek to wear
That 'Tiger Badge' with its crown so fair
Shall I rise with the dawn to polish my shoes?
But if I don't shave I've nought to lose
I check the papers, see the news
Of friends and comrades newly dead
So I drink them a toast and go back to bed
No, there's nothing the matter with me.

Gordon Charkin

The Dreamcatcher

I sat and looked at the dreamcatcher, hanging there
and wished that it would release those dreams
I had when I was young
now, I can't remember
they must have been fun

I sit and dream of what I used to say or do
but never what I dreamt
it is, as if these moments
were caught by the dreamcatcher
and he won't let them go
especially not the dreams of an infant
to an old man
who wouldn't appreciate
their simplicity
or perhaps their complexity
but most of all their honesty

Did I dream of Santa Claus
and did I dream of growing up?
I think I did
but is that the thought of the adult
imagining what he thought as a child
from the adult standpoint?
It makes sense
but, children rarely make sense
except to the dreamcatcher
who has all the answers
concealed in his web of intrigue
and mystery.

David Quenby

The Garden

It's true, the garden is a pleasure
That we all can treasure
Lovely flowers, pretty songbirds and bumblebees
The sweet fruits on the orchard trees.
We may not have money
But we've got plenty of honey
So let's count our blessings today
For tomorrow is another day.

G B Moore

Some Trek

The hills were calling, as I packed my rucksack
My needs were few, but essentials were in a stack
It was summer vacation, one I was going to enjoy
Some said I was silly, at heart I was really a boy

The packing all done and the sun shining bright
My trek was twenty-six miles, over hills and at night
I set off at a steady pace along the valley and dale
Making my first stop as the postman delivered mail

It was at a farmhouse, on its own, way out in the wild
But there was no sign of life, then the cry of a child,
'Can I give you a lift?' said the postman full of glee,
'No thanks,' I said, then motioned towards the valley

My next stop was at another farm, some miles on,
'Good morning,' said the farmer whose name was John.
'Some tea me lad to warm your innards,' said the man,
'Yes,' I said, as he handed me biscuits and tea in a can

My help wasn't required, so I waved a farewell goodbye
Pushing my way along the valley, then up towards the sky
On reaching the top, the view was magnificent and bright
Everything was reduced by a half, making a toy box sight

Some time was spent, taking in the vast panoramic view
But I had to press on, even though this was all very new
Another two miles, and it was an awaited rest for the night
A large hostel was on my route, much to my delight

The next morning was bright with the sun in the sky
But my body was tired and my head wanted me to cry
The journey had taken its toll, I was sore and didn't care
After all I cannot walk, I am confined to a wheelchair.

William A Laws

My Father - The Carpenter

The wood is dry and rotting
The shavings turned to dust
No sound of hammering
The nails have turned to rust.

No singing from the saw
Or smoothing from the plane
The craftsman through the open door
We shall not see again.

He will live on for all to see
In workmanship well done
In polished wood the memory
Can never be outshone.

Kathleen Allison

Wonderful Blessings

Count your blessings every day
There are many coming our way
Sunshine, bright and glowing
Lovely flowers growing
Good food we have each day
Kind friends who came to stay
Green fields, a gentle breeze
The smile of a little child
Bluebells growing wild
Thoughts of holidays well spent
Fun, camping in a tent
Delights of a waterfall
Sunshine over all
Dressed in clothes, looking good
Give thanks to God, we should
All our needs are daily met
Give thanks and never fret
The dear Lord always will provide
His arms for us are open wide
He blesses all who to Him come
So count your blessings, every one.

Lilian Loftus

Poem For Gus

Standing in the sleet of a January day
As a clay-coloured sheet is pulled away
And your body is lowered into wet cold earth.
Is this all your life was worth?

Through eyes blurred with frozen tears
I see your son of sixteen years.
He looks so young to be at this place
Though sad with grief, he wears your face
And I believe a new future has begun
You will live tomorrow through your son.
He will feel the new spring rain
And he will smile and laugh again.
He will see the sky turn blue
And he will sing and dance for you.

I will always feel sad that you are gone
But I know you have passed your future on.

Cheryl Creber

Magical Winter

A touch of frost covers the ground
A bird singing is the only sound
The frost glistens in the early dawn
A new day is about to be born
I walk on following the beautiful song
I hope I don't get there to find it gone
Just round the corner I spot a tree
And a special sight awaits me
It's a robin singing out strong and loud
Such perfection for his adoring crowd
He puffs himself up to keep warm in the frost
But he knows he must find food at all cost
Nature has given us a bird of blood-red
Splash of white and brown from tail to the head
It's a magical winter when you see this sight
Either on a tree or in flight
He sings like an angel day after day
Helping us to go on our way
Just as I leave him to his singing
He is joined by the church bells ringing
I'm on my way home with a happy heart
Thanks to the robin giving me the perfect start . . .

Elaine Potter

A Child Is Born

Joy to our hearts
A child is born.

May we love and care
Enjoy the beauty that we share
The miracle that's been revealed.

Joy to our hearts
A child is born.

May we not forget our God
Who has breathed this breath
And given this baby life.

Joy to our hearts
A child is born.

May we give our God the praise
Praise Father, Son
And Holy Spirit too.

Let Mum and Dad rejoice
And we will with them too
We will, we will
We'll all rejoice
A child is born.

Andrea Koenders-Donnan

Count Our Blessings

The years pass by one cannot forget
But memories never fade away
Come what may, and all the happiness too
Family and friends keep in touch
Some near, some in faraway places
The nearest ones we often see
Which is a blessing too
Family photos are lovely to see
Grandchildren, great-grandchildren
Cousins, relations too
They are treasured souvenirs
Of today and the past
The family tree is growing up now
Which is a blessing for one to see.

F Crawford

Blessèd Rain

Is there any greater blessing
Than lying in a nice warm bed
And listening to the rain?
To hear those gusts of wind
As they throw it to the windowpane?
You lie at peace
With all the world
Within these moments . . . rare
Try to spare a moment
Before you face the world again,
To utter just a few kind words
A little gentle prayer
A thank you for the elements
The wind, the rain, the sun
For this bed, which is your haven
When the long day's work is done
And all your creature comforts
So precious to your heart
Thus fortified - go on your way
As the daily round you start . . .

Joyce Alice Turner

The Cat

Everyone should have a cat
To feed, stroke and give a pat
They ask for little else at all
And come back when you call.

Mind you they don't like the rain
Getting wet can be a pain
They love basking in the heat
Rolling on backs is a treat.

Heaven is basking in the sun
Tickling tummies is great fun
They ask for little in life
Food, comfort and lack of strife.

Ina J Harrington

Change Of Heart

As a matter of fact, I used to hate
People who said to me,
'Count your blessings, life is great,
Stop grumbling, shake yourself free
From self-absorption, envy and greed,
Think of others and what you can do
To gratify their silent need
With a little attention from you.'

But now I'm older and often alone
I begin to think they were right,
Stifling some deep-felt moan
Can keep me awake all night,
It gets me nowhere, that's for sure,
Indulging in miserable news,
I need to rely just more and more
On positive thoughts and fresh views.

So I have to admit that friends who said,
'Things aren't as bad as they seem,
Count your blessings while looking ahead
And work towards your dream,'
Were right all along,
Though it's hard to comply,
And say to myself - I was wrong -
But I'm prepared to give it a try.

S J Dodwell

The Astrologer

Thank you for the smile
And sincerity in your eyes.
I learned to love by post
With a man who's very wise.
I hope one day we'll meet
And yet somehow we've met before,
Somewhere, some time or in another life.
It's hard to trust when you've been hurt.
He taught me to try in a spiritual way,
I'm positive now about my pathway.
I pay a tribute to this man
In the very best way I can.
I want to say 'Anthony'
Thank you.

Margaret Milnes

Wild Flowers

Across the meadow colours stretch
Of scarlet poppy, purple vetch
And further on there is a drift
Of yellow mustard and mauve thrift.

Beyond there is another flow:
Lacy cow parsley, cream yarrow,
And all along the roadside verge
Convolvuluses and clover merge.

With waving grasses and anon
White marguerites and campion
And higher, on the stony soil
A blaze of bright bird's-eye trefoil.

Not far away there is a bank
Which wears a mantle on its flank
For crowding closely, all along
The yellow cowslips densely throng
So close you cannot slide a blade
Between this weft of rich brocade.

But turning homeward down the lane
As I once thought I think again
That what gives me the most delight
In seeing, bathed in warm sunlight
Gold in the golden afternoon
A field of buttercups in bloom.

Evelyn Westwood

Snowdrops

When I was talking with my neighbour
Some time ago
She asked me if I had seen the lovely snowdrops
At the top of the Jephson Gardens
I went up to see them and there
Was a large flower bed covered in glistening white snowdrops
They were quite beautiful.

Some months later my neighbour died
I never see snowdrops now
Without thinking of her.

Irene Lorch

The Gloaming Rise

Hot summer days, I can recall when nettles
Seemed to grow so tall, as blistered legs I rubbed
In vain with dock on leaves to ease the pain
Memories come flooding back, the roads we walked
With haversack, leisure time spent in pursuit of Nathan trout
In shaded nook

Red-spotted sides and yellow flank, regimental in their rank
Suspended in their element, the scent of wild blossoms in the air
And songbirds sing in sweet refrain
Summertime is here again, with trembling hands I tie my fly
And watch as it goes drifting by.

A swirl, a boil, I have a fish, a worthy catch to grace a dish
A chosen spot was our retreat where Dad and I sat down to eat
Our day's catch laid out at our feet and as we watched we had a treat
As blue-coated kingfishers darted past and white-bibbed dippers
Bobbed up and down, resplendent in their coats of brown.

Reminiscence of the day, of caddis in their house of clay
And mayfly hatching on the wing, to herald their flight
The skylarks sing, occasionally a fox's bark, this countryside
Our 'Noah's Ark', oh Nathan, sweet Nathan, your praises I sing

How nature has blessed you with treasures of gold
When winter's upon us we won't feel the cold, our memories
Will warm us as memories unfold, The Rise in the Gloaming
Forever retold.

Alexander Grozier

To My Daughter

I give thanks to creation for the moon at night
And also the stars that twinkle so bright
I give thanks for the sun and morning dew
But most of all for giving me you
I give thanks for blue skies and also the showers
For the birds in the trees and all of the flowers
For giving me strength to start each day anew
But most of all for giving me you
I thank creation for all of these wonderful things
For everything that each new day brings
I can give thanks each minute
My whole life through
But never enough for giving me you.

Joan Hartland

Northern Lights

In the early morning, just before the dawn
I wake from sleep quite suddenly, drowsy and forlorn
From our back bedroom window I scan the northern sky
A few bright, shiny, twinkling lights I suddenly espy
Like tiny fattened glow-worms out on a hunting spree
This way and that, quite slowly cavorting gay and free
Have I gatecrashed a party of comets, asteroids or shooting stars
In a black hole or Milky Way, seeking the path to Mars?
Then suddenly, and sickeningly, I begin to understand
Our house is on a flight path to Heathrow and not to Fairyland
With a wakening reality I move from fantasy and mock lands
To aircraft on their regular flights to London Heathrow and Docklands.
But still I count my blessings as I begin to query
Where have they come from, these night travellers, tired and weary?
From Samarkand or China, from frozen shore or hot land
From Timbuktu or Russian Steppe, maybe from nearby Scotland?
Sometimes I wake on cloudy nights when it is raining
The lights are dimmed or faded and fantasy is draining
No fireflies dance, no velvet skies in mystery surrounded
My lights, my fairyland has gone, the sky completely clouded
But dreams remain of mystery to tear the clouds asunder
When I get up my mind is full of childhood thoughts and wonder!

Jack Scrafton

Like A Rose

Like the bud on a rosebush we curl up tight
Not letting anyone come near our sight
We send out thorns to keep all away
Not knowing what to do or say.

Then someone comes and shows us love
Like the warmth of the sun from above
Gradually we open ourselves to the world
Like the petals of a rose uncurled.

As we open up a fragrance begins to flow
And the beauty inside us begins to show
We all need love to brave facing life
With all its toil and all its strife.

But as we open ourselves to those about
There is in all of us a beauty waiting to come out.

Sylvia Riggs

Lost Child

I could cope with
Losing you to a younger lover
Replacing you with a domineering stepmother, but
You're not leaving me voluntarily without
Putting up a fearsome fight.
Premature dementia has claimed you
I don't know why or how but you're holding on tight.

I'm slowly losing you, day by day by day
Bits and pieces are gradually ebbing away.
I'm missing you like mad, only you're still here
I thought I was brave but cannot face my fear.
Your personality is shrinking, dissolving and fading away
A colour photograph, black to sepia into white
Morning becomes afternoon, dawn to dusk
Black day converges with white night.

I'll always be here for you, you'll see
Painting your nails, brushing your hair, stirring your tea
Repaying the loving care you lavished on me.
I'll stay although you've forgotten my name
No matter what you call, I'll answer all the same.
Memories you've lost, never to regain
My love for you lives eternally on.
There's sunshine after the rain.

Amelia Michael

Gifts Of Love

We have eyes to gaze on love and beauty;
We have eyes to see this world's great needs;
We have eyes to read Your Holy Gospel;
Thank You Lord, for Your precious gift of love.

We have ears to catch the sounds of nature;
We have ears to hear when children cry;
We have ears to listen to Your message;
Thank You Lord, for Your precious gift of love.

We have voices to speak our love and kindness;
We have voices to raise in song and prayer;
We have voices to tell of Christ, our Saviour;
Thank You Lord, for Your precious gift of love.

We have hands to clasp in sign of friendship;
We have hands to work and help and heal;
We have hands to fold in meditation;
Thank You Lord, for Your precious gift of love.

We have hearts to love our friends and neighbours;
We have hearts to share their pain and joy;
We have hearts to feel our love for Jesus;
Thank You Lord, for Your precious gift of love.

We have lives to spend in serving others;
We have lives to use in doing good;
We have lives to offer in Your service;
Thank You Lord, for Your precious gift of love.

God created us in His own image;
And so many gifts on us bestowed;
Let us use them wisely in His service;
Giving thanks for His precious gifts of love.

Eileen N Blackmore

Mother

Breast cancer is what you had
Didn't want you to die like my dad
Over a month you lay in your bed
Enduring terrible pains in feet and legs.

Guilt filled me every single visiting day
Not knowing what to talk about or say
Sitting there by you, you didn't speak
Each day of every single week.

You stared at the walls or went to sleep
Sitting by your bed I'd silently weep
What was going through your mind lying there
I worried about you so much, I do care.

I didn't get there in time to say goodbye
But knew on the way to hospital you'd died
There you lay, all quiet and still
Down my spine went a cold chill.

Kissing your face and stroking your hair
All I could do was cry and stare
You looked so peaceful lying there
Now with the angels for them to take care.

Putting the teddy I'd bought you by your head
He too was now tucked up in bed
Love and miss you, Mum, and sadly goodbye
I walked away with tears in my eyes.

Memories are all I have and all my love
You're with Father now in Heaven above
You'll be forever in my heart, my very precious mum
I count my blessings because you were my special mum.

Ali Ashley

Passionflower

When April with his bellows blew grey smoke above,
When he angrily did hammer down on anvil Earth
His Vulcan fist in cruel cast iron, cloudy glove,
When his whirling, whizzing, wheezing, wind-making mirth
Carded the chamois, mauve and burgundy fettle
Of thistles like filmy fine silk and sent each fair
Blonde daisy and pink seven sister rose petal
Flailing, floundering on his larruped sea of air,
My child's heart beat fast, valour roused a rushing surge
To sally forth across the meadows to converge
Among anxious mice and coal-black, coach-whip snakes
Slithering and scurrying, in shivering quakes,
Shaking, swaying, weedy fields' floss flower verge.

A crossroad cleanly split green meadow on this verge
And at an incline to dark stormy sky laid bare
The wounded passionflower faced the demiurge
Whose added violence hashed his violet flesh, a flair
Of force and fury from the prince of Mother Earth,
While every element screamed with wicked glee.
Grey mice, black snakes and feral cats for all their worth
Drew near and lingered where I stood, transformed and free,
Devoted to the torn, dying passionflower,
Fused in friendship, while the torrents of the shower
Poured down from high above angry fist, iron-gloved,
Until the Lord of Heaven's majesty had shoved
Aside Earth's fuming hordes with bright-shine sun-power.

Yet, nobly we'd return when pastel May arrived, to see
Only thriving may-pops where our passionflower should be.

Edgar Stephens

Country Wedding

In heavy sunlight families
and friends in Butterwick
and Bennington dress
the churchyard in temporary
clusters - not noticing
debris from owls' feastings
spattered on chiselled prayers.

All Saints, in cream, is irrigated
by faith and velvet shade.
Mysteries - spun deeper
by Bach - meet two,
touch two, draw them home.

She watches him: glad.
His breathing matches hers.
His summer odour - inches away -
opens inside her head.
She smiles: he is in balance.

He looks and smiles,
she wears joy in her eyes.
Her skin is the taste of naked suns.
He looks: expectant.
Now she is his world.

Bread breaks to bind two lives,
wine inscribes two tongues
for joy: and death.
They vow to catch
a summertime of days together.

. . . till they come to the end of their lives -
she senses each moment is a memory
of beauty from before.
. . . and are in joyful anticipation of Heaven -
his violet eyes see things that
exist in excess.

Outside cream, dead-nettle crowd steps
and waits - where you lost time for me.

Derek Webster

The Big Day

She stood at the door
And I held my breath,
Her beauty glowed from within
Her ivory gown, sprinkled with pearl
Fell to the ground in a satin swirl
And the veil misted her crown.
The joy in her eyes
And the tentative smile
Took my heart to the edge of tears,
For my child is taking her vows today
And the man of her choice awaits.

As the music begins, she is suddenly there
Standing by his side
And their look of love
Seals the treasured hour
As we hear them utter the words,
Committed now, blessed by God
To a life of sharing all.

And I pray that her loveliness,
God's child and mine,
Will radiate through the years
As I let her go, only mothers know
The sorrowful joy this brings
For the child is leaving, her life has moved on,
And this is how it should be,
But my heart aches with pride
And I'll never forget
How different she looks today,
A beautiful woman and bride.

Jane Ward

Count Your Blessings

Count your blessings, name them one by one,
And it will surprise you what the Lord has done.
The memory of our loved ones still live on,
Inspiring us to greater heights.
They have left behind with us a legacy of beautiful memories
Oh the love that they have given to us.
The lessons we have learned from them.
They taught us faith in God and gave us love.
They have given us something money cannot buy.
They have given us an example of rich faith in God.
Oh, the joy to know that they put their Christianity into practice.
Spoke boldly of their love and trust
In their Saviour, Lord and Master, their great Creator
How they sang those hymns so sweetly
Of Jesus and His love.
By the fireside they sat and told us stories,
Bringing happiness to us that money couldn't buy.
Those happy times they spent with us,
Left behind with us a legacy that money couldn't buy.
Now today I share those stories with my friends
And thank my God for the gift of friendships.
No one is poor who has one true faithful friend,
Who knows all about them and loves them just the same.
No one is poor who has had a godly mother.
So let us count our blessings
And it will surprise us what God has done.
We will have a joy in our hearts and a spring in our step.
Soon we will learn that the richness of our spirits is the wealth of life.

Joy Wilson

Live For Something

An old, old cottage in a very depressed area,
Where people go to the shops in that very old mining community.
They count their blessings every day,
Being born and bred in that very old cottage, with love
Bringing up their children in the very best way.
My great grandchild Mackenzie speaks to me on the phone,
Her daddy and grandpa tell her the story of the old cottage,
Where they all had to work hard in school to escape everywhere in the world
The cottage had done its work.

Dorothy Jane Lewis

A Trilogy Of Presents

My Christmas present (past) is the memory
Of that credible fantasy taught to me in infancy
A tale of wonder that will be always celebrated annually
Within a barn close by an inn, glorified by seraphim
A child was born of a virgin maid
And modestly, in a manger laid.
This child who would a Saviour be
God's gift to all humanity
With His love and faith for evermore
My Christmas present remains secure.
My Christmas present (present) is found in the sound
Of happy children all around and joys of giving that are found
In the togetherness of Christmas time. A seasonal pantomime;
With mistletoe, the Christmas tree, the hopes and the expectancy
The goodwill flowing, embracing all
The pleasures past we love to recall
Within my present I will find the future hope for all mankind.
With love and faith for evermore.
My Christmas present remains secure.
My Christmas present (future) brings a gift of peace
Unholy divisions cease and the unity of faiths increase
Annual festivities celebrate the finality of all feudal hate
The future sows a seed to form a mutual peaceful creed.
Through all the years that are left to me
I will follow that creed and hope to see
That gift of peace eternally surrounding all my family
With this peace and faith for evermore
My Christmas present remains secure.

Stan Coombs

A True Friend

The first time that you saw her
You knew she was the one.
As you gazed into her brown eyes
She looked so full of fun.
You spent the days together,
Never far apart
And surely as you knew it,
She crept into your heart.
But now the years have passed
And she has gone away,
Now as you count your blessings
I'm sure your heart will mend,
As you say a fond farewell
To that special four-legged friend.

Coreen Holmes

Enlightenment

After a restless night, I lay
stitched and bruised from an operation,
so I rose early and drew the curtains,
revealing the darkness preceding a new day.

I freshened myself and waited
for the light of the celestial display,
which began with a tinge of orange,
then rose, and watched the sunrise created.

Seated by the window in a chair,
the vibrant colours of orange,
carmine and violet blended and emerged
through the clouds, letting daylight appear.

The silhouette of the trees,
against this magnificent backdrop,
ignited my spirit of recovery,
once more to feel at peace and at ease.

Suddenly my experiences became like the night,
pushed away by the glory of dawn,
and encouraging me to explore
a fresh scene with new insight.

I resolved to be true to myself
and when back home, felt my spirit
grow and expand, like an opening rose,
the dawn had imbued me with spiritual wealth.

Suzanna Wilson

Nature's Wonders

As I come home at night
The moon follows me, shining bright
Orange, gold or a silvery white
The stars are shining
Watching over us throughout the night
The lightning, thunder and the rain
Bring out the sun
Then a rainbow come
The leaves are all colours
Green, yellow and bronze
Flaming bright
It really is a wonderful sight
The wind, so powerful and strong
Nature's wonders
How wonderful.

Pat Jakes

After The Rain

Falling raindrops were the tears of yesterday,
When all was dark mid tumult of life's storms.
Long night, restless with invading thoughts and
Fitful sleep. Awake, for
Comes the dawn and promise of a new resolve
To cherish life and health and those we love.

The sun has risen now upon our world,
To bring us hope and bid us cast out fear.
Give thanks for this new day,
Untouched by time as yet,
Its history unwritten on the empty page,
God's gift, unchanging in a changing world.

The snowdrop dwelt in darkness, deep in earth,
Yet thrust its way towards the light of day.
The gloom of winter falls away to spring
And life emerges.
We lift our eyes towards the sun, and pray
In gratitude for all of life's good things.

Jean Jackson

The Light Of Hopefulness

Earthquakes, famine, murders and greed,
millions of helpless people in need.
Dictators ruling without mercy and hate,
their people, in vain, for help await.

We are destroying our world, without a care,
Man's selfishness and vanity, unashamedly laid bare.
As I witness all this chaos and madness,
I ask, is our world doomed to eternal sadness?

Then I look into the bleakness once more,
looking with greater care than I did before.
Amongst all that chaos, evil and bleak,
I see the light of a stranger aiding the weak.

Amid the greed, anger, hatred and pain,
I see the light of another, helping once again.
My spirits rise, is there hope after all?
Yes, we may be destroying this spherical ball.

But in the midst of the black, a light shines bright,
gently leading us from the darkness to the light.
The light I saw also there for you to find,
always there in the midst of tragedy,
it's the light of goodness, ever present in mankind.

Patricia Edmondson

Great Aunt Jane

My great aunt Jane, who's eighty-three
And loves inviting me to tea
To what was once great grandma's house
Where happy years were spent with spouse
Her furniture is old, but good
And every piece is solid wood.
Her china glistens, silver gleams
The linen all has homestitched seams
No maid the basement stairs now treat
To fetch and carry or make bed.
Aunt Jane must wait upon herself
And this she'll do while she's in health.
A little prim and set in ways
I do believe she still wears stays
My underwear, or lack of it
She vows, will send her in a fit.
With scorn she views the modern miss
And doesn't like the way they kiss.
'Young men today,' she says, 'are dim.'
I've told you once, she is quite prim.
But once when she had company
And I'd been summoned there to tea
Bored, I quietly left the talk
And thought I'd take me for a walk.
Upstairs I crept without a sound,
Then Aunt Jane's bedroom door I found
Was open, so I tiptoed in
And what I saw was not so prim
A television, hid from sight
A portable in brilliant white.
Then underneath the pin tray heart
I saw a sight that made me start
Ernie bonds and betting slips
A note that bore the latest tips
Oh now I've caught you out, that's plain
But how I love you, dear Aunt Jane.

Joyce Williams

A New Beginning

The gloom which often comes with the new year
Can leave us feeling depressed and inclined to tears
Try to see it as a new beginning
A time to start anew and be intent on winning
Winning your way through the dark days ahead
Coping with whatever may be along the path you tread
There will always be both ups and downs in life
But it is possible to contain the strife
Keep busy, make sure you can occupy your mind
Along with work have a hobby of some kind
Maybe keep a diary of events each day
Have your favourite music which you can play
Spend some time watching the garden birds feed
Relax, have the book you have been wanting to read
There is more to life than work, don't try to do it all
For that is a sure way to make life pall
Give yourself a treat, be it a meal or a makeover
Let your sunny side take over
Meet up with friends both old and new
Making time just for you
Soon you will find that spring is here
With it, it will bring more cheer.

Rachel Green

Yearning

Why do people fall in love?
What eternal force gave me these feelings
And then contrives to keep you from me,
Spreading pain and misery in my life?
The time since last we spoke,
Has been the worst pain to endure,
It's like a part of me is lost,
Perhaps never to return.
I sit here alone at night,
Just waiting for your call,
Although it never seems to come,
But still I sit and wait for you.
I miss you more than words can say,
Am alone without your smile,
My heart beats alone right now,
But it's waiting for your voice.

Simon J Golding

The Clothes Shopper

Her days were spent shopping,
High heels clattering
Like drumsticks
On taut, unyielding pavements,
Or sinking into deep pile carpets
Thick and welcoming.

Caressing silks and satins
In tactile ecstasy,
Tossing some aside
As pecking birds
Discard unwanted seed.

Posing, in lace-trimmed briefs
In front of tilted mirrors;
Passing sumptuous fabrics
Over ivory shoulders
To eager ankles.

Twisting, viewed from all angles.
Unresisting to the velvet gown;
The soft crepe lingerie
Coursing with feverish adrenalin.
Fortifying,
In the silver restaurant.

Gliding from shop to shop
Arms weighed down with shiny bags
Sporting a sparkling logo.
Staring at her trim reflection,
Tempted into scented doorways.

Failing . . .
Legs as heavy as a marathon runner.
Sleeping . . .
Is the only option.
Anticipating . . .
Tomorrow is another day!

Veronica Charlwood Ross

The Wooden Crucifix

That is where I found Him
Hanging in the garret
That is where I saw Him
Hanging all alone
That is where I worshipped
Jesus on a crucifix
The sunlight through the skylight
Shining on His face.

The barrel organ in the corner
The guitar against the wall
The ukulele and the mandolin
Beloved over all
Told this house was full of music
Not long ago
And the wind in the rafters assented
Very, very low.

Was there ever such a collection
Of things so old, yet young?
Old tools, old toys, old books, old joys
Of life not long begun
Ere autumn comes
And the leaves downfall
Then the clearing up begins -
For winter.

That is when I heard the words
Standing in the garret
That is when I understood
Standing all alone
'I am the Way, the Truth and the Life,'
Even in a garret
And in that vivid moment
As I gazed upon His face
That dirty, dismal garret
Became a holy place.

Jessica Boak

Nature's Blessings

The first time I had flown was in September of last year
We went to an Irish wedding of a niece we hold most dear
I'll never forget seeing from the plane's-eye view
The little cirrus clouds edged with a lovely hue.

We took photographs which have turned out very well
Certainly not to be forgotten and they're good enough to sell
As we returned to England, water shapes were seen below
Then as we neared them the reservoirs seemed to ebb and flow.

Where would we be without nature, whether it be winter, summer, autumn or spring?
Just think of all the beauty each season does bring
Beautiful blossoms, colourful flowering bulbs and bees
Autumnal tints, Jack Frost and snowy scenes decorating the trees.

All the animals use instinct in their own natural way
And the songbirds' dawn chorus brightens a day
So enjoy our altering seasons and climate change, if it be so
Thank God we don't have extremes as some countries we know.

Monica Baxter

Hindsight

Suddenly, it seems the children have grown,
They wish to leave the palatial home,
Life on their own they think it is fine,
They're departing from me when I thought they were mine.

The house is so sad, so strange, so quiet,
It seems to have died, I'm alone at night,
The silence is shouting out; how will I cope
My whole world has changed, I just sit and mope.

Realisation sets in; we all do the same,
Not knowing that we are causing real pain,
Parents who've loved and adored them for years,
End up wondering why and shed more real tears.

New families begin, new babies are born,
Parents come round from feeling forlorn,
As nannies etc they find there's new hope
When the house is more noisy and with babies to 'cope'.

Life is now again very grand, the house rings out anew,
Grandchildren galore, they're all the same brew,
The days are now full, more than ever before,
Sadness is an old memory and I'm loving what's in store.

Phyllis Wright

Life's Blessings

We each have different gifts
To offer back to life,
Which may provide the lifts
To help a soul in strife.

A listener we may be
When someone needs an ear.
It's plain for all to see
These benefits are clear.

The gift of time to call
On someone all alone,
Who could have had a fall
And no one would have known!

And what's the good of laughter
If it's not being spread about?
It can bring joy hours after
Reflecting fun no doubt.

Some have gifts of art
Concrete or abstract,
There's acting for a start
And singing, that's a fact.

Even without good health
We all have gifts to share,
Even without much wealth
We've gifts beyond compare.

These gifts are all equal
No matter what the cost.
Here follows the natural sequel -
Life's gifts are never lost!

Lola Perks-Hartnell

When?

If and it decide to be arrogant
Or belligerent; in fact very mean
In mind, thought and heart
They are not fit to preen
Their feathers and strut around
Pleased as punch when in fact
With reality they possess a profound
Depth so deep and still to attract
The Devil who is an unknown quantity
We can and must do without
Because he tempts the sanctity
Of peace and calm full of clout
Knowing and vowing he will win
The spurs of any trial that is thrust
Upon his shoulder is no sin
Because he does know and trust
His power when a wayward mind is open wide
To sin, so please be stronger than temptation
Let mind over matter abide
By counting the blessing of equation.

Beryl Hall

Share Our Blessings

Once I was young and now I am old
I've seen love of God, by the many grow cold
But as I reflect on this wonderful world
All the beauties of nature before us unfurled
I give thanks to our Father for His bounteous love
And the blessings He's showered on us all from above
The joys of our home, of a father and mother
A husband or wife, children, sisters or brother
Our food and our clothing, the stars up above
Someone to love us and some we too can love
Most of these cost us nothing, are there for us all
Though there are many on Earth on whom none of these fall
Let's love one another, help all these to share
In the wonderful blessings around everywhere
So let's not be greedy, but do a good deed
To our brothers of every race, colour or creed
Help all to enjoy all the blessings around
So that peace and goodwill toward all will abound.

Margaret Grice

Depend On Me

Whatever happens
You've always got me
If you're trapped in a pothole
Or stuck up a tree
I'm always on hand
To help you cope
If you need a long ladder
Or a short length of rope.

Whatever the future
Throws out at you
If you've run out of tea bags
Or ruined the stew
Remember I'm here
With a recipe for life
And I'll cook up a solution
To consume all your strife.

Whatever arises
To cloud up your day
Whether it's hot in winter
Or snowing in May
I'll drop everything
To rush to your side
And bring you the sunshine
Only love can provide.

June Waine

Distant Children

When happy sounds of children's play
Echoes through those summer days,
We wonder where the time has gone
Since we were parents keen and young.
When kids are young, it's the busiest time
In whatever occupation parents climb.
Eventually regrets come to the fore,
Do we make the best of them, of
Children's love and delights at times
When faced with life's uncertainties, we
Take for granted those happy sounds?
Future parents who are now just kids,
Will wonder where the time has gone,
When they were parents keen and young.

John L Wigley

Kerena Curtis

I read in the papers, you were well known
An alcoholic - a deadbeat, to me
You were not always like an old crone
Kerena Curtis, young and fair
Wonderful figure, glorious hair.

Young, beautiful, tall and straight
Men clung around you
As fish round good bait
Life in the raw, life in the red
Life in a glass of whisky
You are a long time dead
All the chat-up and bull****
Just to get you in bed.

To chat-up, flatter, ply you with drink
Come on girls, you must learn to think
Before, you look in the mirror
Kerena's face will look back
One smack, you are down
In the heat of the moment
Or cold light of day
A beating will follow
Always ending that way.

The bottle is empty, must be replaced
There's mayhem and murder
The moans, groans, the screams in the night
Are ignored by the neighbours
Can't deal with their fright.

It's cold . . . you are quiet, must have a fag
Now, you can't find your bloody handbag
Blood is the word; it spreads over the ground
It covers the glass, all scattered around
You stumble . . . fumble; must have a drink
But, your two black eyes won't let you blink.

Count Our Blessings

I read the words of your daughter
When you were dead
'Who could do this?'
Anyone . . . once they climb out of bed
For a girl, turns into a woman
Turns into fair game
Can turn into society's trollop
I think it's a shame.

Kerena had a husband, I met him one night
In the lounge bar of 'The Rose'
He was all full of fight
We chatted awhile; laughed
Then they were gone off in the night
Through the years chance meetings we had
She, full of smiles and laughter, never was bad.

Then came the day, I wish I knew when
I could not speak, I did not dare
She looked for a moment, I tried not to stare
The moments ticked by, her pain I could feel
I felt cold, sick
The pain, I could see in her eyes
This was real.

Now . . . the tears fill my eyes
I'll never forget
Not a drunken old crone
That littered the streets
Wouldn't go home
For you were my friend
Full of young grace
'The Body' young men of Bedford
Named you when did . . .
How could the transformation take place?

Eileen Whitmore

Count Your Blessings

I count my blessings when I see
My baby creeping on that knee
Now he is going through his drills
He won't be quiet or ever be still
Determined to reach for that special toy
Soon he will be walking, oh what a joy
By this time having two or four front teeth
And will be getting stronger on his feet
Will stand in his cot and throw the things on the floor
Will move so fast on those knees you must close that door
His mind is active, he is at the learning stage
Will do everything you do, because they mimic at this age
Keep him checked but guided he will grow, and grow
With strong healthy mind and I love him so
Yes, a blessing each day, God's plan for us men
I count them, yes I count them, and we all can.

M Joseph

Each New Day

The early bird sings in the morning
To welcome the new day that's dawning
The grass it is covered with a silvery dew
And the flowers are showing a colourful hue.

On the horizon the sun is shining
The sheep in the fields they are dining
The hens on the range are ready to lay
And the cattle are chewing the cud in the hay.

I leap from my bed with joy
Just like a young girl or boy
To greet the new day for the love it will bring
And I feel I can joyfully sing.

Glory to God in the highest
Glory to the God of the Earth
Praise Him for giving us new life
Praise Him for giving us birth.

Jean Coleman

Appreciation

We so often take for granted
Things so helpful, day by day
Lots of things have been provided
As a help along the way.

Each morning let's say 'Thank You'
To our Creator - God above
Who sustains and helps and keeps us
By His eternal love.

Thank Him for the blessing
He has given us to see
The beauties of this lovely Earth
Our friends and family.

For speech we are so thankful
Helps us comfort, teach or say
Many things so helpful
All along the way.

Thank God for our hearing
At work, at school, at play
This is such a blessing
Each and every day.

How nice to hear the footsteps
Of a long awaited friend
Or join a family conversation
Hear delightful music that has end.

If these were non-existent
How silently we'd live
Be blind and dumb and sightless
Precious little we could give.

So let us all be thankful
For speech, hearing and for sight
These are a source of blessing
And make each day so bright.

Nell Thompson

The Beauty Of Life

For everything we are grateful for in every way
Let's count our blessings each and every day
Good health if we are lucky to have this precious gift
A smile that gives others who are sad a lift
The most important surely will be family and friends
Sometimes your list may never end
A beloved pet who sits by your side
His loyalty given unquestionably to you in his eyes
A neighbour who is always there for you
Who will try to help in everything you have to do
The daffodils and hyacinths on a spring day
When the sun shines and the blackbird sings his heart away
There is so much beauty around us if we only realise
Just to be here is a gift in many people's eyes
We all have something to contribute in this life
So in spite of ups and downs and strife
Let's live each day as if it was our last
And put all sadness and gloom back in the past.

Enid Skelton

Your Father

(Dedicated to a father who was loved and will never be forgotten)

Your father's time has come to go,
Now that God has beckoned him so.
The door of life has opened wide,
To let him through and pass inside.

Who are we to say,
When and where we go?
It is not for us to choose,
Who we love and who we lose.

Before you shed a painful tear,
Whisper in his waiting ear,
'Farewell, my darling dad,
Farewell, for all the love we've had.'

Derek Dobson

New World Surfacing

Lost in a world far beyond the one they know
Testing your faith and everything you believe
Confused by lies told through private parables
Tormented by a past filled with tragedy
In the secret places where emotions flow
There is a consciousness of what comes with death
But is hope alone enough to bring you back
When you are only hanging on by a breath

Well, it's nice to know that you survive
Through whispers that tell you what to do
And a surreal world of escape
From all the things that want to harm you
But a life that's scarred by travesty
Means that things won't be the same again
So is there something to hold on to
Or do you need a new religion

Now that you know that there is a world of pain
You will have to find the strength to make it through
And no doubt it's hard when you've been abandoned
By the same ones that are supposed to save you
It seems that all your cries for help are in vain
Because people can't seem to see with blind eyes
They claim to want to help you but turn away
So now you know that there is a world of lies

Well, since you've been pushing on my dear
Through this world of yours that's surfacing
Maybe it's time that they understood
That it all came from your suffering
But there are still things that you question
Maybe this is one time you won't win
So when doubt starts clouding up your thoughts
Then ask yourself what you believe in

Now they'll know
About a world of pain
Now they'll know
About a world of lies

Steve Morris

My Favourite Place

When I am tired of life's fast pace,
Ev'n weary of the human race,
I long to be in my favourite place,
On the sands of yesteryear.

I used to skip and jump and run,
Of worldly worries there were none,
As children, we would have such fun,
On the sands of yesteryear.

We'd draw, make castles in the sand,
And everyone would lend a hand,
Indeed, we were a merry band,
On the sands of yesteryear.

As years pass by, the pastimes change,
There's cricket, rounders, quite a range,
But, comfort's there . . . nothing's strange,
On the sands of yesteryear.

That's why I go, with time to spare,
To spend some hours, just being there,
To smell the sea, the tang, the air,
On the sands of yesteryear.

The joy to walk along the beach,
Absorbing views, all free to reach,
The treasures that no one can teach,
On the sands of yesteryear.

I travel there now, in my mind,
Calm thoughts come easy and I find
The pressure's gone, I can unwind,
On the sands of yesteryear.

Catherine Buchan

Growing Old

She forgets now
On darkling days
As bowed pedestrians come and go
With unengaging drabness
Through the rutted snow
How
Above the leaden clouds
In places aircraft fly
How over neatly tended rows
Of village gardens in July
How from the energetic faith in children's eyes
A sun of future promise always shines.

Peter Taylor

The Boy

The little boy had spent his day
In hours of everlasting play
He'd kicked his ball, he'd hugged his dog
He'd drawn a cow or so he said
He'd jumped and skipped and danced
Until he found a snail entranced
All rush and hurry when you're two
And little legs are fairly new
Until that is a crashing fall
And Mummy had to kiss you well
At last it's time to pick up Ted and go to bed
Hand in hand, with Dad upstairs
He paused, with infant eyes amazed
The stars, the firmament ablaze
The magic millions twinkle there
More than the grains of sand we hear
He could not speak but fell asleep
Until the dawn, he saw with disbelief, his stars had gone
We dried his eyes and calmed his fear
His stars unseen were truly there
With boys and ted in bed at night
The stars will still be twinkling bright
So off he went another day of everlasting play.

Judy McEwan

His Room

I was on show within four walls of a dream
The wallpaper for fashions, come and gone
Humming volumes in leather, glossed in light cream
Searching in papers and trophies you won

Dressed in beige, you were sitting at your desk, quiet
Your moon-eyes bathing in ancient texts
My soul hung from the Murano light, a riot
Against sparse furniture, swift feelings, next

To hide inside locked cupboards in my blue mind
A courtyard of lost souls in my dream town
A room where starched people open and shut blinds

Doors with airy hands, electric ghosts, clowns
That fall asleep under tight anaesthetic
Hold my bridge of squares in counting magic.

Mariana Zavati Gardner

Invite To A Poem

Found an owl matched to tree
But that bird couldn't fool me.
Very well suited to its hiding place
Yet when it hooted
My dog gave a howl of glee,
Providing more entertainment for free.
Stood there watching as clouds were crossing,
We waited - an owl, a tree, a dog and me.
Our minds combined enabled a scarecrow to speak,
We always knew it was life he did seek.
Join us now, become part of our fraternity,
To see what we see, to hear what we hear.
A tractor growls and treads upon the soil,
A puff of smoke from its engine oil.
A short cut they take, a twilight sun to celebrate,
As shadow ducks fly across the meadow.
As colour from the land is drawn and magic is born,
Falcon swoops, a blackbird stoops, the owl recruits a mouse.
A firework of sparks ignites the night,
An illuminated wizard our scarecrow becomes,
Makes a bonfire dance on the river.
Happiness to our hearts is now delivered.
Sword from stone is drawn
And Arthur sits again upon his throne.

Vann Scytere

The Quiet Garden

I sat in a very quiet garden
With the sun burning down
It was very relaxing and peaceful
With only the birds' sound

I admired all the flowers
As they were shown on parade
They were all beautiful
In their various pretty shades

I saw a bevy of butterflies
Fluttering and flying away
They settled on the flowers
In their pretty, fine array.

Rita Wilde

Count Your Blessings

Has life dealt to you a heavy blow?
Is your heart hardened, the Saviour now you do not wish to know?
Take courage! His love never changes, neither His ways rearrange.
He who once walked this road before us, was rejected and despised,
but the Father's love had kept Him,
He will also keep you.
This walk of life has many pains, I have experienced them myself,
the hurt, the loss and loneliness with many trials too,
yet in my heart I am comforted for I know I am not alone,
as that still small voice echoes in my ears. 'Look up! You are not alone.'
To someone feeling low today, be encouraged for there is a way
even in the lowest valley. Jesus is the way.
This pilgrimage is not always easy, on your journey there could be
many falls, but true enough there are the everlasting arms
which bear you up and dry your tears and sweetly whisper,
'My child, have no fear.'
I too have been in the valleys, dark shadows covered me.
At times it made me wonder, *will a light again shine for me?*
I have also been in the desert, where everything seems so dry,
then I was assured that there was life in the desert
as I drank daily of His supply.
I have travelled up the hills, sometimes I get so tired,
then he whispers, 'Stop a while and be still. I will never leave you.'
There are times I get a glimpse of the mountains and the beauty
all around, and then I am lowered down again,
to continue my journey through.
It is Jesus who brought me out, so I must tell this story all about.
In the rough times I have experienced the power of God.
In my weakness I have experienced His strength.
In my joy I have experienced His blessings.
And with His peace I am embraced in His love.
Then what have you to fear? Give thanks to God, for He is near.

Vida Harris

Rainbow Spectrums

The ghost of Christmas past, New Year too,
The year has a seven at its end, which is deemed lucky too,
So if friends or relatives have deserted you and you're feeling all alone,
Don't you moan, groan, cry, or be a serious clown,
Always remember new happinessings and people are coming your way,
To pick you up when you are feeling somewhat down,
For you have a rainbow of hope inside you, you also have a spectrum of light,
Brighter than the sun, so chase those blues away one by one.
Ignore all bad news, untenable dues, and gently cruise through happinessings,
While concentrating all your consideration, to count your caressing blessings.

Peter Vaughan Williams

Count Our Blessings

It is a very dull Monday morning
The sky is cloudy and grey
But as I look out of my window
What a wonderful sight is displayed

I love all the birds that visit my garden
The blue tits, the great tits and jays
The robins, the blackbirds and so many more
That feast on the nuts every day

I have three lovely pots filled with flowers
Petunias and pansies galore
We had some severe frosts, but happily
These flowers they seemed to ignore

My relations and friends bring such pleasure
From my childhood and in every day
How supportive they've been through the years
What memories I have stored away

I had a stroke two years ago
And that meant a hospital stay
My church friends were really wonderful
Brought my husband to see me each day

The doctors said how well I'd progressed
I knew that my will was so strong
I determined to strive and never give up
And count my blessings all the way along

There are so many things that surround us
In our lives, almost every day
We must make sure that we never forget
All the blessings that come our way.

Trixie Burnham

My Friend

Thank You for my friend, Lord
The answer to my heartfelt prayer
Thank You for my friend, Lord

Her heart overflows with mercy and love
With wisdom she guides who is Yours
A reflection of her Heavenly Father above
Her Heavenly Father who she truly adores.

Thank You for my friend, Lord.

S J Sanders

All These Things

All these things
Mean nothing
Without you

Look about us
For all we've amassed
It counts for little
It counts for less
Than the idle breath
We sigh

Trinkets and rings
Around your neck
Upon your finger
Can't hold a candle
To the light and love
You daily bring

If we were to wear
Rags rather than finery
They couldn't change a thing
As for this home we have
I could settle for the stars
And open skies

We've seen others
Pass blindly down
This path of self-
Satisfaction
Wrapped about each other
As long as the weather's
Fine and set fair
Before fortune fades

We'd still be there
For each other
When the storms
Demand attention
With the look and
Reassuring glance

All these things
Will mean nothing
Without your love.

R R Gould

Company

What is it that fulfils a man
Breathes warmth into his soul?
What is it takes an empty shell
Then makes that person whole?

The presence of another being?
Someone to hold your hand?
Someone to give you a tender gaze,
Someone to share your plans?

It's all these little things, and more,
The sum more than the parts,
A wealth of small, shared, private things,
Makes you ache when you're apart.

To find that lost piece of a jigsaw,
A missing button off a coat,
The times nine, you can't remember,
That you used to chant by rote.

The pen that you've just put down,
To find at last behind your ear.
That's what it's like to have you home,
How it feels to have you near.

Peter Church

Summer On Ashdown Forest

Watching the gentle movement of the leaves
Whispering with the soft presence of a breeze.
A breeze that murmurs a caressing sigh,
With each moment that passes, under summer skies.

Summer skies which hold an abundance of blue,
Warming the landscape, an inspiring message of blue.
The message that conveys summer is at last here,
A season of warming comfort, we all hold dear.

Treasuring summer is a well-known fact,
We relax, absorb the sun's rays, with reserved tact.
Whilst here on Ashdown Forest, a calmness vibrates,
Quality, of calmness a constant joy to relate.

Far away in the distance, trees appear quite still,
Not even a whispering murmur emerges from over the hill.
All appears still, as if tree's dreaming in sleep,
A sign perhaps, they too have a siesta to quietly keep.

Pleasure is a word which conveys how we feel,
Here on Ashdown Forest where we enjoyed a picnic meal.
Here, where the calmness of time graces our being,
Filling our emotions with peaceful gratitude,
Enriched with visually seeing.

Lorna Tippett

Day By Day

If only we could appreciate things before they went,
Then maybe we would never have a day that was ill-spent,
This morning don't forget to kiss your loved ones goodbye,
And don't start out the day with a moan, a groan and sigh,
For the beauty of this life is all around . . . just take a look,
It's in the glory of the flowers, the trees and babbling brook,
It's in the chill of winter, when by the fire you take a book,
It's in the majesty of mountains, of rivers and sunset skies,
It's in the morning birdsong, and beautiful butterflies,
It's in the heat of summer, when your toes caress the sand,
The ocean waves are pounding and your loved one takes your hand,
It's in the cool of evening, when the busy day is done,
There's time to talk, to plan, to reminisce and have some fun!
It's in the smile of loved ones, memories of happy days,
All captured on camera . . . so we can remember as we gaze,
So many things to be thankful for, a mystery to unravel . . .
Who gives us all these good things, as in this life we travel?
We're told in God's word that the best in life is free,
Life in all its fullness, is what's offered to you and me,
Thank you, Lord, for giving us this beautiful world You created,
And placing us in families, with friends and homes as well,
You've given us freedom, health, our safety and choices still to make,
Help us to make good decisions as so much is at stake!

Sue Edwards

The Day I Recycled My Teeth

Where are they now? Heaven knows how
I could lose my teeth. I've looked beneath
Cushions and covers. Even moved Mother's
Antimacassar. It's really bizarre. I took them
Out, without a doubt, but where are they now?

'Have you looked in the bin?' said my neighbour
With a grin. 'Good job it's the bottom, you can't
See you've not got 'em!'

Then I found them at last 'neath the paper and
Glass. In recycling bin, they were lying within.
Smiling at me they knew they'd been found
And saved from recycling mound. Incisors it
Seems have invaded my dreams and with
Molars and grinders, indelible reminders of the
Cardinal sin - of throwing your teeth in the bin!

P J Hale

Pondering

Can you remember that long-forgotten dream
When all our steps were bathed in cream
And every spring, river, fountain stream
Was life?

And now we sit and ponder on our ills
Looking toward the next pain-killing pills
And thoughts of dark satanic mills
Are rife

Where is the zeal born of the young
Where are the deeds now left unsung
How many pearls were never strung
Now lost?

So many questions in so little time
Never asked when in one's prime
When there were many hills to climb
At cost

But

Throughout the years there has been treasure
When sadness gave way to pleasure
Overflowing and with good measure
From God.

Lyn Cave

Love's Blessing

(Inspired by a picture of a mother and her infant)

The smiles exchanged
Between her and her boy
Promise a constant joy
As first love shines out
From deep within his infant eyes.

Oh, to see the sweetness in his gaze
To watch him grow tall and strong
To live as one in the warmth of his sun
And die when old wombed in his ascendant glow
Her life fulfilled, her purpose this first boy.

Katherine Jane Rawlings

Memories Of England

Give me back my old England,
Land I was proud to call my own,
Where streets were walked in safety
And muggings quite unknown.

Give me back my old England,
With children running free,
And respect was found in classrooms
As they learnt their ABC.

Give me back my old England,
When the Sabbath was a day of rest,
When we all enjoyed the Sunday roast
And cooking skills were put to test.

Give me back my old England,
When people found time to talk.
We went to work on buses
But no objections to a walk.

Give me back my old England,
When family life was the done thing.
Couples prepared to keep their vows
And bring up their own offspring.

Give me back my old England,
I want to relive my dream
When material things were unimportant
And folks were happier, or so it seems.

Margaret Meadows

Just Like A Rose

Life is like a rose,
In the summertime,
When all the beauty is there,
It's like the happiness we share.

And when the petals fall,
And all the beauty's gone,
That's when things in our life,
Seem to go wrong.

But things seem to brighten up,
And there is no more gloom,
When that rose once more,
Comes into bloom.

Raymond Wakefield

Flight Fantastic

Emerging from the darkened caverns of the mind
To embrace a light so directional and bright.
A chrysalis once, a butterfly now,
Wings unfolded, taking flight.
A flight not of escape but of liberation.
Brave New World.
What a day, what a night, what a life!

Experiencing a spiritual rebirth,
Breathing a passionate air into my lungs once again,
Like a stiff, bracing breeze energising the soul.
Life is in my eyes once again.
The window on the soul expresses the happiness within.
A childish enthusiasm fills all my days now.
Reawakened, impassioned and wide-eyed as I go out into the world once more.
The freedom of flight is mine now
To land at will wherever fancy takes me
To touch the lives of fellow creative souls
And deliver the message of beauty
In this oft dark world in which we live.
The flight of the butterfly is one to relish.
I urge you to spread your gossamer wings and fly . . .

Lorraine Nicholson

Blessings

Blessings are a pleasure
A treasure you can share
Blessings come in many ways
And many shapes and forms.
So don't forget to share them
A blessing shared with others
Will give you peace of mind.
So as you go along life's way
Count your blessings every day.
I'd like to own a shooting star
And spread my blessings near and far
Love and happiness would follow
And peace throughout the land.
No more suffering, no more sorrow
If you don't do it today
Make sure you do it tomorrow.
So count your blessings one by one
And then make sure you pass them on
Goodnight and God bless to everyone.

Yvonne Cooper

Things That Warm The Heart

When feeling down or out of sorts
It helps to think - I find -
Of things that lift your spirits
Warm your heart or ease your mind -

A smiling face, a cheerful word
An unexpected hug
A snoozing pet, relaxed, contented
Sprawled out on the rug

A treasured item, lost for weeks
That suddenly appears
A phone call from a friend whose voice
You haven't heard in years

An extra cuppa just for pleasure
Something nice to eat
Shrill squeals of happy children
Chasing up and down the street

And on a cold grey morning
What a joy to be aware
Of birdsong - robin, blackbird, blue tit
Trilling in the air

So though no magic wand can make
Our problems go away
Good feelings can bring comfort and
Sustain us day by day.

Helen M Clarke

The Joy Of Living

What a joy it is to wake each morn
And open your eyes to another day,
To experience the wonders that life adorns
Living is so wondrous that way.

To have good health and enjoy life to the full
Live every day as it comes,
Nature provides and over all rules,
Give a smile - here comes the sun.

Brian R Russ

Reflection

Take a moment to reflect on where your path in life has taken you
Look at all the experiences that you have shared with others
See the wonderful people that have a special place in your life
All the memories that you have made, that you can look back upon
Revise all the lessons that life has taught you so far
See how much you have grown
Picture where you fit into others' lives and what you do for them
Make sure that your life is complete, that there are no regrets
Be honest and truthful with others and remember to work on your relationships
Never let a day go by that you forget to tell your loved ones that you love them
Always remember to thank others and be grateful for the small things in life
Remember that family and friends are important
They should never be mistreated or taken advantage of
Remember these things as you turn another corner in your life's path
Knowing that you take these things with you as you ask another to share in your life
Look into the eyes of the special person who has become your friend and lover
Take their hand and walk together down life's path
Facing whatever may come
Working through all the good and bad times together
Looking back every now and then
Making sure that your path in life is going in the right direction.

Julie Banyard

Gratitude

For all the gifts on us You shower
Lord, we thank You every hour
Let us all our voices raise
And forever sing Your praise
For all the seasons of the year
And for all that we hold dear
For the flowers and birds that sing
Grateful thanks to You we bring
For the friends we meet each day
As we go along our way
For all the things we say and do
Lord, we give our thanks to You
At our work or school or play
Please, dear Lord, beside us stay
And when we are put to test
Help us, Lord, to do our best
As each day comes to its end
We ask that You will be our friend
And hear our voices as we lift
Our thanks to You for every gift.

Ian Russell

A Loving Hand

Sometimes a blessing
Is the touch of God
Through a human hand.
Comforting presence
When we feel alone.
Smile from a stranger
Empathy, eye meeting eye.

Blessings of neighbours
Willing to lift me,
Body collapsing
In powerless heap.
Friends ready to help
Yet giving me space,
Allowing me to be me.

My husband's deep love
In a thousand ways.
Grandchildren's letters
Their laughter and chat.
My caring children
With their roles reversed.
Blessings money cannot buy.

So I thank my Lord
For the blessings sent,
Through the touch of a loving hand.

Renee Loynds

Summer Of Yesteryear

A ray of sunshine,
The view at the top of the hill -
Looking out to meadowlands hot and still,
A bird soars high in the sky,
A lovely warm summer's day
And children play in the hay,
A butterfly goes by,
The drone of an aeroplane above -
Mixing with the sound of the bees,
Humming around the wild flowers,
Cows mooing in the meadows,
Dogs barking as owners take them for a walk,
An idyllic summer of yesteryear.

V Harding

The Innocent

Precious baby - my little one
There are some things you don't need to know
Stay close to me - by Mummy's side
For ill winds will surely blow.

Precious baby - my little one
I heard you crying through the night
So I comforted and I cuddled you
When Daddy disappeared from sight.

Precious baby - my little one
You had brothers and sisters too
Was that the sound again of a gun
Now there's only me and you.

I'd like to see you - grow big and strong
Be happy, live life to the full
But Mummy won't always be here
For there's something called a cull . . .

Mummy, you said - not to stray
And I promise I won't go far
Who is that man - Mummy, don't go away
Ma . . .baa . . .baa

I'm lonely here all by myself
And I cannot feel my knees
Mummy - Daddy - where have you gone?
Victims of foot and mouth disease . . .

C Rank

Another World

If the sun
Walking on the water
Or the light reflected
From a thousand polished surfaces,
Washed by the seas
Which run forever
In their secret places,
Reminds me of a world I've made
From whatever pieces came to hand,
How much more
Your entering a room,
Or crying *It's only me*,
Calls forth a world
More real than that
Through which I move.

Richard Henry

Blessings

My granddaughter is a beautiful child,
Very loving and a little bit wild;
Like a rose in bloom, so sweet and fine,
It's a privilege to call her mine.

Then came a lump upon her leg,
We were so worried by the tests;
Cancer, they said, upon the thigh,
All I wanted to do was cry.

After more tests, they found they were wrong,
No cancer there, I felt like singing a song;
I now count my blessings, one by one,
And thank God for the happy outcome.

Thelma Cook

To Matthew With Love

This young man arrived
On bike in combat gear
Chris said, 'This is Matthew'
We were pleased to have him here

A nurse like Chris
We learnt he collected antiques
Visited his house in Brighton
Not for Matthew, flat packs, teak

His garden was amazing
Palms, lamp posts, greenery galore
He worked on the Victorian house
Inside glassware ceiling to floor

The house was sold
We accepted they were gay
They moved in with us
We love our son come what may

Months later you made history
First civil partnership in the land
We were proud you were our family
We kissed and took your hand

The next day you didn't wake
We were all there when you died
You made Chris so happy
Our memories lasting all our lives

We will miss you, Matthew
You made a big impression
We will think of you daily
Till we meet in Heaven.

Diana Cramp

Count Your Blessings

Counting my blessings over the years,
Having good times with our peers.
Going to church and Sunday school,
Where for life we learnt their rules.
Learning always to be forgiving,
Later leaving home to earn our living.
Making new friends, but still valuing the old,
Lifelong friendship which never grew cold.
A great blessing was to live in a home
Where no one ever felt alone,
Where Father loved Mother and Mother loved Father,
Where loving friends and relations would gather.
Later to be wed to the love of my life,
When we lived our lives without any strife.
We lived our lives in harmony,
Which cheers me up as I go along,
As I remember that lovely song,
Blessings should be counted every day,
Even when few come our way.
The greatest gain shall come from loss,
For life for all flows from the Cross.
Sufferers can enter into another's pain
Then their lack of blessing can be a gain.
Theirs is a blessing hard to count
But in reality it's a blessing of large amount.
So we'll count our blessings every day,
Whether good or bad comes our way,
Even if they're small, thankful they're not less,
A thankful heart is a happy heart and always is well blessed.

Janet Richards

September

Last autumn as blackbirds flew
Across the orange sky
My berry-laden trees fed migratory birds well
Hiding behind the door of my old shed
Sits a broken wheelbarrow
Where a family of robins dwell
They will be safe here, from predators
And there will be an abundance
Of fallen fruit to keep them well fed
When winter calls.

J M Stoles

Only A Thought Away

However dark the day may seem,
However grey the sky,
I know your love will still reach out,
A love that cannot die.
You walked with me so long ago
And yet it seems so near,
A time long past and distant now
When I could hold you, dear.
I still reach out and nothing's there,
No warmth where once you lay,
No indentation left behind,
No voice to bid me 'stay'.
Though you have gone, there still remains
My memories of you.
I feel your breath upon my face,
Your own sweet love so true.
The sun, which breaks the leaden sky,
Is your warm touch on me
And in each raindrop I behold
Your love, so full and free.
You're closer now than any time,
Your spirit's with me still,
As you reach out and call to me
I'd climb the highest hill.
I cannot see you, cannot touch
That face I've loved so long,
But in my mind the picture's clear,
It's well refined and strong.
I think of you, and thought gives flight
And brings you to my side.
I feel so blessed to have you still,
Though from the world you hide.
And so I live, and live for you,
Whate'er the world may think,
I've not forgotten you, my love,
And you'll not let me sink
Into despair, or dark and gloom,
You want me still to smile
And so I wait to be with you,
Alone, but for a while.

Jackie Morgan

I Am Lucky

I count my blessings every day
And to God, I often pray,
To keep me well to carry on,
As I am a widow and live alone.

When I look around and see some folk
In wheelchairs, who cannot walk,
I feel so lucky that I am not chair-bound
And that I am privileged to be able to get around.

M Crickmore

Precious Moments With My Granddaughter

When you were a little girl
I loved to push you in your pram
And walk along the country road
And hold your little hand
To stop awhile
And listen to the birds
To pick flowers
Growing near the curb
Those precious moments
I shared with you
And how one day, you lost your shoe
I think I am lucky to have had
Those precious moments
I shared with you
They will always live in my heart
Whenever we are near
Or far apart.

Grace R M Bean

Keep Smiling

Life is for living
Enjoy every day
For just in one second
It can be taken away.

Stop moaning and groaning
No one listens to you
When you laugh and keep smiling
Lots of friends will come your way.

Matilda Stewart Chambers

Children Of My Children

I play their games of hide-and-seek,
Shower them with abundant cuddles,
Thrill them with scary stories,
Organise their continual muddles.

I make them tasty fairy cakes,
But cheat with ready mixtures,
Educate their absorbing minds
With numbers, words and pictures.

We walk for miles in countryside,
Wiggle toes on sandy beaches,
Pick wild and wonderful flowers,
Explore rocks of weird sea creatures.

Children who love to paint my face
With old make-up garish and bright,
Tangle and back-comb my long, thinning hair,
Much to their mischievous delight.

I sing and dance to their nursery rhymes,
Reassure them through fears and trepidation,
Embrace them enthusiastically each day,
Love and perceive them in glowing admiration.

Celia Auld

Life's Little Things

Another New Year bringing the promise of hope
Look to the future, make use of the scope
There are things we can do with no effort at all
Like a friendly hello, warm smile, promised call

Check what you have in your life today
Quite a lot to bring a sunshine ray
Someone who loves you, forgives your faults
Helps you look forward to a brand new tot

Another New Year, use all of it now
We only get one chance, don't wear a frown
Your talent and skills can help so many
Spread them around without seeking a penny

Count your blessings, you'll be in for a shock
How they increase when you have a rock
Take care of them all, young and old
And your many riches will gradually unfold.

Rebecca Keough

Blessings Are Everywhere

(Respectfully dedicated to my very dear mother, Merna, who always knows how to 'count your blessings')

Up, down, left, right, backwards, forwards,
Centre, north, south, east and west -
You will always find them there,
Quite regardless of whenever you might
Happen to search for them.
They can easily be found skywards,
Or on and in an earthly descent.

Persistently look for them
And you will joyfully find them
In every single separate direction.

For they are indeed constantly present
During our own respective lifespans -
If only we can even ever be slightly bothered
To move around in various ways -
We shall always be able to locate accurately,
All of these gloriously gleaming riches for ourselves,
At whatever time of day and night,
We may be strenuously striving to see them,
Both clearly, and even purely,
For ourselves alone, and together.

Michael Crossley-Stalker

Appreciation Of Life

Life is precious when you look around
And behold God's gifts to us abound.
My grateful thanks from me do pour
For my wonderful life I've had and more.

Grief and sadness is hard to bear
Like many others I've had my share.
But if we had no love and affection
There would be no tears and dejection.

My memories remain deep in my heart
And loved ones from me never part.
In life as we are passing through
Keep on smiling for friends so true.

Our life is brief and ever special
Appreciate all things that are essential.
Value our life the way we should
Because being alive is really good.

Always look at life to brighten
Your spirits to raise and heart to lighten.
Truly all troubles will ebb away
So count your blessings every day.

Rosalind Sim

Count Our Blessings

Not being a Hebrew scholar
One has to trust what's told
I'd Yada Know, than Yada Not
Or *'Uns mit Gott'* might be my lot.*

They say it's true if you're a Jew
It's how it's said is what is meant
Whether blessing or curse is thereby sent

I seek an ancient scribe
His name is quite unknown
He wrote a piece 'Didatche'
Guarded in the archives
Of the British Library Zone

There speaks within of a roving curse
That stalks throughout the land
It bends all low 'neath its terrible blow.
Nursing those who kiss his hand.

You can count on this
A Royal bliss in guise of tragic portent.
Each moment of the world's great fray
The past, forever . . . the present.

* Post Script:

The Hebrew verb 'to know'
I know is 'Yada' is it not?
Aber *'Gott mit uns' ist Deutsch*
Inverted Nazis made it rot

I bless this verse to count the curse
In January double-0 seven
The perfect year of the third grand tier of
James & I & us & BoUnd & turn around
And bound again and found to reign with Christ in highest Heaven

Andrew Trevor Polson

The Best Day Of The Week

If the postman brings a letter
Full of cheering news
Or some editor regales me
With excellent reviews
And fills my head with promises
Of publicity I seek
Then that would make a Monday
The best day of the week.

On Tuesday we go out at night
(It's my husband's night off work)
Always to a restaurant
Italian, Chinese, Turk
Sometimes we eat Indian
More often we go Greek
One reason to make Tuesday
The best day of the week.

If Wednesday is a rollover
And I do the lottery
Go home with my ticket
And find the winner's me
Or I find the family heirloom
Is a valuable antique
Then of course that would make Wednesday
The best day of the week.

Thursday night's a quiet night
I sit and watch TV
For Thursday night's the one night
There are things I like to see
I drink some dry white wine
Relax and rest my feet
That's why every Thursday
Is the best day of the week.

Count Our Blessings

Friday night is party night
A night for having fun
The start of the weekend
The working day is done
I dress up in my finery
Something smart and sleek
And go out on the town
On the best day of the week.

Saturday is shopping day
A day to bargain hunt
We take the children to McDonald's
Have quarterpounders for our lunch
Meet up with all our friends
And gossip when we speak
So perhaps that should make Saturday
The best day of the week.

Sunday is a day of rest
I read a magazine
Write letters to the people
That I haven't lately seen
Recharge all my batteries
And get back to my peak
Ready for those seven days
The best ones of the week.

Joyce Walker

My Life

Laughter, love and lots of fun
The blessing of a loving son.
The happiness of a husband true,
Caring parents, watching over you.
I've been lucky in every way
With countless blessings every day.
Family and friends to love
All these blessings from above.
Sunrise, sunset, a rainbow's hue
Breathtaking mountains and ocean view.
Feeling the sun, wind, rain and snow
Or quietly sitting by the fire's glow.
Golden memories enrich and enthral
Blessings, blessings upon me fall.

Christine Clark

The Joys Of Everyday Life

The wonderful smile on a baby's face
The comforting hug of a loved one's embrace

A loving husband, an adoring wife
To comfort the stress of everyday life

A cosy, warm and friendly home
Where all are given a friendly welcome

A garden full of colourful flowers
Which one can enjoy for hours and hours

The joy of children and grandchildren too
With places to go and things to do

A country ride in a comfortable car
With lunch to enjoy in a country bar

The gentle touch of a helping hand
A steady arm to help one stand

A beautiful rainbow in a lowering sky
With attractive colours to delight the eye

These simple joys are as precious as gold
Especially when one is getting old.

Mary Stace

Cold As January

January, how I hate and dread it,
Wet and dark and stormy.
Snow is falling, freezing and icy.
Everlasting and for evermore.

Colds and flu drag me down,
Sneezing and coughing every day.
Nose running, tissues unending,
Aching all over, no voice to say.

Huddle indoors, watching television,
Central heating helps, only a little.
Frosty air to breathe, almost is nectar
Could I be feeling a bit better?

Peace at last, with sleep at nights,
February is coming, bringing good cheer.
Smile and think of spring, enjoy a treat,
January is on its way until another year.

Sheila Rowland

The Secret World

Sirens scream in
Cambridge rain:
What's going on?
Miscreants, mayhem, murder
On the roads?
All I do know is that away
From streets paced
By men with wild eyes
And fearful faces
Lives a secret world.
Here, moorhens slip
Into a clear stream
Draining into the gentle Cam,
Fearless at my tread.
A young girl passes
With flowered bag
Full of innocent promise,
Her face shrouded.
Surprise songbirds startle
From hidden gardens.
No sirens here, thank God,
But only autumn grasses
Sending their breath
Heavenwards.

Colin Shaw

Words Of Comfort

The hush of the wind whispers words of love,
Sent down with the stars from Heaven above,
Our loved ones whisper, 'We're not far away,
But are with you always, day by day.'

Be happy as you go along life's way,
Enjoy every minute of each day.
Don't be afraid, I'm always near,
I'll watch over you, never fear.

Then one day we shall be together,
I'll hold you close forever and ever.
So shed a tear, if you must,
But remember, in me you can trust.

Joan D Bailey

A Little Blessing Goes A Long Way!

I am not rich, I am not poor,
Sometimes what I am, I am not sure!
I am older each day that is passing.
At the end of the day, I count my blessings!

I am alone, my beloved is gone.
With God, family and friends I go on.
These days going on can be smoother,
Modern gadgets, and a mobility scooter!

My limbs are creaking and painful.
I still can write but, not so plentiful!
My sight isn't what it used to be.
Bifocals and computers are helping me.

I am not rich, I am not poor,
Sometimes what I am, I am not sure!
At the end of each passing day,
Thank you, God, I truly say!

Licia Johnston

Small Blessings, Wait And See

A new grandchild, for a new year,
That's what we have now, Rebbeca Jane is here.
She is beautiful, hope for the future, a dream come true,
Her sisters call her Becky Boo,
She is our sixth grandchild, so we feel blessed,
And nothing in the world can make us depressed,
Ours is a growing family,
Wonderful them, lucky me.

Events that occur outside I can't do anything about,
So, there's no point in moaning or having a shout,
Life is sweet and what you make it I am told,
Live it to the full, don't have regrets as you grow old,
Don't look back, the future looks good to me,
We shall have to wait and see,
I have my health, strength and now Becky Boo,
I pray her future will be blessed too.

Maureen Arnold

The Coming Of The Dawn

Darkness, blackness, despair!
Many names to call this place
Of dilemma,
Of unknowing,
Of confusion,
Of non-sensing of your presence
And unhearing of your word.

God, are Your promises a hoax
To tease me and to dump me?
Just false hope,
That seems empty,
That feels illusion,
When expectations of Your intervention
Leave me disappointed and defeated?

Midnight! Low point, darkest hour,
Turn of night toward the dawn.
Waiting acceptance,
Darkness passing,
Hope rekindled.
Daylight seeping, barely perceptible at first,
Dispelling, then repulsing the dark.

Dawn! The coming of the light,
Like God's presence, completely changes perspective.
Accurate seeing,
Increased understanding,
Relationship restored.
Faith and trust rekindled by the light
Reassuring for facing another night's dark.

'Just as darkness turns to day,
So is my light for you,
Predictable,
Promised,
Assured.
I am with you in the darkness of your life.
Trust me, I know the way towards the dawn.'

Margaret Dunn

Blest

Compared with many others,
A privileged life I lead,
I can see, hear, use my arms and legs,
Get myself up and put myself to bed.

When I draw back the curtains each morning,
I gaze on the beauty that surrounds,
The stars are disappearing one by one
And the moon fades in the background.

Most mornings I witness the sunrise,
Sheer beauty to behold,
Or watch the rain nourishing my garden,
The raindrops shining like diamonds as flowers unfold.

I am privileged to remember
The peace and quiet of bygone days,
When vehicles were at a minimum
And a cheery good morning always came my way.

As children we ran and played freely
Through the lanes, fields and woods,
Never a thought that we would be apprehended,
Unless by someone for our own good.

I collected new-laid eggs from our chickens,
Running daily on the grass,
Our milk and cream came straight from the dairy,
Cooled and measured into a jug made of glass.

Our bread was delivered daily,
By a dear old man in a black van,
Our meat was also delivered to the door,
There was no health and safety ban.

Food poisoning was seldom heard of,
Maybe an upset stomach came our way,
The word 'virus' had not been thought of
And for children's complaints, your mum nursed you day by day.

Count Our Blessings

You were given various potions,
Not antibiotics which kill most things in sight,
Sometimes the medicines tasted ghastly
And you turned a paler shade of white.

The coal copper boiler in the kitchen
Was lit on a Monday crack of dawn,
Washing was hurled in in abundance,
Washing machines had not been born.

Our food and clothes were made by a gem of a mother,
Trips were seldom to the shops,
But when we did go, you enjoyed every moment,
We had no car, just once a month on a bus.

I count my blessings daily,
And take solace when in distress,
By thinking of those less fortunate than myself,
Who has been well and truly blest.

Anne-Rose Harris

My Gift, My Son, My Michael

Too deep is the love which dwells in my heart
to convey words, to explain the part
of my life which is wholly devoted to you.
For you're in my all, with me whatever I do.

Each intake of breath or passing thought
has the essence of you, for there is nought
I could be without you there.
Your very soul I hold carefully in prayer.

When the nest you leave and start to fly
I will watch with pride, I don't want to cry
for you, my love, will go with our Lord.
Be true to yourself and follow His word.

You held my hand a moment while you were small,
my gift from God, the greatest gift of all
you were to me, I treasured your being
and forever will, albeit without always seeing.

My lips make a mockery of what my heart wants to say.
So just simply know in your soul, each day
while you fly, free to taste every new emotion,
you'll be wrapped in the prayers of my eternal devotion.

Kay Holmes

Blessings

When you are feeling sad and low,
And you start to think there is no way to go,
Cast your fears aside, you do not need to hide,
Take a look around and you will find,
All the wonders that come flooding into mind.
The beautiful birds that sit in the trees,
They sing us their song as they sway in the breeze,
The sparkling sun that glitters and gleams,
The silver moon that creeps into our dreams.
A place of beauty is this wonderful world,
Such marvellous secrets that have to be unfurled,
We have everything we need as we walk by the sea,
Such beauty all around for everyone to see.
The peace you can find as you stand on a hill,
When everything is quiet and still.
Do not crave for things you cannot find,
Just relax and let the beauty fill your mind.
You do not need silver, you do not need gold,
These gifts are all here for us to behold.
So be happy, so be free, there is everything for you and me.

Christina Sturman

Awakening

A dog barks in hollow tones
The sound of a large truck moans
A fast car sweeps by on a rush of wind
And I lie awakening to the din

The heavy gears of the milk van persist
Slowly and painfully into my brain they insist
Where is the cock crow, long gone I'm afraid
Where are the birdsongs? Somewhere but they fade

My children will soon arise
Sunshine will emit from their cries
Bright light will pour from their eyes
And God again will light up my skies.

Margaret M Cassidy

The Graduation Ceremony

His mother arrived
On a 'Harley Davidson' bike
In a 'Mary Quant' designer dress

Adjusting her black feather boa
He noticed an exposed tattoo
Delicately woven on her shoulder
That read 'Positive Parent'
'Don't worry, son,' she said
'It is part of my new two-week life-coach plan
That will change everything'

Her son forced a smile
As a man got off from the bike
In top hat and tails
And a pink bowtie
'Hi, I'm Solomon, her new guru
I think your mum is very cool'
'Don't worry, son,' she said
'It is step one, make an impact
Part of my two-week life-coach plan
That will change everything'

They were drinking champagne in the bar
When Solomon stood up and played a tune
On his 'Tony Dixon low 'D' flute'
Her son looked on in awe
As his mother started to sing 'Staying Alive'
'What are you doing, Mother?' he gasped
'Don't worry, son,' she said
'It is step two, get the life you want
Part of my two-week life-coach plan
That will change everything'

Seated in row 'F'
Though a little intoxicated
She produced from her handbag
An A4 piece of paper
In 'Dresden Yellow'
And started to write
With her 'Parker Profile' pen
'What are you doing, Mother?' he asked
'Don't worry, son,' she said
'I am composing a speech
It is step three, start succeeding
Part of my two-week life-coach plan
That will change my life'

J Ashford

The Windy Day

I'm feeling very low today
I'm sitting all alone
For Mr Wind he blew me down
And I've broken another bone.

He picked me up and threw me down
Just like a leaf upon the breeze
I thought *oh heck, where will I land?*
On my head or on my knees?

I lay there on the ground quite stunned
Not knowing what to do
A friendly voice said, 'Come on love
I'll take care of you.'

So now I'm a little lazy
I hope you can believe it's true
A car ran over my glasses
I lost an earring too.

But all has turned out OK
I'm feeling fine and grand
And after all that trouble
I only broke my hand.

Kathy French

Grateful

When you see what some people live with day by day
The fighting, the floods, the destruction of homes
And so many lives lost, young and old
We have cause to count our blessings every day
We can go where we please in Great Britain and Wales
Without fear of bombing or men with guns
Shooting at people, and children, regardless who they are
For what reason, no one knows
We should count our blessings each morning we wake
Healthy and able to do what we want
And not in a hospital bed with so much pain
And a future so bleak before you.

Margaret Stumpp

Blessings Bestowed

A troubled world which affects all races,
Sadness, despair upon millions of faces.
We were given a world to fulfil all our needs,
Now being destroyed by disruption and greed.
Life has become gloomy and for many so hard,
Wars raging, abuse, no respect or regard.
We sometimes feel nothing will brighten our day,
A battle to live, hard work and no play.
But, we should count our blessings and not despair,
Beauty abides and there *are* people who care.
To be wanted and loved by our families and friends,
Being able to help others and aid to them send.
Breathtaking beauty of jungles and seas,
Birds on the wing, a whispering breeze.
With nature around us and so much to give,
We should, count our blessings, live and let live.
Animal friends from large to a bee,
Flowers that sway and dance in the breeze.
Cotton-wool clouds, a sky of ice-blue,
Berries so bright and globules of dew.
At the end of the day a mantle of grey,
An ebony sky with diamonds displayed.
A gentle smile on the face of the moon,
Shafts of light that brighten the gloom.
The sun will rise, a ball of spun gold,
A jewel box for the world to behold.
The miracle of birth, a new baby's breath,
Yes, we should count our blessings and inwardly digest.
These are a few of the blessings bestowed,
We must be grateful for these from birth until old.

Ruth James

The Fun Way To Reach 100

(The New Scientist Magazine publishes research on how to live to be 100)

If you're going to reach 100, then you've got to be . . .
Positive and laugh a lot. Eat healthily.
Your brain, it needs exercise, a press-up or two,
Rise to the challenge of . . .
Oriental Sudoku.

You've gotta take some risks, learn to bungee jump,
See the bottle as half full and never get the hump.
You need to get some sunshine, till your skin feels sore,
Get her to rub the cream in. Get her to do it some more!
Your brain it needs exercise, a squat thrust or two,
Rise to the challenge of . . .
Oriental Sudoku.

Make a virtue of a vice, if you know what I mean,
And I have in mind your honey-love, not chocolate or ice cream.
Smile as you jog for miles and do not vegetate,
No use to you that TV set, switched on for hours till late.
Your brain it needs exercise, a sit-up or two,
Rise to the challenge of . . .
Oriental Sudoku.

When you've climbed your next mountain, been pot-holing just for fun,
Joined the circus as an acrobat and been fired from their gun.
Take a leaf from Jamie Oliver, be creative dans la cuisine,
Serve a meal that's truly wonderful with every ingredient ever seen.
Your brain it needs exercise, a pull-up or two,
Rise to the challenge of . . .
Oriental Sudoku.

Don't say it can't be done, check out the roller coaster ride,
Sign up for the thrill-a-minute, see if your pacemaker's on your side.
I know it may not be easy, I know we can't all succeed,
But trying it anyway will add years! Are we all agreed?
Your brain it needs exercise, a push-me-pull-you will do,
Rise to the challenge of . . .
Oriental Sudoku.

John Riddick

The Bay Of Tranquility

From Salen travel west along the narrow lochside road
Close on your left the sea with attendant cape and bay and promontory
Above, upon your right, the rugged hills and slopes clothed with trees
Birch and oak and Caledonian pine, larch plantations, spruce and other evergreens.

Thus for ten miles or so loch and road keep company
Then suddenly the road ascends and sharply turns away
And you find a broad headland and a wide and open view
And Sunart Loch has merged and flowed into the wide sea.
Here there's room to draw aside and absorb the beauty of the scene.

Before you the roadway wends its way across the steep and grassy slope
Below, the steep incline, the green and grassy meadow forming the shape of a horseshoe
And the bay itself clean and white, weed free
Where the gentle waves break into white ripples on the sand
The grassy slopes on either side rising green and smooth and clean.

Well above the water line and sacrosanct
The walled enclosure of the ancient cemetery
The old gravestones take you back to the dawn of time
When the sea was thoroughfare for friend and foe alike.
As for the denizens - who can say?
But they did well to lie forever in this lovely spot.

Joan Mackenzie

The Presence

There is no depth I can sink from you,
There is no height I can climb,
You're in my joys
And my anxious woes.

Before I fall, you are there to catch me,
Your arms of love encircle me,
From the deepest pit you rescue me,
You will not let me go.

Each whisper, each sob, is heard by you,
My innermost thoughts you know,
Your presence is always with me,
Wherever I may go.

Joan Thompson

Winter

Winter's here once again
The sky is full of icy rain,
The temperature is well below
I'm sure we'll soon get some snow.

Then the world will be transformed
Where the sheep and cattle roamed,
It will sparkle white like fairyland
As though the angels waved a wand.

I think of broth and winter food
And while I'm in a pensive mood,
I think of many times when I was young
Mother wrapped me up to protect my lungs.

And when we skated in the park
We stayed there till nearly dark,
I fell through once and got all wet
How they rescued me, I don't know yet.

I love the rain and wind and watery sun
I love to lie when day is done,
In my bed and listen to the wind and rain
Blowing hard down country lanes.

The trees are naked now, and very bare
The branches shiver and gone is the hare,
But will return in the spring
And then once more the birds will sing.

But back to winter and it's cold, cold days
The thunder and lightning and its electric rays,
I love to stand at the window at night
And listen to the thunder and watch the bright light.

No firework display can compete with nature's hand
I'm there till dawn, in my nightie I stand,
I'm thrilled with it all and the feeling it brings
I watch as the rubbish, across the garden, it flings.

Count Our Blessings

Then morning comes and it's quiet once more
Gone are the lights and the thunder's roar,
It's time to look forward to another day
Take the dog out to run and play.

The world is ticking like a clock
You can't hear it tick, you can't hear it tock,
But it functions in the same old way
It goes round and round day after day.

So if you're feeling down and sad
Go for a walk and just be glad,
That you are here to see it all
And don't you dare have the gall

To say it's not nice, this winter of ours
Look under the snow, you'll find little flowers,
Look at the sky and watch the clouds
Float across like big black shrouds.

Nature is wonderful, I can't stress enough
You want the smooth, so take the rough,
And maybe you'll see it in someone else's eyes
Like mine, as I ponder and look at the skies.

Felicity Pigtails

Alex Isn't Walking Yet

'Isn't Alex walking yet?'
'Surely he should be by now!'
'Is that his granny standing near?'
I could hear the whispered words
As I watched his tiny form.
Life is hard. My tears are real,
This noisy group, what do they feel?
I wonder, can they sense my pain?
Alex isn't walking yet! But . . .
A sudden lunge, arms outstretched,
I pick him up, a secret smile,
Life is now very much worthwhile!
I hold him close - he grabs my ear,
I put him down. He has no fear.
Together, we face another year.

Anne Leahy

Light At The End Of The Tunnel

When I first had to live alone
I found it hard but then
I got myself a new routine,
Went back to church again.

I laid the table for my meals
And would not have a tray.
I did enjoy a glass of wine
And do so to this day.

I went out every day I could
And, luckily, still drive.
So I could offer lifts or phone -
My friendships seem to thrive.

I set myself a challenge -
A day out on my own.
I booked a coach seat, going to Bath
And walked around alone.

My next step is to take a break
For maybe several days -
Enjoy a new experience
In many different ways.

There's gardening, music, reading books and other widows, friends,
Life beckons and the spring is near - I will not pity me.
I'm writing with the Lord's support who surely shapes our ends.

Jo Newman

Thanks

Thank God for the past
The good and the bad
The light and the dark
The bright and the grey
For light is brighter in dark
And grey can be calm.
Thanks too
For the might-have-been
That was not
But leaving a lift of the heart
In remembering.
Thank God for a life filled
With living and loving
With making mistakes
With weeping - and laughing.

Diana Good

England's Jewel

Winter is over
No more cold dark nights for me.
Lakeland in springtime is the place to be
Where the mountains touch the sky and sea.
Cascading waterfalls,
Walking through meadows,
Where drifts of daffodils grow,
A tapestry of yellow and green.
Trees are festooned with blossom.
A land of painters and poets
Art galleries are everywhere.
Touring Kendal and Keswick and Ullswater
There are so many places to explore.
Cruising on Windermere
A lake of pewter, slate and gold
Where oystercatchers, curlews and lapwings call.
Waves of silver diamonds caress the shore
Sunsets are a symphony of light and dark.
Where is this spectacular and romantic place?
Where else but Cumbria,
England's jewel.

Sandra Wood

I Am What I Am

I came with nothing in this world
Just a large smile as I embraced my mother's hold
As I faced life's trials and tribulations with fear
The smile has eventually diminished - completely disappeared
I recheck my thoughts and realise my ability
To communicate is an art
To read - a desire I was not born with
But developed with time, a habit lifelong
Guess what? I am writing this rhyme
My heart beats constantly
Representing me
It strengthens and encourages
Even find ways to analyse my motives
I have feelings
Whether sorrowing or rejoicing
I smile
For I am alive.

Angela Nevo Hopkins

Memories

Memories bring blessings untold,
God's greatest gift to Man, I'd say,
Memories to console, unfold
Or memories of joy displayed
- in such a happy face.

When searching for trifle old,
Letters of consolation found;
Memorabilia then is surely,
Source of many blessings sound
- and a contented heart.

Souvenirs are memories too
And can quite unexpectedly
Bring so many blessings new,
But tangibly and visibly
- can warm the very soul.

A postcard old or ribbon,
An invitation from years past
Prompting memories so dim,
But brought to mind, flowing fast:
- thank God for memories.

Janet Bowen

Winter Night

Even the dogs are quiet
And the voices of foxes still
Save for the whispering trees in the woods
And the wind upon the hill

No rowdy revellers rattle now
In the empty street below
For there is only the clear, cold frosty air
And a hint of coming snow

But the past still comes to torment me
With all its wherefores and whys
And sad eyes still come to haunt me
As they say their last sad goodbyes

Till sleep, the friend of the lonely
Comes to dry my inward tears
And the deep, sweet sound of silence
Falls at last on my waiting ears.

Doris Ginsberg

Our Friends

Slowly but surely
I'm pulling through,
The loneliness of bereavement
That left me in two.
Decisions and worries,
I've tried to cope alone,
Till friends rallied round
Saying, 'Don't be on your own.'
They've listened, they've advised,
Giving me strength to go on,
My smile is back, my worries
Hopefully gone.
This poem's to say I never
Forget friends,
You helped me in my hour of need,
Our friendship never ends.

Gwyneth Clarke

I Saw My First Snowdrops Today

I saw my first snowdrops today,
And they made my heart sing,
Pushing through the wet earth,
Heralding the spring.

The crocuses will soon appear,
In white, purple and yellow hue,
They're so bright and cheerful,
And seem to say 'We're here too'.

These are followed by daffodils,
On majestic stalks of green,
Golden trumpets blow in the breeze,
No fairer sight to be seen.

Tulips tall and slender,
Primroses nestle at their feet,
A galaxy of brilliant colour,
Waiting, the warm sun to greet.

The summer brings the roses,
Their fragrance fills the air,
Bees dance lightly among them,
Nestling to sup the nectar there.

I pause to take in this splendour,
It is repeated year after year,
To absorb with sight and senses,
And to know God's hand is here.

Josephine Herron

In The Mood

Feeling depressed, got no go
Unhappy and so full of woe!
So close your eyes, rest your brain
You've had your blessings again and again!
Let your mind drift back into the past
How good it was but went too fast.
Sun, sea, sand, meadows and hills
No worries, no work, no wretched bills!
The bus fare to school - you cheated and ran
Pocketing the money, bought sweets and a can!
Sitting exams, so pleased when you passed
Bursting with pride when parents asked!
Teenage, feeling guilty, Mum mustn't know
What you got up to, supposed not to go!
Falling in love, floating on cloud
Being so very good, sex not allowed.
The longed-for kiss, then married joy
Perhaps first a little girl, followed by boy.
Excitement when you got your own home
Knowing no more would you be alone.
Not rich, not poor, just in-between
What a lovely life this has been!
Of all your wishes, most came true
Happiness, success, prosperity too!
I took them for granted just like you!
Wonderful memories never will die
Everyone has them so that is why
You should count your blessings as above
Life is so good! So full of love.

Roselie B Mills

An Angel Touched

When spring flowers
Touch the winter snow,
When black boughs
Meet the golden globes of light
When ones are lost
At Christmas

An angel touched the snow.

Irene Patricia Kelly

Changes

Since the crash I'm different,
I absolutely know.
I look the same,
I dress the same,
From top of head to toe.

But now I often wonder,
Am I really, really here?
I feel the same,
I talk the same,
But my mind is very clear.

It's clouds that fascinate me now
And seagull cries above.
I see the same,
I hear the same,
But now I think with love.

A friendly conversation,
A gentle pat or smile.
I act the same,
I laugh the same,
But life's a little while.

Will it fade, this observation
Or dim as time flies by?
I pray the same,
I live the same,
Such blessings that are mine.

Jean M Hallam

Granny's Rocking

Granddaughters guide Granny to Markeaton Park, hide as
Granny swings on dangling ropes, hurl old limbs across the brook,
Nosy squirrels pause to look,
Granny crawls up muddy banks, granddaughters give thanks, Granny's in one piece and laughing, a brogue floats off down the stream, three head off for choc ice cream at the Orangerie,
A pot of tea for one, soggy Granny's full of fun,

Ban painful knees, arthritic hips mar this day of pleasure trips,
'til morrow we'll postpone the aches, Gran's return to gentle exercise, over 50s in the cool of a warm, inviting pool, Granny's structured once again in ordered swimming granny lanes
Splash.

Rosemarie Reeves

Lean On Me

Shoulders are for crying on,
Shoulders should be strong,
Shoulders can be shrugged,
Shoulders can be broad . . . and long.

Shoulders droop when you are sad,
Shoulders heave with laughter,
Shoulders tense when you are mad,
Shoulders ache in sport . . . and after.

My shoulders aren't strong,
Aren't broad and aren't long,
They sometimes ache and sometimes droop,
And shake a lot when I get croup.

But when I need some courage,
I put my shoulders back,
Narrow my eyes and take deep breaths,
Using all my bravery tack.

For you, my friend, they are always there,
Whenever you feel the need.
When your spirits are low
And you think your heart
Will break and continue to bleed.

Remember this. It is no con,
Shoulders are for crying on.

Annemarie

A Sort Of Quiet

Far from conflicts
Of all kind
That we met
In human mind
Lies oasis near the sea
Like a mirror it can be
And the waves
Like sound of music
When tuned in
With babies'
Joy, cry and laughter
We find harmony
And happiness that lasts.

Barbro Pattie

Almost Good

Have you ever stopped to wonder,
When we hear such awful news,
It's our kin that takes the thunder,
As we shout and scream our views.

What can we do to help them?
Send them money, take a part.
It would make a lovely emblem,
If it came right from the heart.

Some of us will give support
And go to fight the cause,
Others they will think they ought,
But at the outset, they will pause.

It's nice to go and give a hand,
Support someone in need,
It means alone they will not stand,
With help to take the lead.

But all in all with afterthought,
No problems do we face,
For we relax in homes we've bought,
And live a gentle pace.

J T Bright

Look Around

Look around and you will find blessings abound.
Sun, moon, stars and gentle warming of the Earth
After winter's severest frosts.
Soon the seeds and bulbs resting in the soil
Will blaze forth heralded by the snowdrops, January's blessing.
However we abuse our precious Earth,
She comes back to help us.
Life stirs everywhere, the birds sing,
Nest-building starts and new lambs skip happily after their mothers.
However cruelly the world seems to treat us -
Look around!
Nature will provide solace and healing
And a fresh and happy start for the future.

Ivy Allpress

Star Flowers

How the fog outlines blurred
The island's distant headlands,
Flickering, clustering circles.
The darkened wings and black eyes
Over the rims of wave crests,
Rock needle points, moonlight and starlight
Wild for centuries.
Under the belling clouds, after the full
Evening sunburst
With breaking perfumed mist had achieved
A giant flower gold gleaming galaxy
Then swept and filled the lofty pines
Over the soft blooms sweet sleeping
Angels blessings.
As stream kissed cloudlets are reflected
In the willow pond,
The embracing wind dances in the flower crown
And the diamond dewdrops kaleidoscopes
A thousand jewelleries.

Edward Tanguy

Blessings

Family, friendship,
The warmth of our home.
Time when we need it
For being alone.
The ground that we walk on,
The air which we breathe,
Eyes that we see with,
Our minds which perceive.
All that's around us,
The sun, sea and sky.
Answers to questions
When asking just why.
The newness of babies,
Their making, with love.
All of these things
Are a true treasure trove.
In the millions, these gifts
Then abound, for you and me.
Just open your heart.
You will certainly see
Happiness there.

Meg Wilson

Springtime

Springtime!
Season of nature's awakening
After the cold days of winter.

Sunshine,
Beckoned me into a woodland
To walk on velvet green carpet
Bestrewn with the bright flowers of spring.

Silence,
Breathtaking in its intensity
Compelled me to gaze in wonder
At avenues of tall, stately trees.

Singing!
Melodious chorus of birdsong
Called me to join in thanksgiving
To God, for the miracle of life.

Margaret Haining

Blessings

Have you counted your blessings today?
Or are you too busy and time's slipped away?
Have a look round you and you will find,
There's lots of blessings we can all bring to mind.

Open your eyes - what do you see?
The dawn of a new day with many hours free?
Or are you a pessimist and see only dull and drear sights?
Look round again, I'm sure you'll find light.

What are these blessings you're talking about?
Too numerous to mention, but here are a few:
Look outside, wet or fine, the grass is green,
The sky may be cloudy-grey, but soon will be blue.

People are busy, but give them a smile,
I'm sure they'll return it, so there'll be miles of smiles.
Look at the mother with a new baby, girl or boy,
Her eyes full of love, her heart full of joy.
She is so happy and surprised at what the Lord has done,
As the old saying goes.

W Mary Pearce

Beauty

Walking through life on a spring day
The smell of the country wafts our way
Daffodils are glorious, a sight to see
Blossom appearing on the apple tree

Lambs are skipping up and down
There's a gentle breeze all around
Not a cloud is visible in the sky
And life is great for you and I

Let's take delight in such simple pleasure
These are the days we should treasure
For the beauty here on Earth
Is surrounding us in its girth.

Sandra Noyes

Make Yourself Some Sunshine

It's that corner of the year
When all life feels bleak and drear
And the springtime seems a million miles away
Don't just sit around and mope
Now's not the time to give up hope
Try and put a little sunshine in your day
Bring some plants into the room
Let their colour and perfume
Lighten your heart - send winter blues away
So now get that paintbox out
And then splash some paint about
Paint yourself a picture, put it on display
Plus some bright cushions will add clout
Let your curtains have a shout
And most likely they'd be telling you hooray!
Take a look now in a glass
You'll see what has come to pass
Where once was a frown - a smile goes all the way
So don't mind how bad it seems
Just hang on to all your dreams
Let your life be full of sunshine every day.

Daphne Lodge

The Four Seasons

I look forward to the four seasons with rapt anticipation
Viewing changes they bring forth with avid expectation.
Spring promising new life always arrives on time
Showering the countryside with colour so sublime.
The yellow of the daffodils, such a welcome sight
Accompanied by tulips and crocuses to delight.
Waking trees shoot forth new leaves with blossoms to adorn
Birds sing in perfect harmony at the first glimpse of dawn.

Summer follows all too soon, young animals abound
Baby rabbits, lambs and cubs scamper all around.
Whilst swallows feed their hungry young, many insects they must catch
This applies to other birds when their eggs do hatch.
Flowers grow in abundance, their perfume fills the air
Bringing intense pleasure, a gift for all to share.

Autumn creates a changing scene, leaves turn to red and gold
Berries replacing blossom, their beauty to behold.
Chestnuts in abundance hide amongst the leaves
Attract a busy squirrel, a bonanza to retrieve.
Ripened fruit is gathered in, the harvest's in full swing
Preparing for the winter, who knows what it will bring.

The dazzling white of winter, a season of deep contrast
Frost glitters in the sunlight, snow is falling fast.
Children playing snowballs, having lots of fun
Down hills on their toboggans, a mini Cresta run.
Hibernating wildlife escape the winter they abhor
'Til spring in all its glory returns to reign once more.

Doreen E Kowalska

Hollyhocks

Hollyhocks, your beauty is there to cheer our way,
Stately and tall you stand midst gravel, rocks and clay.
Until this lovely summer, vandals have slashed you down,
But this year they've wrought havoc in other parts of town.

This year they had decided to vandalise our hall,
With toxic dust and water on tables, chairs and wall.
Our brave united stalwarts with Hoover and with broom,
Spent many hours working hard to clear the dirt and gloom.

And so the beauty of God's love
Will triumph over all,
Like hollyhocks in radiant hues
Will bloom whatever befall.

Monica Hurdwell

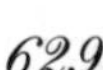

Childhood Memories

When I look back and remember loved ones no longer here
I think of the laughter and love that we shared
I was the youngest of a large family
My father was dead, just my mother, sister, brothers and me.
We were at war, but our life was still good
We had fun as all children should
Each of us had jobs to do every day
Before going to school or out to play.
Our holiday was a trip to the seaside one day every year
On a Sunday school outing with friends all there
I remember the barbed wire guarding the beach
Keeping the enemy, we hoped, well out of reach.

At Christmas a party at school with a present off the tree
Where us children put on a play for our families
We respected the teachers and the village policeman was just fine
For thoughts of the cane or a slap round the head made us toe the line.
I count my blessings in so many ways
For these lovely memories of my childhood days.

Millicent Hewitt

Almost There!

Every cloud has a silver lining, they say,
When darkness comes and obstacles block your way,
Just look for the light at the end of the tunnel.

Hope is the anchor that we all cling to,
When seas are rough and dark, hope it always find you,
Lifting you up, in warm, strong arms.

Feeling alone, no one seems to care,
Courage rises from within when you are least aware,
Giving you strength to face the angry mob.

And when 'The Black Dog' has you in its jaws,
Beautiful peace will come to open up the doors,
Soothing your troubled soul.

Walking into the wind, shoulders hunched, tired head bowed,
You can almost hear the cheering of a watching crowd,
'Almost there!', 'Don't give up!', 'Aim for the goal!', 'Press on for the prize!'

Sue Lake

A Bright Shining Cross In The Sky

Lord, give me words and inspiration.
I need Your help and illumination
To write of the cross so shining and bright,
That cross in the sky so full of light.

Perhaps I was only eight or ten,
The day was clear without any rain.
Outside my father's house at play,
My mother inside cooked the food for the day.

Looking up, I saw to my great delight,
A cross in the sky so shining and bright.
What excitement to see that cross in the sky,
All light, so huge and so very high.

Much brighter than the setting sun.
Hastily to my mother I run
And tell her to come out and see
And she shares the joy of that cross with me.

But that light went dim as I grew older
And my mind forgot and my heart grew colder.
Yet always to me the Lord's been kind
And only in Him can we, new life, find.

I see Him dying on that Cross,
Then risen again to repair our loss.
He's alive from the dead, it still says to me:
'My Lord and my God' for eternity.

David Shrisunder

Opinions

Everybody has an opinion to make
Whether it be right or wrong,
Sometimes it may cause an argument
No one's opinion is ever strong.

But that is not to say though
An opinion is better kept to yourself,
Sometimes you have to give your opinion
And maybe accept another opinion as help.

Everybody has an opinion to give
So respect them for who they are,
Don't let opinions break a friendship
Because our opinion is just who we are.

Niall McManus

It's Up To You

You've been offered a life more abundant, not lack
So whatever you put into life you'll get back

You can set your antennae to 'happy' or 'sad'
Always watching for blessings or locked on to 'bad'

This doesn't just happen - the choice is all yours
Whatever your problems, you're not a lost cause

You can open your arms or close your mind
Seek to encourage or undermine

You can smell the sweet roses or flee from their thorns
Drink in the sun or anticipate storms

You can bask in good memories or rue the past
Wave your flag gladly or fly at half-mast

You can glow with a passion or burn up with rage
Give just for joy or demand a high wage

You can heal other's wounds or reopen your own
Engage with your neighbour or stay quite alone

You can learn from the wise or listen to rumour
Laugh long and loud or stay locked in bad humour

You can travel in hope or put up with your lot
Enjoy all you have or list all you have not

You can marvel at nature or see only strife
And whichever you choose will reflect in your life

It's your choice to see rainbows or just curse the rain
To be one of God's radiators or a drain.

Helen Camplin

It's A Wonderful World

Grey mist surrounding the autumn trees, nature's jewel
Box, that's what the artist paints and sees, all the colours
Look superb, can you explain? Is there a name?

The grass with the dew shining so bright, equivalent
To the stars in the sky at night, church on the hill
Looking forlorn, won't see a soul till Sunday morn.

All will change in an hour or so, might be the same
Tomorrow but we do not know, hopefully the sun
Will shine the rest of the day, leaving us with a lovely
Light as it fades away.

Tomorrow it might be snow or frost, but we can stand
And look, there is no cost, nature and its wonders
Have always interested me, but some folks just go
Through life and never look or see.

Anthony Hull

Count Our Blessings

(January 15th 2004 - January 15th 2007)

It happened oh, so very fast,
The ambulance, Brian and me, aghast.
We didn't know what was wrong,
Finally decided, they weren't long.
I had a stroke, down the right side,
Requiring care and need a guide.
Nurses and doctors were there to prod,
Scans and scopes; and so was God.
He was there to comfort me,
As I lay in bed and drank my tea.
Brian brought chess, as I played half,
The 'bishop', wrong place, I could still laugh.
The nurses in the ward were helpful and keen
As I tried to stand with a tall 'stroke' machine.
Cousins, friends gave mags I couldn't read,
To talk, do numbers, or letters or feed.
As I looked out the window, rabbits were there,
Flowers and shrubs and grass fore'er.
A wheelchair was sent for, there was no doubt,
June came along, I was going out.
Since then and now, I've come a long way,
Such a lot has happened but One Shining Ray.
I was shy, now I'm not, God made me fight
For everything good and purposefully right.

Anne Black

Brian's Laughter

(For Irene)

A light went out in our lives today,
Someone we loved passed away.
Never complaining, no matter what,
The jokes and the laughter were all that we got.
And though we don't see him,
He's still very near.
Just mention his name
And smiles will appear,
For he's left us his gift of laughter,
Not tears.
How far is it to Heaven,
I wonder, is it far?
For every time I think of you,
I'm sure that's where you are.

Patricia Watling

Blessings

Our lives are blessed with many things
That money cannot buy
The smell of earth that follows rain
A sunset in the sky
The soft caress of evening breeze
A walk 'neath stars so bright
The fragrant smell of blossom
Upon a summer night.
A woodland glade with bluebells
The smell of new-mown hay
Crystal drops on spiders' webs
Where autumn sunbeams play
The song of wind among the trees
Sweet flowers that bloom in spring
The comfort of the sun's warm kiss
The peace that prayer can bring
The comfort of a loved one's hand
When you're weary and you falter -
So many blessings fill our lives
These things will never alter.

Vi M Whitehead

I Have A Guardian Angel

I have a guardian angel,
Watching over me,
Day and night she's by my side,
Though I cannot see.
She warns me of all dangers
And keeps me safe and sound,
She stands before Our Father,
Where our hope and faith are found.
She knows when we are happy,
Also when we are sad,
She knows of all the sweet dreams
And nightmares that we've ever had.
She will always be beside me,
For that's what Our Lord commands,
She will forever watch over me,
For that's what Our Lord demands.
You too can have a guardian angel,
To keep watch over you,
Day and night she will be by your side
And take good care of you.

Shirley Sewell

Tipple To Lift Your Spirits

If you need an incentive to help you rise just after dawn,
There is a solution that will prevent you feeling forlorn.

Drag yourself through your ablutions and stumble down every stair,
In the kitchen, plug in and be ready for the treat that will make this early hour easier to bear.

The fact is, this beverage, morning, afternoon and night is a universal panacea,
And doesn't cause the brain to be fuddled, unlike the effect of alcohol, which gives us artificial cheer.

And at a mere few pence a pint, it suits every wallet and purse,
To praise its every aspect is the reason I've put pen to paper to compose this verse.

Its advantages are multitude and whenever a pot is brewing, we know smiles are due,
Which is preferable to the murderous rage incited when giving rum to a pirate crew.

I applaud this drink because for me, every mouthful is a tiny sip of whoopee,
Anxiety is eased and I count my blessings whenever I consume, a refreshing, hot cup of tea.

Joy R Gunstone

Blessings

So, how many blessings
Have we each one?
Stop, think and count,
It will amaze everyone.

Can you walk and talk?
Can you hear and see?
In control of your mind,
Possess a good memory?

Arms, hands and fingers,
Are they free from pain?
Do your feet and legs move?
Can they take the strain?

Are you blessed with friends and family
And, still breathing?
Well, greet a new day!
Thank God for all your blessings
And good health for others pray.

Stella Bush-Payne

His Timing

Another day -
Another way of cracking nut on head -
Sit down, take breath -
A mini prayer; you'll see -
You'll be astounded, bowled back to
Witness such supreme awareness
Love and timing. His timing.
Waves winding over beach.
Wind wafting where there's been no air.
Rain rattling windows where once was parched -
Brilliant blue -
Cotton-wool clouds -
Daisies down meadows -
Super sun glinting down -
Thro' tiniest of town.
Fluffy, sleepy sheep -
Cows a-yawning.
Pigs a-pottering.
Flights of freedom - birds a-soaring.
So when?
His timing - know now.

Jac C Simmons

Child Of Mine

(To my daughter, Stephanie Clare)

Gentle spirit of my dawning day
Child of mine,
Your smiles the rising sun
A radiance that shines throughout my life,
Your laughter light and shade of passing clouds
Playing with the daylight hours,
Your eyes the summer skies, eternally blue
Vibrant with fluttering dreams of
Childish thoughts . . .
Share them with me,
O child of mine . . .
And when the angels call to sleep,
And sunlight weaves moonbeams 'pon your lips,
What secrets are sung in their lullabies?
Do stars take your hand in the realm of night
Flying upon waves of enchanted light
Rocking you softly in the cradle of slumber
Warmly wrapped in fluttering dreams of childish thoughts?
O share them with me,
Dear child of mine . . .

Carolyn Smith

End Of Term Play

As Christmas time at school drew near
The music teacher made it clear
That choir selection soon must start,
So every child should have a part,
To sing a carol, or to read,
One of the lessons they would need
To help to make the Christmas play
To show to parents on the day.
So, class by class, to make a choice
She listened for the perfect voice,
Most were tuneful, but three boys
Made groaning sounds, an awful noise,
But, not to cause them misery,
The 'Three Wise Men,' she said, 'you'll be.'
Which meant their singing voice was 'out',
They only had to stand about
And bring three presents to the King,
And let the other children sing.
The big night came, and parents waited
With eager eyes, anticipated
Just what their darling child could do
A poem, story, song or two.
The Wise Men came, joy to behold,
Dressed in blue and red, and gold,
Each mother proudly raised her head,
'A most important part,' they said.

Derek H Tanton

Christmas Eve, 1968

Its thin crescent shape
Hung low in the
Wintry air, that cold
December night.
Hard, sparkling rime
And vocal carol-strains
Heralded the 'Sally-Ann's'
Blessings 'neath their
Lantern lights.
Opposite the neon-lighted
Supermarket, queues were
Forming by the bus stop . . .
Soon, people would be
Hurrying home.
That night, three spacemen
Journeyed deep into space,
Destined to orbit
The moon.

Terrence St John

Bramble

They say no prayers for him at Friday Mass
but Bramble the dog is on his pavement,
chin on paws and looking for perks.
In the High Street, shoppers scurry like mice
but Bramble? Only his eyes make movement
by the shop where his master works.

The bell rings at Friday Mass but Bramble
has only his tennis ball to offer,
waiting for people to throw it.
When they do, those who walk at an amble,
stop and straighten as if from a fever
and watch him race to retrieve it.

So his days are spent, through Christmas shopping
and noisy children coming home from school:
Bramble the dog chasing a ball.
His tail bristling and his left ear flopping,
till he, stretched out, safe within his own scale,
takes pride in something none will spoil.

Silent people, strolling from Friday Mass,
turn into the High Street and see Bramble
outside his shop, not forgetting.
And new rain, hitting the pavement like Morse,
will not move him or make him dissemble.
Bramble and his ball, still waiting.

Ian Caws

Bedtime

When I can't get off to sleep
And lie awake for hours
Even counting boring sheep
And maybe dreaming of flowers.

I then try counting all the blessings that I've had
Like health, love, family and all the things that make me glad.
To be alive and sharing all the things that come my way
Then, would you believe, eventually sleep comes to me anyway.

Patricia Elvins

He Who Made All Things Good In His Time

Everyone's here for a purpose
It takes time to know what it is
Discipline, training and practise
Experience is ne'er wasted or missed

You'll find you'll have to take risks
Get hurt, be kept waiting or fail
For years, while you feel unsure
Which is your road, your peg or your rail

Carry on with the job that you have
Grow in practise and learning and love
It's not wasted, just wait and you'll see
You're being watched over from way up above

You'll get there because He has said
'I have made you all,' for a reason
So try different jobs or pursuits
Pray often . . . wait . . . in due season.

Petronilla Cockin

Thank You, God

For myriad stars in a dark velvet sky
For the grace of the gulls as they float by
For the rainbow bridge from Cowal to Craigmore
A sight we've seen many times before
For our feathered friends who share our crops
For the secretive deer who retreat to the tops
For the sweet notes of songsters perched up high
For a loving daughter who keeps a watchful eye
For the privilege of a busy, happy life
For the peace of Bute away from strife
For a cosy home with view over the Clyde
Where Beth and I in retirement abide
For the special gift of great, grand waens
And families who to keep in touch take pains
For the most important blessing of my life
Fifty-five years shared with my beloved wife
Lord, my heartfelt thanks I raise to Thee
You have indeed been good to me!

Deryck Southgate

My Mansion

We lived in a parlour terrace,
Complete with blinds and lace,
With a long hall at the entrance,
Leading to a long staircase.
My mother sometimes let me play,
In a corner by the door.
And it became my mansion
Though it was on the floor.
The fireguard was my trellis,
A cushion was my chair,
A shoebox was my cradle
With my dolly lying there.
Oh, how I loved my mansion,
Though only four feet wide,
But in my imagination,
It was bigger than the tide.
Well now I'm in a chalet
With a wide sweep for a drive,
And a lovely squared bay window,
Complete with louvre blinds.
But I'd trade my lovely chalet,
Garage, garden, car and all,
Just to go back to my mansion
Where I played when I was small.

Ina Higginson

Brandy And Ben

My two dogs both go for their jog,
Brandy is rough and ready,
Ben is calm and steady.
Brandy gets a stick,
Oh, is going to perform a trick.

No chewing it up in a bit!

Then taking a jumping fit
They two decide to fight,
Oh, what a sight.
Brandy is not light,
Ben brings him down to the ground,
With a thump and gives him a bump.

Marie Coyles

The Sport Of Kings

Some oppose the sport of hunting
Where the fox becomes the prey
Forgetting all the harm they do
Stealing chicks by night and day

They feel sorry for the victim
And think the sport should cease
I wonder would they feel the same
When watching performing fleas?

For three weeks they've been trained
A bicycle to ride
Then robed in ballet dress
They hop from side to side

Their standard food is blood
Which they love themselves to suck
But now it's served up for them
Which needs no joy or pluck

They love to live together
In cats and dogs to sting
I wonder if an animal lover
Would accept this sort of thing?

And so we have to ask ourselves
Where do we draw the line
Twixt animal and insect
And life of any kind?

Bridget Monahan

A Warning

Beware of men who make a fuss
And think most things are obvious;
(Some, keen to shatter our illusions
May also jump to false conclusions).

Who was it who first said that God
Was in men's minds - and with a nod -
Said pain and woes of our existence
Made *us* make *Him* for our 'assistance'!

Oh, let us never be deceived
Like Dr X who once believed
He'd hit the nail right on the head,
But missed - and hit his thumb instead.

Anthony Manville

Wishes Good And Sad

Young brothers and sister,
Decide when grown up,
My wish will be sister,
To own my own home.
Mine is for a car of my own,
To take you all about.
Mine is for sons to protect me,
Just like my brothers do.
One more brother's wish,
Is to be a big soldier.
One little brother left,
To have your bedroom, sister.
Wishes all carried out
And all fulfilled,
Some right down to flowers and shapes
For Heaven's rest home.
A dartboard for one,
A filled heart for another,
Just a spray for me, sister.
Well baby brother, no flowers,
Or cars, no service for me,
You all did it through my days
Of young and middle aged.
So baby brother, fifteen months time,
You get a good, hard-earned wish.
Old age pension and still have me,
Seventy-three isn't a bad age,
I can still peel the spuds,
Parsnips, carrots and onions.
The way to a man's heart
Is through his stomach.

M Clark

I Did Love Them

If I never find love,
Always remember the family that brought me here.
Remember those loved ones I never thanked,
One unkind, forgotten December.
Always remind yourself and don't shed a tear
If I never found love
I knew you loved me, were here
In all my selfishness and unkindness
Amidst my dumb and blindness
Remember kindly, I did love them.

Barry Powell

Nature

The sun cascading on a grassy knoll, filters through the leaves,
As birds chirp and chatter idly, carried on a summer breeze.
Beneath the canopy of blue and a multitude of green, I walk barefoot
On dew-covered grass to the silver, bubbling stream.
I sit and watch the darting minnows as they play a game of hide-and-seek
Amongst the moss-laden pebbles, only inches from my feet.
I sigh and take a deep breath, meadow-sweet the scented air.
Hares are running swiftly, they tumble as they leap,
Acknowledging the sunshine which has lulled them softly from their sleep.
Far off in the distance, cows feed upon the grass,
Their tails twitching fervently to keep the flies at bay.
I spy the old church steeple, surrounded by tall trees and the clock tower on the hill,
Whose bronze fingers have turned green.
I see the ploughman in his fields and I can smell the heavy earth,
And as the sun beats down upon my back, I whisper a silent prayer -
If God is to be found anywhere, then it surely must be here.

R T Clark

So Lucky

I don't need assistance
Or help to be fed
To put on my clothes
Or tilt back my head

I don't need to call you
To tidy my hair
Or use a stair-lift
To get down the stairs

I've no need for tablets
To help me survive
No transplanted organs
To keep me alive

No doctors or nurses
Surrounding my bed
No constant pain
So I wish I was dead

I'm able to see you
To walk by your side
To hold you and love you
So lucky am I.

Ray Perkins

Count Your Blessings

How often have you felt sad, and feel life has passed you by
And looking back at memories only makes you cry?
Often when you look back, and start to reminisce,
Suddenly you realise, is there something you have missed?

Seems you have forgotten all the happy times you have had,
But what you must remember, the good outweigh the bad.
Think of all the people who are far worse off then you,
Take the time to look around, you will find that it is true.

Wealth is not just being rich, it is the love you have inside,
It's the love of those around you, try and carry it with pride.
Be proud of all that you have achieved and do not be dismayed,
Life is but a game of chance and is the way in which it's played.

So count your blessings every day and put them in one heap
And throw away the worries, those you need not keep.
All of us, some time in our lives, have had a cross to bear,
Most important thing for us, is never to despair.

Be strong, be brave, be positive and keep an open mind,
Be proud of who you are, and remember to be kind.
So count your blessings every day, make it a thing to do,
And don't forget that quite nearby, there is someone far worse off than you.

Joan Morris

What A Wonderful World We Live In

I wake up in the morning to the birds calling
Often the raindrops are falling
Sometimes we are on our mooring
Trees swaying to and fro, saying hello
Their roots stretching deep below
The swans moving with the flow
The farmers' wives making the dough
The early morning call of the crow
What a wonderful world we live in
I am counting my blessings, trying not to live in sin
And drink that bottle of gin
I am counting my blessings into it heart and soul
Running alongside the foal
Out to reach my goal
I must not tread on that mole or fall in that hole
What a wonderful world we live in.

Maureen Butcher

Jesus Said

Jesus said:
'Come follow me
Do not follow any other.

I am
Your God, your King
And Everlasting Friend
Your Teacher and your Brother.'

Jesus said:
'I am
The Way, the Truth,
The Life Eternal,
Your Father and your Mother.

You come follow Me
Do not follow any other.'

Jesus said:
'Be born again
Become a new creation.

I am
The life for those who do,
For I have chosen you,
Your Lord and closest relation.'

Jesus said:
'Walk in the light,
The truth will set you free.

I am
The Light of Revelation,
Walk not the darkness of disbelief
But in the light with Me.
Place your footsteps close to Mine,
I am always very near,
My love will always on you shine.

Come walk in the light,
Walk in the light with Me.'

Joan Ibell

Notions On A Day

Some days are dull and gloomy, when all aches and pains appear
Your thoughts just seem to match the clouds, low, grey and drear
Don't sit procrastinating, on a downward spiral you will go
Get up, do something useful, tidy cupboards, clean the windows,
Wash the floor, phone a friend, arrange a meeting, write a letter
Go to the shop
On the way give passers-by a smile, even do some skips, or even hop
Soon as your spirits brighten, think of pleasant incidents
Sunrays piercing through clouds, colours of flowers and their scents
Little birds a-hopping, so grateful for the crumbs
The red breast of a robin, children laughing with their chums
So many things to cheer you, a breeze undulating through a grassy lea
Dewdrops trembling along a web, sunlight dancing on the sea
Kind words, an understanding look, arms clasped in a warm embrace
Then miraculously, of your depression there seems to be no trace
Savour each delightful moment, enfold each thought with love
Give a sincere prayer of thanks to God who gives guidance from above.

Marjorie Leyshon

Mentia

The scattered wisdoms of my life play out
on an ultraviolet screen. These truths and
deepenings, are seen in the eyes of the willing,
able, and the ably infused. There's an inconsistency
in the artistry of many men, they coax the worst from
people. But like a blue-red flower left to bask in
brilliant sunlight, the fury of invention and life stays
with me as ever.
  My heart speaks a language of laughter,
love and hopeful learning, but dreams can only
be quantified in sure actions. As those loop-
filled memories spill and re-spill like the froth
on the height of a spume of boiling water,
I'll find my way back to the heart of my own
loving intention. And with the hopes and dreams
of a man entering the brilliant reality of
real life, I'll find my way, and stay whole . . .
hopefully.

D Finlay

Faith

Once I had nothing;
Nothing to live for, hard work and no reward,
Continuing ill health, nothing to ease the pain and misery,
Felt I could not look forward.
Gradually, began to have faith,
Faith in myself, in God, in life,
Don't know how it began,
But gone was all the strife.

Began to write poetry, and prose,
With a fair amount of success,
Went to church, my life I began to bless.
At this late stage in my life,
Have begun to live,
No longer sit in doom and gloom,
Feel as if I want to give.

The loneliness, and isolation, seem to have left me,
There is beauty in everything I see.
Have been to Bible class,
Enjoy the discussions we have there.
Feel as if I make a contribution,
No longer have problems I can't bear.
Listen to problems of others,
Feel I'm with sisters and brothers.

Not self-satisfied, just have reason
To enjoy life now.
Can just sit and listen to good music,
Enjoy writing, am happy doing my own thing.
Do not understand the person I used to be,
To be in the doldrums is not now me.

Want to be kind to all people and give,
If this is living with Jesus,
Pray that my faith will live.
And all the blessings that helped me mend,
Will stay with me till the end.

Olive Young

My Cancer (How I Fought It And Won)

It should have been a new century, new beginning, a new year
I was having trouble with my prostate and felt a chill of fear
Went to see a doctor who said I needed a test
Hospital sent for me, my partner wished me all the best
Sitting in the waiting room, I was the last on the list
When I was told I had cancer, my eyes clouded over in mist
I had to change my lifestyle and give the treatment a go
Or I was going to die, this I do know
My partner was a solid rock, told me I needed to fight
Would not let me give up, said we'd be alright
For five long years, through hope and despair
She was with me all the way, even felt the pain I bear
With my good days when I was up, and bad days when down
We would share laughter and joy, even the odd frown
Some days her being with me, I forgot I was ill
Keeping me on an even keel, helping my days to fill
My partner I owe everything, for me being here
If not for her, I don't think I would have fought this fear
But fight I did, and I am able to tell this tale
To all of you who suffer from cancer, fight like a blowing gale.

(I do count my blessings, every one, every day.)

Robert Henry

Hope And Faith

When you feel down
and things seem out of reach.
Do not despair
pray and hope
for better times.
It will bring
a ray of light
to glimmer
in the darkness;
reach out in faith,
pray and hope.

Penny Kirby

The cows are coming down the road, the clock strikes half-past four
The light be only just enough, 'twas dark an hour afore.
An' farmer says, 'Get 'long wi 'ee,' mid many a nonesuch word
An' thwacks his stick agin o' them and ricochets the herd.

They amble by and downalong, a-through the village street
Their phantom shapes a memory o' ways now obsolete.
Whence from the milking-stall becomes the clank of chain and churn
The blare of cattle, and all that, that makes the sleeper turn.

Methinks now, Daisy, Cowslip, May, and Buttercup live on
Those gentle beasts indigenous to Ebenezer John.
Yea, Farmer John, I see thee now, thy crookéd staff in hand
Thy slouched hat on thy head askant, wi' feather-boa band.

A snippet of the countryside in ev'rybody's eye
A yeoman, who's a-family that's been yer years abye.
A medieval farm was thine and many velds beyond,
The water chute, the pigeon cote, the school and church and pond.

I see thy pedestrian gait, in corduroys and smock,
Thy wind-blown, craggy, bearded face, as supine as thy stock.
'Get 'long wi' ee,' thou taps a rump, the straggler do start -
How sad that time despoiled such a rich Arcadian heart.

Derek Haskett-Jones

Dreaming

I was thinking the other day
of how hard life can be,
how each day is a struggle
and how I'd like to break free.
I'd dream I won the lottery
and how my life would change,
a quaint house in the country
an open fire in the range.
Maybe a couple of horses,
roaming free on the land,
how life would be different,
if our fate was planned.
Then I took a look around me
and realised that I'm quite blessed,
and that dreaming is the antidote
for when you're feeling stressed.

Anne Leeson

Dream Of A Lifetime

(This poem is dedicated to my young brother, who died aged 29 on January 1st 1969. A book of my poetry was left in The Church Of St George in the Pines, Banff, Canada)

On a road in Banff, I met a lady in white,
The road was empty, no one in sight.
'I'm on a pilgrimage,' I said,
'To find a church to which I've been led.'

She looked at me, and her face just beamed,
To England, she'd been on such a quest it seemed.
We had the same empathy, I could see the signs,
As I asked her the way to St George in the Pines.

The tiny church was quiet, I felt at ease in this place,
As I called to mind my young brother's face.
A prayer was said and a memory made,
Of a young man who at rest is laid.

He'd intended to emigrate and start a new life,
When forty years ago, I was a young mother and wife.
In this life, his dream went unfulfilled,
When fate took a hand and he was cruelly killed.

I'm back at home now, it seems so far away,
The little church in the pines where I knelt to pray.
But, a little bit of my brother is there I feel,
When I went to Canada and living the dream was real.

Anne Roberts

A Dream Of Heaven

Is there a Heaven for long-lost trees,
For meadows of buttercups gold?
For hedges of hawthorn, snowy and sweet
Which we children knew of old?
Those halcyon summers of seven to ten
When we played with never a fear,
Nor thought of the murder in Flanders' fields
And the 'Kaiser's War' so near?
We heard of death, but the Lord of Life
Who rose on Easter Day
Two thousand years past, still rules the Earth,
And yearly bids us say,
'God so loved the world that He gave His Son'
That we in the midst of strife,
Should no longer fear, as death draws near,
But join Him in endless life.

Kathleen M Hatton

Hey Ho, The Wind And The Rain

A malevolent wind whipped my face,
As I struggled home in the torrential rain.
Cars took a perverse delight in driving through puddles,
Drenching me in the process, adding to my misery.

Counting my blessings was not foremost in my mind,
As I battled against the elements, relentlessly unkind.

Then I saw him, huddled in a doorway,
His thin pinched face and lacklustre eyes,
Denoting his down-and-out status, his sense of despair,
Rejected by society, not deemed a deserving case.

Guiltily, I thought of home awaiting me, with food, light and heat,
How blest was I compared to those sleeping on the street.

When sorrows overwhelm us, blessings seem far away,
But they will come, often in surprising, insignificant ways.
The smile of a stranger, the smell of newly mown hay,
The melodious song of a blackbird, a golden sunset.

Lord, Your goodness is such that when we cannot sleep,
Counting our blessings takes longer than counting sheep.

A M Drever

A Cascade Of Blessings

The blessings began when the ambulance came
Two knocks on the door and they called me by name
Tenderly stretchered and carried at speed
The journey so urgent no one must impede.
X-rayed with precision and handled with care
Throughout the proceedings the nurses were there
A trip to the theatre, anaesthetic applied
Always the attendants were there by my side.
The surgeons, the process of healing began
Confirmed as successful by the following scan
Greetings cards arrived from friends far and near
Blessings they intended my spirit to cheer.
The love of my family each day was expressed
Showing me truly how much I am blessed.
Count my blessings? I learned that I should
And starting that moment I vowed that I would.
Within it all was the sign of God's love
For all of Earth's blessings come down from above.

Eric Bentley

Blessings Counted

I start gloomily another day
With yet another bill to pay
No money have I to settle the account
And so my depression begins to mount
The bathroom's unfinished, the walls are bare
I need so much, it's so unfair
The kitchen wall is damp and bleak
There is no carpet beneath my feet
There is so much I want to do
That I am just unable to
I need new clothes, I need new shoes
My hair's a mess, I have the blues
The money I need to end my plight
Out of my reach and out of my sight
And as I wallow in my misery
Only the depths of despair I see
And then a voice inside my head it shouted
Have you today your blessings counted?
And so, one by one, my blessings I named
And all at once, I felt so ashamed
I have a roof above my head
I have a warm and comfortable bed
Never will I have to go through
The pain of hunger that others do
I have a man who loves me truly
I'm not perturbed by ill health unduly
I have a dog who gives so much love to me
I am humbled by its purity
I have a family whose love never falters
All through my life, it never alters
It's there for me to reach out and touch
The love of a family that means so much
I live in a country not at war
I feel safe when I walk through my door
No bullets flying, no bodies lying, no people dying
In my heaven on Earth
What must my blessings be worth?

Count Our Blessings

When I walk out of my door I see
Views of open fields and trees
Pheasants come to visit me
Goose and duck and swan
Fly above me in the sun
I walk through air fresh from the sea
Down country lanes, my dog and me
Just how lucky can you be
When I think what I have got
Compared to others who have not
Most of all the love around me
And all the good things that surround me
I have so much I start to cry
I really have it all don't I?
And I wonder why my life I doubted
Now I have my blessings counted.

Lynda Hughes

Dear Alfie

For five years a delightful furry visitor to my garden and home,
Then six wonderful months living with me most happily.
Despite being 11 years, always utterly kittenish,
Engaging in every way -
A most delicious tiny bundle of love and fun to cherish.
Then on Christmas Eve, most unexpectedly,
Alfie crawled indoors very poorly indeed.
Warmly cuddled, we drove to the on-call vet
And kidney failure took him to rest quietly.
Oh my, what a perfect gift of love and gentleness
For our Maker on such a day!
Immense shock and many tears
Yet I instantly smile when I think of all he gave me,
With joyous eyes sparkling, lively ears and tail
Ever alert to my comings and goings.
The dearest of characters, so full of life and warmth
And very aware of all around him.
Overflowing with love simply expressed.
My picture of the Nativity scene
Will always include a small, affectionate black cat
With lively ears, tail, curious and loving.

Margaret Ann Wheatley

My Christmas Story

Christmas is special
We all see our nearest and dearest
Time for singing carols and praising God
Making the Christmas cake
Hoping it turns out alright
Putting icing on all frosty and white.

The Christmas tree all trimmed with decorations
Used year by year and added to each year
Has a memory of someone or some place.

Christmas is a time we look back over the year to see
What we have achieved
What work we have done
If we have helped people enough and can we do better next year.

Christmas night all children fast asleep after
Putting a mince pie and drink of pop out for Santa.
All is quiet,

Early morning, moving feet crackling papers, parcels different
Shapes, it's still not light, too excited to sleep,
Hope it will soon be morning.

Waking up with cries of, 'Mum, Dad, look what Father Christmas
Has brought me.' The long-awaited beautiful doll or train.
Looking in the stocking for orange, nuts and a few sweets,
Someone finds a whistle, no more sleep today,
Everyone wishes each other Merry Christmas.

Look outside, it's started to snow.
'Can we build a snowman, Mum?'
'Quick, have some breakfast, it's time for church.'
We can slide all the way there.
'Yes, you can take one toy each with you.'
We meet our friends. 'Merry Christmas everyone!'

We thank God for all our wonderful gifts of life and presents.
Back home to see how the turkey is cooking.
Must get dinner over to hear the Queen's speech
And relax, thinking about Christmases gone by.

Yes, Christmas is a magical time.

Mavis Wilson

My Reply To George

Dear George, what a shock I got
To hear that you have bought a plot

When first I heard I felt scared
But like a boy scout be prepared

I hope the plot is long and wide
With room for you to fit inside

I'm glad you've got one with a view
Because there's not much else to do

But lie about and look around
And watch stray dogs pee on your ground

Friends asked you to buy a plot
To share with them the Scottish lot

But you said no, you couldn't stand
The noise of bagpipes on your land

But George, this is a long way off
Provided you lose that nasty cough.

Jean M Eyre

Reflections

As I gaze at a beautiful sunset
Or stars that dance on the sea,
Often do I wonder,
Why you were taken from me.

As I peruse apple blossom
And inhale delights of spring,
I am prone to wonder
Why cheerful birds still sing.

As I look upon hope, the rainbow,
Arcing my leaden skies,
My thoughts once more go wandering
To the question why.

I do not have an answer,
Maybe nature has a clue,
For as my heart lives her beauty,
I see reflections of you.

Jeannie Caldwell

King Solomon Singing

When King Solomon sang his songs of love
It was to very lucky woman
Caring words
Sharing feelings wise yet human
Thy belly is a mound if wheat underneath thy veil
That's sweet
Was she pregnant?
Imagine two exhausted bodies collapsed into one
On woven tasselled cushions scented with bergamot
Did her hands smooth the curve of his dear tum
Shy yet knowing
And teasing pillow her head on his royal saggy bum
Gentle caresses clinging mingling
Rose swirls of sunset
Fire-red embers, echoes
Swish of the tent screen
Passion in repose, rhythm of the heart
In the hot, ash-white sand of the desert.

Sue Woodbine

People . . .

There was a time for quite a while
I used to sit and think
That people weren't very nice
And the world was on the brink.

But trouble knocked upon my door
Then suddenly I realised
That everyone was good and kind
This made me open up my eyes.

Once more I looked at people
And saw I'd been unfair
For had I looked for good points
I'd have found that they were there.

So if you look upon a man
And faults are all that you can view
Look swiftly back within yourself
And ask, what does he see in you?

Agnes McLaren

Climbing The Mountain

I put my foot upon the rung
But have no strength to climb,
I know I need to look ahead
But oh! I'm running out of time!

What will the future bring?
Can I muster strength enough
To see this work through to its end
Before running out of breath?

Then I remember cherry picking,
Labouring in the sun,
Reaching out for glossy fruit,
The joy of work well done!

God, give me a head for heights,
I've plumbed the depths too long,
But keep my feet upon the ground
When my heart is so headstrong!

When my spirit takes wing to fly
Show me the way ahead,
Never let me rust away
Or spend my life in bed!

Guard my soul, whichever course,
You know I'm not easily led,
Nothing easy shall I know,
That's not the way I've been bred.

Graham K A Walker

Blessings Counted

When we wake up each morning
And look forward to our day,
Do we ever think of the good things
We take for granted along life's way?
All of us have our ups and downs,
That's life as we all know it,
But think about God's blessings,
That keep on flowing through it.
Sunshine, love and happiness,
Are just a little few,
Yet if you start to count God's blessings,
Time will run out on you.

Ellen Walt

Fed Up, Who Me?

You look nice today, Mum. *Well, thank you very much*
But I'm not going anywhere, I have no one to see
There's a basket full of washing upstairs waiting for me
Dad's gone down the job centre, he's had to take the bus
He needs to find a job real soon to earn a daily crust
Washing machine turned on with the socks and underwear
I'll make a cup of tea and have a sit down in the chair
Time to make the dinner, put the rubbish in the bin
Perhaps I'll have a liquid lunch, I need a double gin
Oh, I do get fed up with the same things to do
I don't sit around all day, I'm unable to see my friends
Since we moved away
Some days I want to leave the chores and find someone
To talk or maybe buy a dog and go out for a walk
On days like this when I feel fed up, the kids won't talk to me
Because I snap and shout at them until they make me see
You are our mum, you are the best, you always treat us as your guests
It's nice to come home and find you here, we like to be hugged
And feel you near
So come on, Mum and cheer yourself, you know it will be alright.
Thank you for washing our clothes, they are always clean, warm and bright.
Now Dad's got a job he'll be working on the post
So we can look forward to a special Sunday roast
Our food is always on the table, you give us nice things to eat
And there's a little surprise for those of us
Who don't eat meat
Mum, you needn't feel fed up, in fact you are quite smart
Remember every day, Mum, you're right here in our hearts.
You look great today, Mum.

Mary Ward

Togetherness

That magic moment when eyes meet, a tantalising transient treat.
When two as one seem to relate, in recognition of their fate.

Togetherness provides the key that symbolises harmony.
To us a perfect complement, a blessing surely Heaven-sent.

Through many years of blissfulness we will enjoy much tenderness
Despite dark days of deep despair when cruel times are deemed unfair.

Interspersed with apprehension, children add a new dimension.
For life indeed now rearranges, introducing many changes.

Tranquillity will be disturbed, impromptu action must be curbed.
The kids now take priority, for that's the way it has to be.

To count our blessings as we may, symbolises each new day.
Their coming has enhanced our lives, no longer simply man and wife.

When love is tested and succeeds it has fulfilled our every need
And we'll remain, right to the end, lifelong lovers, faithful friends.

Stan Taylor

Summer For Me

Summer for me is the yellow of grass bleached by the sun
The bluest of sky, the smile of the day
In a young man's eye, the hope of better things to come
Passing the home-made bakery, eying a creamy bun, yum!

Summer for me is a rosy apple on a tree
Wearing cotton crisp clothes, open shoes and feeling free
In all the busy streets where tourists stop to buy
No one to say hello or hi, why?
Yet summer for me is beautiful just the same
Memories of joy, love and pain.

Young and old live and enjoy
Doing simple things
Playing in the park or swimming in the sea.

Summer for me makes sense of life
And all that it throws at you
The fears, the tears, the end of another chapter
Another life too . . .

Then summer is gone!
Like a whisper, like a kiss, like a tear
Big yellow flower, king of the sky
Enrapture this earth with a passionate eye.

Pamela Hanover

I'll Put The Kettle On

Shut the door behind me, home once again,
Shake myself dry, drenched from the rain,
Utterly fed up, umbrella broke,
Innards and everything completely soaked,
Kick the cat out the way, want to go to bed,
Aching heart and aching head,
But thoughts of the day dissolved and gone,
As soon as I put the kettle on.

The bus didn't stop, it drove on by,
Late for appointments, monumental sigh,
Had to wait for another, at the bus stop huddled,
As car after car passed through the nearby puddle,
And what is more, I lost my bus fare,
Life, it would seem, is totally unfair,
But things aren't so bad, you will see,
Once you sip the first sip of tea.

Forgot my library card and couldn't get through,
So now my books are overdue,
Fine, I thought, so I popped to the shops
And set off the alarm - oh, this is the tops!
In the 'ten items or less' queue, someone had eleven
And two dozen, I had seven,
It came to five pounds and a penny in sum,
So I had to break into a tenner, not having a penny of one,
The change rattled in my pocket all the way down the road,
(And the hole in my pocket certainly lightened the load!)
But now I don't feel quite so fed up,
Due to the leafy contents of my favourite cup.

When I arrived at work, I was wearing odd socks,
Only spam emails filled my inbox,
By lunchtime the day hadn't improved,
For only coffee at noon, I remained unsoothed,
While chewing my pen, it leaked bluey-black,
So now my teeth a definite whiteness lack,
Then to add insult to injury, how absurd,
Somebody had already filled in the crossword,
Except the impossible clue, fourteen down,
An English beverage, milky-brown.

But thankfully I have to my haven returned,
The mug in front of me for which I have yearned,
I've locked the door to the world outside,
And immersed myself in this tea-bag paradise,
And after having had the day from Hell,
I think I might have a digestive as well!

Ruth Morris

Nature's Calming Hand

On the banks of its reedy river
I sit for hours
Listening to nature talk
Soothing and so pure the water gently flows
Down through the fields standing tall
In meadow grass soon to be harvested

Where on a morning a trail is marked out
By a fox coming home
One leg trailing from an old injury
Sustained when as a fun-loving young cub
It became too brave
And got caught on a jagged thorn tree

I wait till midday
Listening to the larks sing and water's soft tones
As swifts fly high above and swallows fly low
Above water coloured a sparkling blue
But not half as shocking as the kingfisher hiding
In the hanging weeping willows below

For the king of the river is a dazzling blue
Of which I have seen but few
Remembering every one
A sparkling diamond in nature's crown
Seen as fishermen in June cast off their winter vest
I sit there, at peace - my mind and body completely at rest.

Maurice Hope

Sharing And Caring

A hundred times a thank you
A hundred times a day
Is when I say my prayer
How grateful I do feel.

Looking back at life gone past
The kindness I received
The world is open to us all
Its friendship we do seek.

There is no price tag to the love
For it is given freely
We have to show that we do care
When we are among the needy.

Open up your heart
Let the love spread out
There is no limit in our soul
So give it freely now.

Elisabeth-Anna

The Dark Valley Of Depression

As I walked through the long dark valley of depression,
Each step taken is never-ending in the winding path of remission.
The whole world is black as black as the ace of spades,
Every tree, bush, the grass and all the flowers have faded.

Each part of the body from head to toe has grown weary,
There's nothing in this world for this body, everything is dreary.
All God's creatures have gone, the animals aren't any fun.
Looking up in the sky, there's no blue, there are no clouds,
It's grey with no sun.

There are no people in this world, I'm frightened and all alone.
Where have the horses, cows and sheep gone? There are none in the field.
Please tell me where have all the crops gone? There isn't any yield.

One day whilst struggling along the dark valley of depression,
A bright light appeared.
As I neared the end of the valley, the light was so overpowering,
It never seemed to disappear.

The sky turned blue, the sun came out, all the birds began to sing.
All the trees, the bushes and the flowers too were slowly dancing in the breeze.

Is this a new world outside the valley of depression with a familiar ring?
Little lambs started to frolic in the field, the cows and horses prancing around.
There are friendly people hustling and bustling in the town,
Is this a new world on the ground?

C M A Hughes

Memories

As I sit here all alone
Thinking how fast the years have flown
With memories which will stay forever
Of holidays we shared together.
Especially the last in Barcelona, Spain
Where wonderful thoughts will always remain
Daily swimming in calm, blue seas
And enjoying tasty Spanish teas.
Walking along the busy Las Ramblas
With all its flower stalls to pass
These memories will never leave me
Until my loved one once more I see.

D Yewdall

Count Our Blessings

Whenever I am feeling blue
I always know just what to do.
A walk through nature's wonderland
Shows what I need so close to hand.

No clocks to keep my eyes upon,
The noise and rushing round has gone.
Another world I can now see,
So calm and peaceful, I feel free.

Each season brings its own reward,
Leaves fall in autumn, squirrels hoard.
Cold winter snow and frozen lake,
Soon all of nature will awake.

Now spring renews earth's sleepy bed,
The joys of nature lie ahead.
Summer flowers and busy bees,
The leaves and blossoms on the trees.

I count my blessings, that I know
Another world where I can go,
Back to nature, a brand new start,
You can have both worlds in your heart.

Sheila Maureen St Clair

Emotions

To stand alone on a clifftop high
The space, fresh air and in the heather can lie
To be on your own with one's thoughts
Speculate dream and emotions one has fought
To think of all your worldly things
To wonder what future your life will bring
With loves that have gone you may wonder about
To loves present, you know you have no doubt
Life and death now being so surreal
Bringing heartache and sorrow with a letter can seal
But still you stand with the birds winging above
Dreaming of all the things that you would love
Life is very hard and can be unjustified
Disease of a loved one brings tears to your eyes
Turning your back on your clifftop stand
Finding your partner then taking his hand
Trying to forget what your life has been dealt
A smile to show them, the love that is felt.

Linda Meadows

To Mum

Thank you for your sense of fun, those silly Irish jokes,
Those Christmas gifts, those seaside trips,
Those stories of your folks.

Thank you for that fighting spirit, your will to overcome,
Those wartime tales, that stubborn pride
And drive to get things done.

Your shining path stays in our hearts to lead us on our way,
Carved out despite life's cruellest blows
To guide us should we stray.

As pain attacks and body breaks, as darkened days descend,
Your constant faith from deep within,
Victorious till the end.

So now look down with pride and smile, and take a bow or two,
For what you see and who we are
It's all because of you.

Tony Bennett

Searching For Love

I've never asked too much from life:
I've not caused trouble, grief or strife.
So why is it in all this time,
I've yet to find my valentine?

Some people say that love is blind;
Now surely that's all in the mind.
But, moon and stars would brightly shine,
If I could find my valentine.

The course of love does not run smooth;
Has peaks and troughs, in honest truth.
Yet, simple pleasures would be mine,
If I should find my valentine.

They claim that true love knows no bounds,
No barriers, no alien grounds.
To tops of mountains I would climb,
To try to find my valentine.

I think that I'm a gentle man,
No criminal, no hooligan.
For pure affection I shall pine,
Until I find my valentine.

Brian M Wood

Forever Locked In Your Heart

How do I begin to try and comfort you?
You have lost someone you loved dearly
There are no words I can say to heal the pain you are feeling
But know that I am here for you, night or day
Somehow you will find a way to go on
The love you shared together
Wonderful memories and special times
Will always be a part of you
Who you were together and who you are now
Nobody can take that away
It is that which will get you through this
That love so precious and so true
It is a rare thing; you have forever locked in your heart

Jacqui Watson

Moses On The Mobile

(One of the greatest blessings is a sense of humour.
I cannot believe in a God who does not laugh)

'Oh Lord, won't You buy me a mobile phone?
Less hard on the back than those tablets of stone,
And You could send orders for my eyes alone.'

Replied the Almighty, but slightly perplexed,
'Thou good, faithful servant, oh whatever next?
Take these new Commandments to form the first text.

Look after your neighbour, close by or remote,
Remember *Old Labour* when you go to vote,
Applaud the musician who strikes the right note,
Be kind to the poet whose verses you quote,
Pass on to your children the books that he wrote.

You butchers and bakers good victuals provide,
Cry 'Health' to the farmer at rich harvest tide,
When sat in your motor, drive careful and wide,
Leave room in the road for a cyclist to ride,
Care well for the woodlands where treasures abide.

The flora and fauna perhaps you can't name,
Exist for your pleasure, you know, just the same,
When life isn't perfect don't badger or blame,
But hope at the gathering to hear them declaim,
'They were funny old folk, but we're glad that they came!''

John Guy

What Is Love?

What is love? Is it doing the chores?
Making life comfortable - cooking the food?
Years pass so quickly - you do your best
And you hope each day to complete the rest.

Once life was worthwhile - you liked to help
But as you grow older, health fails and you yelp,
It isn't much fun working hard at the sink
But it keeps others happy - they need to drink.
Is this love?

Food does not automatically fall on the plate,
It has to be bought, carried home and replaced,
Put in the fridge, removed and cooked,
It will soon be eaten - so never be late,
Is this love?

Washing piles up - of course machines help you fend
Cleaning dust is a daily task - but it wins in the end,
If you look at things closely, what do you see?
More and more mess - you are never free.
Is this love?

Things that surround you remind you of friends,
They make you happy, but you know it soon ends.
I look back and remember what they did for me -
It was love at the time, which kept me free -
For a while anyway!

Doris E Pullen

Magic Moments

In life with many, we share love,
With our children and our friends,
Then comes one who makes the Earth move,
On whom happiness depends.

Love is one of life's real blessings,
It brings us so much pleasure,
It happens to the lowly and to kings
And is something we must treasure.

When the loved one is taken,
We're left with a broken heart,
But our memories can never be shaken
And the love will never depart.

D M Carne

My Dream

The other night I had a dream,
My love and I sat by a stream.
On its journey it said to me,
'Come with me out to the sea.

I'll take you to the ocean wide,
On a leaf with ease you will ride.
We'll see big ships and foreign places,
Swim with dolphins, meet different races.'

A great big bird sat next to me,
'Come with me, much more you'll see.
Upon my back safely you will fly,
We'll touch the clouds as we pass by.

We'll see the night stars all aglow,
Explore forests where orchids grow,
Mountains, castles, sunshine or snow,
Wherever you would like to go.'

'But, my love,' he said to me,
'My delights are best to see.
I will take you by the hand,
We don't need a foreign land.

Together we will tread life's path,
Through laughter, tears, joy and wrath.
And when our time on Earth is past,
I will have loved you till the last.'

Then I awoke to see the dawn
And my lovely dream had gone.
Now, my love, I know you'll wait,
To meet me at Heaven's Gate.

Joyce Curtis

To Grace

The touch of her hand on that first morn
The day our grandchild, Grace, was born
As we watch her grow each day
We are very lucky, we have to say

This precious gift sent from above
Brings such joy and oh, so much love
Grandchildren so special, we hope for more
A kiss and a cuddle as they come through the door.

Josie Corbett

All Jewels And Gems

They come as little gems day by day
Not even knowing sometimes how or why
But blessings, countless, they be for you, for me
All in the struggles that beset our well-worn way
Where may you see a smile to lift a tired sigh.

And soon we know amidst heartache and pain
A friend comes to comfort and bring peace
Assuring us that loved ones lost in love . . .
Their love lives on and forever will remain
Because love is eternal - it will never cease.

Joy and sadness walk together side by side
As a loved one is taken - new life we see again
Reminding us for always, wherever we be
New babies smile - and soon our tears we hide
Just as the sun which shines through clouds and rain.

So blessings we are given to help us smile once more
Are those kind hearts and loved ones very dear
All jewels and gems - no matter what their name
Maybe today they will again come to your door
Countless blessings all - and hopefully all sincere.

Irene A Dalzell

Blessings

He sat in his bower of sweet peas,
Sweet-smelling, colourful, bowing
To his rocking in his old rocking chair.
His blue eyes twinkled, the wind ruffled
His silver hair. He was at peace.
'Count your blessings, my child,' he said,
My great uncle. That's how I
Shall always remember you.
Teller of stories, teaser of wife,
A vicar's daughter, loving but sometimes
Disapproving of stories too far-fetched
For truth. 'Willie, how could you!
Don't believe him, child!' But I did
And I always will. And, more importantly,
I shall do as he said, and always
Count my blessings.

Elizabeth Morris

It's In You To Be Happy

How hard is it to change the negativity of being sad?
Just what can we do to stop feeling so bad?
Think back to happier times and places,
Remember when you last had fun and saw lots of smiling faces.
Times of loss can send you to the depths of despair,
You don't want help, instead you just sit and blankly stare.
At times like this, the change can only come from within you,
The start comes from being fed up with feeling blue.

Having suffered a time of deep depression,
Support from family and close friends left a lasting impression.
I learnt that I had people around who really cared,
That the whole ghastly experience wasn't just me, but shared.
I accept now that in life there are ups and downs,
It's not all smiles and fun, it's OK for an occasional frown.
The times spent with my grandchildren, where I can act the fool,
Without doubt, laughter is a powerful tool.

I'm a fan of laughter-makers of every type,
It doesn't have to be the famous ones with all their hype.
It could be a friend or colleague from the workplace,
With a natural ability to entertain, but knows not to be in your face.
People soon tire of a miserable soul,
Another good reason to make happiness your goal.
I'm not saying there aren't days when I don't feel down,
I believe, though, a smile is better than a frown.

Robert Humphrey

Ellie

(For Eleanor, 1980-2006. Love always)

The winter wanes, the sun seeps through,
I think I feel the warmth of you.
The warmth of love you gave to me,
Although I can no longer touch or see.
I feel that love most every day,
Though where you are, I cannot say.
I see you in Heaven and never in Hell,
Where you are, I cannot tell.
But that warmth of love you gave to me,
It helps me see, it helps me see.
It helps me see the love in You,
That you gave to me, Lord,
Let it be, just let it be.

Gareth Thomas

For Gordon, 1930-2005

The sea loved him
Loved him for the sturdy ship
He gave for her to enjoy
Culled by his hand from a strip
Of larch; eager for his employ;
In a remote ravine somewhere in Wales.

The timber loved him
And bent to his will and skill
With adze and plane; steam
And copper clench; wanting still
To grow anew, to strake and beam
Reincarnate copse of heart's desire

His students loved him
Welcomed the contagion from his hands
Into their mind's eye so their wood
Or steel or silver broke the chrysalis bands
And butterflied in a glorifying flood.
True discipline of true disciples

And we all loved him
For his wit and wisdom, strength and
Un-fly-hurting tolerance, boyish elation;
Scratched into time's immutable sand.
His goal in life was ever pure creation
And God can now embrace a fellow creator.

Tony Jennett

Count Our Blessings

Our blessings are meant to be bestowed
And readily made aware,
With a purpose ready-made to share.
In this great mart of least compassion,
They're humanity's currency of care.
An equality of benefit and endowment.

Carrying a loveliness.

The soul's satisfaction of beneficence
From those who may walk with us awhile
Leaving a lastingness that shines out its blessedness.

Ray Dite

Special Moments

If you're really lucky, on a beautiful spring day,
There's my favourite part of the common,
Where rabbits come out to play.
If it's the right part of the day
And you are very still,
I swear they really will.
It was a bright blue sky, it made the rabbits frisky,
Even bold and kind of risky.
Twitching noses and soft brown eyes,
No defence, not even much of a size.
The birds were singing sweetly, building their nest,
To attract a mate they gave it their best.
There were six rabbits so near, then there were three,
And one of them came right up to me.
The grass was so green, flowers on the ground,
The rabbits finished playing, then were gone without a sound.
Apart from the one by my feet lingered on,
Our eyes met and how its brown eyes shone.
Then it bobbed and turned, got ready to run,
I swear that little rabbit looked back at me,
As if I had something to say,
Then it seemed to change its mind,
Instead, it was as if it gave a little smile,
Before it turned and bobbed off on its way.
And as I sat deserted, it came to me quite clear,
This was a 'special moment', it was not by chance I was here.
I'd met my guardian angel, who'd given me a sign,
Regardless what my horrors were,
I'm not alone and things will turn out fine.
I can't say how long I pondered,
The sun had set and it was night
And as I set off to walk home,
For all there was no moon,
The path had never seemed so bright.

Jan Anderson

Count Your Blessings

We must make the most of all the lovely things we see,
When in the month of January with no blossom on the trees.
To see a newborn baby in her mother's arms,
Looking lovingly at her daughter, keeping her from harm.
Some people have such sadness, it really is a shame,
We'll never understand it, there is no one to blame.
We have to count our blessings and live from day-to-day,
We'll think of all the beautiful things that have come our way.
Like animals to look at, lovely sunsets at night,
Blue skies and green meadows when the sun shines bright.
The sand so soft upon our feet, we go on holiday and family meet.
Then to the theatre, what a treat, so count your blessings instead of sheep.

Carole Andrews

Life's Treasures

So bleak, so dark, so cold it seems
Whilst summer fades into our dreams
We long so much for daylight hours
To sit and dream amongst the flowers

But wait, somewhere I can hear a song
On the other hand I could be wrong
No, there he is, with his lovely red breast
Singing his heart out - he's just the best

My family's coming to have some tea,
'I wonder just how long they'll be'
No sooner said - the doorbell rings
And in they come with toys and things

Johnny has made a racing car
He's trying to make it go very far
While Lucy climbs up to sit on my knee
Some chance of me having my cup of tea

Fluffy, my cat, so soft and so sweet
Is sat by the fire, just by my feet
She's purring to tell us that everything's fine
I feel so lucky that all this is mine

It's still cold and wet, through the window I see
But today has been 'summer' for them and for me
And when they've gone home and I am still here
I will think of the day that I'll always hold dear.

Josephine Western

Badgers In The Moonlight

January, February bring wanton weather
Christmas family no longer visiting together
Dusty decorations all packed away
Alone, by the cottage window I watch trees sway

The ferocious wind reaches its height
As ships seek sanctuary in Holyhead Bay
Screeching seagulls struggle in flight
Everyone needs shelter from the storm
As trees from their roots are torn
And raging rain lashes down all day
'Please let this gale end soon,' I pray.

Deep darkness falls, suddenly all is calm
Black, angry clouds disappear
Like magic from the night sky
Stars flash silver, nature's neon lights
Surround a munificent mellow moon so clear
Along the moonlit path three badgers make their way.

I watch in silence, wonder why
Humans destroy so much to try
And be supreme gods of all they survey.
Here on this quiet mountainside
These shy, cautious creatures forage and play
Unaware of how special they are.
I watch them and feel blessed
They are more real than any celebrity star.
Daylight dawns and no one could have guessed
That three badgers had a moonlight stroll
Before returning to their deeply dug hole.
We should count our blessings
Let all of nature's wonders enrich our soul.

Jean Charlotte Houghland

Precious Moments

A glimpse of Heaven in a rainbow
A sunset moment we can share
The first cry of a baby
The cherished words 'I care'
The moment when your wish comes true
When you doubted far too long
The pleasure of a friendship
The joy of love in a song

The sudden song of a skylark
As it rises up so high
The soothing sound the river makes
As it goes gurgling by
The caressing warmth of the summer sun
That strokes you into sleep
The fleeting glimpse of a butterfly
That's too beautiful to keep

The tender touch of a loved one
As you hold each other's hand
What more can life envisage
We know that all was planned
How can we then not marvel
At all things great and small
The cricket and the grasshopper
The trees so strong and tall
These all are precious moments
We live with and enjoy
Each with its special message
Of beauty that does not cloy.

Vera May Coote

Switch On!

On Saturday the heating went off,
My home went very cold,
I wouldn't mind if I were young
But I am ninety years old.

So blessing electricity
I carried convector in,
Then boiled electric kettle
For two bottles needed filling.

Next I turned on washing machine,
It keeps the kitchen warm
And when the clothes are clean and dry
I'll use my electric iron, early in the morn

At lunchtime I stopped for an hour or two,
It gave me time to think,
While I eat muesli and three fresh fruit
And microwave my nice hot drink.

Snuggled in my armchair
I switch the TV on
To watch the afternoon movie
Till the light is almost gone.

Drawing blinds and curtains
And switching on the lights,
Blessing again electricity,
I really hate dark nights.

And so to bed, it's time to go,
I'm lovely and warm, my face aglow,
My goodnight drink from microwave,
Oh! Blessed electricity, today it's me you saved!

Millicent Blanche Colwell

We Praise And Thank You, O Lord

We praise and thank You, O Lord,
For Your wonderful creation,
For the warmth of the sun and refreshing rain,
The shade from clouds on summer days,
The snow and frost in winter.

We praise and thank You, O Lord,
For Your wonderful creation,
For all the kinds of fruit we eat,
The variety of shape and colour,
Of apples, bananas, oranges and pears.

We praise and thank You, O Lord,
For Your wonderful creation,
The birds' different songs, colour and size,
For the beauty, fragrance and colour of flowers
Whether wild or grown in a garden.

We praise and thank You, O Lord,
For Your wonderful creation,
For trees in the woods standing so tall,
The mighty oak, ash and beech,
Small shrubs and trees that brighten our gardens.

We praise and thank You, O Lord,
For Your wonderful creation,
For vegetables rich in flavour,
Green, white, red, so good for us,
Some cooked, some can be eaten raw.

We praise and thank You, O Lord,
For Your wonderful creation,
For loving pets like dogs and cats
Who welcome us each day,
And other pets which give us joy.

We praise and thank You, O Lord,
For Your wonderful creation,
For loving friends and caring families,
Help us to respect all Your creation
To love and show loving care for all things,
We praise and thank You, O Lord,
For Your wonderful creation.

Jean Martin-Doyle

'Only Connect'

On a cold and grey January morning,
Alice, weathered backpacker, independent and wise,
Pushed through East Street market,
Unaware that a plastic bag had stuck to her left shoe.

A gentle tap on her shoulder
Caused her to look round
And recognise the stallholder from whom
She had just bought nylon stockings.

Engagingly, he pointed to her feet,
Bent down and released the tacky film.
Touched by his courtesy, Alice smiled, thanked him
And moved on, musing.

The far-away image of a bedouin boy came into her mind.
He, too, had come forward to help her
When she had stumbled through the ruins
Of the monastery of the Essenes
And had almost fallen, picking up a stone.

The man returned to his unguarded stall,
Thinking of his time as a paramedic
When he had rescued many a victim of a fall
And had conveyed them to hospital.

The paths of these people would not cross again -
- Foil and stone a connecting karmic line.

Elise Henden

Let's Count Our Blessings Now

There are things in life which we accept and don't appreciate
Quite often we just count our blessings when it is too late.
So from now on let's stop and think, life's gone before you know it
A thank you or a smiling glance means love, so why not show it.
Sit down - take stock - think hard and you'll be glad
To find that all the happy days by far outweigh the sad.

Sheila Henrietta Birkett

Far-Gone Days

Whenever you're feeling really sad,
Or even a little down, or a little blue,
Stop and look out through a window into your garden,
Imagine what you can see, not what you need to do.

We all pass through some bleak times,
This is when we need to dream,
Of all that is good and beautiful,
So nothing is as bad as it is, or as bad as it seems.

Some people say life is what you make it,
But that's hard to believe when you're in the depths of despair,
Especially when you're not responsible for what is happening,
When you just need someone to understand, someone to care.

Sometimes you need a helping hand,
To guide you through the maze,
Till all is well and good again,
Till the bad is left in far-gone days.

We can't be happy all of the time,
But we don't wish to be always sad,
Try to do something special for yourself,
Don't be ashamed if good times are had.

You can find a dream in a rainbow,
You can find a dream in sunshine, also in the rain,
Tears always fall for a reason,
Sometimes because we are happy, not just tears from pain.

So look to the skies above you,
See the beauty of what it holds,
Think of the space it covers,
Now you have a dream ready to be told.

Gillian S Gill

Kindness Of Friends

The new year uplifts
And brings us new hope -
For the fulfilment
Of all daily needs.
With strength of purpose
We're able to cope
And friends encourage -
With kind words and deeds.
Then as world's problems
Continue to mount,
We feel quiet peace
Within our glad hearts -
And daily blessings
Continue to count,
From concern for others -
Ne'er to depart
And as Father Time
Decrees new year's end -
Goodwill to all men
We see has been done -
When those classed as foe
We all now befriend.
Once more our blessings
We count one by one.

Marian Curtis-Jones

Count Our Blessings

We moan about the weather,
Decide whether to go out - or not
We moan about the sunshine,
If sublime, we decide that it's too hot!

We grumble if it's raining
Without explaining that it's needed
We grumble at the flooded lawn
Often scorn, it can be re-seeded.

The remedy is shoes that punch
You flinch, although no time to scoff
My silent cough, that you will smile
All the while they're taken off!

Marian Acres

Silver Season

It is the silver season,
When branches of the bare trees
Sparkle and gleam in weak sun;
They seem to set out to please.

Jack Frost creeps up in the night,
Leaving his silvery hue,
And people are unhappy
With their toes and fingers blue.

Rime lies on the rooftops,
Dangles in cold icicles:
Now in winter's icy grip,
Dangerous to ride bicycles.

Birds are silent as the dead,
Their little feet must be cold;
Huddled by the chimney stack,
They prefer harvest gold.

Cattle shiver in the fields,
They should not really be out.
Coughing their breath on the air,
Waiting a warm shippon, no doubt.

Fine cobwebs from fairyland,
Adorn the barren hedges;
Twinkling like lovely jewels,
On myriad silken ledges.

There's little water in the stream,
It is edged and frilled with ice;
The earth is rock-hard, like stone,
And outdoor swimming - no dice!

Telephone wires hum and sing;
Silver frost has covered the land.
Nature stands completely still,
Yet spring is already planned!

J Millington

Terry - True Love Lives On Forever

(Dedicated with love and pride beyond compare to my beloved husband, Terry Reynolds - loved and missed by us all. With love always to my precious granddaughter, Liseanne, and her darling baby, Terry-Kai, due to be born on 'Mother's Day' - March 18th 07. True love lives on forever)

Our saddest day was in December
Although you'd fought so hard to stay
Cruel cancer won its victory
And God took your pain away

Our lives have been so empty
Without your laughter, help and love
But we all know you are watching us
And guiding from above

Beloved husband, dad and grandad
Missed beyond any words we could ever say
Your loss has been our cross to bear
But . . . soon comes a brighter day

Our happiest, proudest day will be in March
When a brand new life will make us smile . . . and cry
For we'll rejoice and welcome back a part of you
When we say hello to dearest, darling baby Terry-Kai

So we'll 'count our blessings' every day
For we know that's what you'd want us all to do
And thank God for this precious little life
When we see Terry-Kai live on through you.

Sylvia E L Reynolds

Silent Movie

The sky is like a silent movie on a widescreen
Faces of parents, children, loving pets all act in the scenes
I watch the stars of this silent movie go to and fro
They seem to follow me, everywhere I go!

I count my blessings daily for my sight, so I can see
The wonderful actors in this movie, looking down at me
As the clouds change, or even in the glow of moonlight
I know all those actors make sure I'm alright!

This magical silent movie shows in the sky so high
Helps me every day, gives me hope as years fly by
Thro' clouds thick or thin, hail, rain or snow
I thank God for my sight, to let me see this show!

Maisie Roberts

Count Our Blessings

Count our blessings for the NHS,
Even if it seems to be in a mess.
Be prepared to find a way,
When, for no reason, your job's gone astray.
Always keep a healthy table,
So as to feed your family if you are able.
Which brings to mind a question of money,
Save for rainy days which are sometimes too many.
Be practical in all you do,
Or there may come a day that you could rue.
Thank the Lord for every day,
For the food we buy and the food we eat.
Thank the Lord as we go on our way,
Thank You for the shoes on our feet.
Many people have *none!*
Cut your cloth according to means,
Or your dreams could never be seen.
Count our health instead of our wealth.
Count our blessings that you are able to walk.
Count our blessings that you are able to talk.
Count our blessings that we are able to shop.
Some can't - which are quite a lot.
Thank the Lord for the way we live,
For which, their lives, some people would give.
Through indiscriminate wars.
Last but not least, thank the Lord above,
Who watches over us with eternal love.

Rosemary Peach

Blessings To Share

Life is a gift
To treasure each day
Each morning will bring something new
To be blessed with good health
Is worth much more than wealth
Life will bring blessings untold
Blessings to share with the sick and disabled
And those growing frail and old
To see the sunny smile of a child
Such a joy to behold
The moon and the stars
The sun and the rain
The majesty of a great tree
The four winds that blow
And the rivers that flow
The mighty roar of the sea
The loved ones who care
Who will always be there
To share the troubles that life may bring
And what can compare with the sound of a bird
Singing to welcome the spring
As we count all our blessings
We offer a prayer
Giving thanks for so much pleasure
We know that all these gifts we share
Will be ours to treasure forever.

Pat Booker

Count Our Blessings

You said to me, 'Look at all you have got,
A wonderful home, family and friends
and are you ever hungry?'
'Thank you for telling me that,' I said.
(It's good to have friends who are honest!)
Yes, I looked and gave thanks
For my warm, comfortable home,
For a husband who loves and cares for me,
For two amazing sons, gone now out into the world.
And as I watched the sunset in the west,
and the moon and stars come out,
I realised that we must always take time
To stop and count our blessings.

Jane Wade

Shades

defeated - never
foiled not nor
vanquished by all
this life's lumbering rot

so many chances
infinitesimal games
disguising themselves
under multitudinous names

deceit and pity
woes - so sorry
the passing
of one's melancholy

yet hope brushes, bristling
bedrocked beneath
conquer, banish
that bouquet of
sadness' wreath

seemingly unstitching
all worldly seams
be forgetful not
of touchable dreams

flickering, perhaps
or fading slight
dulling with curious shadows
of once-time surefire
bright

renewed, optimistic
not disillusioned, now brave
no more yesteryears' doubts
or uncertainty's slave

gripped by that hand of
fresh starts
- consequences -
untainted emotions
all adrenaline's senses

enraptured, enlivened
remoulded, recast
inner turmoil, self-critical
cast off
in the past

Jamie Caddick

To A Sweet Gem

The day my world stopped turning and darkness fell upon my life
was the grim day my wife passed on.
Although the sun shone on, in clear blue, cloudless skies,
to me, a stygian gloom suffused my mind.
There was no light, no sun, no bright blue sky,
just utter misery, soul-destroying loneliness
and dark, dark thoughts of death.

But there now has come, into my life,
a lovely girl who quelled my loneliness.
Her visits helped dispel the emptiness and
by spending a short time, now and then, with me
she has made me feel far less bereft.
It is surprising that one so young should have
such depth of thoughtfulness, kindness and feeling.

She has helped to make me feel that my life is worth living again,
with her happy smile and her inner light
which is now brightening my days.
My world once more has begun to turn.
The reason can't be sex, for I am far too old.
Nor love, for the beautiful child is much too young
to be affected by such feelings yet.

But she, by calling in and caring,
has brought back to my life a reason to exist.
I thank her from the depths of my being.

D G W Garde

Expressions Of God's Love

Not like St Paul and his 'on the road to Damascus revelation'
but every day in my life there has been the realisation
that the love of God encompasses me - I always know
that whatever occurs it is for my good and wherever I may go
is covered by His grace and however many times I fall short
of His expectations He is always there to exhort
and to comfort me for my failings from the day of my birth
I'm sure if I was the only sinner on God's wonderful Earth
He would still have sent His Son, Jesus, only me to redeem
this is a very personal matter from God to me, between
just the two of us. So how can I fail to adore
the Saviour who loves me so much He gave His only Son for -
me and, of course, all of the people on the Earth He created.
Whatever happens in my life His love has never abated.
Although to fathom His mysteries is not what I am here for
and now I am getting older the list of those 'gone before'
is lengthening year by year until it sometimes seems
there are more 'over there' waiting for me (I see them in my dreams)
than are left here, so I know that when God calls me to be by His side
still supporting me, by His grace, in His love I'll forever abide.

Florence Broomfield

Spider's Web

I watched a spider weave its web
From tiny little bits of silver thread
It grew into a masterpiece.

In awe I saw it catch a fly
And while I watched it slowly die
It became wrapped up like a present.

The spider stored his meal away
To be eaten on another day
When it hungered for a treat.

It ran out to repair a rip
That the fly had made at the end of its trip
And the spider's new home had been broken.

Fascinated, I continued to watch
As it darted out each time to catch
Its dinner, lunch and supper.

Every time the web vibrated
The spider appeared and deliberated
Over which meal this one would become.

Raindrops now falling from the overhead cloud
The spider checks the web; he's very house-proud
And finds the web now dripping with crystal jewels.

The rain has stopped, the sun has appeared
And to the web I find I've neared
To see the amazing light display.

What a perfect hour I've just spent
Watching the spider become content
And seeing the delights of nature unfolding.

Joanne Hale

Winter Observation

When dark December glooms the days
And takes our autumn joys away;
When short and scant the sunbeam throws,
Upon the weary waste of snow,
A cold and profitless regard
Like patron on a needy bard;
When silvan occupations done,
And o'er the chimney rests the gun,
And hang, in idle trophy, near,
The game-pouch, fishing rod and spear;
When wiry terrier, rough and grim,
And greyhound, with his length of limb,
And pointer, now employ'd no more,
Cumber our parlour's narrow floor;
When in his stall the impatient steed,
Is long condemn'd to rest and feed;
When from our snow-encircled home,
Scarce cares, the hardiest step to roam,
Since path is none, save that to bring
The needful water from the spring;
When wrinkled news' page, thrice turned over,
Beguiles the dreary hour no more,
And darkling politician cross'd,
In weighs against the lingering post,
And answering housewife sore complains of carriers,
Snow impeded wains;
When such the country cheer, I come,
Well pleased, to seek our city home;
For converse, and for books, to change.
The forest's melancholy range.
And welcome, with renew'd delight
The busy day, and social night.

M Titcombe

Flotsam And Jetsam

The sea rolls in daily,
And each tide regurgitates
A fresh trail of treasures.
Surprisingly all similar,
Yet each time something different.

Rows of odd shoes of all sizes and colours,
(There must be many one-legged people around!)
Next day all-change to broken buckets and pails,
Then brushes and brooms, so many varieties.
All babies must be wailing when the dummies float up.

Joseph Cornell boxes never had so much choice
As when the aged and smooth wooden sculptures
Save hours of whittling
Created by the passages of time.

Plastic off-cuts,
All that remains of someone's favoured craft
Help to compose psychedelic assemblages.

Carefully drilled roundels,
Where now, strong masts,
Live, locked together,
Automated like machines.

Glass pebbles glow
As in Neptune's locker,
Tumbled into nature's gems.

Gnarled seaweed roots like Triffid's claws
Weave mystery and intrigue
While so many colourful knots unwind the traveller's woe.

Yvonne Adams

A to Z of Authors

Count Our Blessings

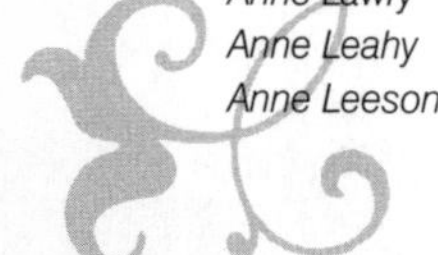

Count Our Blessings

Jill K Gilbert	390	John L Wigley	573
Jim Anderton	260	John Michael Scott	273
Jim E Dolbear	120	John Morrison	305
Jimmy Sinclair	492	John Neal	117
Jim Pritchard	534	John Paulley	105
J Johnson	361	John Pegg	142
J LeC Smith	71	John Pert	91
J M Drinkhill	229	John Pierrepont	69
J Millington	680	John Riddick	614
J M Stoles	596	John Robinson	442
J Nicoll	390	John Walker	360
Jo Allen	406	John W Hewing	148
Joan-Pamela Moore	479	Jo Howson	285
Joana Efua Sam-Avor	122	Jo Lewis	522
Joan C Igesund	83	Jo Newman	618
Joan D Bailey	605	Jonis Pastit	106
Joan Earle Broad	198	Joseph Broadley	358
Joan Gallen	428	Josephine Herron	621
Joan Gladys Cashford	360	Josephine Sexton	163
Joan Hammond	333	Josephine Western	672
Joan Hartland	555	Josie Corbett	667
Joan H Callister	84	Josie Pepper	108
Joan Ibell	645	Josie Smith	462
Joan Lister	346	Joyce Alice Turner	551
Joan Mackenzie	615	Joyce Curtis	667
Joan Mathers	332	Joyce Dunkley	34
Joan McClung	80	Joyce E Pugh	225
Joan McQuoid	223	Joyce Hallifield	61
Joan M E Gray	362	Joyce Hammond	103
Joan Morris	644	Joyce Hammond	212
Joan M Waller	417	Joyce Hudspith	453
Joanna Maria John	317	Joyce Le Vicount	355
Joanne Hale	686	Joyce Walker	603
Joanne Manning	198	Joyce Williams	566
Joan R Gilmour	101	Joyce Willis	179
Joan Thompson	615	Joy D Richardson	351
Joan Yvonne Matthews	153	Joy R Gunstone	635
Joan Zambelli	337	Joy Saunders	54
Jodie Grant	200	Joy Wilson	562
Joe Staunton	506	J R Burr	140
Jo Hawksworth	18	JRH Graham	84
John Ball	490	J T Bright	625
John Beazley	221	Judith Herrington	318
John Birkett	352	Judy McEwan	581
John Cole	139	Julia Pegg	147
John David Robertson	432	Julie Banyard	592
John Eccles	197	Julie Colleen Duffy	524
John Eldridge	95	Julie Dawe	187
John Faucett	441	Julie Marie Laura Shearing	325
John F McCartney	442	June Allum	510
John Gaze	209	June Daniels	257
John Goulding	220	June Davies	499
John Greenslade	68	June Sweeney	127
John Guy	665	June Waine	573
John Harwood	394	J Unsworth	410
John Liberkowski	538	J Webb	274

Count Our Blessings

Forward Press Information

We hope you have enjoyed reading this book - and that you will continue to enjoy it in the coming years.
If you like reading and writing poetry drop us a line, or give us a call, and we'll send you a free information pack.
Alternatively if you would like to order further copies of this book or any of our other titles, then please give us a call or email us at info@forwardpress.co.uk

Forward Press Ltd. Information
Remus House
Coltsfoot Drive
Peterborough
PE2 9JX
(01733) 898101